Machine Learning in Non-Stationary Environments

Adaptive Computation and Machine Learning
Thomas Dietterich, Editor

Christopher Bishop, David Heckerman, Michael Jordan, and Michael Kearns, Associate Editors

A complete list of the books published in this series can be found at the back of the book.

MACHINE LEARNING IN NON-STATIONARY ENVIRONMENTS

Introduction to Covariate Shift Adaptation

Masashi Sugiyama and Motoaki Kawanabe

The MIT Press
Cambridge, Massachusetts
London, England

© 2012 Massachusetts Institute of Technology

All rights reserved. No part of this book may be reproduced in any form by any electronic or mechanical means (including photocopying, recording, or information storage and retrieval) without permission in writing from the publisher.

For information about special quantity discounts, please email special_sales@mitpress.mit.edu

This book was set in Syntex and TimesRoman by Newgen.
Printed and bound in the United States of America.

Library of Congress Cataloging-in-Publication Data

Sugiyama, Masashi, 1974–
Machine learning in non-stationary environments : introduction to covariate shift adaptation / Masashi Sugiyama and Motoaki Kawanabe.
 p. cm. — (Adaptive computation and machine learning series)
Includes bibliographical references and index.
ISBN 978-0-262-01709-1 (hardcover : alk. paper)
1. Machine learning. I. Kawanabe, Motoaki. II. Title.
Q325.5.S845 2012
006.3′1—dc23
                                                                                                2011032824

10 9 8 7 6 5 4 3 2 1

Contents

Foreword   xi
Preface   xiii

I   INTRODUCTION

1   Introduction and Problem Formulation   3
1.1   Machine Learning under Covariate Shift   3
1.2   Quick Tour of Covariate Shift Adaptation   5
1.3   Problem Formulation   7
    1.3.1   Function Learning from Examples   7
    1.3.2   Loss Functions   8
    1.3.3   Generalization Error   9
    1.3.4   Covariate Shift   9
    1.3.5   Models for Function Learning   10
    1.3.6   Specification of Models   13
1.4   Structure of This Book   14
    1.4.1   Part II: Learning under Covariate Shift   14
    1.4.2   Part III: Learning Causing Covariate Shift   17

II   LEARNING UNDER COVARIATE SHIFT

2   Function Approximation   21
2.1   Importance-Weighting Techniques for Covariate Shift Adaptation   22
    2.1.1   Importance-Weighted ERM   22
    2.1.2   Adaptive IWERM   23
    2.1.3   Regularized IWERM   23
2.2   Examples of Importance-Weighted Regression Methods   25
    2.2.1   Squared Loss: Least-Squares Regression   26
    2.2.2   Absolute Loss: Least-Absolute Regression   30
    2.2.3   Huber Loss: Huber Regression   31
    2.2.4   Deadzone-Linear Loss: Support Vector Regression   33
2.3   Examples of Importance-Weighted Classification Methods   35

        2.3.1 Squared Loss: Fisher Discriminant Analysis   36
        2.3.2 Logistic Loss: Logistic Regression Classifier   38
        2.3.3 Hinge Loss: Support Vector Machine   39
        2.3.4 Exponential Loss: Boosting   40
  2.4 Numerical Examples   40
        2.4.1 Regression   40
        2.4.2 Classification   41
  2.5 Summary and Discussion   45

3 Model Selection   47
  3.1 Importance-Weighted Akaike Information Criterion   47
  3.2 Importance-Weighted Subspace Information Criterion   50
        3.2.1 Input Dependence vs. Input Independence in Generalization Error Analysis   51
        3.2.2 Approximately Correct Models   53
        3.2.3 Input-Dependent Analysis of Generalization Error   54
  3.3 Importance-Weighted Cross-Validation   64
  3.4 Numerical Examples   66
        3.4.1 Regression   66
        3.4.2 Classification   69
  3.5 Summary and Discussion   70

4 Importance Estimation   73
  4.1 Kernel Density Estimation   73
  4.2 Kernel Mean Matching   75
  4.3 Logistic Regression   76
  4.4 Kullback–Leibler Importance Estimation Procedure   78
        4.4.1 Algorithm   78
        4.4.2 Model Selection by Cross-Validation   81
        4.4.3 Basis Function Design   82
  4.5 Least-Squares Importance Fitting   83
        4.5.1 Algorithm   83
        4.5.2 Basis Function Design and Model Selection   84
        4.5.3 Regularization Path Tracking   85
  4.6 Unconstrained Least-Squares Importance Fitting   87
        4.6.1 Algorithm   87
        4.6.2 Analytic Computation of Leave-One-Out Cross-Validation   88
  4.7 Numerical Examples   88
        4.7.1 Setting   90
        4.7.2 Importance Estimation by KLIEP   90
        4.7.3 Covariate Shift Adaptation by IWLS and IWCV   92
  4.8 Experimental Comparison   94
  4.9 Summary   101

5 Direct Density-Ratio Estimation with Dimensionality Reduction   103
  5.1 Density Difference in Hetero-Distributional Subspace   103
  5.2 Characterization of Hetero-Distributional Subspace   104

Contents

         5.3   Identifying Hetero-Distributional Subspace   106
                5.3.1 Basic Idea   106
                5.3.2 Fisher Discriminant Analysis   108
                5.3.3 Local Fisher Discriminant Analysis   109
         5.4   Using LFDA for Finding Hetero-Distributional Subspace   112
         5.5   Density-Ratio Estimation in the Hetero-Distributional Subspace   113
         5.6   Numerical Examples   113
                5.6.1 Illustrative Example   113
                5.6.2 Performance Comparison Using Artificial Data Sets   117
         5.7   Summary   121

6   Relation to Sample Selection Bias   125
         6.1   Heckman's Sample Selection Model   125
         6.2   Distributional Change and Sample Selection Bias   129
         6.3   The Two-Step Algorithm   131
         6.4   Relation to Covariate Shift Approach   134

7   Applications of Covariate Shift Adaptation   137
         7.1   Brain–Computer Interface   137
                7.1.1 Background   137
                7.1.2 Experimental Setup   138
                7.1.3 Experimental Results   140
         7.2   Speaker Identification   142
                7.2.1 Background   142
                7.2.2 Formulation   142
                7.2.3 Experimental Results   144
         7.3   Natural Language Processing   149
                7.3.1 Formulation   149
                7.3.2 Experimental Results   151
         7.4   Perceived Age Prediction from Face Images   152
                7.4.1 Background   152
                7.4.2 Formulation   153
                7.4.3 Incorporating Characteristics of Human Age Perception   153
                7.4.4 Experimental Results   155
         7.5   Human Activity Recognition from Accelerometric Data   157
                7.5.1 Background   157
                7.5.2 Importance-Weighted Least-Squares Probabilistic Classifier   157
                7.5.3 Experimental Results   160
         7.6   Sample Reuse in Reinforcement Learning   165
                7.6.1 Markov Decision Problems   165
                7.6.2 Policy Iteration   166
                7.6.3 Value Function Approximation   167
                7.6.4 Sample Reuse by Covariate Shift Adaptation   168
                7.6.5 On-Policy vs. Off-Policy   169
                7.6.6 Importance Weighting in Value Function Approximation   170
                7.6.7 Automatic Selection of the Flattening Parameter   174

7.6.8 Sample Reuse Policy Iteration 175
 7.6.9 Robot Control Experiments 176

III LEARNING CAUSING COVARIATE SHIFT

8 Active Learning 183
 8.1 Preliminaries 183
  8.1.1 Setup 183
  8.1.2 Decomposition of Generalization Error 185
  8.1.3 Basic Strategy of Active Learning 188
 8.2 Population-Based Active Learning Methods 188
  8.2.1 Classical Method of Active Learning for Correct Models 189
  8.2.2 Limitations of Classical Approach and Countermeasures 190
  8.2.3 Input-Independent Variance-Only Method 191
  8.2.4 Input-Dependent Variance-Only Method 193
  8.2.5 Input-Independent Bias-and-Variance Approach 195
 8.3 Numerical Examples of Population-Based Active Learning Methods 198
  8.3.1 Setup 198
  8.3.2 Accuracy of Generalization Error Estimation 200
  8.3.3 Obtained Generalization Error 202
 8.4 Pool-Based Active Learning Methods 204
  8.4.1 Classical Active Learning Method for Correct Models and Its Limitations 204
  8.4.2 Input-Independent Variance-Only Method 205
  8.4.3 Input-Dependent Variance-Only Method 206
  8.4.4 Input-Independent Bias-and-Variance Approach 207
 8.5 Numerical Examples of Pool-Based Active Learning Methods 209
 8.6 Summary and Discussion 212

9 Active Learning with Model Selection 215
 9.1 Direct Approach and the Active Learning/Model Selection Dilemma 215
 9.2 Sequential Approach 216
 9.3 Batch Approach 218
 9.4 Ensemble Active Learning 219
 9.5 Numerical Examples 220
  9.5.1 Setting 220
  9.5.2 Analysis of Batch Approach 221
  9.5.3 Analysis of Sequential Approach 222
  9.5.4 Comparison of Obtained Generalization Error 222
 9.6 Summary and Discussion 223

10 Applications of Active Learning 225
 10.1 Design of Efficient Exploration Strategies in Reinforcement Learning 225
  10.1.1 Efficient Exploration with Active Learning 225
  10.1.2 Reinforcement Learning Revisited 226
  10.1.3 Decomposition of Generalization Error 228

        10.1.4 Estimating Generalization Error for Active Learning   229
        10.1.5 Designing Sampling Policies   230
        10.1.6 Active Learning in Policy Iteration   231
        10.1.7 Robot Control Experiments   232
   10.2 Wafer Alignment in Semiconductor Exposure Apparatus   234

IV CONCLUSIONS

11 Conclusions and Future Prospects   241
   11.1 Conclusions   241
   11.2 Future Prospects   242

   Appendix: List of Symbols and Abbreviations   243
   Bibliography   247
   Index   259

Foreword

Modern machine learning faces a number of grand challenges. The ever growing World Wide Web, high throughput methods in genomics, and modern imaging methods in brain science, to name just a few, pose ever larger problems where learning methods need to scale, to increase their efficiency, and algorithms need to become able to deal with million-dimensional inputs at terabytes of data. At the same time it becomes more and more important to efficiently and robustly model highly complex problems that are structured (e.g., a grammar underlies the data) and exhibit nonlinear behavior. In addition, data from the real world are typically *non-stationary*, so there is a need to compensate for the non-stationary aspects of the data in order to map the problem back to stationarity. Finally, when explaining that while machine learning and modern statistics generate a vast number of algorithms that tackle the above challenges, it becomes increasingly important for the practitioner not only to predict and generalize well on unseen data but to also to explain the nonlinear predictive learning machine, that is, to harvest the prediction capability for making inferences about the world that will contribute to a better understanding of the sciences.

The present book contributes to one aspect of the above-mentioned grand challenges: namely, the world of non-stationary data is addressed. Classically, learning always assumes that the underlying probability distribution of the data from which inference is made stays the same. In other words, it is understood that there is no change in distribution between the sample from which we learn to and the novel (unseen) out-of-sample data. In many practical settings this assumption is incorrect, and thus standard prediction will likely be suboptimal.

The present book very successfully assembles the state-of-the-art research results on learning in non-stationary environments—with a focus on the covariate shift model—and has embedded this body of work into the general literature from machine learning (semisupervised learning, online learning, transductive learning, domain adaptation) and statistics (sample selection bias). It will be an excellent starting point for future research in machine learning, statistics, and engineering that strives for truly autonomous learning machines that are able to learn under non-stationarity.

Klaus-Robert Müller
Machine Learning Laboratory, Computer Science Department
Technische Universität Berlin, Germany

Preface

In the twenty-first century, theory and practical algorithms of machine learning have been studied extensively, and there has been a rapid growth of computing power and the spread of the Internet. These machine learning methods are usually based on the presupposition that the data generation mechanism does not change over time. However, modern real-world applications of machine learning such as image recognition, natural language processing, speech recognition, robot control, bioinformatics, computational chemistry, and brain signal analysis often violate this important presumption, raising a challenge in the machine learning and statistics communities.

To cope with this non-stationarity problem, various approaches have been investigated in machine learning and related research fields. They are called by various names, such as covariate shift adaptation, sample selection bias, semisupervised learning, transfer learning, and domain adaptation. In this book, we consistently use the term *covariate shift adaptation*, and cover issues including theory and algorithms of function approximation, model selection, active learning, and real-world applications.

We were motivated to write the present book when we held a seminar on machine learning in a non-stationary environment at the Mathematisches Forschungsinstitut Oberwolfach (MFO) in Germany in 2008, together with Prof. Dr. Klaus-Robert Müller and Mr. Paul von Bünau of the Technische Universität Berlin. We thank them for their constant support and their encouragement to finishing this book.

Most of this book is based on the journal and conference papers we have published since 2005. We acknowledge all the collaborators for their fruitful discussions: Takayuki Akiyama, Hirotaka Hachiya, Shohei Hido, Tsuyoshi Ide, Yasuyuki Ihara, Takafumi Kanamori, Hisashi Kashima, Matthias Krauledat, Shin-ichi Nakajima, Hitemitsu Ogawa, Jun Sese, Taiji Suzuki, Ichiro Takeuchi, Yuta Tsuboi, Kazuya Ueki, and Makoto Yamada. Finally, we thank the Ministry of Education, Culture, Sports, Science and Technology in Japan, the Alexander von Humboldt Foundation in Germany, the Okawa Foundation, the Microsoft Institute for Japanese Academic Research Collaboration's Collaborative Research Project, the IBM Faculty Award, the Mathematisches Forschungsinstitut Oberwolfach Research-in-Pairs Program, the Asian Office of Aerospace Research and Development, the Support Center for Advanced Telecommunications Technology Research Foundation, the Japan Society for the Promotion of Science, the Funding Program for World-Leading Innovative R&D on Science and Technology, the Federal Ministry of Economics and Technology, Germany, and the IST program of the European Community under the PASCAL2 Network of Excellence for their financial support.

Picture taken at Mathematisches Forschungsinstitut Oberwolfach (MFO) in October 2008. From right to left, Masashi Sugiyama, Prof. Dr. Klaus-Robert Müller, Motoaki Kawanabe, and Mr. Paul von Bünau. Photo courtesy of Archives of the Mathematisches Forschungsinstitut Oberwolfach.

INTRODUCTION

1 Introduction and Problem Formulation

In this chapter, we provide an introduction to covariate shift adaptation toward machine learning in a non-stationary environment.

1.1 Machine Learning under Covariate Shift

Machine learning is an interdisciplinary field of science and engineering studying that studies mathematical foundations and practical applications of systems that learn. Depending on the type of learning, paradigms of machine learning can be categorized into three types:

- *Supervised learning* The goal of supervised learning is to infer an underlying input–output relation based on input–output samples. Once the underlying relation can be successfully learned, output values for unseen input points can be predicted. Thus, the learning machine can generalize to unexperienced situations. Studies of supervised learning are aimed at letting the learning machine acquire the best generalization performance from a small number of training samples. The supervised learning problem can be formulated as a function approximation problem from samples.

- *Unsupervised learning* In contrast to supervised learning, output values are not provided as training samples in unsupervised learning. The general goal of unsupervised learning is to extract valuable information hidden behind data. However, its specific goal depends heavily on the situation, and the unsupervised learning problem is sometimes not mathematically well-defined. Data clustering aimed at grouping similar data is a typical example. In data clustering, how to measure the similarity between data samples needs to be predetermined, but there is no objective criterion that can quantitatively evaluate the validity of the affinity measure; often it is merely subjectively determined.

• *Reinforcement learning*   The goal of reinforcement learning is to acquire a policy function (a mapping from a state to an action) of a computer agent. The policy function is an input–output relation, so the goal of reinforcement learning is the same as that of supervised learning. However, unlike supervised learning, the output data cannot be observed directly. Therefore, the policy function needs to be learned without supervisors. However, in contrast to unsupervised learning, rewards are provided as training samples for an agent's action. Based on the reward information, reinforcement learning tries to learn the policy function in such a way that the sum of rewards the agent will receive in the future is maximized.

The purpose of this book is to provide a comprehensive overview of theory, algorithms, and applications of supervised learning under the situation called *covariate shift*.

When developing methods of supervised learning, it is commonly assumed that samples used as a training set and data points used for testing the generalization performance[1] follow the same probability distribution (e.g., [195, 20, 193, 42, 74, 141]). However, this common assumption is not fulfilled in recent real-world applications of machine learning such as robot control, brain signal analysis, and bioinformatics. Thus, there is a strong need for theories and algorithms of supervised learning under such a changing environment. However, if there is no connection between training data and test data, nothing about test data can be learned from training samples. This means that a reasonable assumption is necessary for relating training samples to test data.

Covariate shift is one of the assumptions in supervised learning. The situation where the training input points and test input points follow different probability distributions, but the conditional distributions of output values given input points are unchanged, is called the covariate shift [145]. This means that the target function we want to learn is unchanged between the training phase and the test phase, but the distributions of input points are different for training and test data.

A situation of supervised learning where input-only samples are available in addition to input–output samples is called semisupervised learning [30]. The covariate shift adaptation techniques covered in this book fall into the category of semisupervised learning since input-only samples drawn from the test distribution are utilized for improving the generalization performance under covariate shift.

---

[1]. Such test points are not available during the training phase; they are given in the future after training has been completed.

1.2 Quick Tour of Covariate Shift Adaptation

Before going into the technical detail, in this section we briefly describe the core idea of covariate shift adaptation, using an illustrative example. To this end, let us consider a regression problem of learning a function $f(x)$ from its samples $\{(x_i^{tr}, y_i^{tr})\}_{i=1}^{n_{tr}}$. Once a good approximation fuction $\widehat{f}(x)$ is obtained, we can predict the output value y^{te} at an unseen test input point x^{te} by means of $\widehat{f}(x^{te})$.

Let us consider a covariate shift situation where the training and test input points follow different probability distributions, but the learning target function $f(x)$ is common to both training and test samples. In the toy regression example illustrated in figure 1.1a, training samples are located in the left-hand side of the graph and test samples are distributed in the right-hand side. Thus, this is an *extrapolation problem* where the test samples are located outside the

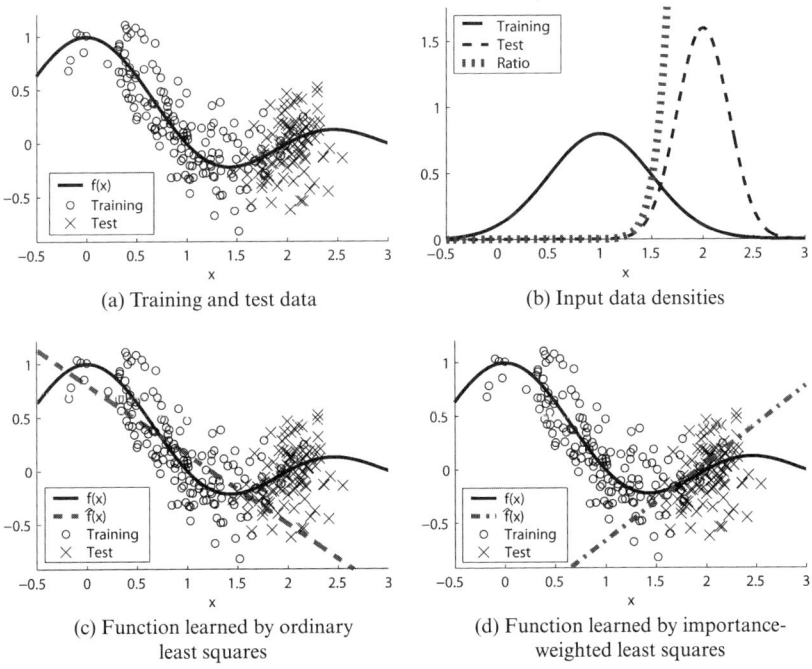

Figure 1.1
A regression example with covariate shift. (a) The learning target function $f(x)$ (the solid line), training samples (○), and test samples (×). (b) Probability density functions of training and test input points and their ratio. (c) Learned function $\widehat{f}(x)$ (the dashed line) obtained by ordinary least squares. (d) Learned function $\widehat{f}(x)$ (the dashed-dotted line) obtained by importance-weighted least squares. Note that the test samples are not used for function learning.

training region. Note that the test samples are not given to us in the training phase; they are plotted in the graph only for illustration purposes. The probability densities of the training and test input points, $p_{\mathrm{tr}}(x)$ and $p_{\mathrm{te}}(x)$, are plotted in figure 1.1b.

Let us consider straight-line function fitting by the method of least squares:

$$\min_{\theta_1,\theta_2}\left[\sum_{i=1}^{n_{\mathrm{tr}}}\left(\widehat{f}(x_i^{\mathrm{tr}})-y_i^{\mathrm{tr}}\right)^2\right],$$

where

$$\widehat{f}(x)=\theta_1 x+\theta_2.$$

This ordinary least squares gives a function that goes through the training samples well, as illustrated in figure 1.1c. However, the function learned by least squares is not useful for predicting the output values of the test samples located in the right-hand side of the graph.

Intuitively, training samples that are far from the test region (say, training samples with $x<1$ in figure 1.1a) are less informative for predicting the output values of the test samples located in the right-hand side of the graph. This gives the idea that ignoring such less informative training samples and learning only from the training samples that are close to the test region (say, training samples with $x>1.2$ in figure 1.1a) is more promising. The key idea of covariate shift adaptation is to (softly) choose informative training samples in a systematic way, by considering the *importance* of each training sample in the prediction of test output values. More specifically, we use the ratio of training and test input densities (see figure 1.1b),

$$\frac{p_{\mathrm{te}}(x_i^{\mathrm{tr}})}{p_{\mathrm{tr}}(x_i^{\mathrm{tr}})},$$

as a weight for the i-th training sample in the least-squares fitting:

$$\min_{\theta_1,\theta_2}\left[\sum_{i=1}^{n_{\mathrm{tr}}}\frac{p_{\mathrm{te}}(x_i^{\mathrm{tr}})}{p_{\mathrm{tr}}(x_i^{\mathrm{tr}})}\left(\widehat{f}(x_i^{\mathrm{tr}})-y_i^{\mathrm{tr}}\right)^2\right].$$

Then we can obtain a function that extrapolates the test samples well (see figure 1.1d). Note that the test samples are *not* used for obtaining this function. In this example, the training samples located in the left-hand side of the graph (say, $x<1.2$) have almost zero importance (see figure 1.1b). Thus, these samples are essentially ignored in the above importance-weighted least-squares method, and informative samples in the middle of the graph are automatically selected by importance weighting.

As illustrated above, importance weights play an essential role in covariate shift adaptation. Below, the problem of covariate shift adaptation is formulated more formally.

1.3 Problem Formulation

In this section, we formulate the supervised learning problem, which includes regression and classification. We pay particular attention to covariate shift and *model misspecification*; these two issues play the central roles in the following chapters.

1.3.1 Function Learning from Examples

Let us consider the supervised learning problem of estimating an unknown input–output dependency from training samples. Let

$$\{(\boldsymbol{x}_i^{\text{tr}}, y_i^{\text{tr}})\}_{i=1}^{n_{\text{tr}}}$$

be the training samples, where the training input point

$$\boldsymbol{x}_i^{\text{tr}} \in \mathcal{X} \subset \mathbb{R}^d, \quad i = 1, 2, \ldots, n_{\text{tr}}$$

is an *independent and identically distributed* (i.i.d.) sample following a probability distribution $P_{\text{tr}}(\boldsymbol{x})$ with density $p_{\text{tr}}(\boldsymbol{x})$:

$$\{\boldsymbol{x}_i^{\text{tr}}\}_{i=1}^{n_{\text{tr}}} \stackrel{\text{i.i.d.}}{\sim} P_{\text{tr}}(\boldsymbol{x}).$$

The training output value

$$y_i^{\text{tr}} \in \mathcal{Y} \subset \mathbb{R}, \quad i = 1, 2, \ldots, n_{\text{tr}}$$

follows a conditional probability distribution $P(y|\boldsymbol{x})$ with conditional density $p(y|\boldsymbol{x})$.

$$y_i^{\text{tr}} \sim P(y|\boldsymbol{x} = \boldsymbol{x}_i^{\text{tr}}).$$

$P(y|\boldsymbol{x})$ may be regarded as the superposition of the true output $f(\boldsymbol{x})$ and noise ϵ:

$$y = f(\boldsymbol{x}) + \epsilon.$$

We assume that noise ϵ has mean 0 and variance σ^2. Then the function $f(x)$ coincides with the conditional mean of y given x.

The above formulation is summarized in figure 1.2.

1.3.2 Loss Functions

Let $\text{loss}(x, y, \widehat{y})$ be the loss function which measures the discrepancy between the true output value y at an input point x and its estimate $\widehat{y}$. In the regression scenarios where $\mathcal{Y}$ is continuous, the *squared loss* is often used.

$$\text{loss}(x, y, \widehat{y}) = (\widehat{y} - y)^2.$$

On the other hand, in the binary classification scenarios where $\mathcal{Y} = \{+1, -1\}$, the following *0/1-loss* is a typical choice since it corresponds to the *misclassification rate*.

$$\text{loss}(x, y, \widehat{y}) = \begin{cases} 0 & \text{if } \text{sgn}(\widehat{y}) = y, \\ 1 & \text{otherwise,} \end{cases}$$

where $\text{sgn}(\widehat{y})$ denotes the sign of $\widehat{y}$:

$$\text{sgn}(\widehat{y}) := \begin{cases} +1 & \text{if } \widehat{y} > 0, \\ 0 & \text{if } \widehat{y} = 0, \\ -1 & \text{if } \widehat{y} < 0. \end{cases}$$

Although the above loss functions are independent of x, the loss can generally depend on x [141].

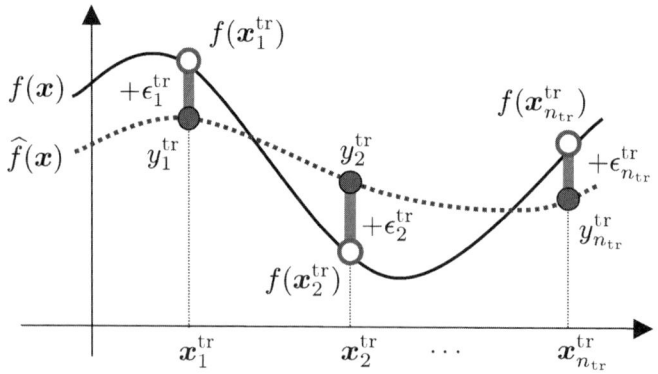

Figure 1.2
Framework of supervised learning.

1.3.3 Generalization Error

Let us consider a test sample (x^{te}, y^{te}), which is not given in the training phase but will be given in the test phase. $x^{te} \in \mathcal{X}$ is a test input point following a test distribution $P_{te}(x)$ with density $p_{te}(x)$, and $y^{te} \in \mathcal{Y}$ is a test output value following the conditional distribution $P(y|x = x^{te})$ with conditional density $p(y|x = x^{te})$. Note that the conditional distribution is common to both training and test samples. The test error expected over all test samples (or the *generalization error*) is expressed as

$$\text{Gen} = \mathop{\mathbb{E}}_{x^{te}} \mathop{\mathbb{E}}_{y^{te}} \left[\text{loss}(x^{te}, y^{te}, \widehat{f}(x^{te}; \boldsymbol{\theta})) \right],$$

where $\mathbb{E}_{x^{te}}$ denotes the expectation over x^{te} drawn from $P_{te}(x)$ and $\mathbb{E}_{y^{te}}$ denotes the expectation over y^{te} drawn from $P(y|x = x^{te})$. The goal of supervised learning is to determine the value of the parameter $\boldsymbol{\theta}$ so that the generalization error is minimized, that is, output values for unseen test input points can be accurately estimated in terms of the expected loss.

1.3.4 Covariate Shift

In standard supervised learning theories (e.g., [195,20,193,42,74,141,21]), the test input distribution $P_{te}(x)$ is assumed to agree with the training input distribution $P_{tr}(x)$. However, in this book we consider the situation under covariate shift [145], that is, the test input distribution $P_{te}(x)$ and the training input distribution $P_{tr}(x)$ are generally different:

$$P_{tr}(x) \neq P_{te}(x).$$

Under covariate shift, most of the standard machine learning techniques do not work properly due to the differing distributions. The main goal of this book is to provide machine learning methods that can mitigate the influence of covariate shift.

In the following chapters, we assume that the ratio of test to training input densities is bounded, that is,

$$\frac{p_{te}(x)}{p_{tr}(x)} < \infty \text{ for all } x \in \mathcal{X}.$$

This means that the support of the test input distribution must be contained in that of the training input distribution. The above ratio is called the *importance* [51], and it plays a central role in covariate shift adaptation.

1.3.5 Models for Function Learning

Let us employ a parameterized function $\widehat{f}(x; \theta)$ for estimating the output value y, where

$$\theta = (\theta_1, \theta_2, \ldots, \theta_b)^\top \in \Theta \subset \mathbb{R}^b.$$

Here, $^\top$ denotes the transpose of a vector or a matrix, and Θ denotes the domain of parameter θ.

1.3.5.1 Linear-in-Input Model

The simplest choice of parametric model would be the *linear-in-input model*:

$$\widehat{f}(x; \theta) = \sum_{k=1}^{d} \theta_k x^{(k)} + \theta_{d+1}, \tag{1.1}$$

where

$$x = (x^{(1)}, x^{(2)}, \ldots, x^{(d)})^\top.$$

This model has linearity in both input variable x and parameter θ, and the number b of parameters is $d+1$, where d is the dimensionality of x. The linear-in-input model can represent only a linear input–output relation, so its expressibility is limited. However, since the effect of each input variable $x^{(k)}$ can be specified directly by the parameter θ_k, it would have high interpretability. For this reason, this simple model is still often used in many practical data analysis tasks such as natural language processing, bioinformatics, and computational chemistry.

1.3.5.2 Linear-in-Parameter Model

A slight extension of the linear-in-input model is the *linear-in-parameter* model:

$$\widehat{f}(x; \theta) = \sum_{\ell=1}^{b} \theta_\ell \varphi_\ell(x), \tag{1.2}$$

where $\{\varphi_\ell(x)\}_{\ell=1}^{b}$ are fixed, linearly independent functions. This model is linear in parameter θ, and we often refer to it as the *linear model*. Popular choices of basis functions include *polynomials* and *trigonometric polynomials*.

When the input dimensionality is $d = 1$, the polynomial basis functions are given by

$$\{\varphi_\ell(x)\}_{\ell=1}^{b} = \{1, x, x^2, \ldots, x^t\},$$

1.3. Problem Formulation

where $b = t + 1$. The trigonometric polynomial basis functions are given by

$$\{\varphi_\ell(x)\}_{\ell=1}^{b} = \{1, \sin x, \cos x, \sin 2x, \cos 2x, \ldots, \sin cx, \cos cx\},$$

where $b = 2c + 1$.

For multidimensional cases, basis functions are often built by combining one-dimensional basis functions. Popular choices include the *additive model* and the *multiplicative model*. The additive model is given by

$$\widehat{f}(\boldsymbol{x}; \boldsymbol{\theta}) = \sum_{k=1}^{d} \sum_{\ell=1}^{c} \theta_{k,\ell} \varphi_\ell(x^{(k)}).$$

Thus, a one-dimensional model for each dimension is combined with the others in an additive manner (figure 1.3a). The number of parameters in the additive model is

$$b = cd.$$

The multiplicative model is given by

$$\widehat{f}(\boldsymbol{x}; \boldsymbol{\theta}) = \sum_{\ell_1, \ell_2, \ldots, \ell_d = 1}^{c} \theta_{\ell_1, \ell_2, \ldots, \ell_d} \prod_{k=1}^{d} \varphi_{\ell_k}(x^{(k)}).$$

Thus, a one-dimensional model for each dimension is combined with the others in a multiplicative manner (figure 1.3b). The number of parameters in the multiplicative model is

$$b = c^d.$$

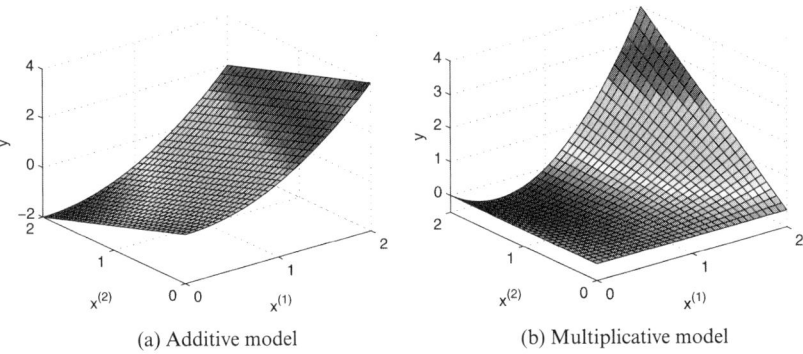

(a) Additive model   (b) Multiplicative model

Figure 1.3
Examples of an additive model $\widehat{f}(\boldsymbol{x}) = (x^{(1)})^2 - x^{(2)}$ and of a multiplicative model $\widehat{f}(\boldsymbol{x}) = -x^{(1)}x^{(2)} + x^{(1)}(x^{(2)})^2$.

In general, the multiplicative model can represent more complex functions than the additive model (see figure 1.3). However, the multiplicative model contains exponentially many parameters with respect to the input dimensionality d—such a phenomenon is often referred to as the curse of dimensionality [12]. Thus, the multiplicative model is not tractable in high-dimensional problems. On the other hand, the number of parameters in the additive model increases only linearly with respect to the input dimensionality d, which is more preferable in high-dimensional cases [71].

1.3.5.3 Kernel Model The number of parameters in the linear-in-parameter model is related to the input dimensionality d. Another means for determining the number of parameters is to relate the number of parameters to the number of training samples, n_{tr}. The *kernel model* follows this idea, and is defined by

$$\widehat{f}(\boldsymbol{x};\boldsymbol{\theta}) = \sum_{\ell=1}^{n_{\text{tr}}} \theta_\ell K(\boldsymbol{x}, \boldsymbol{x}_\ell^{\text{tr}}),$$

where $K(\cdot,\cdot)$ is a *kernel function*. The *Gaussian kernel* would be a typical choice (see figure 1.4):

$$K(\boldsymbol{x},\boldsymbol{x}') = \exp\left(-\frac{\|\boldsymbol{x}-\boldsymbol{x}'\|^2}{2h^2}\right), \qquad (1.3)$$

where h (> 0) controls the width of the Gaussian function.

In the kernel model, the number b of parameters is set to n_{tr}, which is independent of the input dimensionality d. For this reason, the kernel model is often preferred in high-dimensional problems. The kernel model is still linear in parameters, so it is a kind of linear-in-parameter model; indeed, letting

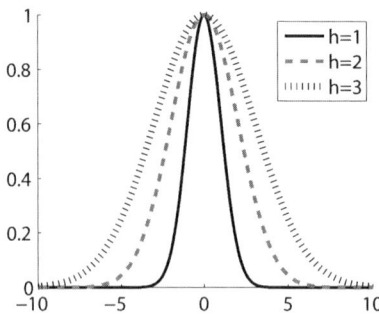

Figure 1.4
Gaussian functions (equation 1.3) centered at the origin with width h.

1.3. Problem Formulation

$b = n_{tr}$ and $\varphi_\ell(x) = K(x, x_\ell^{tr})$ in the linear-in-parameter model (equation 1.2) yields the kernel model. Thus, many learning algorithms explained in this book could be applied to both models in the same way.

However, when we discuss convergence properties of the learned function $\widehat{f}(x; \theta)$ when the number of training samples is increased to infinity, the kernel model should be treated differently from the linear-in-parameter model because the number of parameters increases as the number of training samples grows. In such a case, standard asymptotic analysis tools such as the *Cramér-Rao paradigm* are not applicable. For this reason, statisticians categorize the linear-in-parameter model and the kernel model in different classes: the linear-in-parameter model is categorized as a *parametric model*, whereas the kernel model is categorized as a *nonparametric model*. Analysis of the asymptotic behavior of nonparametric models is generally more difficult than that of parametric models, and highly sophisticated mathematical tools are needed (see, e.g., [191, 192, 69]).

A practical compromise would be to use a fixed number of kernel functions, that is, for fixed b,

$$\widehat{f}(x; \theta) = \sum_{\ell=1}^{b} \theta_\ell K(x, c_\ell),$$

where, for example, $\{c_\ell\}_{\ell=1}^{b}$ are template points for example chosen randomly from the domain or from the training input points $\{x_i^{tr}\}_{i=1}^{n_{tr}}$ without replacement.

1.3.6 Specification of Models

A model $\widehat{f}(x; \theta)$ is said to be correctly specified if there exists a parameter θ^* such that

$$\widehat{f}(x; \theta^*) = f(x).$$

Otherwise, the model is said to be *misspecified*. In practice, the model used for learning would be misspecified to a greater or lesser extent since we do not generally have strong enough prior knowledge to correctly specify the model. Thus, it is important to consider misspecified models when developing machine learning algorithms.

On the other hand, it is meaningless to discuss properties of learning algorithms if the model is *totally* misspecified—for example, approximating highly nonlinearly fluctuated functions by a straight line does not provide meaningful prediction (figure 1.5). Thus, we effectively consider the situation where the model at hand is not correctly specified but is approximately correct.

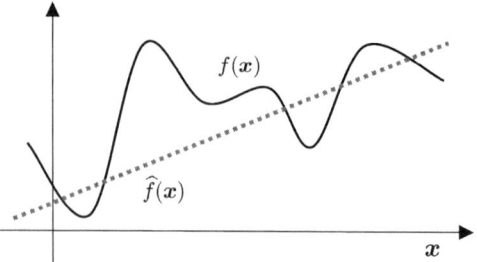

Figure 1.5
Approximating a highly nonlinear function $f(x)$ by the linear-in-input model $\widehat{f}(x)$, which is totally misspecified.

This approximate correctness plays an important role when designing model selection algorithms (chapter 3) and active learning algorithms (chapter 8).

1.4 Structure of This Book

This book covers issues related to the covariate shift problems, from fundamental learning algorithms to state-of-the-art applications.

Figure 1.6 summarizes the structure of chapters.

1.4.1 Part II: Learning under Covariate Shift

In part II, topics on learning under covariate shift are covered.

In chapter 2, function learning methods under covariate shift are introduced. Ordinary *empirical risk minimization* learning is not consistent under covariate shift for misspecified models, and this inconsistency issue can be resolved by considering *importance-weighted loss functions*. Here, various importance-weighted empirical risk minimization methods are introduced, including *least squares* and *Huber's method* for regression, and *Fisher discriminant analysis, logistic regression, support vector machines*, and *boosting* for classification. Their adaptive and regularized variants are also introduced. The numerical behavior of these importance-weighted learning methods is illustrated through experiments.

In chapter 3, the problem of model selection is addressed. Success of machine learning techniques depends heavily on the choice of *hyperparameters* such as *basis functions*, the *kernel bandwidth*, the *regularization parameter*, and the *importance-flattening parameter*. Thus, model selection is one of the most fundamental and crucial topics in machine learning. Standard model selection schemes such as the *Akaike information criterion, cross-validation*, and the *subspace information criterion* have their own theoretical justification

1.4. Structure of This Book

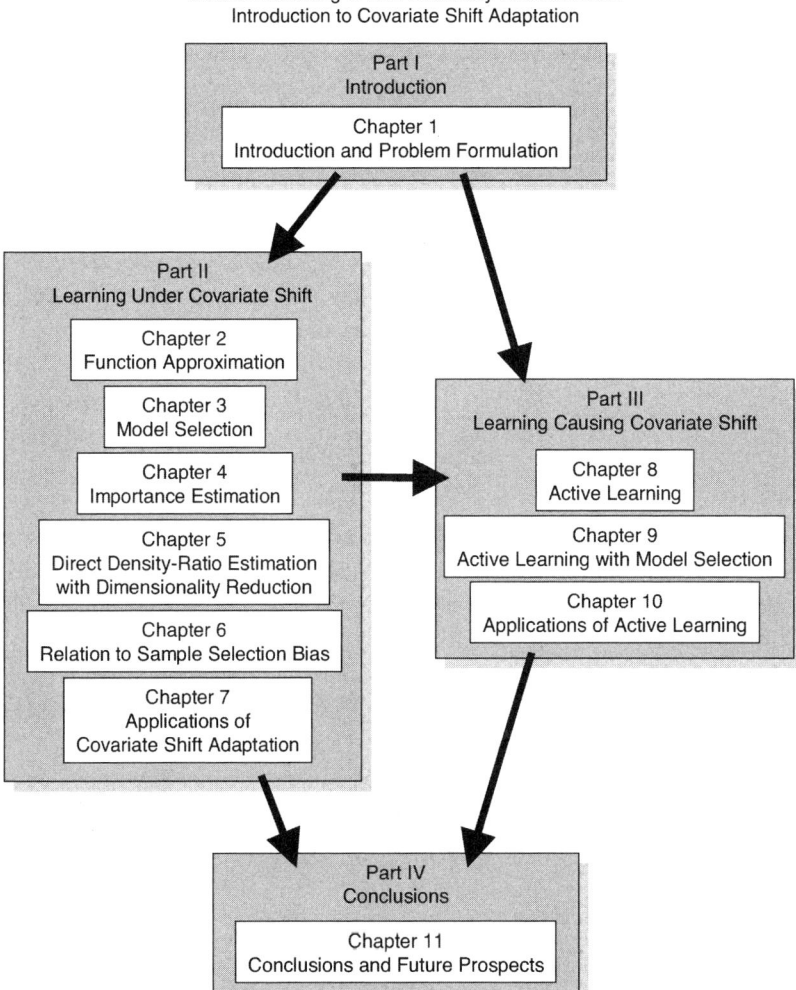

Figure 1.6
Structure of this book.

in terms of the unbiasedness as generalization error estimators. However, such theoretical guarantees are no longer valid under covariate shift. In this chapter, various their modified variants using importance-weighting techniques are introduced, and the modified methods are shown to be properly unbiased even under covariate shift. The usefulness of these modified model selection criteria is illustrated through numerical experiments.

In chapter 4, the problem of *importance estimation* is addressed. As shown in the preceding chapters, importance-weighting techniques play essential roles in covariate shift adaptation. However, the importance values are usually unknown a priori, so they must be estimated from data samples. In this chapter, importance estimation methods are introduced, including importance estimation via *kernel density estimation*, the *kernel mean matching* method, a *logistic regression* approach, the *Kullback–Leibler importance estimation procedure*, and the *least-squares importance fitting* methods. The latter methods allow one to estimate the importance weights without performing through density estimation. Since density estimation is known to be difficult, the direct importance estimation approaches would be more accurate and preferable in practice. The numerical behavior of direct importance estimation methods is illustrated through experiments. Characteristics of importance estimation methods are also discussed.

In chapter 5, a dimensionality reduction scheme for density-ratio estimation, called *direct density-ratio estimation with dimensionality reduction* (D^3; pronounced as "D-cube"), is introduced. The basic idea of D^3 is to find a low-dimensional subspace in which training and test densities are significantly different, and estimate the density ratio only in this subspace. A supervised dimensionality reduction technique called *local Fisher discriminant analysis* (LFDA) is employed for identifying such a subspace. The usefulness of the D^3 approach is illustrated through numerical experiments.

In chapter 6, the covariate shift approach is compared with related formulations called *sample selection bias*. Studies of correcting sample selection bias were initiated by Heckman [77,76], who received the Nobel Prize in economics for this achievement in 2000. We give a comprehensive review of Heckman's correction model, and discuss its relation to covariate shift adaptation.

In chapter 7, state-of-the-art applications of covariate shift adaptation techniques to various real-world problems are described. This chapter includes non-stationarity adaptation in brain–computer interfaces, speaker identification through change in voice quality, domain adaptation in natural language processing, age prediction from face images under changing illumination conditions, user adaptation in human activity recognition, and efficient sample reuse in autonomous robot control.

1.4.2 Part III: Learning Causing Covariate Shift

In part III, we discuss the situation where covariate shift is intentionally caused by users in order to improve generalization ability.

In chapter 8, the problem of *active learning* is addressed. The goal of active learning is to find the most "informative" training input points so that learning can be successfully achieved from only a small number of training samples. Active learning is particularly useful when the cost of data sampling is expensive. In the active learning scenario, covariate shift—mismatch of training and test input distributions—occurs naturally occurs since the training input distribution is designed by users, while the test input distribution is determined by the environment. Thus, covariate shift is inevitable in active learning. In this chapter, active learning methods for regression are introduced in light of covariate shift. Their mutual relation and numerical examples are also shown. Furthermore, these active learning methods are extended to the *pool-based scenarios*, where a set of input-only samples is provided in advance and users want to specify good input-only samples to gather output values.

In chapter 9, the problem of *active learning with model selection* is addressed. As explained in the previous chapters, model selection and active learning are two important challenges for successful learning. A natural desire is to perform model selection and active learning at the same time, that is, we want to choose the best model and the best training input points. However, this is actually a chicken-and-egg problem since training input samples should have been fixed for performing model selection and models should have been fixed for performing active learning. In this chapter, several compromise approaches, such as the sequential approach, the batch approach, and the ensemble approach, are discussed. Then, through numerical examples, limitations of the sequential and batch approaches are pointed out, and the usefulness of the *ensemble active learning* approach is demonstrated.

In chapter 10, applications of active learning techniques to real-world problems are shown. This chapter includes efficient exploration for autonomous robot control and efficient sensor design in semiconductor wafer alignment.

II LEARNING UNDER COVARIATE SHIFT

2 Function Approximation

In this chapter, we introduce learning methods that can cope with covariate shift.

We employ a parameterized function $\widehat{f}(x;\theta)$ for approximating a target function $f(x)$ from training samples $\{(x_i^{\text{tr}}, y_i^{\text{tr}})\}_{i=1}^{n_{\text{tr}}}$ (see section 1.3.5).

A standard method to learn the parameter θ would be *empirical risk minimization* (ERM) (e.g., [193, 141]):

$$\widehat{\theta}_{\text{ERM}} := \operatorname*{argmin}_{\theta}\left[\frac{1}{n_{\text{tr}}}\sum_{i=1}^{n_{\text{tr}}}\text{loss}(x_i^{\text{tr}}, y_i^{\text{tr}}, \widehat{f}(x_i^{\text{tr}};\theta))\right],$$

where $\text{loss}(x, y, \widehat{y})$ is a loss function (see section 1.3.2). If $P_{\text{tr}}(x) = P_{\text{te}}(x)$, $\widehat{\theta}_{\text{ERM}}$ is known to be *consistent*[1] [145]. Under covariate shift where $P_{\text{tr}}(x) \neq P_{\text{te}}(x)$, however, the situation differs: ERM still gives a consistent estimator if the model is correctly specified, but it is no longer consistent if the model is misspecified [145]:

$$\operatorname*{plim}_{n_{\text{tr}} \to \infty}\left[\widehat{\theta}_{\text{ERM}}\right] \neq \theta^*,$$

where "plim" denotes *convergence in probability*, and θ^* is the optimal parameter in the model:

$$\theta^* := \operatorname*{argmin}_{\theta}[\text{Gen}].$$

---

1. For correctly specified models, an estimator is said to be consistent if it converges to the true parameter in probability. For misspecified models, we use the term "consistency" for convergence to the optimal parameter in the model (i.e., the optimal approximation to the learning target function in the model under the generalization error Gen).

Gen is the generalization error defined as

$$\text{Gen} = \mathop{\mathbb{E}}_{x^{te}} \mathop{\mathbb{E}}_{y^{te}} \left[\text{loss}(x^{te}, y^{te}, \widehat{f}(x^{te}; \boldsymbol{\theta}))\right],$$

where $\mathbb{E}_{x^{te}}$ denotes the expectation over x^{te} drawn from the test input distribution $P_{te}(x)$, and $\mathbb{E}_{y^{te}}$ denotes the expectation over y^{te} drawn from the conditional distribution $P(y|x = x^{te})$.

This chapter is devoted to introducing various techniques of covariate shift adaptation in function learning.

2.1 Importance-Weighting Techniques for Covariate Shift Adaptation

In this section, we show how the inconsistency of ERM can be overcome.

2.1.1 Importance-Weighted ERM

The failure of the ERM method comes from the fact that the training input distribution is different from the test input distribution. *Importance sampling* (e.g., [51]) is a standard technique to compensate for the difference of distributions. The following identity shows the essential idea of importance sampling. For a function g,

$$\mathop{\mathbb{E}}_{x^{te}}[g(x^{te})] = \int g(x) p_{te}(x) dx$$

$$= \int g(x) \frac{p_{te}(x)}{p_{tr}(x)} p_{tr}(x) dx$$

$$= \mathop{\mathbb{E}}_{x^{tr}}\left[g(x^{tr}) \frac{p_{te}(x^{tr})}{p_{tr}(x^{tr})}\right],$$

where $\mathbb{E}_{x^{tr}}$ and $\mathbb{E}_{x^{te}}$ denote the expectation over x drawn from $p_{tr}(x)$ and $p_{te}(x)$, respectively. The quantity

$$\frac{p_{te}(x)}{p_{tr}(x)}$$

is called the *importance*. The above identity shows that the expectation of a function g over x^{te} can be computed by the *importance-weighted* expectation of the function over x^{tr}. Thus, the difference of distributions can be systematically adjusted by importance weighting. This is the key equation that plays a central role of in covariate shift adaptation throughout the book.

2.1. Importance-Weighting Techniques for Covariate Shift Adaptation

Under covariate shift, *importance-weighted ERM* (IWERM),

$$\widehat{\boldsymbol{\theta}}_{\text{IWERM}} := \underset{\boldsymbol{\theta}}{\operatorname{argmin}} \left[\frac{1}{n_{\text{tr}}} \sum_{i=1}^{n_{\text{tr}}} \frac{p_{\text{te}}(\boldsymbol{x}_i^{\text{tr}})}{p_{\text{tr}}(\boldsymbol{x}_i^{\text{tr}})} \text{loss}(\boldsymbol{x}_i^{\text{tr}}, y_i^{\text{tr}}, \widehat{f}(\boldsymbol{x}_i^{\text{tr}}; \boldsymbol{\theta})) \right],$$

is shown to be consistent even for misspecified models [145], that is, it satisfies

$$\underset{n_{\text{tr}} \to \infty}{\operatorname{plim}} \left[\widehat{\boldsymbol{\theta}}_{\text{IWERM}} \right] = \boldsymbol{\theta}^*.$$

2.1.2 Adaptive IWERM

As shown above, IWERM gives a consistent estimator. However, it also can produce an unstable estimator, and therefore IWERM may not be the best possible method for finite samples [145]—in practice, a slightly stabilized variant of IWERM would be preferable, that is, one achieved by slightly "flattening" the importance weight in IWERM. We call this variant *adaptive IWERM* (AIWERM):

$$\widehat{\boldsymbol{\theta}}_\gamma := \underset{\boldsymbol{\theta}}{\operatorname{argmin}} \left[\frac{1}{n_{\text{tr}}} \sum_{i=1}^{n_{\text{tr}}} \left(\frac{p_{\text{te}}(\boldsymbol{x}_i^{\text{tr}})}{p_{\text{tr}}(\boldsymbol{x}_i^{\text{tr}})} \right)^\gamma \text{loss}(\boldsymbol{x}_i^{\text{tr}}, y_i^{\text{tr}}, \widehat{f}(\boldsymbol{x}_i^{\text{tr}}; \boldsymbol{\theta})) \right], \quad (2.1)$$

where γ ($0 \leq \gamma \leq 1$) is called the *flattening parameter*.

The flattening parameter controls stability and consistency of the estimator; $\gamma = 0$ corresponds to ordinary ERM (the uniform weight, which yields a stable but inconsistent estimator), and $\gamma = 1$ corresponds to IWERM (the importance weight, which yields a consistent but unstable estimator). An intermediate value of γ would provide the optimal control of the trade-off between stability and consistency (which is also known as the *bias–variance trade-off*).

A good choice of γ would roughly depend on the number n_{tr} of training samples. When n_{tr} is large, bias usually dominates variance, and thus a smaller bias estimator obtained by large γ is preferable. On the other hand, when n_{tr} is small, variance generally dominates bias, and hence a smaller variance estimator obtained by small γ is appropriate. However, a good choice of γ may also depend on many unknown factors, such as the learning target function and the noise level. Thus, the flattening parameter γ should be determined carefully by a reliable model selection method (see chapter 3).

2.1.3 Regularized IWERM

Instead of flattening the importance weight, we may add a *regularizer* to the empirical risk term. We call this *regularized IWERM*:

$$\widehat{\boldsymbol{\theta}}_\lambda := \underset{\boldsymbol{\theta}}{\arg\min} \left[\frac{1}{n_{\text{tr}}} \sum_{i=1}^{n_{\text{tr}}} \frac{p_{\text{te}}(\boldsymbol{x}_i^{\text{tr}})}{p_{\text{tr}}(\boldsymbol{x}_i^{\text{tr}})} \text{loss}(\boldsymbol{x}_i^{\text{tr}}, y_i^{\text{tr}}, \widehat{f}(\boldsymbol{x}_i^{\text{tr}}; \boldsymbol{\theta})) + \lambda R(\boldsymbol{\theta}) \right], \tag{2.2}$$

where $R(\boldsymbol{\theta})$ is a regularization function, and λ (≥ 0) is the regularization parameter that controls the strength of regularization. For some $c(\lambda)$ (≥ 0), the solution of equation 2.2 also can be obtained by solving the following constrained optimization problem:

$$\widehat{\boldsymbol{\theta}}_\lambda = \underset{\boldsymbol{\theta}}{\arg\min} \left[\frac{1}{n_{\text{tr}}} \sum_{i=1}^{n_{\text{tr}}} \frac{p_{\text{te}}(\boldsymbol{x}_i^{\text{tr}})}{p_{\text{tr}}(\boldsymbol{x}_i^{\text{tr}})} \text{loss}(\boldsymbol{x}_i^{\text{tr}}, y_i^{\text{tr}}, \widehat{f}(\boldsymbol{x}_i^{\text{tr}}; \boldsymbol{\theta})) \right],$$

subject to $R(\boldsymbol{\theta}) \leq c(\lambda)$.

A typical choice of the regularization function $R(\boldsymbol{\theta})$ is the squared ℓ_2-norm (see figure 2.1):

$$R(\boldsymbol{\theta}) = \sum_{\ell=1}^{b} \theta_\ell^2.$$

This is differentiable and convex, so it is often convenient to use it in devising computationally efficient optimization algorithms. The feasible region (where the constraint $R(\boldsymbol{\theta}) \leq c(\lambda)$ is satisfied) is illustrated in figure 2.2a.

Another useful choice is the ℓ_1-norm (see figure 2.1):

$$R(\boldsymbol{\theta}) = \sum_{\ell=1}^{b} |\theta_\ell|.$$

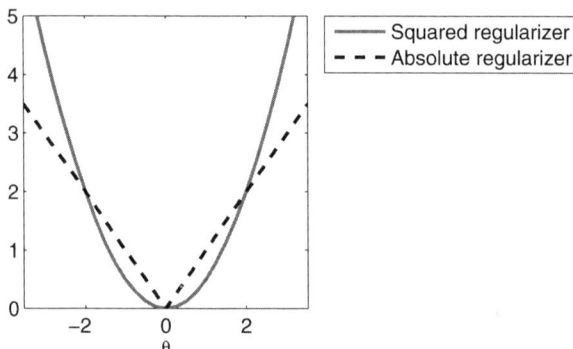

Figure 2.1
Regularization functions: squared regularizer (θ^2) and absolute regularizer ($|\theta|$).

2.2. Examples of Importance-Weighted Regression Methods

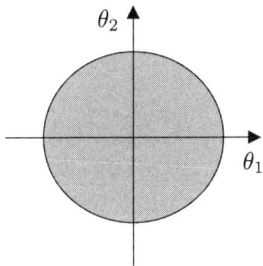
(a) Squared regularization

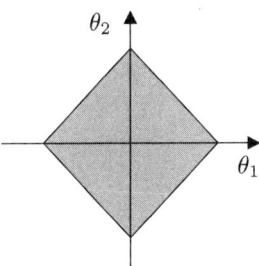
(b) Absolute regularization

Figure 2.2
Feasible regions by regularization.

This is not differentiable, but it is still convex. It is known that the absolute regularizer induces a *sparse* solution, that is, the parameters $\{\theta_\ell\}_{\ell=1}^b$ tend to become zero [200, 183, 31]. When the solution $\widehat{\boldsymbol{\theta}}$ is sparse, output values $\widehat{f}(\boldsymbol{x}; \widehat{\boldsymbol{\theta}})$ may be computed efficiently, which is a useful property if the number of parameters is very large. Furthermore, when the linear-in-input model (see section 1.3.5)

$$\widehat{f}(\boldsymbol{x}; \boldsymbol{\theta}) = \sum_{k=1}^{d} \theta_k x^{(k)} + \theta_{d+1} \tag{2.3}$$

is used, making a solution sparse corresponds to choosing a subset of input variables $\{x^{(k)}\}_{k=1}^d$ which are responsible for predicting output values y. This is highly useful when each input variable has some meaning (type of experiment, etc.), and we want to interpret the "reason" for the prediction. Such a technique can be applied in bioinformatics, natural language processing, and computational chemistry. The feasible region of the absolute regularizer is illustrated in figure 2.2b.

The reason why the solution becomes sparse by absolute regularization may be intuitively understood from figure 2.3, where the squared loss is adopted. The feasible region of the absolute regularizer has "corners" on axes, and thus the solution tends to be on one of the corners, which is sparse. On the other hand, such sparseness is not available when the squared regularizer is used.

2.2 Examples of Importance-Weighted Regression Methods

The above importance-weighting idea is very general, and can be applied to various learning algorithms. In this section, we provide examples of regression methods including least squares and robust regression. Classification methods will be covered in section 2.3.

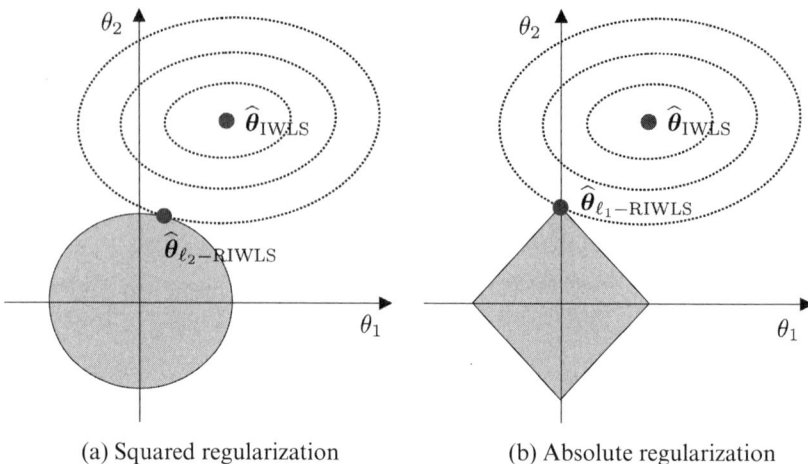

(a) Squared regularization (b) Absolute regularization

Figure 2.3
Sparseness brought by absolute regularization.

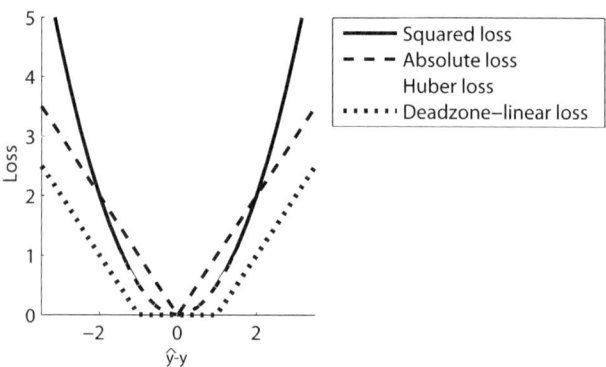

Figure 2.4
Loss functions for regression.

2.2.1 Squared Loss: Least-Squares Regression

Least squares (LS) is one of the most fundamental regression techniques in statistics and machine learning. The adaptive importance-weighting method for the squared loss, called *adaptive importance-weighted LS* (AIWLS), is given as follows (see figure 2.4):

$$\widehat{\boldsymbol{\theta}}_\gamma = \operatorname*{argmin}_{\boldsymbol{\theta}} \left[\frac{1}{n_{\text{tr}}} \sum_{i=1}^{n_{\text{tr}}} \left(\frac{p_{\text{te}}(\boldsymbol{x}_i^{\text{tr}})}{p_{\text{tr}}(\boldsymbol{x}_i^{\text{tr}})} \right)^\gamma \left(\widehat{f}(\boldsymbol{x}_i^{\text{tr}}; \boldsymbol{\theta}) - y_i^{\text{tr}} \right)^2 \right], \tag{2.4}$$

2.2. Examples of Importance-Weighted Regression Methods

where $0 \leq \gamma \leq 1$. Let us employ the linear-in-parameter model (see section 1.3.5.2) for learning:

$$\widehat{f}(x; \theta) = \sum_{\ell=1}^{b} \theta_\ell \varphi_\ell(x), \tag{2.5}$$

where $\{\varphi_\ell(x)\}_{\ell=1}^{b}$ are fixed, linearly independent functions. Then the above minimizer $\widehat{\theta}_\gamma$ is given analytically, as follows.

Let X^{tr} be the *design matrix*, that is, X^{tr} is the $n_{tr} \times b$ matrix with the (i, ℓ)-th element

$$X^{tr}_{i,\ell} = \varphi_\ell(x_i^{tr}).$$

Then we have

$$(\widehat{f}(x_1; \theta), \widehat{f}(x_2; \theta), \ldots, \widehat{f}(x_{n_{tr}}; \theta))^\top = X^{tr}\theta,$$

and thus equation 2.4 is expressed in a matrix form as

$$\frac{1}{n_{tr}}(X^{tr}\theta - y^{tr})^\top W_\gamma^{tr}(X^{tr}\theta - y^{tr})$$

$$= \frac{1}{n_{tr}}\theta^\top X^{tr\top} W_\gamma^{tr} X^{tr}\theta - \frac{2}{n_{tr}}\theta^\top X^{tr\top} W_\gamma^{tr} y^{tr} + \text{Constant},$$

where W_γ^{tr} is the diagonal matrix with the i-th diagonal element

$$[W_\gamma]_{i,i} = \left(\frac{p_{te}(x_i^{tr})}{p_{tr}(x_i^{tr})}\right)^\gamma,$$

and

$$y^{tr} = (y_1^{tr}, y_2^{tr}, \ldots, y_{n_{tr}}^{tr})^\top.$$

Taking its derivative with respect to θ and equating it to zero yields

$$X^{tr\top} W_\gamma^{tr} X^{tr}\theta = X^{tr\top} W_\gamma^{tr} y^{tr}.$$

Let L_γ be the *learning matrix* given by

$$L_\gamma = (X^{tr\top} W_\gamma^{tr} X^{tr})^{-1} X^{tr\top} W_\gamma^{tr},$$

where we assume that the inverse of $X^{tr\top} W_\gamma^{tr} X^{tr}$ exists. Then $\widehat{\boldsymbol{\theta}}_\gamma$ is given by

$$\widehat{\boldsymbol{\theta}}_\gamma = L_\gamma y^{tr}. \tag{2.6}$$

A MATLAB® implementation of adaptive importance-weighted LS is available from http://sugiyama-www.cs.titech.ac.jp/~sugi/software/IWLS/.

The above analytic solution is easy to implement and useful for theoretical analysis of the solution. However, when the number of parameters is very large, computing the solution by means of equation 2.6 may not be tractable since the matrix $X^{tr\top} W_\gamma^{tr} X^{tr}$ that we need to invert is very high-dimensional.[2] Another way to obtain the solution is *gradient descent*—the parameter $\boldsymbol{\theta}$ is updated so that the squared-error term is reduced, and this procedure is repeated until convergence (see figure 2.5):

$$\theta_\ell \leftarrow \theta_\ell - \varepsilon \sum_{i=1}^{n_{tr}} \left(\frac{p_{te}(\boldsymbol{x}_i^{tr})}{p_{tr}(\boldsymbol{x}_i^{tr})}\right)^\gamma \left(\sum_{\ell'=1}^{b} \theta_{\ell'} \varphi_{\ell'}(\boldsymbol{x}_i^{tr}) - y_i^{tr}\right) \varphi_\ell(\boldsymbol{x}_i^{tr}) \quad \text{for all } \ell,$$

where ε (> 0) is a learning-rate parameter, and the rest of the second term corresponds to the gradient of the objective function (equation 2.4). If ε is large, the solution goes down the slope very fast (see figure 2.5a); however, it can overshoot the bottom of the objective function and fluctuate around the

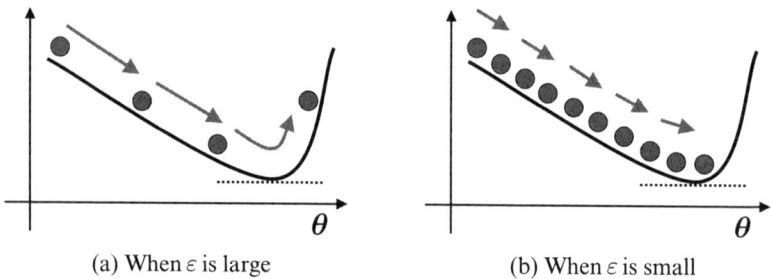

(a) When ε is large (b) When ε is small

Figure 2.5
Schematic illustration of gradient descent.

2. In practice, we may solve the following linear equation,

$$X^{tr\top} W_\gamma^{tr} X^{tr} \widehat{\boldsymbol{\theta}}_\gamma = X^{tr\top} W_\gamma^{tr} y^{tr},$$

for computing the solution. This would be slightly more computationally efficient than computing the solution by means of equation 2.6. However, solving this equation would still be intractable when the number of parameters is very large.

2.2. Examples of Importance-Weighted Regression Methods

bottom. On the other hand, if ε is small, the speed of going down the slope is slow, but the solution stably converges to the bottom (see figure 2.5b). A suitable scheme would be to start from large ε to quickly go down the slope, and then gradually decrease the value of ε so that it properly converges to the bottom of the objective function. However, determining appropriate scheduling of ε is highly problem-dependent, and it is easy to appropriately choose ε in practice.

Note that in general, the gradient method is guaranteed only to be able to find one of the local optima, whereas in the case of LS for linear-in-parameter models (equation 2.5), we can always find the globally optimal solution thanks to the *convexity* of the objective function (see, e.g., [27]).

When the number n_{tr} of training samples is very large, computing the gradient as above is rather time-consuming. In such a case, the following *stochastic gradient method* [7] is computationally more efficient—for a randomly chosen sample index $i \in \{1, 2, \ldots, n_{\mathrm{tr}}\}$ in each iteration, repeat the following single-sample update until convergence:

$$\theta_\ell \leftarrow \theta_\ell - \varepsilon \left(\frac{p_{\mathrm{te}}(x_i^{\mathrm{tr}})}{p_{\mathrm{tr}}(x_i^{\mathrm{tr}})} \right)^\gamma \left(\sum_{\ell'=1}^{b} \theta_{\ell'} \varphi_{\ell'}(x_i^{\mathrm{tr}}) - y_i^{\mathrm{tr}} \right) \varphi_\ell(x_i^{\mathrm{tr}}) \quad \text{for all } \ell.$$

Convergence of the stochastic gradient method is guaranteed in the probabilistic sense.

The AIWLS method can easily be extended to kernel models (see section 1.3.5.3) by letting $b = n_{\mathrm{tr}}$ and $\varphi_\ell(x) = K(x, x_\ell^{\mathrm{tr}})$, where $K(\cdot, \cdot)$ is a kernel function:

$$\widehat{f}(x; \theta) = \sum_{\ell=1}^{n_{\mathrm{tr}}} \theta_\ell K(x, x_\ell^{\mathrm{tr}}).$$

The *Gaussian kernel* is a popular choice:

$$K(x, x') = \exp\left(-\frac{\|x - x'\|^2}{2h^2} \right),$$

where $h > 0$ controls the width of the Gaussian function. In this case, the design matrix X^{tr} becomes the kernel Gram matrix K^{tr}, that is, K^{tr} is the $n_{\mathrm{tr}} \times n_{\mathrm{tr}}$ matrix with the (i, ℓ)-th element

$$K_{i,\ell}^{\mathrm{tr}} := K(x_i^{\mathrm{tr}}, x_\ell^{\mathrm{tr}}).$$

Then the learned parameter $\widehat{\boldsymbol{\theta}}_\gamma$ can be obtained by means of equation 2.6 with the learning matrix $\boldsymbol{L}_\gamma$ given as

$$\boldsymbol{L}_\gamma = (\boldsymbol{K}^{\mathrm{tr}} \boldsymbol{W}_\gamma^{\mathrm{tr}} \boldsymbol{K}^{\mathrm{tr}})^{-1} \boldsymbol{K}^{\mathrm{tr}} \boldsymbol{W}_\gamma^{\mathrm{tr}},$$

using the fact that the kernel matrix $\boldsymbol{K}^{\mathrm{tr}}$ is *symmetric*:

$$(\boldsymbol{K}^{\mathrm{tr}})^\top = \boldsymbol{K}^{\mathrm{tr}}.$$

The (stochastic) gradient descent method is similarly available by replacing b and $\varphi_\ell(\boldsymbol{x})$ with n_{tr} and $K(\boldsymbol{x}, \boldsymbol{x}_\ell^{\mathrm{tr}})$, respectively, which is still guaranteed to converge to the globally optimal solution.

2.2.2 Absolute Loss: Least-Absolute Regression

The LS method often suffers from excessive sensitivity to *outliers* (i.e., irregular values) and less reliability. Here, we introduce an alternative approach to LS based on the *least-absolute* (LA) method, which we refer to as *adaptive importance-weighted least-absolute regression* (AIWLAR)—instead of the squared loss, the absolute loss is used (see figure 2.4):

$$\widehat{\boldsymbol{\theta}}_\gamma = \underset{\boldsymbol{\theta}}{\operatorname{argmin}} \left[\frac{1}{n_{\mathrm{tr}}} \sum_{i=1}^{n_{\mathrm{tr}}} \left(\frac{p_{\mathrm{te}}(\boldsymbol{x}_i^{\mathrm{tr}})}{p_{\mathrm{tr}}(\boldsymbol{x}_i^{\mathrm{tr}})} \right)^\gamma |\widehat{f}(\boldsymbol{x}_i^{\mathrm{tr}}; \boldsymbol{\theta}) - y_i^{\mathrm{tr}}| \right]. \tag{2.7}$$

The LS regression method actually estimates the conditional mean of output y given input $\boldsymbol{x}$. This may be intuitively understood from the fact that minimization under the squared loss amounts to obtaining the mean of samples $\{z_i\}_{i=1}^n$:

$$\underset{c}{\operatorname{argmin}} \left[\sum_{i=1}^n (z_i - c)^2 \right] = \operatorname{mean}(\{z_i\}_{i=1}^n) = \frac{1}{n} \sum_{i=1}^n z_i.$$

If one of the values in the set $\{z_i\}_{i=1}^n$ is extremely large or small due to, for instance, some measurement error, the mean will be strongly affected by that outlier sample. Thus, *all* the values $\{z_i\}_{i=1}^n$ are responsible for the mean, and therefore even a *single* outlier observation can significantly damage the learned function.

On the other hand, the LA regression method is actually estimates the conditional median of output y, given input $\boldsymbol{x}$. Indeed, minimization under the

2.2. Examples of Importance-Weighted Regression Methods

absolute loss amounts to obtaining the median:

$$\underset{c}{\mathrm{argmin}} \left[\sum_{i=1}^{2n+1} |z_i - c| \right] = \mathrm{median}(\{z_i\}_{i=1}^{2n+1}) = z_{n+1},$$

where $z_1 \leq z_2 \leq \cdots \leq z_{2n+1}$. The median is not influenced by the magnitude of the values $\{z_i\}_{i \neq n}$, but only by their *order*. Thus, as long as the order is kept unchanged, the median is not affected by outliers—in fact, the median is known to be the most robust estimator in the light of *breakdown-point analysis* [83, 138].

The minimization problem (equation 2.7) looks cumbersome due to the absolute value operator, which is non-differentiable. However, the following mathematical trick mitigates this issue [27]:

$$|x| = \min_{b} b \quad \text{subject to } -b \leq x \leq b.$$

Then the minimization problem (equation 2.7) is reduced to the following optimization problem:

$$\begin{cases} \displaystyle\min_{\theta, \{b_i\}_{i=1}^{n_{\mathrm{tr}}}} \sum_{i=1}^{n_{\mathrm{tr}}} \left(\frac{p_{\mathrm{te}}(x_i^{\mathrm{tr}})}{p_{\mathrm{tr}}(x_i^{\mathrm{tr}})} \right)^{\gamma} b_i, \\ \text{subject to} \quad -b_i \leq \widehat{f}(x_i^{\mathrm{tr}}; \theta) - y_i^{\mathrm{tr}} \leq b_i, \ \forall i. \end{cases}$$

If the linear-in-parameter model (equation 2.5) is used for learning, the above optimization problem is reduced to a *linear program* [27] which can be solved efficiently by using a standard optimization software.

The number of constraints is n_{tr} in the above linear program. When n_{tr} is large, we may employ sophisticated optimization techniques such as *column generation* by considering increasing sets of active constraints [37] for efficiently solving the linear programming problem. Alternatively, an approximate solution can be obtained by gradient descent or (quasi-)Newton methods if the absolute loss is approximated by a smooth loss (see section 2.2.3).

2.2.3 Huber Loss: Huber Regression

The LA regression is useful for suppressing the influence of outliers. However, when the training output noise is Gaussian, the LA method is not statistically efficient, that is, it tends to have a large variance when there are no outliers. A popular alternative is the *Huber loss* [83], which bridges the LS and LA methods. The adaptive importance-weighting method for the Huber loss, called *adaptive importance-weighted Huber regression* (AIWHR), is follows:

$$\widehat{\boldsymbol{\theta}}_\gamma = \underset{\boldsymbol{\theta}}{\mathrm{argmin}} \left[\frac{1}{n_{\mathrm{tr}}} \sum_{i=1}^{n_{\mathrm{tr}}} \left(\frac{p_{\mathrm{te}}(\boldsymbol{x}_i^{\mathrm{tr}})}{p_{\mathrm{tr}}(\boldsymbol{x}_i^{\mathrm{tr}})} \right)^\gamma \rho_\tau \left(\widehat{f}(\boldsymbol{x}_i^{\mathrm{tr}}; \boldsymbol{\theta}) - y_i^{\mathrm{tr}} \right) \right],$$

where τ (≥ 0) is the robustness parameter and ρ_τ is the Huber loss, defined as follows (see figure 2.4):

$$\rho_\tau(y) := \begin{cases} \frac{1}{2} y^2 & \text{if } |y| \leq \tau, \\ \tau |y| - \frac{1}{2} \tau^2 & \text{if } |y| > \tau. \end{cases}$$

Thus, the squared loss is applied to "good" samples with small fitting error, and the absolute loss is applied to "bad" samples with large fitting error. Note that the Huber loss is a convex function, and therefore the unique global solution exists.

The Huber loss function is rather intricate, but for the linear-in-parameter model (equation 2.5), the solution can be obtained by solving the following convex *quadratic programming problem* [109]:

$$\min_{\boldsymbol{\theta}, \{u_i, v_i\}_{i=1}^{n_{\mathrm{tr}}}} \left[\sum_{i=1}^{n_{\mathrm{tr}}} \left(\frac{p_{\mathrm{te}}(\boldsymbol{x}_i^{\mathrm{tr}})}{p_{\mathrm{tr}}(\boldsymbol{x}_i^{\mathrm{tr}})} \right)^\gamma \left(\frac{1}{2} u_i^2 + \tau v_i \right) \right],$$

subject to $-v_i \leq \sum_{\ell=1}^{b} \theta_\ell \varphi_\ell(\boldsymbol{x}_i^{\mathrm{tr}}) - y_i^{\mathrm{tr}} - u_i \leq v_i$ for all i.

Another way to obtain the solution is gradient descent (notice that the Huber loss is once differentiable):

$$\theta_\ell \leftarrow \theta_\ell - \varepsilon \sum_{i=1}^{n_{\mathrm{tr}}} \left(\frac{p_{\mathrm{te}}(\boldsymbol{x}_i^{\mathrm{tr}})}{p_{\mathrm{tr}}(\boldsymbol{x}_i^{\mathrm{tr}})} \right)^\gamma \Delta \rho_\tau \left(\sum_{\ell'=1}^{b} \theta_{\ell'} \varphi_{\ell'}(\boldsymbol{x}_i^{\mathrm{tr}}) - y_i^{\mathrm{tr}} \right) \varphi_\ell(\boldsymbol{x}_i^{\mathrm{tr}}) \quad \text{for all } \ell,$$

where ε (> 0) is a learning rate parameter, and $\Delta \rho_\tau$ is the derivative of ρ_τ given by

$$\Delta \rho_\tau(y) = \begin{cases} y & \text{if } |y| \leq \tau, \\ \tau & \text{if } y > \tau, \\ -\tau & \text{if } y < -\tau. \end{cases}$$

Its stochastic version is

$$\theta_\ell \leftarrow \theta_\ell - \varepsilon \left(\frac{p_{\text{te}}(\boldsymbol{x}_i^{\text{tr}})}{p_{\text{tr}}(\boldsymbol{x}_i^{\text{tr}})}\right)^\gamma \Delta \rho_\tau \left(\sum_{\ell'=1}^b \theta_{\ell'}\varphi_{\ell'}(\boldsymbol{x}_i^{\text{tr}}) - y_i^{\text{tr}}\right) \varphi_\ell(\boldsymbol{x}_i^{\text{tr}}) \quad \text{for all } \ell,$$

where the sample index $i \in \{1, 2, \ldots, n_{\text{tr}}\}$ is randomly chosen in each iteration, and the above gradient descent process is repeated until convergence.

2.2.4 Deadzone-Linear Loss: Support Vector Regression

Another variant of the absolute loss is the *deadzone-linear loss* (see figure 2.4):

$$\widehat{\boldsymbol{\theta}}_\gamma = \underset{\boldsymbol{\theta}}{\operatorname{argmin}} \left[\frac{1}{n_{\text{tr}}}\sum_{i=1}^{n_{\text{tr}}}\left(\frac{p_{\text{te}}(\boldsymbol{x}_i^{\text{tr}})}{p_{\text{tr}}(\boldsymbol{x}_i^{\text{tr}})}\right)^\gamma \left|\widehat{f}(\boldsymbol{x}_i^{\text{tr}};\boldsymbol{\theta}) - y_i^{\text{tr}}\right|_\epsilon\right],$$

where $|\cdot|_\epsilon$ is the *deadzone-linear loss* defined by

$$|x|_\epsilon := \begin{cases} 0 & \text{if } |x| \leq \epsilon, \\ |x| - \epsilon & \text{if } |x| > \epsilon. \end{cases}$$

That is, if the magnitude of the residual $\left|\widehat{f}(\boldsymbol{x}_i^{\text{tr}};\boldsymbol{\theta}) - y_i^{\text{tr}}\right|$ is less than ϵ, no error is assessed. This loss is also called the ϵ-*insensitive loss* and is used in *support vector regression* [193]. We refer to this method as *adaptive importance-weighted support vector regression* (AIWSVR).

When $\epsilon = 0$, the deadzone-linear loss is reduced to the absolute loss (see section 2.2.2). Thus the deadzone-linear loss and the absolute loss are related to one another. However, the effect of the deadzone-linear loss is quite different from that of the absolute loss when $\epsilon > 0$—the influence of "good" samples (with small residual) is deemphasized in the deadzone-linear loss, while the absolute loss tends to suppress the influence of "bad" samples (with large residual) compared with the squared loss.

The solution $\widehat{\boldsymbol{\theta}}_\gamma$ can be obtained by solving the following optimization problem [27]:

$$\begin{cases} \underset{\boldsymbol{\theta},\{b_i\}_{i=1}^{n_{\text{tr}}}}{\min} & \sum_{i=1}^{n_{\text{tr}}}\left(\frac{p_{\text{te}}(\boldsymbol{x}_i^{\text{tr}})}{p_{\text{tr}}(\boldsymbol{x}_i^{\text{tr}})}\right)^\gamma b_i \\ \text{subject to} & -b_i - \epsilon \leq \widehat{f}(\boldsymbol{x}_i^{\text{tr}};\boldsymbol{\theta}) - y_i^{\text{tr}} \leq b_i + \epsilon, \\ & b_i \geq 0, \forall i. \end{cases}$$

If the linear-in-parameter model (equation 2.5) is used for learning, the above optimization problem is reduced to a *linear program* [27] which can be solved efficiently by using a standard optimization software.

The support vector regression was shown to be equivalent to minimizing the *conditional value-at-risk* (CVaR) of the absolute residuals [180]. The CVaR corresponds to the mean of the error for a set of "bad" samples (see figure 2.6), and is a popular risk measure in finance [137].

More specifically, let us consider the cumulative distribution of the *absolute residuals* $|\widehat{f}(\boldsymbol{x}_i^{tr}; \boldsymbol{\theta}) - y_i^{tr}|$ over all training samples $\{(\boldsymbol{x}_i^{tr}, y_i^{tr})\}_{i=1}^{n_{tr}}$:

$$\Phi(\alpha|\boldsymbol{\theta}) := \text{Prob}_{tr}\left(\left|\widehat{f}(\boldsymbol{x}_i^{tr}; \boldsymbol{\theta}) - y_i^{tr}\right| \leq \alpha\right),$$

where Prob_{tr} denotes the probability over training samples $\{(\boldsymbol{x}_i^{tr}, y_i^{tr})\}_{i=1}^{n_{tr}}$. For $\beta \in [0, 1)$, let $\alpha_\beta(\boldsymbol{\theta})$ be the 100th β-percentile of the distribution of absolute residuals:

$$\alpha_\beta(\boldsymbol{\theta}) := \mathop{\text{argmin}}_\alpha \text{ subject to } \Phi(\alpha|\boldsymbol{\theta}) \geq \beta.$$

Thus, only the fraction $(1 - \beta)$ of the absolute residuals $|\widehat{f}(\boldsymbol{x}_i^{tr}; \boldsymbol{\theta}) - y_i^{tr}|$ exceeds the threshold $\alpha_\beta(\boldsymbol{\theta})$. $\alpha_\beta(\boldsymbol{\theta})$ is referred to as the *value-at-risk* (VaR).

Let us consider the β-tail distribution of the absolute residuals:

$$\Phi_\beta(\alpha|\boldsymbol{\theta}) \equiv \begin{cases} 0 & \text{if } \alpha < \alpha_\beta(\boldsymbol{\theta}), \\ \dfrac{\Phi(\alpha|\boldsymbol{\theta}) - \beta}{1 - \beta} & \text{if } \alpha \geq \alpha_\beta(\boldsymbol{\theta}). \end{cases}$$

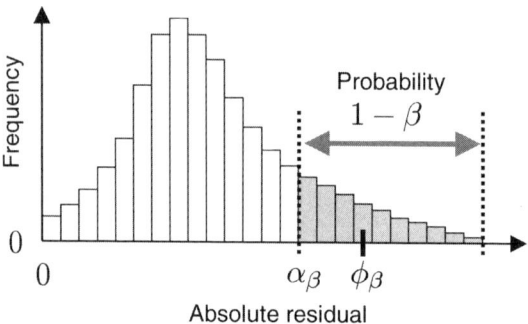

Figure 2.6
The conditional value-at-risk (CVaR).

Let $\phi_\beta(\boldsymbol{\theta})$ be the mean of the β-tail distribution of the absolute residuals:

$$\phi_\beta(\boldsymbol{\theta}) \equiv \mathbb{E}_{\Phi_\beta}\left[|\widehat{f}(\boldsymbol{x}_i^{\text{tr}};\boldsymbol{\theta}) - y_i^{\text{tr}}|\right],$$

where $\mathbb{E}_{\Phi_\beta}$ denotes the expectation over the distribution Φ_β. $\phi_\beta(\boldsymbol{\theta})$ is called the CVaR. By definition, the CVaR of the absolute residuals is reduced to the mean absolute residuals if $\beta = 0$, and it converges to the worst absolute residual as β tends to 1. Thus, the CVaR smoothly bridges the LA approach and the *Chebyshev approximation* (a.k.a. *minimax*) method. CVaR is also referred to as the *expected shortfall*.

2.3 Examples of Importance-Weighted Classification Methods

In this section, we provide examples of importance-weighted classification methods including *Fisher discriminant analysis* [50, 57], *logistic regression* [74], *support vector machines* [26, 193, 141], and *boosting* [52, 28, 53]. For simplicity, we focus on the binary classification case where $\mathcal{Y} = \{+1, -1\}$. Let n_{tr}^+ and n_{tr}^- be the numbers of training samples in classes $+1$ and -1, respectively.

In the classification setup, the following *0/1-loss* is typically used as the error metric since it corresponds to the *misclassification rate*.

$$\text{loss}(\boldsymbol{x}, y, \widehat{y}) = \begin{cases} 0 & \text{if sgn}(\widehat{y}) = \text{sgn}(y), \\ 1 & \text{otherwise,} \end{cases}$$

where y is the true output value at an input point $\boldsymbol{x}$, $\widehat{y}$ is an estimate of y, and $\text{sgn}(\widehat{y})$ denotes the sign of $\widehat{y}$:

$$\text{sgn}(\widehat{y}) := \begin{cases} +1 & \text{if } \widehat{y} > 0, \\ 0 & \text{if } \widehat{y} = 0, \\ -1 & \text{if } \widehat{y} < 0. \end{cases}$$

This means that, in classification scenarios, the *sign* of $\widehat{y}$ is important, and the magnitude of $\widehat{y}$ does not affect the misclassification error.

The above 0/1-loss can be equivalently expressed as

$$\text{loss}(\boldsymbol{x}, y, \widehat{y}) = \begin{cases} 0 & \text{if sgn}(y\widehat{y}) = 1, \\ 1 & \text{otherwise.} \end{cases}$$

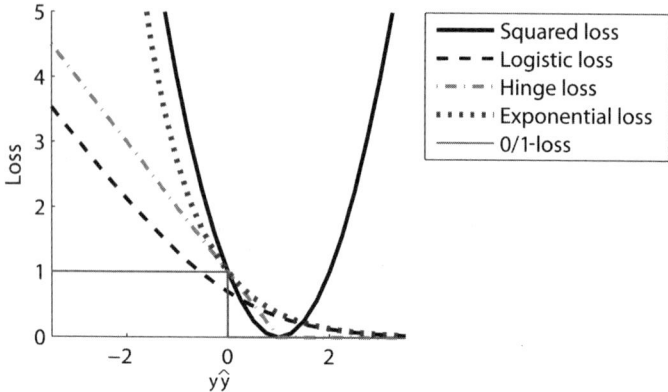

Figure 2.7
Loss functions for classification. y are the true output value at an input point x and $\widehat{y}$ is an estimate of y.

For this reason, the loss function in classification is often expressed in terms of $y\widehat{y}$, which is called the *margin*. The profile of the 0/1-loss is illustrated as a function of $y\widehat{y}$ in figure 2.7.

Minimizing the 0/1-loss is the ultimate goal of classification. However, since the 0/1-loss is not a convex function, optimization under it is hard. To cope with this problem, alternative convex loss functions have been proposed for classification scenarios (figure 2.7). In this section, we review classification methods with such convex loss functions.

2.3.1 Squared Loss: Fisher Discriminant Analysis

Fisher discriminant analysis (FDA) is one of the classical classification methods [50]. In FDA, the input samples are first projected onto a one-dimensional subspace (i.e., a line), and then the projected samples are linearly separated into two classes by thresholding; for multiclass extension, see, for example, [57].

Let μ, μ^+, and μ^- be the means of $\{x_i^{tr}\}_{i=1}^{n_{tr}}$, $\{x_i^{tr} | y_i^{tr} = +1\}_{i=1}^{n_{tr}}$, and $\{x_i^{tr} | y_i^{tr} = -1\}_{i=1}^{n_{tr}}$, respectively:

$$\mu := \frac{1}{n_{tr}} \sum_{i=1}^{n_{tr}} x_i^{tr},$$

$$\mu^+ := \frac{1}{n_{tr}^+} \sum_{i: y_i^{tr} = +1} x_i^{tr},$$

$$\mu^- := \frac{1}{n_{tr}^-} \sum_{i: y_i^{tr} = -1} x_i^{tr},$$

2.3. Examples of Importance-Weighted Classification Methods

where $\sum_{i:y_i^{tr}=+1}$ denotes the summation over index i such that $y_i^{tr} = +1$. Let S^b and S^w be the *between-class scatter matrix* and the *within-class scatter matrix*, respectively, defined as

$$S^b := n_{tr}^+(\mu^+ - \mu)(\mu^+ - \mu)^\top + n_{tr}^-(\mu^- - \mu)(\mu^- - \mu)^\top,$$

$$S^w := \sum_{i:y_i^{tr}=+1} (x_i^{tr} - \mu^+)(x_i^{tr} - \mu^+)^\top + \sum_{i:y_i^{tr}=-1} (x_i^{tr} - \mu^-)(x_i^{tr} - \mu^-)^\top.$$

The FDA projection direction $\phi_{\text{FDA}} \in \mathbb{R}^d$ is defined as

$$\phi_{\text{FDA}} := \underset{\phi \in \mathbb{R}^d}{\operatorname{argmax}} \left[\frac{\phi^\top S^b \phi}{\phi^\top S^w \phi} \right].$$

That is, FDA seeks a projection direction ϕ with large between-class scatter and small within-class scatter after projection.

The above ratio is called the *Rayleigh quotient*. A strong advantage of the Rayleigh quotient formulation is that globally optimal solutions can be computed *analytically* even though the objective function is not convex. Indeed, the FDA projection direction ϕ_{FDA} is given by

$$\phi_{\text{FDA}} = \phi_{\max},$$

where $\phi_{\max}$ is the generalized eigenvector associated with the largest generalized eigenvalue of the following generalized eigenvalue problem:

$$S^b \phi = \beta S^w \phi.$$

Thanks to the analytic solution, the FDA projection direction can be computed efficiently. Finally, the projected samples are classified by thresholding.

The FDA solution can be also obtained in the LS regression framework where $\mathcal{Y} = \mathbb{R}$. Suppose the training output values $\{y_i^{tr}\}_{i=1}^{n_{tr}}$ are

$$y_i^{tr} \propto \begin{cases} 1/n_{tr}^+ & \text{if } x_i^{tr} \text{ belongs to class} + 1, \\ -1/n_{tr}^- & \text{if } x_i^{tr} \text{ belongs to class} - 1. \end{cases}$$

We use the linear-in-input model (equation 2.3) for learning, and the classification result $\widehat{y}^{te}$ of a test sample x^{te} is obtained by the sign of the output of the learned function.

$$\widehat{y}^{te} = \text{sgn}\left(\widehat{f}(x^{te}; \boldsymbol{\theta})\right).$$

In this setting, if the parameter $\boldsymbol{\theta}$ is learned by the LS method, this classification method is essentially equivalent to FDA [42, 21].

Under covariate shift, the adaptive importance-weighting idea can be employed in FDA, which we call *adaptive importance-weighted FDA* (AIWFDA):

$$\widehat{\boldsymbol{\theta}}_\gamma = \underset{\boldsymbol{\theta}}{\text{argmin}} \left[\frac{1}{n_{tr}} \sum_{i=1}^{n_{tr}} \left(\frac{p_{te}(x_i^{tr})}{p_{tr}(x_i^{tr})} \right)^\gamma \left(\widehat{f}(x_i^{tr}; \boldsymbol{\theta}) - y_i^{tr} \right)^2 \right].$$

The solution is given analytically in exactly the same way as the regression case (see section 2.2.1).

As explained in the beginning of this section, the margin $y_i^{tr} \widehat{f}(x_i^{tr}; \boldsymbol{\theta})$ plays an important role in classification. If $y^{tr} = \pm 1$, the squared error used above can be expressed in terms of the margin as

$$\left(\widehat{f}(x_i^{tr}; \boldsymbol{\theta}) - y_i^{tr} \right)^2 = (y_i^{tr})^2 \left(\frac{\widehat{f}(x_i^{tr}; \boldsymbol{\theta})}{y_i^{tr}} - 1 \right)^2$$

$$= \left(1 - y_i^{tr} \widehat{f}(x_i^{tr}; \boldsymbol{\theta}) \right)^2,$$

where we used the facts that $(y_i^{tr})^2 = 1$ and $y_i^{tr} = 1/y_i^{tr}$. This expression of the squared loss is illustrated in figure 2.7, showing that the above squared loss is a convex upper bound of the 0/1-loss. Therefore, minimizing the error under the squared loss corresponds to minimizing the upper bound of the 0/1-loss error, although the bound is rather loose.

2.3.2 Logistic Loss: Logistic Regression Classifier

Logistic regression (LR)—which sounds like a regression method—is a classifier that gives a *confidence value* (the class-posterior probability) for the classification results [74].

The LR classifier employs a parametric model of the following form for expressing the class-posterior probability $p(y|x)$:

$$\widehat{p}(y|x) = \frac{1}{1 + \exp\left(-y\widehat{f}(x; \boldsymbol{\theta})\right)}.$$

The parameter $\boldsymbol{\theta}$ is usually learned by *maximum likelihood estimation* (MLE). Since the negative log-likelihood can be regarded as the empirical error, the

2.3. Examples of Importance-Weighted Classification Methods

adaptive importance-weighting idea can be employed in LR, which we call *adaptive importance-weighted LR* (AIWLR):

$$\widehat{\boldsymbol{\theta}}_\gamma = \underset{\boldsymbol{\theta}}{\operatorname{argmin}} \left[\sum_{i=1}^{n_{\text{tr}}} \left(\frac{p_{\text{te}}(\boldsymbol{x}_i^{\text{tr}})}{p_{\text{tr}}(\boldsymbol{x}_i^{\text{tr}})} \right)^\gamma \log \left(1 + \exp\left(-y_i^{\text{tr}} \widehat{f}(\boldsymbol{x}_i^{\text{tr}}; \boldsymbol{\theta}))\right)\right) \right].$$

The profile of the above loss function, which is called the *logistic loss*, is illustrated in figure 2.7 as a function of margin $y\widehat{f}(\boldsymbol{x})$.

Since the above objective function is convex when a linear-in-parameter model (2.5) is used, the global optimal solution can be obtained by standard nonlinear optimization methods such as the gradient descent method, the conjugate gradient method, Newton's method, and quasi-Newton methods [117]. The gradient descent update rule is given by

$$\theta_\ell \leftarrow \theta_\ell + \varepsilon \sum_{i=1}^{n_{\text{tr}}} \left(\frac{p_{\text{te}}(\boldsymbol{x}_i^{\text{tr}})}{p_{\text{tr}}(\boldsymbol{x}_i^{\text{tr}})} \right)^\gamma \frac{y_i^{\text{tr}} \varphi_\ell(\boldsymbol{x}_i^{\text{tr}}) \exp\left(-y_i^{\text{tr}} \sum_{\ell'=1}^{b} \theta_{\ell'} \varphi_{\ell'}(\boldsymbol{x}_i^{\text{tr}})\right)}{1 + \exp\left(-y_i^{\text{tr}} \sum_{\ell''=1}^{b} \theta_{\ell''} \varphi_{\ell''}(\boldsymbol{x}_i^{\text{tr}})\right)}$$

for all ℓ.

A C-language implementation of importance-weighted kernel logistic regression is available from the Web page http://sugiyama-www.cs.titech.ac.jp/~yamada/iwklr.html.

2.3.3 Hinge Loss: Support Vector Machine

The *support vector machine* (SVM) [26, 193, 141] is a popular classification technique that finds a separating hyperplane with *maximum margin*. Although the original SVM was derived within the framework of the *Vapnik–Chervonenkis theory* and the *maximum margin principle*, the SVM learning criterion can be equivalently expressed in the following form[3] [47]:

$$\min_{\boldsymbol{\theta}} \left[\sum_{i=1}^{n_{\text{tr}}} \max \left(0, 1 - y_i^{\text{tr}} \widehat{f}(\boldsymbol{x}_i^{\text{tr}}; \boldsymbol{\theta})\right) \right].$$

This implies that SVM is actually similar to FDA and LR; only the loss function is different. The profile of the above loss function, which is called the *hinge loss*, is illustrated in figure 2.7. As shown in the graph, the hinge loss is a convex upper bound of the 0/1-loss and is sharper than the squared loss.

---

3. For simplicity, we have omitted the regularization term.

Adaptive importance weighting can be applied to SVM, which we call *adaptive importance-weighted SVM* (AIWSVM):

$$\widehat{\boldsymbol{\theta}}_\gamma = \underset{\boldsymbol{\theta}}{\operatorname{argmin}} \left[\sum_{i=1}^{n_{\text{tr}}} \left(\frac{p_{\text{te}}(\boldsymbol{x}_i^{\text{tr}})}{p_{\text{tr}}(\boldsymbol{x}_i^{\text{tr}})} \right)^\gamma \max\left(0, 1 - y_i^{\text{tr}} \widehat{f}(\boldsymbol{x}_i^{\text{tr}}; \boldsymbol{\theta}))\right) \right].$$

The support vector classifier was shown to minimize the *conditional value-at-risk* (CVaR) of the margin [181] (see section 2.2.4 for the definition of CVaR).

2.3.4 Exponential Loss: Boosting

Boosting is an iterative learning algorithm that produces a convex combination of base classifiers [52]. Although boosting has its origin in the framework of *probably approximately correct* (PAC) learning [190], it can be regarded as a stagewise optimization of the *exponential loss* [28, 53]:

$$\min_{\boldsymbol{\theta}} \left[\sum_{i=1}^{n_{\text{tr}}} \exp\left(-y_i^{\text{tr}} \widehat{f}(\boldsymbol{x}_i^{\text{tr}}; \boldsymbol{\theta})\right) \right].$$

The profile of the exponential loss is illustrated in figure 2.7. The exponential loss is a convex upper bound of the 0/1-loss that is looser than the hinge loss.

The adaptive importance-weighting idea can be applied to boosting, a process we call *adaptive importance-weighted boosting* (AIWB):

$$\widehat{\boldsymbol{\theta}}_\gamma = \underset{\boldsymbol{\theta}}{\operatorname{argmin}} \left[\sum_{i=1}^{n_{\text{tr}}} \left(\frac{p_{\text{te}}(\boldsymbol{x}_i^{\text{tr}})}{p_{\text{tr}}(\boldsymbol{x}_i^{\text{tr}})} \right)^\gamma \exp\left(-y_i^{\text{tr}} \widehat{f}(\boldsymbol{x}_i^{\text{tr}}; \boldsymbol{\theta})\right) \right].$$

2.4 Numerical Examples

In this section we illustrate how ERM, IWERM, and AIWERM behave, using toy regression and classification problems.

2.4.1 Regression

We assume that the conditional distribution $P(y|x)$ has mean $f(x)$ and variance σ^2, that is, output values contain independent additive noise. Let the learning target function $f(x)$ be the *sinc function*:

$$f(x) = \operatorname{sinc}(x) := \begin{cases} 1 & \text{if } x = 0, \\ \dfrac{\sin(\pi x)}{\pi x} & \text{otherwise.} \end{cases}$$

2.4. Numerical Examples

Let the training and test input densities be

$$p_{\mathrm{tr}}(x) = N(x; 1, (1/2)^2),$$
$$p_{\mathrm{te}}(x) = N(x; 2, (1/4)^2),$$

where $N(x; \mu, \sigma^2)$ denotes the Gaussian density with mean μ and variance σ^2. The profiles of the densities are plotted in figure 2.8a. Since the training input points are distributed in the left-hand side of the input domain and the test input points are distributed in the right-hand side, we are considering a (weak) extrapolation problem. We create the training output value $\{y_i^{\mathrm{tr}}\}_{i=1}^{n_{\mathrm{tr}}}$ as

$$y_i^{\mathrm{tr}} = f(x_i^{\mathrm{tr}}) + \epsilon_i^{\mathrm{tr}},$$

where $\{\epsilon_i^{\mathrm{tr}}\}_{i=1}^{n_{\mathrm{tr}}}$ are i.i.d. noise drawn from

$$N(\epsilon; 0, (1/4)^2).$$

We let the number of training samples be $n_{\mathrm{tr}} = 150$, and we use a linear-in-input model (see section 1.3.5.1) for function learning:

$$\widehat{f}(x; \boldsymbol{\theta}) = \theta_1 x + \theta_2.$$

If ordinary least squares (OLS, which is an ERM method with the squared loss) is used for fitting the straight-line model, we have a good approximation of the left-hand side of the sinc function (see figure 2.8b). However, this is not an appropriate function for estimating the test output values (× in the figure). Thus, OLS results in a large test error. Figure 2.8d depicts the learned function obtained by importance-weighted LS (IWLS). IWLS gives a better function for estimating the test output values than OLS, although it is rather unstable. Figure 2.8c depicts a learned function obtained by AIWLS with $\gamma = 0.5$ (see section 2.2.1), which yields better estimation of the test output values than IWLS (AIWLS with $\gamma = 1$) and OLS (AIWLS with $\gamma = 0$).

2.4.2 Classification

Through the above regression examples, we found that importance weighting tends to improve the prediction performance in regression scenarios. Here, we apply the importance-weighting technique to a toy classification problem.

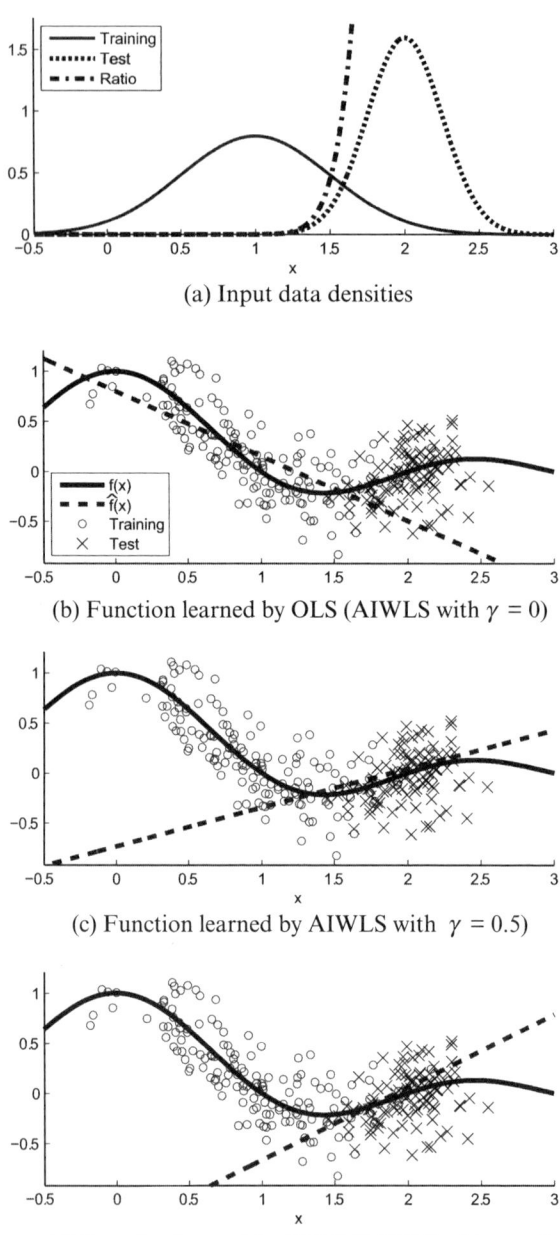

Figure 2.8
An illustrative regression example with covariate shift. (a) The probability density functions of the training and test input points and their ratio. (b)–(d) The learning target function $f(x)$ (the solid line), training samples (○), a learned function $\widehat{f}(x)$ (the dashed line), and test samples (×). Note that the test samples are not used for function learning.

2.4. Numerical Examples

Let us consider a binary classification problem in the two-dimensional input space ($d = 2$). We define the class-posterior probabilities, given input x, by

$$p(y=+1|x) = \frac{1 + \tanh\left(x^{(1)} + \min(0, x^{(2)})\right)}{2}, \quad (2.8)$$

where $x = (x^{(1)}, x^{(2)})^\top$ and

$$p(y=-1|x) = 1 - p(y=+1|x).$$

The optimal decision boundary, that is, a set of all x such that

$$p(y=+1|x) = p(y=-1|x),$$

is illustrated in figure 2.9a.

Let the training and test input densities be

$$p_{\mathrm{tr}}(x) = \frac{1}{2}N\left(x; \begin{bmatrix} -2 \\ 3 \end{bmatrix}, \begin{bmatrix} 1 & 0 \\ 0 & 4 \end{bmatrix}\right) + \frac{1}{2}N\left(x; \begin{bmatrix} 2 \\ 3 \end{bmatrix}, \begin{bmatrix} 1 & 0 \\ 0 & 4 \end{bmatrix}\right), \quad (2.9)$$

$$p_{\mathrm{te}}(x) = \frac{1}{2}N\left(x; \begin{bmatrix} 0 \\ -1 \end{bmatrix}, \begin{bmatrix} 1 & 0 \\ 0 & 1 \end{bmatrix}\right) + \frac{1}{2}N\left(x; \begin{bmatrix} 4 \\ -1 \end{bmatrix}, \begin{bmatrix} 1 & 0 \\ 0 & 1 \end{bmatrix}\right), \quad (2.10)$$

where $N(x; \mu, \Sigma)$ is the multivariate Gaussian density with mean μ and covariance matrix Σ. This setup implies that we are considering a (weak) extrapolation problem. Contours of the training and test input densities are illustrated in figure 2.9(a).

Let the number of training samples be $n_{\mathrm{tr}} = 500$. We create training input points $\{x_i^{\mathrm{tr}}\}_{i=1}^{n_{\mathrm{tr}}}$ following $p_{\mathrm{tr}}(x)$ and training output labels $\{y_i^{\mathrm{tr}}\}_{i=1}^{n_{\mathrm{tr}}}$ following $p(y|x = x_i^{\mathrm{tr}})$. Similarly, let the number of test samples be $n_{\mathrm{te}} = 500$. We create n_{te} test input points $\{x_j^{\mathrm{te}}\}_{j=1}^{n_{\mathrm{te}}}$ following $p_{\mathrm{te}}(x)$ and test output labels $\{y_j^{\mathrm{te}}\}_{j=1}^{n_{\mathrm{te}}}$ following $p(y|x = x_j^{\mathrm{te}})$.

We use the linear-in-input model for function learning:

$$\widehat{f}(x; \theta) = \theta_1 x^{(1)} + \theta_2 x^{(2)} + \theta_3,$$

and determine the parameter θ by AIWFDA (see section 2.3.1).

Figure 2.9b depicts an example of realizations of training and test samples, as well as decision boundaries obtained by AIWFDA with $\gamma = 0, 0.5, 1$. In this particular realization, $\gamma = 0.5$ or 1 works better than $\gamma = 0$.

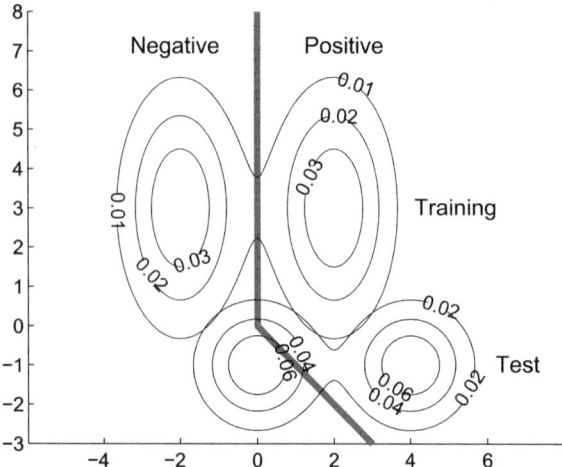

(a) Optimal decision boundary (the thick solid line) and contours of training and test input densities (thin solid lines).

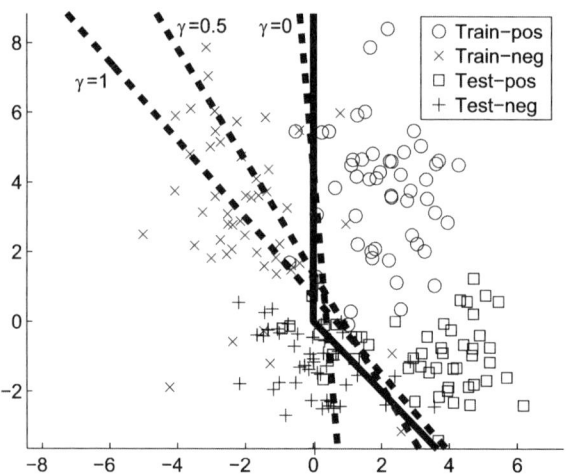

(b) Optimal decision boundary (solid line) and learned boundaries (dashed lines). ○ and × denote the positive and negative training samples, while □ and + denote the positive and negative test samples. Note that the test samples are not given in the training phase; they are plotted in the figure for illustration purposes.

Figure 2.9
An illustrative classification example with covariate shift.

2.5 Summary and Discussion

Most of the standard machine learning methods assume that the data generating mechanism does not change over time (e.g., [195, 193, 42, 74, 141, 21]). However, this fundamental prerequisite is often violated in many practical problems, such as off-policy reinforcement learning [174, 66, 67, 4], spam filtering [18], speech recognition [204], audio tagging [198], natural language processing [186], bioinformatics [10, 25], face recognition [188], and brain–computer interfacing [201, 160, 102]. When training and test distributions are different, ordinary estimators are biased and therefore good generalization performance may not be obtained.

If the training and test distributions have nothing in common, we may not be able to learn anything about the test distribution from training samples. Thus, we need a reasonable assumption that links the training and test distributions. In this chapter, we focused on a specific type of distribution change called covariate shift [145], where the input distribution changes but the conditional distribution of outputs given inputs does not change—extrapolation would be a typical example of covariate shift.

We have seen that the use of importance weights contributes to reducing the *bias* caused by covariate shift and allows us to obtain consistent estimators even under covariate shift (section 2.1.1). However, a naive use of the importance weights does not necessarily produce reliable solutions since importance-weighted estimators tend to have large variance. This is because training samples which are not "typical" in the test distribution are downweighted, and thus the effective number of training samples becomes smaller. This is the price we have to pay for bias reduction. In order to mitigate this problem, we introduced stabilization techniques in sections 2.1.2 and 2.1.3. flattening the importance-weights and regularizing the solution. The importance-weighting techniques have a wide range of applicability, and any learning methods can be adjusted in a systematic manner as long as they are based on the empirical error (or the log-likelihood). We have shown examples of such learning methods in regression (section 2.2) and in classification (section 2.3). Numerical results illustrating the behavior of these methods were presented in section 2.4.

The introduction of stabilizers such as the flattening parameter and the regularization parameter raises another important issue to be addressed; how to optimally determine these trade-off parameters. This is a *model selection* problem and will be discussed in detail in chapter 3.

3 Model Selection

As shown in chapter 2, adaptive importance-weighted learning methods are promising in the covariate shift scenarios, given that the *flattening parameter* γ is chosen appropriately. Although $\gamma = 0.5$ worked well for both the regression and the classification scenarios in the numerical examples in section 2.4, $\gamma = 0.5$ is not always the best choice; a good value of γ may depend on the learning target function, the models, the noise level in the training samples, and so on. Therefore, *model selection* needs to be appropriately carried out for enhancing the generalization capability under covariate shift.

The goal of model selection is to determine the model (e.g., basis functions, the flattening parameter γ, and the regularization parameter λ) so that the generalization error is minimized [1, 108, 2, 182, 142, 135, 35, 3, 136, 144, 195, 45, 118, 96, 85, 193, 165, 161, 159]. The true generalization error is not accessible since it contains the unknown learning target function. Thus, some generalization error estimators need to be used instead. However, standard generalization error estimators such as cross-validation are heavily biased under covariate shift, and thus are no longer reliable. In this chapter, we describe generalization error estimators that possess proper unbiasedness even under covariate shift.

3.1 Importance-Weighted Akaike Information Criterion

In density estimation problems, the *Akaike information criterion* (AIC) [2] is an asymptotic unbiased estimator of the *Kullback–Leibler divergence* [97] from the true density to an estimated density, up to a constant term. AIC can be employed in supervised learning if the supervised learning problem is formulated as the problem of estimating the conditional density of output values, given input points. However, the asymptotic unbiasedness of AIC is no longer true under covariate shift; a variant of AIC which we refer to as *importance-weighted AIC* (IWAIC) is instead asymptotically unbiased [145]:

$$\text{IWAIC} := -\frac{1}{n_{\text{tr}}} \sum_{i=1}^{n_{\text{tr}}} \frac{p_{\text{te}}(\mathbf{x}_i^{\text{tr}})}{p_{\text{tr}}(\mathbf{x}_i^{\text{tr}})} \text{loss}(\mathbf{x}_i^{\text{tr}}, y_i^{\text{tr}}, \widehat{f}(\mathbf{x}_i^{\text{tr}}; \widehat{\boldsymbol{\theta}})) + \frac{1}{n_{\text{tr}}} \text{tr}(\widehat{\boldsymbol{F}} \widehat{\boldsymbol{G}}^{-1}), \tag{3.1}$$

where $\widehat{\boldsymbol{\theta}}$ is a learned parameter vector, and $\widehat{\boldsymbol{F}}$ and $\widehat{\boldsymbol{G}}$ are the matrices with the (ℓ, ℓ')-th element

$$\widehat{F}_{\ell,\ell'} := \frac{1}{n_{\text{tr}}} \sum_{i=1}^{n_{\text{tr}}} \left(\frac{p_{\text{te}}(\mathbf{x}_i^{\text{tr}})}{p_{\text{tr}}(\mathbf{x}_i^{\text{tr}})} \right)^2 \frac{\partial \text{loss}(\mathbf{x}_i^{\text{tr}}, y_i^{\text{tr}}, \widehat{f}(\mathbf{x}_i^{\text{tr}}; \widehat{\boldsymbol{\theta}}))}{\partial \theta_\ell}$$

$$\times \frac{\partial \text{loss}(\mathbf{x}_i^{\text{tr}}, y_i^{\text{tr}}, \widehat{f}(\mathbf{x}_i^{\text{tr}}; \widehat{\boldsymbol{\theta}}))}{\partial \theta_{\ell'}},$$

$$\widehat{G}_{\ell,\ell'} := -\frac{1}{n_{\text{tr}}} \sum_{i=1}^{n_{\text{tr}}} \frac{p_{\text{te}}(\mathbf{x}_i^{\text{tr}})}{p_{\text{tr}}(\mathbf{x}_i^{\text{tr}})} \frac{\partial^2 \text{loss}(\mathbf{x}_i^{\text{tr}}, y_i^{\text{tr}}, \widehat{f}(\mathbf{x}_i^{\text{tr}}; \widehat{\boldsymbol{\theta}}))}{\partial \theta_\ell \partial \theta_{\ell'}}.$$

When $p_{\text{tr}}(\mathbf{x}) = p_{\text{te}}(\mathbf{x})$, IWAIC is reduced to

$$\text{TIC} := -\frac{1}{n_{\text{tr}}} \sum_{i=1}^{n_{\text{tr}}} \text{loss}(\mathbf{x}_i^{\text{tr}}, y_i^{\text{tr}}, \widehat{f}(\mathbf{x}_i^{\text{tr}}; \widehat{\boldsymbol{\theta}})) + \frac{1}{n_{\text{tr}}} \text{tr}(\widehat{\boldsymbol{F}}' \widehat{\boldsymbol{G}}'^{-1}),$$

where $\widehat{\boldsymbol{F}}'$ and $\widehat{\boldsymbol{G}}'$ are the matrices with the (ℓ, ℓ')-th elements

$$\widehat{F}'_{\ell,\ell'} := \frac{1}{n_{\text{tr}}} \sum_{i=1}^{n_{\text{tr}}} \frac{\partial \text{loss}(\mathbf{x}_i^{\text{tr}}, y_i^{\text{tr}}, \widehat{f}(\mathbf{x}_i^{\text{tr}}; \widehat{\boldsymbol{\theta}}))}{\partial \theta_\ell} \frac{\partial \text{loss}(\mathbf{x}_i^{\text{tr}}, y_i^{\text{tr}}, \widehat{f}(\mathbf{x}_i^{\text{tr}}; \widehat{\boldsymbol{\theta}}))}{\partial \theta_{\ell'}},$$

$$\widehat{G}'_{\ell,\ell'} := -\frac{1}{n_{\text{tr}}} \sum_{i=1}^{n_{\text{tr}}} \frac{\partial^2 \text{loss}(\mathbf{x}_i^{\text{tr}}, y_i^{\text{tr}}, \widehat{f}(\mathbf{x}_i^{\text{tr}}; \widehat{\boldsymbol{\theta}}))}{\partial \theta_\ell \partial \theta_{\ell'}}.$$

This is called the *Takeuchi information criterion* (TIC) [182]. Furthermore, when the model $\widehat{f}(\mathbf{x}; \boldsymbol{\theta})$ is correctly specified, $\widehat{\boldsymbol{F}}'$ agrees with $\widehat{\boldsymbol{G}}'$. Then TIC is reduced to

$$\text{AIC} := -\frac{1}{n_{\text{tr}}} \sum_{i=1}^{n_{\text{tr}}} \text{loss}(\mathbf{x}_i^{\text{tr}}, y_i^{\text{tr}}, \widehat{f}(\mathbf{x}_i^{\text{tr}}; \widehat{\boldsymbol{\theta}})) + \frac{\dim(\boldsymbol{\theta})}{n_{\text{tr}}},$$

3.1. Importance-Weighted Akaike Information Criterion

where $\dim(\boldsymbol{\theta})$ denotes the dimensionality of the parameter vector $\boldsymbol{\theta}$. This is the original Akaike information criterion [2].

Thus, IWAIC would be regarded as a natural extension of AIC. Note that in the derivation of IWAIC (and also of TIC and AIC), proper *regularity conditions* are assumed (see, e.g., [197]). This excludes the use of nonsmooth loss functions such as the 0/1-loss or nonidentifiable models such as multilayer perceptrons and Gaussian mixture models [196].

Let us consider the following Gaussian linear regression scenario:

- The conditional density $p(y|\boldsymbol{x})$ is Gaussian with mean $f(\boldsymbol{x})$ and variance σ^2:

$$p(y|\boldsymbol{x}) = N(y; f(\boldsymbol{x}), \sigma^2),$$

where $N(y; \mu, \sigma^2)$ denotes the Gaussian density with mean μ and variance σ^2.

- The linear-in-parameter model is used (see section 1.3.5.2) is used:

$$\widehat{f}(\boldsymbol{x}; \boldsymbol{\theta}) = \sum_{\ell=1}^{b} \theta_\ell \varphi_\ell(\boldsymbol{x}),$$

where b is the number of parameters and $\{\varphi_\ell(\boldsymbol{x})\}_{\ell=1}^{b}$ are fixed, linearly independent functions.

- The parameter is learned by a *linear learning* method, that is, the learned parameter $\widehat{\boldsymbol{\theta}}$ is given by

$$\widehat{\boldsymbol{\theta}} = \boldsymbol{L} \boldsymbol{y}^{\text{tr}},$$

where $\boldsymbol{L}$ is a $b \times n_{\text{tr}}$ learning matrix that is independent of the training output noise contained in $\boldsymbol{y}^{\text{tr}}$, and

$$\boldsymbol{y}^{\text{tr}} := (y_1^{\text{tr}}, y_2^{\text{tr}}, \ldots, y_{n_{\text{tr}}}^{\text{tr}})^\top.$$

- The generalization error is defined as

$$\text{Gen} := \mathop{\mathbb{E}}_{\boldsymbol{x}^{\text{te}}} \mathop{\mathbb{E}}_{y^{\text{te}}} \left[\left(\widehat{f}(\boldsymbol{x}^{\text{te}}; \widehat{\boldsymbol{\theta}}) - y^{\text{te}} \right)^2 \right],$$

that is, the squared loss is used.

To make the following discussion simple, we subtract constant terms from the generalization error:

$$\mathrm{Gen}' := \mathrm{Gen} - C' - \sigma^2, \tag{3.2}$$

where C' is defined as

$$C' := \mathop{\mathbb{E}}_{\boldsymbol{x}^{\mathrm{te}}}\left[f^2(\boldsymbol{x}^{\mathrm{te}})\right].$$

Note that C' is independent of the learned function.

Under this setup, the generalization error estimator based on IWAIC is given as follows [145]:

$$\widehat{\mathrm{Gen}}_{\mathrm{IWAIC}} = \langle \widehat{\boldsymbol{U}}\boldsymbol{L}\boldsymbol{y}^{\mathrm{tr}}, \boldsymbol{L}\boldsymbol{y}^{\mathrm{tr}}\rangle - 2\langle \widehat{\boldsymbol{U}}\boldsymbol{L}\boldsymbol{y}^{\mathrm{tr}}, \boldsymbol{L}_1\boldsymbol{y}^{\mathrm{tr}}\rangle + 2\mathrm{tr}(\widehat{\boldsymbol{U}}\boldsymbol{L}\widehat{\boldsymbol{Q}}\boldsymbol{L}_1^\top),$$

where $\langle \cdot, \cdot \rangle$ denotes the inner product,

$$\widehat{\boldsymbol{U}} := \frac{1}{n_{\mathrm{tr}}}\boldsymbol{X}^{\mathrm{tr}\top}\boldsymbol{W}\boldsymbol{X}^{\mathrm{tr}},$$

and $\widehat{\boldsymbol{Q}}$ is the diagonal matrix with the i-th diagonal element

$$\widehat{Q}_{i,i} := (y_i^{\mathrm{tr}} - \widehat{f}(\boldsymbol{x}_i^{\mathrm{tr}}; \widehat{\boldsymbol{\theta}}))^2.$$

IWAIC is asymptotically unbiased even under covariate shift; more precisely, IWAIC satisfies

$$\mathop{\mathbb{E}}_{\{\boldsymbol{x}_i^{\mathrm{tr}}\}_{i=1}^{n_{\mathrm{tr}}}} \mathop{\mathbb{E}}_{\{y_i^{\mathrm{tr}}\}_{i=1}^{n_{\mathrm{tr}}}} [\widehat{\mathrm{Gen}}_{\mathrm{IWAIC}} - \mathrm{Gen}'] = o(n_{\mathrm{tr}}^{-1}), \tag{3.3}$$

where $\mathbb{E}_{\{\boldsymbol{x}_i^{\mathrm{tr}}\}_{i=1}^{n_{\mathrm{tr}}}}$ denotes the expectations over $\{\boldsymbol{x}_i^{\mathrm{tr}}\}_{i=1}^{n_{\mathrm{tr}}}$ drawn i.i.d. from $p_{\mathrm{tr}}(\boldsymbol{x})$, and $\mathbb{E}_{\{y_i^{\mathrm{tr}}\}_{i=1}^{n_{\mathrm{tr}}}}$ denotes the expectations over $\{y_i^{\mathrm{tr}}\}_{i=1}^{n_{\mathrm{tr}}}$, each drawn from $p(y|\boldsymbol{x} = \boldsymbol{x}_i^{\mathrm{tr}})$.

3.2 Importance-Weighted Subspace Information Criterion

IWAIC has nice theoretical properties such as asymptotic lack of bias (equation 3.3). However, there are two issues for possible improvement—input independence and model specification.

3.2.1 Input Dependence vs. Input Independence in Generalization Error Analysis

The first issue for improving IWAIC is the way lack of bias is evaluated. In IWAIC, unbiasedness is evaluated in terms of the expectations over *both* training input points and training output values (see equation 3.3). However, in practice we are given only a single training set $\{(\boldsymbol{x}_i^{\text{tr}}, y_i^{\text{tr}})\}_{i=1}^{n_{\text{tr}}}$, and ideally we want to predict the *single-trial* generalization error, that is, the generalization error for a single realization of the training set at hand. From this viewpoint, we do not want to average out the random variables; we want to plug the realization of the random variables into the generalization error and evaluate the realized value of the generalization error.

However, we may not be able to avoid taking the expectation over the training output values $\{y_i^{\text{tr}}\}_{i=1}^{n_{\text{tr}}}$ (i.e., the expectation over the training output noise) since the training output noise is inaccessible. In contrast, the location of the training input points $\{\boldsymbol{x}_i^{\text{tr}}\}_{i=1}^{n_{\text{tr}}}$ is accessible. Therefore, it would be advantageous to predict the generalization error *without* taking the expectation over the training input points, that is, to predict the *conditional* expectation of the generalization error, given training input points. Below, we refer to estimating the conditional expectation of the generalization error as *input-dependent analysis of the generalization error*. On the other hand, estimating the full expectation of the generalization error is referred to as *input-independent analysis of the generalization error*.

In order to illustrate a possible advantage of the input-dependent approach, let us consider a simple model selection scenario where we have only one training sample (x, y) (see figure 3.1). The solid curves in figure 3.1a depict $G_{M_1}(y|x)$, the generalization error for a model M_1 as a function of the (noisy) training output value y, given a training input point x. The three solid curves correspond to the cases where the realization of the training input point x is x', x'', and x''', respectively. The value of the generalization error for the model M_1 in the input-independent approach is depicted by the dash-dotted line, where the expectation is taken over both the training input point x and the training output value y (this corresponds to the mean of the values of the three solid curves). The values of the generalization error in the input-dependent approach are depicted by the dotted lines, where the expectation is taken over only the training output value y, conditioned on $x = x'$, x'', and x''', respectively (this corresponds to the mean of the values of each solid curve). The graph in figure 3.1b depicts the generalization errors for a model M_2 in the same manner.

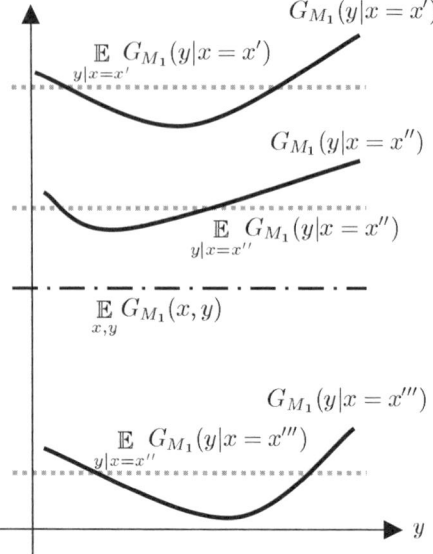

(a) Generalization error for model M_1

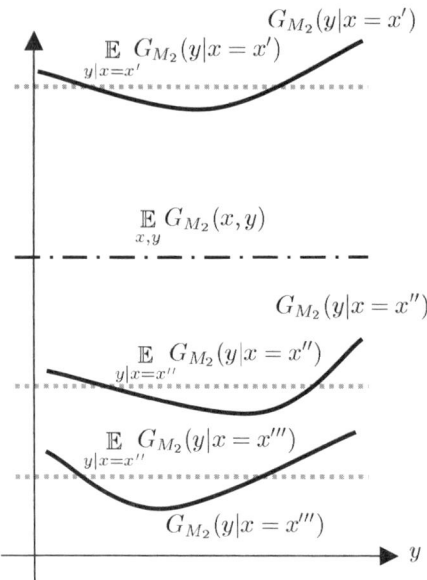

(b) Generalization error for model M_2

Figure 3.1
Schematic illustrations of the input-dependent and input-independent approaches to generalization error estimation.

3.2. Importance-Weighted Subspace Information Criterion

In the input-independent framework, the model M_1 is judged to be better than M_2, regardless of the realization of the training input point, because the dash-dotted line in figure 3.1a is lower than that in figure 3.1b. However, M_2 is actually better than M_1 if x'' is realized as x. In the input-dependent framework, the goodness of the model is *adaptively* evaluated, depending on the realization of the training input point x. This illustrates a possibility that input-dependent analysis of the generalization error allows one to choose a better model than input-independent analysis.

3.2.2 Approximately Correct Models

The second issue for improving IWAIC is model misspecification. IWAIC has the same asymptotic accuracy for *all* models (see equation 3.3). However, in practice it may not be so difficult to distinguish good models from completely useless (i.e., heavily misspecified) models since the magnitude of the generalization error is significantly different. This means that we are essentially interested in choosing a very good model from a set of reasonably good models. In this scenario, if a generalization error estimator is more accurate for better models (in other words, approximately correct models), the model selection performance will be further improved.

In order to formalize the concept of "approximately correct models," let us focus on the following setup:

- The squared-loss (see section 1.3.2) is used:

$$\text{loss}(x, y, \widehat{y}) = (\widehat{y} - y)^2.$$

- Noise in training and test output values is assumed to be i.i.d. with mean zero and variance σ^2. Then the generalization error is expressed as follows (see section 1.3.3):

$$\begin{aligned}
\text{Gen} &:= \mathop{\mathbb{E}}_{x^{te}} \mathop{\mathbb{E}}_{y^{te}} \left[\left(\widehat{f}(x^{te}; \widehat{\boldsymbol{\theta}}) - y^{te} \right)^2 \right] \\
&= \mathop{\mathbb{E}}_{x^{te}} \mathop{\mathbb{E}}_{y^{te}} \left[\left(\widehat{f}(x^{te}; \widehat{\boldsymbol{\theta}}) - f(x^{te}) + f(x^{te}) - y^{te} \right)^2 \right] \\
&= \mathop{\mathbb{E}}_{x^{te}} \left[\left(\widehat{f}(x^{te}; \widehat{\boldsymbol{\theta}}) - f(x^{te}) \right)^2 \right] + \mathop{\mathbb{E}}_{y^{te}} \left[(f(x^{te}) - y^{te})^2 \right] \\
&\quad + 2 \mathop{\mathbb{E}}_{x^{te}} \left[\widehat{f}(x^{te}; \widehat{\boldsymbol{\theta}}) - f(x^{te}) \right] \mathop{\mathbb{E}}_{y^{te}} \left[f(x^{te}) - y^{te} \right] \\
&= \mathop{\mathbb{E}}_{x^{te}} \left[\left(\widehat{f}(x^{te}; \widehat{\boldsymbol{\theta}}) - f(x^{te}) \right)^2 \right] + \sigma^2,
\end{aligned}$$

where $\mathbb{E}_{\boldsymbol{x}^{\text{te}}}$ denotes the expectation over $\boldsymbol{x}^{\text{te}}$ drawn from $p_{\text{te}}(\boldsymbol{x})$, and $\mathbb{E}_{y^{\text{te}}}$ denotes the expectation over y^{te} drawn from $p(y|\boldsymbol{x}=\boldsymbol{x}^{\text{te}})$.

- A linear-in-parameter model (see section 1.3.5.1) is used:

$$\widehat{f}(\boldsymbol{x};\boldsymbol{\theta}) = \sum_{\ell=1}^{b} \theta_\ell \varphi_\ell(\boldsymbol{x}),$$

where b is the number of parameters and $\{\varphi_\ell(\boldsymbol{x})\}_{\ell=1}^{b}$ are fixed, linearly independent functions.

Let $\boldsymbol{\theta}^*$ be the optimal parameter under the above-defined generalization error:

$$\boldsymbol{\theta}^* := \operatorname*{argmin}_{\boldsymbol{\theta}} \text{Gen}.$$

Then the learning target function $f(\boldsymbol{x})$ can be decomposed as

$$f(\boldsymbol{x}) = \widehat{f}(\boldsymbol{x};\boldsymbol{\theta}^*) + \delta r(\boldsymbol{x}), \tag{3.4}$$

where $\delta r(\boldsymbol{x})$ is the residual. $r(\boldsymbol{x})$ is orthogonal to the basis functions $\{\varphi_\ell(\boldsymbol{x})\}_{\ell=1}^{n_{\text{tr}}}$ under $p_{\text{te}}(\boldsymbol{x})$:

$$\mathbb{E}_{\boldsymbol{x}^{\text{te}}}\left[r(\boldsymbol{x}^{\text{te}})\varphi_\ell(\boldsymbol{x}^{\text{te}})\right] = 0 \text{ for } \ell = 1, 2, \ldots, b.$$

The function $r(\boldsymbol{x})$ governs the nature of the model error, and δ is the possible magnitude of this error. In order to separate these two factors, we impose the following normalization condition on $r(\boldsymbol{x})$:

$$\mathbb{E}_{\boldsymbol{x}^{\text{te}}}\left[r^2(\boldsymbol{x}^{\text{te}})\right] = 1.$$

The above decomposition is illustrated in figure 3.2. An "approximately correct model" refers to the model with small δ (but $\delta \neq 0$). Rather informally, a good model should have a small model error δ.

3.2.3 Input-Dependent Analysis of Generalization Error

Based on input-dependent analysis (section 3.2.1) and approximately correct models (section 3.2.2), a generalization error estimator called the *subspace information criterion* (SIC) [165, 161] has been developed for linear regression, and has been extended to be able to cope with covariate shift [162]. Here we review the derivation of this criterion, which we refer to

3.2. Importance-Weighted Subspace Information Criterion

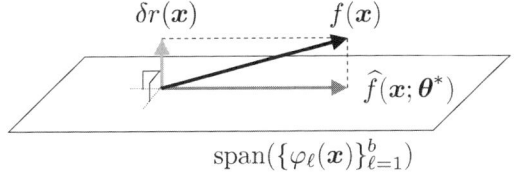

Figure 3.2
Orthogonal decomposition of $f(x)$. An approximately correct model is a model with small model error δ.

as *importance-weighted SIC* (IWSIC). More specifically, we first derive the basic form of IWSIC, "pre-IWSIC," in equation 3.8. Then versions of IWSIC for various learning methods are derived, including linear learning (equation 3.11, and affine learning (equation 3.11)), smooth nonlinear learning (equation 3.17), and general nonlinear learning (equation 3.18).

3.2.3.1 Preliminaries Since $\widehat{f}(x;\widehat{\boldsymbol{\theta}})$ and $r(x)$ are orthogonal to one another (see figure 3.2), Gen$'$ defined by equation 3.2 can be written as

$$\begin{aligned}
\text{Gen}' &= \mathop{\mathbb{E}}_{x^{\text{te}}}\left[\widehat{f}(x^{\text{te}};\widehat{\boldsymbol{\theta}})^2\right] - 2\mathop{\mathbb{E}}_{x^{\text{te}}}\left[\widehat{f}(x^{\text{te}};\widehat{\boldsymbol{\theta}})f(x^{\text{te}})\right] \\
&= \mathop{\mathbb{E}}_{x^{\text{te}}}\left[\widehat{f}(x^{\text{te}};\widehat{\boldsymbol{\theta}})^2\right] - 2\mathop{\mathbb{E}}_{x^{\text{te}}}\left[\widehat{f}(x^{\text{te}};\widehat{\boldsymbol{\theta}})\left(\widehat{f}(x^{\text{te}};\boldsymbol{\theta}^*)+r(x^{\text{te}})\right)\right] \\
&= \langle \boldsymbol{U}\widehat{\boldsymbol{\theta}},\widehat{\boldsymbol{\theta}}\rangle - 2\langle \boldsymbol{U}\widehat{\boldsymbol{\theta}},\boldsymbol{\theta}^*\rangle,
\end{aligned} \tag{3.5}$$

where $\boldsymbol{U}$ is the $b \times b$ matrix with the (ℓ, ℓ')-th element

$$U_{\ell,\ell'} := \mathop{\mathbb{E}}_{x^{\text{te}}}\left[\varphi_\ell(x^{\text{te}})\varphi_{\ell'}(x^{\text{te}})\right].$$

A basic concept of IWSIC is to replace the unknown $\boldsymbol{\theta}^*$ in equation 3.5 with the *importance-weighted least-squares* (IWLS) estimator $\widehat{\boldsymbol{\theta}}_1$ (see section 2.2.1):

$$\widehat{\boldsymbol{\theta}}_1 := \boldsymbol{L}_1 \boldsymbol{y}^{\text{tr}},$$

where

$$\boldsymbol{L}_1 := (\boldsymbol{X}^{\text{tr}\top}\boldsymbol{W}_1 \boldsymbol{X}^{\text{tr}})^{-1}\boldsymbol{X}^{\text{tr}\top}\boldsymbol{W}_1, \tag{3.6}$$
$$\boldsymbol{y}^{\text{tr}} := (y_1^{\text{tr}}, y_2^{\text{tr}}, \ldots, y_{n_{\text{tr}}}^{\text{tr}})^\top.$$

X^{tr} is the $n_{\mathrm{tr}} \times b$ design matrix with the (i, ℓ)-th element

$$X_{i,\ell} := \varphi_\ell(x_i^{\mathrm{tr}}),$$

and W_1 is the diagonal matrix with the i-th diagonal element

$$[W_1]_{i,i} := \frac{p_{\mathrm{te}}(x_i^{\mathrm{tr}})}{p_{\mathrm{tr}}(x_i^{\mathrm{tr}})}.$$

However, simply replacing $\boldsymbol{\theta}^*$ with $\widehat{\boldsymbol{\theta}}_1$ causes a bias since the sample y^{tr} is also used for obtaining the target parameter $\widehat{\boldsymbol{\theta}}$. The bias is expressed as

$$\mathbb{E}_{\{y_i^{\mathrm{tr}}\}_{i=1}^{n_{\mathrm{tr}}}} \left[\langle U\widehat{\boldsymbol{\theta}}, \widehat{\boldsymbol{\theta}}_1 \rangle - \langle U\widehat{\boldsymbol{\theta}}, \boldsymbol{\theta}^* \rangle \right],$$

where $\mathbb{E}_{\{y_i^{\mathrm{tr}}\}_{i=1}^{n_{\mathrm{tr}}}}$ denotes the expectations over $\{y_i^{\mathrm{tr}}\}_{i=1}^{n_{\mathrm{tr}}}$, each of which is drawn from $p(y|x = x_i^{\mathrm{tr}})$. Below, we study the behavior of this bias.

3.2.3.2 Approximate Bias Correction and pre-IWSIC The output values $\{\widehat{f}(x_i^{\mathrm{tr}}; \boldsymbol{\theta}^*)\}_{i=1}^{n_{\mathrm{tr}}}$ can be expressed as

$$(\widehat{f}(x_1^{\mathrm{tr}}; \boldsymbol{\theta}^*), \widehat{f}(x_2^{\mathrm{tr}}; \boldsymbol{\theta}^*), \ldots, \widehat{f}(x_{n_{\mathrm{tr}}}^{\mathrm{tr}}; \boldsymbol{\theta}^*))^\top = X^{\mathrm{tr}}\boldsymbol{\theta}^*.$$

Let r^{tr} be the n_{tr}-dimensional vector defined by

$$r^{\mathrm{tr}} = (r(x_1^{\mathrm{tr}}), r(x_2^{\mathrm{tr}}), \ldots, r(x_{n_{\mathrm{tr}}}^{\mathrm{tr}}))^\top,$$

where $r(x)$ is the residual function (see figure 3.2). Then the training output vector y^{tr} can be expressed as

$$y^{\mathrm{tr}} = X^{\mathrm{tr}}\boldsymbol{\theta}^* + \delta r^{\mathrm{tr}} + \boldsymbol{\epsilon}^{\mathrm{tr}},$$

where δ is the model error (see figure 3.2), and

$$\begin{aligned}\boldsymbol{\epsilon}^{\mathrm{tr}} &:= y^{\mathrm{tr}} - X^{\mathrm{tr}}\boldsymbol{\theta}^* - \delta r^{\mathrm{tr}} \\ &= y^{\mathrm{tr}} - \mathbb{E}_{\{y_i^{\mathrm{tr}}\}_{i=1}^{n_{\mathrm{tr}}}}\left[y^{\mathrm{tr}}\right]\end{aligned}$$

3.2. Importance-Weighted Subspace Information Criterion

is the vector of training output noise. Due to the i.i.d. noise assumption, ϵ^{tr} satisfies

$$\mathbb{E}_{\{y_i^{tr}\}_{i=1}^{n_{tr}}} [\epsilon^{tr}] = \mathbf{0}_{n_{tr}},$$

$$\mathbb{E}_{\{y_i^{tr}\}_{i=1}^{n_{tr}}} [\epsilon^{tr} \epsilon^{tr\top}] = \sigma^2 \mathbf{I}_{n_{tr}},$$

where $\mathbf{0}_{n_{tr}}$ denotes the n_{tr}-dimensional vector with all zeros and $\mathbf{I}_{n_{tr}}$ is the n_{tr}-dimensional identity matrix.

For a parameter vector $\widehat{\boldsymbol{\theta}}$ learned from $\mathbf{y}^{tr}$, the bias caused by replacing $\boldsymbol{\theta}^*$ with $\widehat{\boldsymbol{\theta}}_1$ can be expressed as

$$\begin{aligned}
& \mathbb{E}_{\{y_i^{tr}\}_{i=1}^{n_{tr}}} \left[\langle \mathbf{U}\widehat{\boldsymbol{\theta}}, \widehat{\boldsymbol{\theta}}_1 \rangle - \langle \mathbf{U}\widehat{\boldsymbol{\theta}}, \boldsymbol{\theta}^* \rangle \right] \\
&= \mathbb{E}_{\{y_i^{tr}\}_{i=1}^{n_{tr}}} \left[\langle \mathbf{U}\widehat{\boldsymbol{\theta}}, \mathbf{L}_1(\mathbf{X}^{tr}\boldsymbol{\theta}^* + \delta \mathbf{r}^{tr} + \epsilon^{tr}) \rangle - \langle \mathbf{U}\widehat{\boldsymbol{\theta}}, \mathbf{L}_1 \mathbf{X}^{tr}\boldsymbol{\theta}^* \rangle \right] \\
&= \mathbb{E}_{\{y_i^{tr}\}_{i=1}^{n_{tr}}} \left[\langle \mathbf{U}\widehat{\boldsymbol{\theta}}, \mathbf{L}_1 \epsilon^{tr} \rangle + \delta \langle \mathbf{U}\widehat{\boldsymbol{\theta}}, \mathbf{L}_1 \mathbf{r}^{tr} \rangle \right],
\end{aligned} \quad (3.7)$$

where $\mathbb{E}_{\{y_i^{tr}\}_{i=1}^{n_{tr}}}$ denotes the expectations over $\{y_i^{tr}\}_{i=1}^{n_{tr}}$, each of which is drawn from $p(y|\mathbf{x}=\mathbf{x}_i^{tr})$. In the above derivation, we used the fact that $\mathbf{L}_1 \mathbf{X}^{tr} = \mathbf{I}_b$, which follows from equation 3.6. Based on the above expression, we define "pre-IWSIC" as follows.

$$\widehat{\mathrm{Gen}}_{\text{preIWSIC}} := \langle \mathbf{U}\widehat{\boldsymbol{\theta}}, \widehat{\boldsymbol{\theta}} \rangle - 2\langle \mathbf{U}\widehat{\boldsymbol{\theta}}, \mathbf{L}_1 \mathbf{y}^{tr} \rangle + 2 \mathbb{E}_{\{y_i^{tr}\}_{i=1}^{n_{tr}}} \left[\langle \mathbf{U}\widehat{\boldsymbol{\theta}}, \mathbf{L}_1 \epsilon^{tr} \rangle \right], \quad (3.8)$$

that is, $\mathbb{E}_{\{y_i^{tr}\}_{i=1}^{n_{tr}}} \left[\delta \langle \mathbf{U}\widehat{\boldsymbol{\theta}}, \mathbf{L}_1 \mathbf{r}^{tr} \rangle \right]$ in equation 3.7 was ignored. Below, we show that pre-IWSIC is asymptotically unbiased even under covariate shift. More precisely, it satisfies

$$\mathbb{E}_{\{y_i^{tr}\}_{i=1}^{n_{tr}}} [\widehat{\mathrm{Gen}}_{\text{preIWSIC}} - \mathrm{Gen}'] = \mathcal{O}_p(\delta n_{tr}^{-\frac{1}{2}}), \quad (3.9)$$

where $\mathcal{O}_p$ denotes the asymptotic order in probability with respect to the distribution of $\{\mathbf{x}_i^{tr}\}_{i=1}^{n_{tr}}$.

[Proof of equation 3.9:] $\mathbf{L}_1 \mathbf{r}^{tr}$ is expressed as

$$\mathbf{L}_1 \mathbf{r}^{tr} = \left(\frac{1}{n_{tr}} \mathbf{X}^{tr\top} \mathbf{W}_1 \mathbf{X}^{tr} \right)^{-1} \frac{1}{n_{tr}} \mathbf{X}^{tr\top} \mathbf{W}_1 \mathbf{r}^{tr}.$$

Then the *law of large numbers* [131] asserts that

$$\underset{n_{\mathrm{tr}}\to\infty}{\mathrm{plim}}\left[\left(\frac{1}{n_{\mathrm{tr}}}X^{\mathrm{tr}\top}W_1X^{\mathrm{tr}}\right)\right]_{\ell,\ell'} = \underset{n_{\mathrm{tr}}\to\infty}{\mathrm{plim}}\frac{1}{n_{\mathrm{tr}}}\sum_{i=1}^{n_{\mathrm{tr}}}\frac{p_{\mathrm{te}}(x_i^{\mathrm{tr}})}{p_{\mathrm{tr}}(x_i^{\mathrm{tr}})}\varphi_\ell(x_i^{\mathrm{tr}})\varphi_{\ell'}(x_i^{\mathrm{tr}})$$

$$= \int \frac{p_{\mathrm{te}}(x)}{p_{\mathrm{tr}}(x)}\varphi_\ell(x)\varphi_{\ell'}(x)p_{\mathrm{tr}}(x)dx$$

$$= \int p_{\mathrm{te}}(x)\varphi_\ell(x)\varphi_{\ell'}(x)dx$$

$$< \infty,$$

where "plim" denotes *convergence in probability*. This implies that

$$\left(\frac{1}{n_{\mathrm{tr}}}X^{\mathrm{tr}\top}W_1X^{\mathrm{tr}}\right)^{-1} = \mathcal{O}_p(1).$$

On the other hand, when n_{tr} is large, the *central limit theorem* [131] asserts that

$$\left[\frac{1}{n_{\mathrm{tr}}}X^{\mathrm{tr}\top}W_1r^{\mathrm{tr}}\right]_\ell = \frac{1}{n_{\mathrm{tr}}}\sum_{i=1}^{n_{\mathrm{tr}}}\frac{p_{\mathrm{te}}(x_i^{\mathrm{tr}})}{p_{\mathrm{tr}}(x_i^{\mathrm{tr}})}\varphi_\ell(x_i^{\mathrm{tr}})r(x_i^{\mathrm{tr}})$$

$$= \int \frac{p_{\mathrm{te}}(x)}{p_{\mathrm{tr}}(x)}\varphi_\ell(x)r(x)p_{\mathrm{tr}}(x)dx + \mathcal{O}_p(n_{\mathrm{tr}}^{-\frac{1}{2}})$$

$$= \int p_{\mathrm{te}}(x)\varphi_\ell(x)r(x)dx + \mathcal{O}_p(n_{\mathrm{tr}}^{-\frac{1}{2}})$$

$$= \mathcal{O}_p(n_{\mathrm{tr}}^{-\frac{1}{2}}),$$

where we use the fact that $\varphi_\ell(x)$ and $r(x)$ are orthogonal to one another under $p_{\mathrm{te}}(x)$ (see figure 3.2). Then we have

$$L_1r^{\mathrm{tr}} = \mathcal{O}_p(n_{\mathrm{tr}}^{-\frac{1}{2}}).$$

This implies that when $\widehat{\boldsymbol{\theta}}$ is convergent,

$$\delta\langle U\widehat{\boldsymbol{\theta}}, L_1r^{\mathrm{tr}}\rangle = \mathcal{O}_p(\delta n_{\mathrm{tr}}^{-\frac{1}{2}}),$$

and therefore we have equation 3.9.

Note that IWSIC's asymptotic lack of bias shown above is in terms of the expectation *only* over the training output values $\{y_i^{\mathrm{tr}}\}_{i=1}^{n_{\mathrm{tr}}}$; training input points $\{x_i^{\mathrm{tr}}\}_{i=1}^{n_{\mathrm{tr}}}$ are fixed (i.e., input-dependent analysis; cf. input-independent analysis,

3.2. Importance-Weighted Subspace Information Criterion

explained in section 3.1). The asymptotic order of the bias of pre-IWSIC is proportional to the model error δ, implying that pre-IWSIC is more accurate for "better" models; if the model is correct (i.e., $\delta = 0$), pre-IWSIC is *exactly* unbiased with finite samples.

Below, for types of parameter learning including linear, affine, smooth nonlinear, and general nonlinear, we show how to approximate the third term of pre-IWSIC,

$$\mathbb{E}_{\{y_i^{tr}\}_{i=1}^{n_{tr}}} \left[\langle U\widehat{\boldsymbol{\theta}}, \boldsymbol{L}_1 \boldsymbol{\epsilon}^{tr} \rangle \right],$$

from the training samples $\{(\boldsymbol{x}_i^{tr}, y_i^{tr})\}_{i=1}^{n_{tr}}$. In the above equation, $\mathbb{E}_{\{y_i^{tr}\}_{i=1}^{n_{tr}}}$ essentially means the expectation over training output noise $\{\epsilon_i^{tr}\}_{i=1}^{n_{tr}}$. Below, we stick to using $\mathbb{E}_{\{y_i^{tr}\}_{i=1}^{n_{tr}}}$ for expressing the expectation over $\{\epsilon_i^{tr}\}_{i=1}^{n_{tr}}$.

3.2.3.3 Linear Learning First, let us consider *linear learning*, that is, the learned parameter $\widehat{\boldsymbol{\theta}}$ is given by

$$\widehat{\boldsymbol{\theta}} = \boldsymbol{L} \boldsymbol{y}^{tr}, \tag{3.10}$$

where $\boldsymbol{L}$ is a $b \times n_{tr}$ learning matrix which is independent of the training output noise. This independence assumption is essentially used as

$$\mathbb{E}_{\{y_i^{tr}\}_{i=1}^{n_{tr}}} \left[\widehat{\boldsymbol{\theta}} \right] = \mathbb{E}_{\{y_i^{tr}\}_{i=1}^{n_{tr}}} \left[\boldsymbol{L} \boldsymbol{y}^{tr} \right] = \boldsymbol{L} \mathbb{E}_{\{y_i^{tr}\}_{i=1}^{n_{tr}}} \left[\boldsymbol{y}^{tr} \right].$$

Linear learning includes *adaptive importance-weighted least squares* (see section 2.2.1) and *importance-weighted least squares with the squared regularizer* (see section 2.1.3).

For linear learning (equation 3.10), we have

$$\mathbb{E}_{\{y_i^{tr}\}_{i=1}^{n_{tr}}} \left[\langle U\widehat{\boldsymbol{\theta}}, \boldsymbol{L}_1 \boldsymbol{\epsilon}^{tr} \rangle \right] = \mathbb{E}_{\{y_i^{tr}\}_{i=1}^{n_{tr}}} \left[\langle \boldsymbol{U}\boldsymbol{L}(\boldsymbol{X}^{tr}\boldsymbol{\theta}^* + \delta \boldsymbol{r}^{tr} + \boldsymbol{\epsilon}^{tr}), \boldsymbol{L}_1 \boldsymbol{\epsilon}^{tr} \rangle \right]$$

$$= \langle \boldsymbol{U}\boldsymbol{L}(\boldsymbol{X}^{tr}\boldsymbol{\theta}^* + \delta \boldsymbol{r}^{tr}), \boldsymbol{L}_1 \mathbb{E}_{\{y_i^{tr}\}_{i=1}^{n_{tr}}} \left[\boldsymbol{\epsilon}^{tr} \right] \rangle$$

$$+ \mathbb{E}_{\{y_i^{tr}\}_{i=1}^{n_{tr}}} \left[\langle \boldsymbol{U}\boldsymbol{L}\boldsymbol{\epsilon}^{tr}, \boldsymbol{L}_1 \boldsymbol{\epsilon}^{tr} \rangle \right]$$

$$= 0 + \operatorname{tr}(\boldsymbol{U}\boldsymbol{L} \mathbb{E}_{\{y_i^{tr}\}_{i=1}^{n_{tr}}} [\boldsymbol{\epsilon}^{tr} \boldsymbol{\epsilon}^{tr\top}] \boldsymbol{L}_1^\top)$$

$$= \sigma^2 \operatorname{tr}(\boldsymbol{U}\boldsymbol{L}\boldsymbol{L}_1^\top),$$

where σ^2 is the unknown noise variance. We approximate the noise variance σ^2 by

$$\widehat{\sigma}^2 := \frac{\|\bm{y}^{\mathrm{tr}} - \bm{X}^{\mathrm{tr}}\bm{L}_0\bm{y}^{\mathrm{tr}}\|^2}{n_{\mathrm{tr}} - \mathrm{tr}(\bm{X}^{\mathrm{tr}}\bm{L}_0)},$$

where $\bm{L}_0$ is the learning matrix of the ordinary least-squares estimator:

$$\bm{L}_0 := (\bm{X}^{\mathrm{tr}\top}\bm{X}^{\mathrm{tr}})^{-1}\bm{X}^{\mathrm{tr}\top}.$$

Then IWSIC for linear learning is given by

$$\widehat{\mathrm{Gen}}_{\mathrm{IWSIC}} := \langle \bm{U}\bm{L}\bm{y}^{\mathrm{tr}}, \bm{L}\bm{y}^{\mathrm{tr}}\rangle - 2\langle \bm{U}\bm{L}\bm{y}^{\mathrm{tr}}, \bm{L}_1\bm{y}^{\mathrm{tr}}\rangle + 2\widehat{\sigma}^2\mathrm{tr}(\bm{U}\bm{L}\bm{L}_1^{\top}). \quad (3.11)$$

When the model is correctly specified (i.e., $\delta = 0$), $\widehat{\sigma}^2$ is an unbiased estimator of σ^2 with finite samples. However, for misspecified models (i.e., $\delta \neq 0$), it is biased even asymptotically:

$$\mathbb{E}_{\{y_i^{\mathrm{tr}}\}_{i=1}^{n_{\mathrm{tr}}}}\left[\widehat{\sigma}^2\right] = \sigma^2 + \mathcal{O}_p(1).$$

On the other hand, $\mathrm{tr}(\bm{U}\bm{L}\bm{L}_1^{\top}) = \mathcal{O}_p(n_{\mathrm{tr}}^{-1})$ yields

$$\mathbb{E}_{\{y_i^{\mathrm{tr}}\}_{i=1}^{n_{\mathrm{tr}}}}\left[\widehat{\sigma}^2\mathrm{tr}(\bm{U}\bm{L}\bm{L}_1^{\top})\right] = \mathcal{O}_p(n_{\mathrm{tr}}^{-1}),$$

implying that even for misspecified models, IWSIC still satisfies

$$\mathbb{E}_{\{y_i^{\mathrm{tr}}\}_{i=1}^{n_{\mathrm{tr}}}}[\widehat{\mathrm{Gen}}_{\mathrm{IWSIC}} - \mathrm{Gen}'] = \mathcal{O}_p(\delta n_{\mathrm{tr}}^{-\frac{1}{2}}). \quad (3.12)$$

In section 8.2.4, we introduce another input-dependent estimator of the generalization error under the *active learning* setup—it is interesting to note that the constant terms ignored above (see the definition of Gen' in equation 3.2) and the constant terms ignored in active learning (equation 8.2) are different.

The appearance of IWSIC above rather resembles IWAIC under linear regression scenarios:

$$\widehat{\mathrm{Gen}}_{\mathrm{IWAIC}} = \langle \widehat{\bm{U}}\bm{L}\bm{y}^{\mathrm{tr}}, \bm{L}\bm{y}^{\mathrm{tr}}\rangle - 2\langle \widehat{\bm{U}}\bm{L}\bm{y}^{\mathrm{tr}}, \bm{L}_1\bm{y}^{\mathrm{tr}}\rangle + 2\mathrm{tr}(\widehat{\bm{U}}\bm{L}\widehat{\bm{Q}}\bm{L}_1^{\top}),$$

3.2. Importance-Weighted Subspace Information Criterion

where

$$\widehat{U} := \frac{1}{n_{\mathrm{tr}}} X^{\mathrm{tr}\top} W X^{\mathrm{tr}},$$

and $\widehat{Q}$ is the diagonal matrix with the i-th diagonal element

$$\widehat{Q}_{i,i} := (y_i^{\mathrm{tr}} - \widehat{f}(x_i^{\mathrm{tr}}; \widehat{\theta}))^2.$$

Asymptotic unbiasedness of IWAIC in the input-dependent framework is given by

$$\mathbb{E}_{\{y_i^{\mathrm{tr}}\}_{i=1}^{n_{\mathrm{tr}}}} [\widehat{\mathrm{Gen}}_{\mathrm{IWAIC}} - \mathrm{Gen}'] = \mathcal{O}_p(n_{\mathrm{tr}}^{-\frac{1}{2}}),$$

that is, the model error δ does not affect the speed of convergence. This difference is significant when we are comparing the performance of "good" models (with small δ).

3.2.3.4 Affine Learning Next, we consider a simple nonlinear learning method called *affine learning*. That is, for a $b \times n_{\mathrm{tr}}$ matrix L and a b-dimensional vector c, both of which are independent of the noise ϵ^{tr}, the learned parameter vector $\widehat{\theta}$ is given by

$$\widehat{\theta} = L y^{\mathrm{tr}} + c. \tag{3.13}$$

This includes *additive regularization learning* [121]:

$$\min_{\theta} \left[\sum_{i=1}^{n_{\mathrm{tr}}} \left(\widehat{f}(x_i^{\mathrm{tr}}) - y_i^{\mathrm{tr}} - \lambda_i \right)^2 + \|\theta\|^2 \right],$$

where

$$\lambda := (\lambda_1, \lambda_2, \ldots, \lambda_{n_{\mathrm{tr}}})^\top$$

is a tuning parameter vector. The learned parameter vector $\widehat{\theta}$ is given by equation 3.13 with

$$L = (X^{\mathrm{tr}\top} X^{\mathrm{tr}} + I_b)^{-1} X^{\mathrm{tr}\top},$$
$$c = (X^{\mathrm{tr}\top} X^{\mathrm{tr}} + I_b)^{-1} X^{\mathrm{tr}\top} \lambda,$$

where I_b denotes the b-dimensional identity matrix.

For affine learning (equation 3.13), it holds that

$$\mathbb{E}_{\{y_i^{\text{tr}}\}_{i=1}^{n_{\text{tr}}}} \left[\langle U\widehat{\boldsymbol{\theta}}, \boldsymbol{L}_1 \boldsymbol{\epsilon}^{\text{tr}} \rangle \right] = \mathbb{E}_{\{y_i^{\text{tr}}\}_{i=1}^{n_{\text{tr}}}} \left[\langle U(\boldsymbol{L} \boldsymbol{y}^{\text{tr}} + \boldsymbol{c}), \boldsymbol{L}_1 \boldsymbol{\epsilon}^{\text{tr}} \rangle \right]$$

$$= \sigma^2 \text{tr}(\boldsymbol{U} \boldsymbol{L} \boldsymbol{L}_1^\top).$$

Thus, we can still use linear IWSIC (equation 3.11) for affine learning without sacrificing its unbiasedness.

3.2.3.5 Smooth Nonlinear Learning Let us consider a *smooth nonlinear learning* method. That is, using an *almost differentiable* [148] operator $\boldsymbol{L}$, $\widehat{\boldsymbol{\theta}}$ is given by

$$\widehat{\boldsymbol{\theta}} = \boldsymbol{L}(\boldsymbol{y}^{\text{tr}}). \tag{3.14}$$

This includes *Huber's robust regression* (see section 2.2.3):

$$\min_{\boldsymbol{\theta}} \left[\sum_{i=1}^{n_{\text{tr}}} \rho_\tau(\widehat{f}(\boldsymbol{x}_i^{\text{tr}}; \boldsymbol{\theta}) - y_i^{\text{tr}}) \right],$$

where τ (≥ 0) is a tuning parameter and

$$\rho_\tau(y) := \begin{cases} \frac{1}{2} y^2 & \text{if } |y| \leq \tau, \\ \tau |y| - \frac{1}{2}\tau^2 & \text{if } |y| > \tau. \end{cases}$$

Note that $\rho_\tau(y)$ is twice almost differentiable, which yields a once almost differentiable operator $\boldsymbol{L}$.

Let $\boldsymbol{V}$ be the $n_{\text{tr}} \times n_{\text{tr}}$ matrix with the (i, i')-th element

$$V_{i,i'} := \nabla_i [\boldsymbol{L}_1^\top \boldsymbol{U} \boldsymbol{L}]_{i'}(\boldsymbol{y}^{\text{tr}}), \tag{3.15}$$

where ∇_i is the partial derivative operator with respect to the i-th element of input $\boldsymbol{y}^{\text{tr}}$ and $[\boldsymbol{L}_1^\top \boldsymbol{U} \boldsymbol{L}]_{i'}(\boldsymbol{y}^{\text{tr}})$ denotes the i'-th element of the output of the vector-valued function $[\boldsymbol{L}_1^\top \boldsymbol{U} \boldsymbol{L}](\boldsymbol{y}^{\text{tr}})$.

Suppose that the noise $\boldsymbol{\epsilon}^{\text{tr}}$ is Gaussian. Then, for smooth nonlinear learning (equation 3.14), we have

$$\mathbb{E}_{\{y_i^{\text{tr}}\}_{i=1}^{n_{\text{tr}}}} \left[\langle U\widehat{\boldsymbol{\theta}}, \boldsymbol{L}_1 \boldsymbol{\epsilon}^{\text{tr}} \rangle \right] = \sigma^2 \mathbb{E}_{\{y_i^{\text{tr}}\}_{i=1}^{n_{\text{tr}}}} \left[\text{tr}(\boldsymbol{V}) \right]. \tag{3.16}$$

3.2. Importance-Weighted Subspace Information Criterion

This result follows from *Stein's identity* [148]: for an n_{tr}-dimensional i.i.d. Gaussian vector $\boldsymbol{\epsilon}^{\text{tr}}$ with mean $\mathbf{0}_{n_{\text{tr}}}$ and covariance matrix $\sigma^2 \boldsymbol{I}_{n_{\text{tr}}}$, and for any almost-differentiable function $h(\cdot): \mathbb{R}^{n_{\text{tr}}} \to \mathbb{R}$, it holds that

$$\mathbb{E}_{\{y_i^{\text{tr}}\}_{i=1}^{n_{\text{tr}}}} \left[\epsilon_{i'}^{\text{tr}} h(\boldsymbol{\epsilon}^{\text{tr}}) \right] = \sigma^2 \mathbb{E}_{\{y_i^{\text{tr}}\}_{i=1}^{n_{\text{tr}}}} \left[\nabla_{i'} h(\boldsymbol{\epsilon}^{\text{tr}}) \right],$$

where $\epsilon_{i'}^{\text{tr}}$ is the i'-th element of $\boldsymbol{\epsilon}^{\text{tr}}$. If we let

$$\boldsymbol{h}(\boldsymbol{\epsilon}) = [\boldsymbol{L}_1^\top \boldsymbol{U} \boldsymbol{L}](\boldsymbol{y}^{\text{tr}}),$$

$\boldsymbol{h}(\boldsymbol{\epsilon})$ is almost differentiable since $\boldsymbol{L}(\boldsymbol{y}^{\text{tr}})$ is almost differentiable. Then an elementwise application of Stein's identity to a vector-valued function $\boldsymbol{h}(\boldsymbol{\epsilon})$ establishes equation 3.16.

Based on this, we define *importance-weighted linearly approximated SIC* (IWLASIC) as

$$\widehat{\text{Gen}}_{\text{IWLASIC}} = \langle \boldsymbol{U}\widehat{\boldsymbol{\theta}}, \widehat{\boldsymbol{\theta}} \rangle - 2\langle \boldsymbol{U}\widehat{\boldsymbol{\theta}}, \boldsymbol{L}_1 \boldsymbol{y}^{\text{tr}} \rangle + 2\sigma^2 \text{tr}(\boldsymbol{V}), \tag{3.17}$$

which still maintains the same lack of bias as the linear case under the Gaussian noise assumption. It is easy to confirm that equation 3.17 is reduced to the original form (equation 3.11) when $\widehat{\boldsymbol{\theta}}$ is obtained by linear learning (equation 3.10). Thus, IWLASIC may be regarded as a natural extension of the original IWSIC.

Note that IWLASIC (equation 3.17) is defined for the *true* noise variance σ^2; if σ^2 in IWLASIC is replaced by an estimator $\widehat{\sigma}^2$, unbiasedness of IWLASIC can no longer be guaranteed. On the other hand, IWSIC for linear and affine learning (see equation 3.11) is defined with an unbiased noise variance estimator $\widehat{\sigma}^2$, but it is still guaranteed to be unbiased.

3.2.3.6 General Nonlinear Learning
Finally, let us consider general nonlinear learning methods. That is, for a general nonlinear operator $\boldsymbol{L}$, the learned parameter vector $\boldsymbol{\theta}$ is given by

$$\widehat{\boldsymbol{\theta}} = \boldsymbol{L}(\boldsymbol{y}^{\text{tr}}).$$

This includes *importance-weighted least squares with the absolute regularizer* (see section 2.1.3).

---

1. Obtain the learned parameter vector $\widehat{\boldsymbol{\theta}}$, using the training samples $\{(\boldsymbol{x}_i^{\text{tr}}, y_i^{\text{tr}})\}_{i=1}^{n_{\text{tr}}}$ as usual.
2. Estimate the noise by $\{\widehat{\epsilon}_i^{\text{tr}} \mid \widehat{\epsilon}_i^{\text{tr}} = y_i^{\text{tr}} - \widehat{f}(\boldsymbol{x}_i^{\text{tr}}; \widehat{\boldsymbol{\theta}})\}_{i=1}^{n_{\text{tr}}}$.
3. Create bootstrap noise samples $\{\widetilde{\epsilon}_i^{\text{tr}}\}_{i=1}^{n_{\text{tr}}}$ by sampling with replacement from $\{\widehat{\epsilon}_i^{\text{tr}}\}_{i=1}^{n_{\text{tr}}}$.
4. Obtain the learned parameter vector $\widetilde{\boldsymbol{\theta}}$ using the bootstrap samples $\{(\boldsymbol{x}_i^{\text{tr}}, \widetilde{y}_i^{\text{tr}}) \mid \widetilde{y}_i^{\text{tr}} = \widehat{f}(\boldsymbol{x}_i^{\text{tr}}) + \widetilde{\epsilon}_i^{\text{tr}}\}_{i=1}^{n_{\text{tr}}}$.
5. Calculate $\langle \boldsymbol{U}\widetilde{\boldsymbol{\theta}}, \boldsymbol{L}_1 \widetilde{\boldsymbol{\epsilon}}^{\text{tr}} \rangle$.
6. Repeat steps 3 to 5 a number of times and output the mean of $\langle \boldsymbol{U}\widetilde{\boldsymbol{\theta}}, \boldsymbol{L}_1 \widetilde{\boldsymbol{\epsilon}}^{\text{tr}} \rangle$.

Figure 3.3
Bootstrap procedure in IWBASIC.

For general nonlinear learning, we estimate the third term $\mathbb{E}_{\{y_i^{\text{tr}}\}_{i=1}^{n_{\text{tr}}}} \left[\langle \boldsymbol{U}\widehat{\boldsymbol{\theta}}, \boldsymbol{L}_1 \boldsymbol{\epsilon}^{\text{tr}} \rangle \right]$ in pre-IWSIC (equation 3.8), using the *bootstrap* method [43, 45]:

$$\mathbb{E}_{\{y_i^{\text{tr}}\}_{i=1}^{n_{\text{tr}}}} \left[\langle \boldsymbol{U}\widehat{\boldsymbol{\theta}}, \boldsymbol{L}_1 \boldsymbol{\epsilon}^{\text{tr}} \rangle \right] \approx \widetilde{\mathbb{E}}_{\{y_i^{\text{tr}}\}_{i=1}^{n_{\text{tr}}}} \left[\langle \boldsymbol{U}\widetilde{\boldsymbol{\theta}}, \boldsymbol{L}_1 \widetilde{\boldsymbol{\epsilon}}^{\text{tr}} \rangle \right],$$

where $\widetilde{\mathbb{E}}_{\{y_i^{\text{tr}}\}_{i=1}^{n_{\text{tr}}}}$ denotes the expectation over the bootstrap replication, and $\widetilde{\boldsymbol{\theta}}$ and $\widetilde{\boldsymbol{\epsilon}}^{\text{tr}}$ correspond to the learned parameter vector $\widehat{\boldsymbol{\theta}}$ and the training output noise vector $\boldsymbol{\epsilon}^{\text{tr}}$ estimated from the bootstrap samples, respectively. More specifically, we compute $\widetilde{\mathbb{E}}_{\{y_i^{\text{tr}}\}_{i=1}^{n_{\text{tr}}}} \left[\langle \boldsymbol{U}\widetilde{\boldsymbol{\theta}}, \boldsymbol{L}_1 \widetilde{\boldsymbol{\epsilon}}^{\text{tr}} \rangle \right]$ by *bootstrapping residuals* as described in figure 3.3.

Based on this bootstrap procedure, *importance-weighted bootstrap-approximated SIC* (IWBASIC) is defined as

$$\widehat{\text{Gen}}_{\text{IWBASIC}} = \langle \boldsymbol{U}\widehat{\boldsymbol{\theta}}, \widehat{\boldsymbol{\theta}} \rangle - 2\langle \boldsymbol{U}\widehat{\boldsymbol{\theta}}, \boldsymbol{L}_1 \boldsymbol{y}^{\text{tr}} \rangle + 2 \widetilde{\mathbb{E}}_{\{y_i^{\text{tr}}\}_{i=1}^{n_{\text{tr}}}} \left[\langle \boldsymbol{U}\widetilde{\boldsymbol{\theta}}, \boldsymbol{L}_1 \widetilde{\boldsymbol{\epsilon}}^{\text{tr}} \rangle \right]. \tag{3.18}$$

3.3 Importance-Weighted Cross-Validation

IWAIC and IWSIC do not accept the 0/1-loss (see section 1.3.2). Thus, they cannot be employed for estimating the misclassification rate in classification scenarios. In this section, we describe a more general model selection method that can be applied to an arbitrary loss function including the 0/1-loss. Below, we consider the generalization error in the following general form:

$$\text{Gen} := \mathbb{E}_{\boldsymbol{x}^{\text{te}}} \mathbb{E}_{y^{\text{te}}} \left[\text{loss}(\boldsymbol{x}^{\text{te}}, y^{\text{te}}, \widehat{f}(\boldsymbol{x}^{\text{te}}; \boldsymbol{\theta})) \right].$$

3.3. Importance-Weighted Cross-Validation

One of the popular techniques for estimating the generalization error for arbitrary loss functions is *cross-validation* (CV) [150, 195]. CV has been shown to give an *almost* unbiased estimate of the generalization error with finite samples [105, 141]. However, such unbiased estimation is no longer possible under covariate shift. To cope with this problem, a variant of CV called *importance-weighted CV* (IWCV) has been proposed [160]. Let us randomly divide the training set $\mathcal{Z} = \{(\mathbf{x}_i^{\text{tr}}, y_i^{\text{tr}})\}_{i=1}^{n_{\text{tr}}}$ into k disjoint nonempty subsets $\{\mathcal{Z}_i\}_{i=1}^{k}$ of (approximately) the same size. Let $\widehat{f}_{\mathcal{Z}_i}(\mathbf{x})$ be a function learned from $\{\mathcal{Z}_{i'}\}_{i' \neq i}$ (i.e., without $\mathcal{Z}_i$). Then the *k-fold IWCV* (kIWCV) estimate of the generalization error Gen is given by

$$\widehat{\text{Gen}}_{k\text{IWCV}} = \frac{1}{k} \sum_{i=1}^{k} \frac{1}{|\mathcal{Z}_i|} \sum_{(\mathbf{x},y) \in \mathcal{Z}_i} \frac{p_{\text{te}}(\mathbf{x})}{p_{\text{tr}}(\mathbf{x})} \text{loss}(\mathbf{x}, y, \widehat{f}_{\mathcal{Z}_i}(\mathbf{x})),$$

where $|\mathcal{Z}_i|$ is the number of samples in the subset $\mathcal{Z}_i$ (see figure 3.4).

When $k = n_{\text{tr}}$, kIWCV is called *IW leave-one-out CV* (IWLOOCV):

$$\widehat{\text{Gen}}_{\text{IWLOOCV}} = \frac{1}{n_{\text{tr}}} \sum_{i=1}^{n_{\text{tr}}} \frac{p_{\text{te}}(\mathbf{x}_i^{\text{tr}})}{p_{\text{tr}}(\mathbf{x}_i^{\text{tr}})} \text{loss}(\mathbf{x}_i^{\text{tr}}, y_i^{\text{tr}}, \widehat{f}_i(\mathbf{x}_i^{\text{tr}})),$$

where $\widehat{f}_i(\mathbf{x})$ is a function learned from all samples without $(\mathbf{x}_i^{\text{tr}}, y_i^{\text{tr}})$. It has been proved that IWLOOCV gives an *almost* unbiased estimate of the generalization error even under covariate shift [160]. More precisely, IWLOOCV for n_{tr} training samples gives an unbiased estimate of the generalization error for

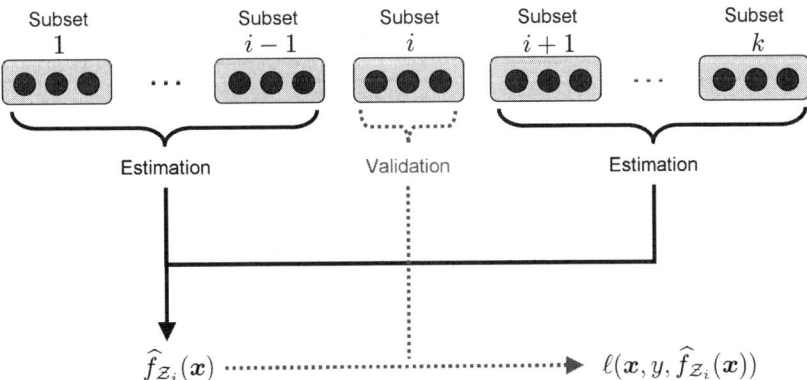

Figure 3.4
Cross-validation.

$n_{\mathrm{tr}} - 1$ training samples:

$$\mathbb{E}_{\{x_i^{\mathrm{tr}}\}_{i=1}^{n_{\mathrm{tr}}}} \mathbb{E}_{\{y_i^{\mathrm{tr}}\}_{i=1}^{n_{\mathrm{tr}}}} \left[\widehat{\mathrm{Gen}}_{\mathrm{IWLOOCV}}\right] = \mathbb{E}_{\{x_i^{\mathrm{tr}}\}_{i=1}^{n_{\mathrm{tr}}}} \mathbb{E}_{\{y_i^{\mathrm{tr}}\}_{i=1}^{n_{\mathrm{tr}}}} [\mathrm{Gen}_{n_{\mathrm{tr}}-1}]$$

$$\approx \mathbb{E}_{\{x_i^{\mathrm{tr}}\}_{i=1}^{n_{\mathrm{tr}}}} \mathbb{E}_{\{y_i^{\mathrm{tr}}\}_{i=1}^{n_{\mathrm{tr}}}} [\mathrm{Gen}],$$

where $\mathbb{E}_{\{x_i^{\mathrm{tr}}\}_{i=1}^{n_{\mathrm{tr}}}}$ denotes the expectation over $\{x_i^{\mathrm{tr}}\}_{i=1}^{n_{\mathrm{tr}}}$ drawn i.i.d. from $p_{\mathrm{tr}}(x)$, $\mathbb{E}_{\{y_i^{\mathrm{tr}}\}_{i=1}^{n_{\mathrm{tr}}}}$ denotes the expectations over $\{y_i^{\mathrm{tr}}\}_{i=1}^{n_{\mathrm{tr}}}$, each of which is drawn from $p(y|x = x_i^{\mathrm{tr}})$, and $\mathrm{Gen}_{n_{\mathrm{tr}}-1}$ denotes the generalization error for $n_{\mathrm{tr}} - 1$ training samples. A similar proof is possible for kIWCV, but the bias is slightly larger [74].

Almost unbiasedness of IWCV holds for any loss function, any model, and any parameter learning method; even nonidentifiable models [196] or nonparametric learning methods (e.g., [141]) are allowed. Thus, IWCV is very flexible and useful in practical model selection under covariate shift.

Unbiasedness of IWCV shown above is within the input-independent framework (see section 3.2.1); in the input-dependent framework, unbiasedness of IWCV is described as

$$\mathbb{E}_{\{y_i^{\mathrm{tr}}\}_{i=1}^{n_{\mathrm{tr}}}} [\widehat{\mathrm{Gen}}_{\mathrm{IWCV}} - \mathrm{Gen}] = \mathcal{O}_p(n_{\mathrm{tr}}^{-\frac{1}{2}}).$$

This is the same asymptotic order as in IWAIC and IWSIC. However, since it is independent of the model error δ, IWSIC would be more accurate in regression scenarios with good models.

3.4 Numerical Examples

Here we illustrate how IWAIC, IWSIC, and IWCV behave.

3.4.1 Regression

Let us continue the one-dimensional regression simulation of section 2.4.1.

As shown in figure 2.8 in section 2.4.1, adaptive importance-weighted least squares (AIWLS) with flattening parameter $\gamma = 0.5$ appears to work well for that particular realization. However, the best value of γ depends on the realization of samples. In order to investigate this issue systematically, let us repeat the simulation 1000 times with different random seeds. That is, in each run, $\{(x_i^{\mathrm{tr}}, \epsilon_i^{\mathrm{tr}})\}_{i=1}^{n_{\mathrm{tr}}}$ are randomly drawn and the scores of tenfold IWCV, IWSIC, IWAIC, and tenfold CV are calculated for $\gamma = 0, 0.1, 0.2, \ldots, 1$. The means and standard deviations of the generalization error Gen and its estimate by each method are depicted as functions of γ in figure 3.5.

3.4. Numerical Examples

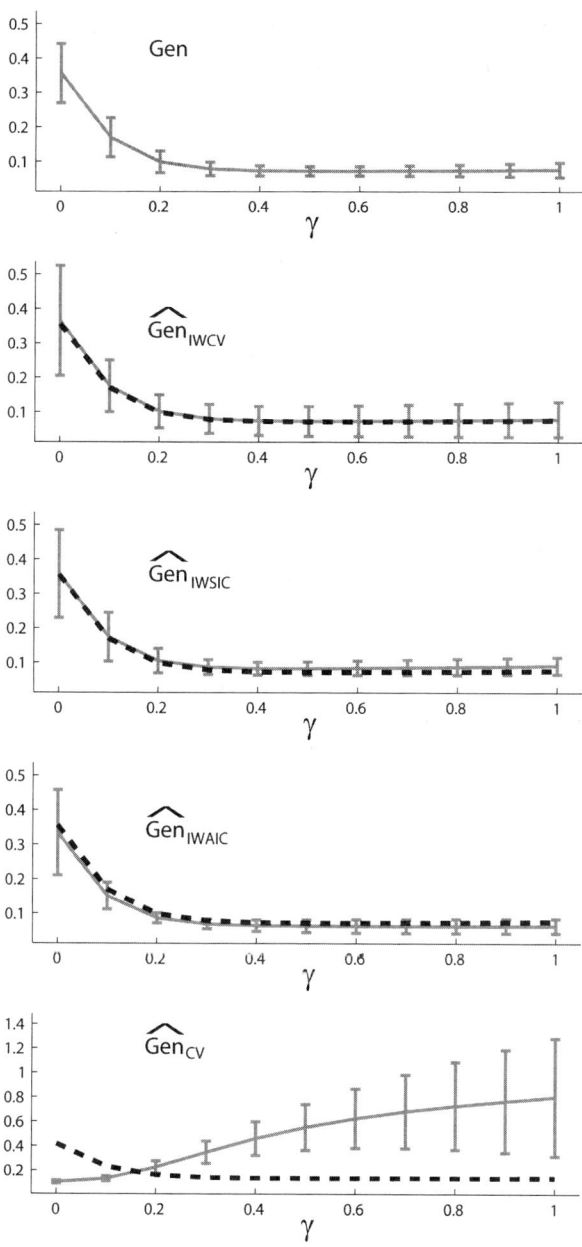

Figure 3.5
Generalization error and its estimates as functions of the flattening parameter γ in adaptive importance-weighted least squares (AIWLS) for the regression examples in figure 2.8. Dashed curves in the bottom four graphs depict the true generalization error for clear comparison. Note that the vertical scale of CV is different from others since it takes a wider range of values. Also note that IWAIC and IWSIC are estimators of the generalization error up to some constants (see equations 3.3 and 3.12). For clear comparison, we included those ignored constants in the plots, which does not essentially change the result.

Note that IWAIC and IWSIC are estimators of the generalization error up to some constants (see equations 3.3 and 3.12). For clear comparison, we included those ignored constants in the plots, which does not essentially change the result. The graphs show that IWCV, IWSIC, and IWAIC give reasonably good unbiased estimates of the generalization error, while CV is heavily biased. The variance of IWCV is slightly larger than those of IWSIC and IWAIC, which would be the price we have to pay in compensation for generality (as discussed in section 3.3, IWCV is a much more general method than IWSIC and IWAIC). Fortunately, as shown below, this rather large variance appears not to affect the model selection performance so much.

Next we investigate the model selection performance: the flattening parameter γ (see section 2.1.2) is chosen from $\{0, 0.1, 0.2, \ldots, 1\}$ so that the score of each method is minimized. The mean and standard deviation of the generalization error Gen of the learned function obtained by each method over 1000 runs are described in the top row of table 3.1. This shows that IWCV, IWSIC, and IWAIC give significantly smaller generalization errors than CV under the *t-test* [78] at the significance level of 5 percent. IWCV, IWSIC, and IWAIC are comparable to each other. For reference, the generalization error when the flattening parameter γ is chosen optimally (i.e., for each trial, γ is chosen so that the true generalization error is minimized) is described as OPT in the table. The result shows that the generalization error values of IWCV, IWSIC, and IWAIC are rather close to the optimal value.

The bottom row of table 3.1 describes the results when the polynomial model of order 2 is used for learning. This shows that IWCV and IWSIC still work well, and outperform IWAIC and CV. When the second-order polynomial model is used, the target function is rather realizable in the test region (see figure 2.8). Therefore, IWSIC tends to be more accurate (see section 3.2.3).

Table 3.1
The mean and standard deviation of the generalization error Gen obtained by each method for the toy regression data set

(n_{tr}, k)	IWCV	IWSIC	IWAIC	CV	OPT
(150, 1)	°0.077 ± 0.020	°0.077 ± 0.023	°0.076 ± 0.019	0.356 ± 0.086	0.069 ± 0.011
(100, 2)	°0.104 ± 0.113	°0.101 ± 0.103	0.113 ± 0.135	0.110 ± 0.135	0.072 ± 0.014

The best method and comparable ones by the *t*-test at the 5 percent significance level 5% are indicated by ○. For reference, the generalization error obtained with the optimal γ (i.e., the minimum generalization error) is described as OPT. n_{tr} is the number of training samples, while k is the order of the polynomial regression model. $(n_{tr}, k) = (150, 1)$ and $(100, 2)$ roughly correspond to *"misspecified and large sample size,"* and *"approximately correct and small sample size,"* respectively.

The good performance of IWCV is maintained thanks to the almost total lack of bias unbiasedness. Ordinary CV is not extremely poor due to the the fact that it is almost realizable, but it is still inferior to IWCV and IWSIC. IWAIC tends to work rather poorly since $n_{tr} = 100$ is relatively small compared with the high complexity of the second-order model, and hence the asymptotic results are not valid (see sections 3.1 and 3.2.3).

The above simulation results illustrate that IWCV performs quite well in regression under covariate shift; its performance is comparable to that of IWSIC, which is a generalization error estimator specialized for linear regression with linear parameter learning.

3.4.2 Classification

Let us continue the toy classification simulation in section 2.4.2. IWSIC and IWAIC cannot be applied to classification problems because they do not accept the 0/1-loss. For this reason, we compare only IWCV and ordinary CV here.

In figure 2.9b in section 2.4.2, adaptive importance-weighted Fisher discriminant analysis (AIWFDA) with a middle/large flattening parameter γ appears to work well for that particular realization. Here, we investigate the choice of the flattening parameter value by IWCV and CV more extensively. Figure 3.6 depicts the means and standard deviations of the generalization error Gen (which corresponds to the misclassification rate) and its estimate by each method over 1000 runs, as functions of the flattening parameter γ in AIWFDA. The graphs clearly show that IWCV gives much better estimates of the generalization error than CV does.

Next we investigate the model selection performance: the flattening parameter γ is chosen from $\{0, 0.1, 0.2, \ldots, 1\}$ so that the score of each model selection criterion is minimized. The mean and standard deviation of the generalization error Gen of the learned function obtained by each method over 1000 runs are described in table 3.2. The table shows that IWCV gives significantly smaller test errors than CV does.

Table 3.2
The mean and standard deviation of the generalization error Gen (i.e., the misclassification Rate) obtained by each method for the toy classification data set

IWCV	CV	OPT
∘0.108 ± 0.027	0.131 ± 0.029	0.091 ± 0.009

The best method and comparable ones by the t-test at the 5 percent significance level are indicated by ∘. For reference, the generalization error obtained with the optimal γ (i.e., the minimum generalization error) is described as OPT.

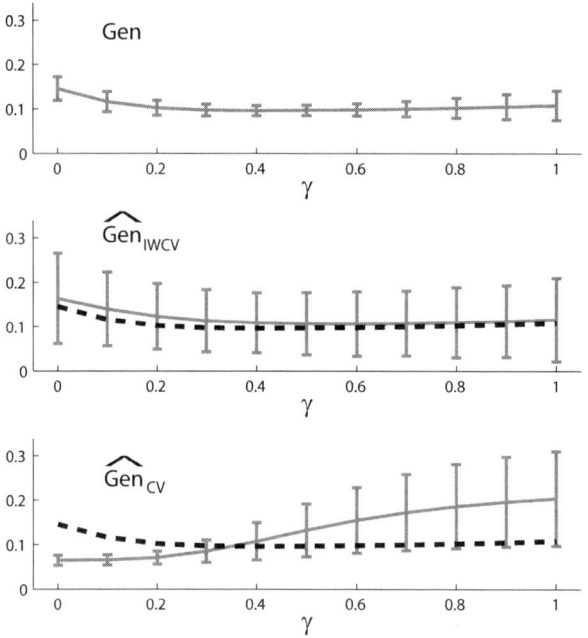

Figure 3.6
The generalization error Gen (i.e., the misclassification rate) and its estimates as functions of the tuning parameter γ in adaptive importance-weighted Fisher discriminant analysis (AIWFDA) for the toy classification examples in figure 2.9. Dashed curves in the bottom two graphs depict the true generalization error in the top graph for clear comparison.

This simulation result illustrates that IWCV also is useful in classification under covariate shift.

3.5 Summary and Discussion

In this chapter, we have addressed the model selection problem under the covariate shift paradigm—training input points and test input points are drawn from different distributions (i.e., $P_{train}(x) \neq P_{test}(x)$), but the functional relation remains unchanged (i.e., $P_{train}(y|x) = P_{test}(y|x)$). Under covariate shift, standard model selection schemes such as the Akaike information criterion (AIC), the subspace information criterion (SIC), and cross-validation (CV) are heavily biased and do not work as desired. On the other hand, their importance-weighted counterparts, IWAIC (section 3.1), IWSIC (section 3.2), and IWCV (section 3.3) have been shown to possess proper unbiasedness.

3.5. Summary and Discussion

Through simulations (section 3.4), the importance-weighted model selection criteria were shown to be useful for improving the generalization performance under covariate shift.

Although the importance-weighted model selection criteria were shown to work well, they tend to have larger variance, and therefore the model selection performance can be unstable. Investigating the effect of large variance on model selection performance will be an important direction to pursue, such as following the line of [151] and [6].

In the experiments in section 3.4, we assumed that the importance weights are known. However, this may not be the case in practice. We will discuss how the importance weights can be accurately estimated from data in chapter 4.

4 Importance Estimation

In chapters 2 and 3, we have seen that the importance weight

$$w(x) = \frac{p_{\text{te}}(x)}{p_{\text{tr}}(x)}$$

can be used for asymptotically canceling the bias caused by covariate shift. However, the importance weight is unknown in practice, and needs to be estimated from data. In this chapter, we give a comprehensive overview of importance estimation methods.

The setup in this chapter is that in addition to the i.i.d. training input samples

$$\{x_i^{\text{tr}}\}_{i=1}^{n_{\text{tr}}} \overset{\text{i.i.d.}}{\sim} P_{\text{tr}}(x),$$

we are given i.i.d. test input samples

$$\{x_j^{\text{te}}\}_{j=1}^{n_{\text{te}}} \overset{\text{i.i.d.}}{\sim} P_{\text{te}}(x).$$

Although this setup is similar to *semisupervised learning* [30], our attention is directed to covariate shift adaptation.

The goal of importance estimation is to estimate the importance function $w(x)$ (or the importance values at the training input points, $\{w(x_i^{\text{tr}})\}_{i=1}^{n_{\text{tr}}}$) from $\{x_i^{\text{tr}}\}_{i=1}^{n_{\text{tr}}}$ and $\{x_j^{\text{te}}\}_{j=1}^{n_{\text{te}}}$.

4.1 Kernel Density Estimation

Kernel density estimation (KDE) is a nonparametric technique to estimate a probability density function $p(x)$ from its i.i.d. samples $\{x_i\}_{i=1}^{n}$. For the

Gaussian kernel

$$K_\sigma(x, x') = \exp\left(-\frac{\|x - x'\|^2}{2\sigma^2}\right),\tag{4.1}$$

KDE is expressed as

$$\widehat{p}(x) = \frac{1}{n(2\pi\sigma^2)^{d/2}} \sum_{i=1}^{n} K_\sigma(x, x_i).$$

The performance of KDE depends on the choice of the kernel width σ. It can be optimized by cross-validation (CV) as follows [69]. First, divide the samples $\{x_i\}_{i=1}^{n}$ into k disjoint subsets $\{\mathcal{X}_r\}_{r=1}^{k}$ of (approximately) the same size. Then obtain a density estimate $\widehat{p}_{\mathcal{X}_r}(x)$ from $\{\mathcal{X}_i\}_{i \neq r}$ (i.e., without $\mathcal{X}_r$), and compute its log-likelihood for $\mathcal{X}_r$:

$$\frac{1}{|\mathcal{X}_r|} \sum_{x \in \mathcal{X}_r} \log \widehat{p}_{\mathcal{X}_r}(x),$$

where $|\mathcal{X}_r|$ denotes the number of elements in the set $\mathcal{X}_r$. Repeat this procedure for $r = 1, 2, \ldots, k$, and choose the value of σ such that the average of the above holdout log-likelihood over all r is maximized. Note that the average holdout log-likelihood is an almost unbiased estimate of the Kullback–Leibler divergence from $p(x)$ to $\widehat{p}(x)$, up to some irrelevant constant.

KDE can be used for importance estimation by first obtaining density estimators $\widehat{p}_{\text{tr}}(x)$ and $\widehat{p}_{\text{te}}(x)$ separately from $\{x_i^{\text{tr}}\}_{i=1}^{n_{\text{tr}}}$ and $\{x_j^{\text{te}}\}_{j=1}^{n_{\text{te}}}$, respectively, and then estimating the importance by

$$\widehat{w}(x) = \frac{\widehat{p}_{\text{te}}(x)}{\widehat{p}_{\text{tr}}(x)}.$$

However, a potential limitation of this naive approach is that KDE suffers from the *curse of dimensionality* [193, 69], that is, the number of samples needed to maintain the same approximation quality grows exponentially as the dimension of the input space increases. This is critical when the number of available samples is limited. Therefore, the KDE-based approach may not be reliable in high-dimensional problems.

In the following sections, we consider *directly* estimating the importance $w(x)$ without going through density estimation of $p_{\text{tr}}(x)$ and $p_{\text{te}}(x)$. An intuitive advantage of this direct estimation approach is that knowing the densities $p_{tr}(x)$ and $p_{te}(x)$ implies knowing the importance $w(x)$, but not vice versa—the importance $w(x)$ cannot be uniquely decomposed into $p_{tr}(x)$ and $p_{te}(x)$. Thus, estimating the importance $w(x)$ could be substantially simpler than estimating the densities $p_{tr}(x)$ and $p_{te}(x)$.

The Russian mathematician *Vladimir Vapnik*—who developed one of the most successful classification algorithms, the *support vector machine*—advocated the following principle [193]: *One should not solve more difficult intermediate problems when solving a target problem.* The support vector machine follows this principle by directly learning the decision boundary that is sufficient for pattern recognition instead of solving a more general, and thus more difficult, problem of estimating the data generation probability.

The idea of direct importance estimation would also follow Vapnik's principle since one can avoid solving a substantially more difficult problem of estimating the densities $p_{tr}(x)$ and $p_{te}(x)$.

4.2 Kernel Mean Matching

Kernel mean matching (KMM) allows one to directly obtain an estimate of the importance values without going through density estimation [82]. The basic idea of KMM is to find $\widehat{w}(x)$ such that the mean discrepancy between nonlinearly transformed samples drawn from $p_{tr}(x)$ and $p_{te}(x)$ is minimized in a universal *reproducing kernel Hilbert space* (RKHS) [149]. The Gaussian kernel (equation 4.1) is an example of kernels that induce a universal RKHS, and it has been shown that the solution of the following optimization problem agrees with the true importance values:

$$\min_{w(x)} \left\| \mathbb{E}_{x^{te}}\left[K_\sigma(x^{te}, \cdot)\right] - \mathbb{E}_{x^{tr}}\left[K_\sigma(x^{tr}, \cdot) w(x^{tr})\right] \right\|_{\mathcal{H}}^2 \tag{4.2}$$

subject to $\mathbb{E}_{x^{tr}}\left[w(x^{tr})\right] = 1$ and $w(x) \geq 0$,

where $\|\cdot\|_{\mathcal{H}}$ denotes the norm in the Gaussian RKHS, $K_\sigma(x, x')$ is the Gaussian kernel (equation 4.1), and $\mathbb{E}_{x^{tr}}$ and $\mathbb{E}_{x^{te}}$ denote the expectation over x^{tr} and x^{te} drawn from $P_{tr}(x)$ and $P_{te}(x)$, respectively. Note that for each *fixed* x, $K_\sigma(x, \cdot)$ is a function belonging to the RKHS $\mathcal{H}$.

An empirical version of the above problem is reduced to the following quadratic program (QP):

$$\min_{\{w_i\}_{i=1}^{n_{tr}}} \left[\frac{1}{2} \sum_{i,i'=1}^{n_{tr}} w_i w_{i'} K_\sigma(\boldsymbol{x}_i^{tr}, \boldsymbol{x}_{i'}^{tr}) - \sum_{i=1}^{n_{tr}} w_i \kappa_i \right]$$

subject to $\quad \dfrac{1}{n_{tr}} \left| \displaystyle\sum_{i=1}^{n_{tr}} w_i - n_{tr} \right| \leq \epsilon \quad \text{and} \quad 0 \leq w_1, w_2, \ldots, w_{n_{tr}} \leq B,$

where

$$\kappa_i = \frac{n_{tr}}{n_{te}} \sum_{j=1}^{n_{te}} K_\sigma(\boldsymbol{x}_i^{tr}, \boldsymbol{x}_j^{te}).$$

B (≥ 0) and ϵ (≥ 0) are tuning parameters that control the regularization effects. The solution $\{\widehat{w}_i\}_{i=1}^{n_{tr}}$ is an estimate of the importance at $\{\boldsymbol{x}_i^{tr}\}_{i=1}^{n_{tr}}$.

Since KMM does not involve density estimation, it is expected to work well even in high-dimensional cases. However, its performance depends on the choice of the tuning parameters B, ϵ, and σ, and they cannot be simply optimized by, for instance, CV, since estimates of the importance are available only at $\{\boldsymbol{x}_i^{tr}\}_{i=1}^{n_{tr}}$. As shown in [90], an inductive variant of KMM (i.e., the entire importance function is estimated) exists. This allows one to optimize B and ϵ by CV over the objective function (equation 4.2). However, the Gaussian kernel width σ may not be appropriately determined by CV since changing the value of σ means changing the RKHSs; the objective function (equation 4.2) is defined using the RKHS norm, and thus the objective values for different norms are not comparable.

A popular heuristic to choose σ is to use the median distance between samples as the Gaussian width σ [141, 147]. However, there seems to be no strong justification for this heuristic. For the choice of ϵ, a theoretical result given in [82] can be used as guidance. However, it is still hard to determine the best value of ϵ in practice.

4.3 Logistic Regression

Another approach to directly estimating importance is to use a probabilistic classifier. Let us assign a selector variable $\eta = -1$ to samples drawn from $p_{tr}(\boldsymbol{x})$ and $\eta = 1$ to samples drawn from $p_{te}(\boldsymbol{x})$. That is, the two densities are written as

$p_{tr}(\boldsymbol{x}) = p(\boldsymbol{x}|\eta = -1),$

$p_{te}(\boldsymbol{x}) = p(\boldsymbol{x}|\eta = 1).$

4.3. Logistic Regression

Note that η is regarded as a random variable.

An application of Bayes's theorem shows that the importance can be expressed in terms of η, as follows [128, 32, 17]:

$$w(\boldsymbol{x}) = \frac{p(\eta=-1)}{p(\eta=1)} \frac{p(\eta=1|\boldsymbol{x})}{p(\eta=-1|\boldsymbol{x})}.$$

The ratio $p(\eta=-1)/p(\eta=1)$ may be easily estimated by the ratio of the numbers of samples:

$$\frac{p(\eta=-1)}{p(\eta=1)} \approx \frac{n_{\mathrm{tr}}}{n_{\mathrm{te}}}.$$

The conditional probability $p(\eta|\boldsymbol{x})$ can be approximated by discriminating $\{\boldsymbol{x}_i^{\mathrm{tr}}\}_{i=1}^{n_{\mathrm{tr}}}$ and $\{\boldsymbol{x}_j^{\mathrm{te}}\}_{j=1}^{n_{\mathrm{te}}}$, using a *logistic regression* (LR) classifier, where η plays the role of a class variable. Below we briefly explain the LR method.

The LR classifier employs a parametric model of the following form for expressing the conditional probability $p(\eta|\boldsymbol{x})$:

$$\widehat{p}(\eta|\boldsymbol{x}) = \frac{1}{1 + \exp\left(-\eta \sum_{\ell=1}^{m} \zeta_\ell \phi_\ell(\boldsymbol{x})\right)},$$

where m is the number of basis functions and $\{\phi_\ell(\boldsymbol{x})\}_{\ell=1}^{m}$ are fixed basis functions. The parameter $\boldsymbol{\zeta}$ is learned so that the negative regularized log-likelihood is minimized:

$$\widehat{\boldsymbol{\zeta}} = \operatorname*{argmin}_{\boldsymbol{\zeta}} \Bigg[\sum_{i=1}^{n_{\mathrm{tr}}} \log\left(1 + \exp\left(\sum_{\ell=1}^{m} \zeta_\ell \phi_\ell(\boldsymbol{x}_i^{\mathrm{tr}})\right)\right) \\ + \sum_{j=1}^{n_{\mathrm{te}}} \log\left(1 + \exp\left(-\sum_{\ell=1}^{m} \zeta_\ell \phi_\ell(\boldsymbol{x}_j^{\mathrm{te}})\right)\right) + \lambda \boldsymbol{\zeta}^\top \boldsymbol{\zeta} \Bigg].$$

Since the above objective function is convex, the global optimal solution can be obtained by standard nonlinear optimization methods such as the gradient method and the (quasi-)Newton method [74, 117]. Then the importance estimator is given by

$$\widehat{w}(\boldsymbol{x}) = \frac{n_{\mathrm{tr}}}{n_{\mathrm{te}}} \exp\left(\sum_{\ell=1}^{m} \zeta_\ell \phi_\ell(\boldsymbol{x})\right). \tag{4.3}$$

This model is often called the *log-linear model*.

An advantage of the LR method is that model selection (i.e., the choice of the basis functions $\{\phi_\ell(x)\}_{\ell=1}^m$ as well as the regularization parameter λ) is possible by standard CV since the learning problem involved above is a standard supervised classification problem.

When multiclass LR classifiers are used, importance values among multiple densities can be estimated simultaneously [16]. However, training LR classifiers is rather time-consuming. A computationally efficient alternative to LR, called the *least-squares probabilistic classifier* (LSPC), has been proposed [155]. LSPC would be useful in large-scale density-ratio estimation.

4.4 Kullback–Leibler Importance Estimation Procedure

The *Kullback–Leibler importance estimation procedure* (KLIEP) [164] directly gives an estimate of the importance function without going through density estimation by matching the two distributions in terms of the *Kullback–Leibler divergence* [97].

4.4.1 Algorithm

Let us model the importance weight $w(x)$ by means of the following linear-in-parameter model (see section 1.3.5.2):

$$\widehat{w}(x) = \sum_{\ell=1}^{t} \alpha_\ell \varphi_\ell(x), \tag{4.4}$$

where t is the number of parameters,

$$\boldsymbol{\alpha} = (\alpha_1, \alpha_2, \ldots, \alpha_t)^\top$$

are parameters to be learned from data samples, $^\top$ denotes the transpose, and $\{\varphi_\ell(x)\}_{\ell=1}^t$ are basis functions such that

$\varphi_\ell(x) \geq 0$ for all $x \in \mathcal{D}$ and $\ell = 1, 2, \ldots, t$.

Note that t and $\{\varphi_\ell(x)\}_{\ell=1}^t$ can depend on the samples $\{x_i^{\text{tr}}\}_{i=1}^{n_{\text{tr}}}$ and $\{x_j^{\text{te}}\}_{j=1}^{n_{\text{te}}}$, so kernel models are also allowed. Later, we explain how the basis functions $\{\varphi_\ell(x)\}_{\ell=1}^t$ are designed in practice.

An estimate of the density $p_{\text{te}}(x)$ is given by using the model $\widehat{w}(x)$ as

$$\widehat{p}_{\text{te}}(x) = \widehat{w}(x) p_{\text{tr}}(x).$$

4.4. Kullback–Leibler Importance Estimation Procedure

In KLIEP, the parameters $\boldsymbol{\alpha}$ are determined so that the Kullback–Leibler divergence from $p_{\text{te}}(\boldsymbol{x})$ to $\widehat{p}_{\text{te}}(\boldsymbol{x})$ is minimized:

$$\text{KL}(\boldsymbol{\alpha}) := \mathop{\mathbb{E}}_{\boldsymbol{x}^{\text{te}}} \left[\log \frac{p_{\text{te}}(\boldsymbol{x}^{\text{te}})}{\widehat{w}(\boldsymbol{x}^{\text{te}}) p_{\text{tr}}(\boldsymbol{x}^{\text{te}})} \right]$$

$$= \mathop{\mathbb{E}}_{\boldsymbol{x}^{\text{te}}} \left[\log \frac{p_{\text{te}}(\boldsymbol{x}^{\text{te}})}{p_{\text{tr}}(\boldsymbol{x}^{\text{te}})} \right] - \mathop{\mathbb{E}}_{\boldsymbol{x}^{\text{te}}} \left[\log \widehat{w}(\boldsymbol{x}^{\text{te}}) \right],$$

where $\mathbb{E}_{\boldsymbol{x}^{\text{te}}}$ denotes the expectation over $\boldsymbol{x}^{\text{te}}$ drawn from $P_{\text{te}}(\boldsymbol{x})$. The first term is a constant, so it can safely be ignored. We define the negative of the second term by KL$'$:

$$\text{KL}'(\boldsymbol{\alpha}) := \mathop{\mathbb{E}}_{\boldsymbol{x}^{\text{te}}} \left[\log \widehat{w}(\boldsymbol{x}^{\text{te}}) \right]. \tag{4.5}$$

Since $\widehat{p}_{\text{te}}(\boldsymbol{x})$ ($= \widehat{w}(\boldsymbol{x}) p_{\text{tr}}(\boldsymbol{x})$) is a probability density function, it should satisfy

$$1 = \int_{\mathcal{D}} \widehat{p}_{\text{te}}(\boldsymbol{x}) d\boldsymbol{x} = \int_{\mathcal{D}} \widehat{w}(\boldsymbol{x}) p_{\text{tr}}(\boldsymbol{x}) d\boldsymbol{x} = \mathop{\mathbb{E}}_{\boldsymbol{x}^{\text{tr}}} \left[\widehat{w}(\boldsymbol{x}^{\text{tr}}) \right]. \tag{4.6}$$

Consequently, the KLIEP optimization problem is given by replacing the expectations in equations 4.5 and 4.6 with empirical averages as

$$\max_{\{\alpha_\ell\}_{\ell=1}^t} \left[\sum_{j=1}^{n_{\text{te}}} \log \left(\sum_{\ell=1}^{t} \alpha_\ell \varphi_\ell(\boldsymbol{x}_j^{\text{te}}) \right) \right]$$

subject to $\dfrac{1}{n_{\text{tr}}} \sum_{\ell=1}^{t} \alpha_\ell \left(\sum_{i=1}^{n_{\text{tr}}} \varphi_\ell(\boldsymbol{x}_i^{\text{tr}}) \right) = 1$ and $\alpha_1, \alpha_2, \ldots, \alpha_t \geq 0$.

This is a convex optimization problem, and the global solution—which tends to be sparse [27]—can be obtained, for example, simply by performing gradient ascent and feasibility satisfaction iteratively. A pseudo code is summarized in figure 4.1.

Properties of KLIEP-type algorithms are theoretically investigated in [128, 32, 171, 120]. In particular, the following facts are known regarding the convergence properties:

- When a fixed set of basis functions (i.e., a parametric model) is used for importance estimation, KLIEP converges to the optimal parameter in the model with convergence rate $\mathcal{O}_p(n^{-\frac{1}{2}})$ under $n = n_{\text{tr}} = n_{\text{te}}$, where $\mathcal{O}_p$ denotes the

```
Input: m = {φ_ℓ(x)}_{ℓ=1}^{t}, {x_i^{tr}}_{i=1}^{n_{tr}}, and {x_j^{te}}_{j=1}^{n_{te}}
Output: ŵ(x)

A_{j,ℓ} ⟵ φ_ℓ(x_j^{te})      for j = 1, 2, ..., n_{te} and ℓ = 1, 2, ..., t;
b_ℓ ⟵ (1/n_{tr}) Σ_{i=1}^{n_{tr}} φ_ℓ(x_i^{tr})    for ℓ = 1, 2, ..., t;
Initialize α (> 0_t) and ε (0 < ε ≪ 1);
Repeat until convergence
    α ⟵ α + εA^⊤(1_{n_{te}}./Aα);   % Gradient ascent
    α ⟵ α + (1 − b^⊤α)b/(b^⊤b);    % Constraint satisfaction
    α ⟵ max(0_t, α);                % Constraint satisfaction
    α ⟵ α/(b^⊤α);                   % Constraint satisfaction
end
ŵ(x) ⟵ Σ_{ℓ=1}^{t} α_ℓ φ_ℓ(x);
```

Figure 4.1
Pseudo code of KLIEP. 0_t denotes the t-dimensional vector with all zeros, and $1_{n_{te}}$ denotes the n_{te}-dimensional vector with all ones. ./ indicates the elementwise division, and $^\top$ denotes the transpose. Inequalities and the "max" operation for vectors are applied elementwise.

asymptotic order in probability. This is the optimal convergence rate in the parametric setup. Furthermore, KLIEP has asymptotic normality around the optimal solution.

• When a nonparametric model (e.g., kernel basis functions centered at test samples; see section 4.4.3) is used for importance estimation, KLIEP converges to the optimal solution with a convergence rate slightly slower than $\mathcal{O}_p(n^{-\frac{1}{2}})$. This is the optimal convergence rate in the minimax sense.

Note that the importance model of KLIEP is the linear-in-parameter model (equation 4.4), while that of LR is the *log-linear model* (equation 4.3). A variant of KLIEP for log-linear models has been studied in [185, 120], which is computationally more efficient when the number of test samples is large. The KLIEP idea also can be applied to *Gaussian mixture models* [202] and *probabilistic principal-component-analyzer mixture models* [205].

4.4.2 Model Selection by Cross-Validation

The performance of KLIEP depends on the choice of basis functions $\{\varphi_\ell(x)\}_{\ell=1}^{b}$. Here we explain how they can be appropriately chosen from data samples.

Since KLIEP is based on the maximization of KL′ (see equation 4.5), it would be natural to select the model such that KL′ is maximized. The expectation over $p_{te}(x)$ involved in KL′ can be numerically approximated by cross-validation (CV) as follows. First, divide the test samples $\{x_j^{te}\}_{j=1}^{n_{te}}$ into

4.4. Kullback–Leibler Importance Estimation Procedure

k disjoint subsets $\{\mathcal{X}_r^{\text{te}}\}_{r=1}^k$ of (approximately) the same size. Then obtain an importance estimate $\widehat{w}_{\mathcal{X}_r^{\text{te}}}(\boldsymbol{x})$ from $\{\mathcal{X}_j^{\text{te}}\}_{j \neq r}$ (i.e., without $\mathcal{X}_r^{\text{te}}$), and approximate KL' using $\mathcal{X}_r^{\text{tr}}$ as

$$\widehat{\text{KL}}'_r := \frac{1}{|\mathcal{X}_r^{\text{te}}|} \sum_{x \in \mathcal{X}_r^{\text{te}}} \log \widehat{w}_{\mathcal{X}_r^{\text{te}}}(\boldsymbol{x}).$$

This procedure is repeated for $r = 1, 2, \ldots, k$, and the average $\widehat{\text{KL}}'$ is used as an estimate of KL':

$$\widehat{\text{KL}}' := \frac{1}{k} \sum_{r=1}^k \widehat{\text{KL}}'_r. \tag{4.7}$$

For model selection, we compute $\widehat{\text{KL}}'$ for all model candidates (the basis functions $\{\varphi_\ell(\boldsymbol{x})\}_{\ell=1}^t$ in the current setting), and choose the one that minimizes $\widehat{\text{KL}}'$. A pseudo code of the CV procedure is summarized in figure 4.2.

One of the potential limitations of CV in general is that it is not reliable for small samples since data splitting by CV further reduces the sample size. On the other hand, in our CV procedure the data splitting is performed only over the *test input samples* $\{\boldsymbol{x}_j^{\text{te}}\}_{j=1}^{n_{\text{te}}}$, not over the training samples. Therefore, even when the number of training samples is small, our CV procedure does not suffer from the small sample problem as long as a large number of test input samples are available.

Input: $\mathcal{M} = \{m | m = \{\varphi_\ell(\boldsymbol{x})\}_{\ell=1}^t\}$, $\{\boldsymbol{x}_i^{\text{tr}}\}_{i=1}^{n_{\text{tr}}}$, and $\{\boldsymbol{x}_j^{\text{te}}\}_{j=1}^{n_{\text{te}}}$
Output: $\widehat{w}(\boldsymbol{x})$

Split $\{\boldsymbol{x}_j^{\text{te}}\}_{j=1}^{n_{\text{te}}}$ into k disjoint subsets $\{\mathcal{X}_j'\}_{j=1}^k$;
for each model $m \in \mathcal{M}$
    for each split $r = 1, 2, \ldots, k$
        $\widehat{w}_{\mathcal{X}_r^{\text{te}}}(\boldsymbol{x}) \longleftarrow \text{KLIEP}(m, \{\boldsymbol{x}_i^{\text{tr}}\}_{i=1}^{n_{\text{tr}}}, \{\mathcal{X}_j^{\text{te}}\}_{j \neq r})$;
        $\widehat{\text{KL}}_r(m) \longleftarrow \frac{1}{|\mathcal{X}_r^{\text{te}}|} \sum_{\boldsymbol{x} \in \mathcal{X}_r^{\text{te}}} \log \widehat{w}_{\mathcal{X}_r^{\text{te}}}(\boldsymbol{x})$;
    end
    $\widehat{\text{KL}}'(m) \longleftarrow \frac{1}{k} \sum_{r=1}^k \widehat{\text{KL}}'_r(m)$;
end
$\widehat{m} \longleftarrow \text{argmax}_{m \in \mathcal{M}} \widehat{\text{KL}}'(m)$;
$\widehat{w}(\boldsymbol{x}) \longleftarrow \text{KLIEP}(\widehat{m}, \{\boldsymbol{x}_i^{\text{tr}}\}_{i=1}^{n_{\text{tr}}}, \{\boldsymbol{x}_j^{\text{te}}\}_{j=1}^{n_{\text{te}}})$;

Figure 4.2
Pseudo code of CV-based model selection for KLIEP.

4.4.3 Basis Function Design

A good model may be chosen by the above CV procedure, given that a set of promising model candidates is prepared. As model candidates we use a Gaussian kernel model centered at the *test* input points $\{x_j^{\text{te}}\}_{j=1}^{n_{\text{te}}}$. That is,

$$\widehat{w}(x) = \sum_{\ell=1}^{n_{\text{te}}} \alpha_\ell K_\sigma(x, x_\ell^{\text{te}}),$$

where $K_\sigma(x, x')$ is the Gaussian kernel with width σ:

$$K_\sigma(x, x') := \exp\left(-\frac{\|x - x'\|^2}{2\sigma^2}\right).$$

Our reason for choosing the test input points $\{x_j^{\text{te}}\}_{j=1}^{n_{\text{te}}}$ as the Gaussian centers, not the training input points $\{x_i^{\text{tr}}\}_{i=1}^{n_{\text{tr}}}$, is as follows. By definition, the importance $w(x)$ tends to take large values if the training input density $p_{\text{tr}}(x)$ is small and the test input density $p_{\text{te}}(x)$ is large; conversely, $w(x)$ tends to be small (i.e., close to zero) if $p_{\text{tr}}(x)$ is large and $p_{\text{te}}(x)$ is small. When a nonnegative function is approximated by a Gaussian kernel model, many kernels may be needed in the region where the output of the target function is large; on the other hand, only a small number of kernels will be enough in the region where the output of the target function is close to zero (see figure 4.3). Following this heuristic, we decided to allocate many kernels at high *test* input density regions, which can be achieved by setting the Gaussian centers at the test input points $\{x_j^{\text{te}}\}_{j=1}^{n_{\text{te}}}$.

Alternatively, we may locate $(n_{\text{tr}} + n_{\text{te}})$ Gaussian kernels at both $\{x_i^{\text{tr}}\}_{i=1}^{n_{\text{tr}}}$ and $\{x_j^{\text{te}}\}_{j=1}^{n_{\text{te}}}$. However, this seems not to further improve the performance, but slightly increases the computational cost. When n_{te} is very large, just using all the test input points $\{x_j^{\text{te}}\}_{j=1}^{n_{\text{te}}}$ as Gaussian centers is already computationally

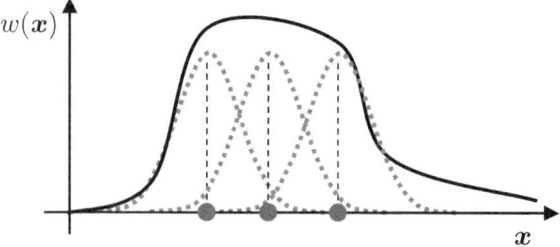

Figure 4.3
Heuristic of Gaussian center allocation. Many kernels may be needed in the region where the output of the target function is large, and only a small number of kernels will be enough in the region where the output of the target function is close to zero.

4.5. Least-Squares Importance Fitting

rather demanding. To ease this problem, a subset of $\{x_j^{\text{te}}\}_{j=1}^{n_{\text{te}}}$ may in practice be used as Gaussian centers for computational efficiency. That is,

$$\widehat{w}(x) = \sum_{\ell=1}^{t} \alpha_\ell K_\sigma(x, c_\ell), \qquad (4.8)$$

where c_ℓ is a template point randomly chosen from $\{x_j^{\text{te}}\}_{j=1}^{n_{\text{te}}}$ and t ($\leq n_{\text{te}}$) is a prefixed number.

A MATLAB® implementation of the entire KLIEP algorithm is available from http://sugiyama-www.cs.titech.ac.jp/~sugi/software/KLIEP/.

4.5 Least-Squares Importance Fitting

KLIEP employed the Kullback-Leibler divergence for measuring the discrepancy between two densities. *Least-squares importance fitting* (LSIF) [88] uses the squared-loss for importance function fitting.

4.5.1 Algorithm

The importance $w(x)$ is again modeled by the linear-in-parameter model (equation 4.4). The parameters $\{\alpha_\ell\}_{\ell=1}^t$ in the model $\widehat{w}(x)$ are determined so that the following squared error J is minimized:

$$\begin{aligned}
J(\alpha) &:= \frac{1}{2} \mathop{\mathbb{E}}_{x^{\text{tr}}} \left[\left(\widehat{w}(x^{\text{tr}}) - w(x^{\text{tr}}) \right)^2 \right] \\
&= \frac{1}{2} \mathop{\mathbb{E}}_{x^{\text{tr}}} \left[\widehat{w}^2(x^{\text{tr}}) \right] - \mathop{\mathbb{E}}_{x^{\text{tr}}} \left[\widehat{w}(x^{\text{tr}}) w(x^{\text{tr}}) \right] + \frac{1}{2} \mathop{\mathbb{E}}_{x^{\text{tr}}} \left[w^2(x^{\text{tr}}) \right], \\
&= \frac{1}{2} \mathop{\mathbb{E}}_{x^{\text{tr}}} \left[\widehat{w}^2(x^{\text{tr}}) \right] - \mathop{\mathbb{E}}_{x^{\text{te}}} \left[\widehat{w}(x^{\text{te}}) \right] + \frac{1}{2} \mathop{\mathbb{E}}_{x^{\text{tr}}} \left[w^2(x^{\text{tr}}) \right],
\end{aligned}$$

where the last term is a constant, and therefore can be safely ignored. Let us denote the first two terms by J':

$$\begin{aligned}
J'(\alpha) &:= J(\alpha) - \frac{1}{2} \mathop{\mathbb{E}}_{x^{\text{tr}}} \left[w^2(x^{\text{tr}}) \right] \\
&= \frac{1}{2} \mathop{\mathbb{E}}_{x^{\text{tr}}} \left[\widehat{w}^2(x^{\text{tr}}) \right] - \mathop{\mathbb{E}}_{x^{\text{te}}} \left[\widehat{w}(x) \right].
\end{aligned}$$

Approximating the expectations in J' by empirical averages, we obtain

$$\widehat{J}'(\alpha) := \frac{1}{2n_{\text{tr}}} \sum_{i=1}^{n_{\text{tr}}} \widehat{w}^2(x_i^{\text{tr}}) - \frac{1}{n_{\text{te}}} \sum_{j=1}^{n_{\text{te}}} \widehat{w}(x_j^{\text{te}})$$

$$= \frac{1}{2}\sum_{\ell,\ell'=1}^{t}\alpha_\ell\alpha_{\ell'}\left(\frac{1}{n_{\text{tr}}}\sum_{i=1}^{n_{\text{tr}}}\varphi_\ell(\boldsymbol{x}_i^{\text{tr}})\varphi_{\ell'}(\boldsymbol{x}_i^{\text{tr}})\right) - \sum_{\ell=1}^{t}\alpha_\ell\left(\frac{1}{n_{\text{te}}}\sum_{j=1}^{n_{\text{te}}}\varphi_\ell(\boldsymbol{x}_j^{\text{te}})\right)$$

$$= \frac{1}{2}\boldsymbol{\alpha}^\top\widehat{\boldsymbol{H}}\boldsymbol{\alpha} - \widehat{\boldsymbol{h}}^\top\boldsymbol{\alpha},$$

where $\widehat{\boldsymbol{H}}$ is the $t \times t$ matrix with the (ℓ, ℓ')-th element

$$\widehat{H}_{\ell,\ell'} := \frac{1}{n_{\text{tr}}}\sum_{i=1}^{n_{\text{tr}}}\varphi_\ell(\boldsymbol{x}_i^{\text{tr}})\varphi_{\ell'}(\boldsymbol{x}_i^{\text{tr}}), \tag{4.9}$$

and $\widehat{\boldsymbol{h}}$ is the t-dimensional vector with the ℓ-th element

$$\widehat{h}_\ell := \frac{1}{n_{\text{te}}}\sum_{j=1}^{n_{\text{te}}}\varphi_\ell(\boldsymbol{x}_j^{\text{te}}). \tag{4.10}$$

Taking into account the nonnegativity of the importance function $w(\boldsymbol{x})$, the optimization problem is formulated as follows.

$$\min_{\boldsymbol{\alpha}}\left[\frac{1}{2}\boldsymbol{\alpha}^\top\widehat{\boldsymbol{H}}\boldsymbol{\alpha} - \widehat{\boldsymbol{h}}^\top\boldsymbol{\alpha} + \lambda\boldsymbol{1}_t^\top\boldsymbol{\alpha}\right]$$

subject to $\boldsymbol{\alpha} \geq \boldsymbol{0}_t$, \hfill (4.11)

where $\boldsymbol{1}_t$ and $\boldsymbol{0}_t$ are the t-dimensional vectors with all ones and zeros, respectively. The vector inequality $\boldsymbol{\alpha} \geq \boldsymbol{0}_t$ is applied in the elementwise manner, that is,

$\alpha_\ell \geq 0$ for $\ell = 1, 2, \ldots, t$.

In equation 4.11, a penalty term $\lambda\boldsymbol{1}_t^\top\boldsymbol{\alpha}$ is included for regularization purposes, where λ (≥ 0) is a regularization parameter. Equation 4.11 is a convex quadratic programming problem, and therefore the unique global optimal solution can be computed efficiently by a standard optimization package.

4.5.2 Basis Function Design and Model Selection

Basis functions may be designed in the same way as KLIEP, that is, Gaussian basis functions centered at (a subset of) the test input points $\{\boldsymbol{x}_j^{\text{te}}\}_{j=1}^{n_{\text{te}}}$ (see section 4.4).

Model selection of the Gaussian width σ and the regularization parameter λ is possible by CV: First, $\{\boldsymbol{x}_i^{\text{tr}}\}_{i=1}^{n_{\text{tr}}}$ and $\{\boldsymbol{x}_j^{\text{te}}\}_{j=1}^{n_{\text{te}}}$ are divided into k disjoint subsets

4.5. Least-Squares Importance Fitting

$\{\mathcal{X}_i^{\text{tr}}\}_{i=1}^{k}$ and $\{\mathcal{X}_j^{\text{te}}\}_{j=1}^{k}$, respectively. Then an importance estimate $\widehat{w}_{\mathcal{X}_r^{\text{tr}},\mathcal{X}_r^{\text{te}}}(x)$ is obtained using $\{\mathcal{X}_i^{\text{tr}}\}_{i \neq r}$ and $\{\mathcal{X}_j^{\text{te}}\}_{j \neq r}$ (i.e., without $\mathcal{X}_r^{\text{tr}}$ and $\mathcal{X}_r^{\text{te}}$), and the cost J' is approximated using the holdout samples $\mathcal{X}_r^{\text{tr}}$ and $\mathcal{X}_r^{\text{te}}$ as

$$\widehat{J}'_r := \frac{1}{2|\mathcal{X}_r^{\text{tr}}|} \sum_{x^{\text{tr}} \in \mathcal{X}_r^{\text{tr}}} \widehat{w}^2_{\mathcal{X}_r^{\text{tr}},\mathcal{X}_r^{\text{te}}}(x^{\text{tr}}) - \frac{1}{|\mathcal{X}_r^{\text{te}}|} \sum_{x^{\text{te}} \in \mathcal{X}_r^{\text{te}}} \widehat{w}_{\mathcal{X}_r^{\text{tr}},\mathcal{X}_r^{\text{te}}}(x^{\text{te}}).$$

This procedure is repeated for $r = 1, 2, \ldots, k$, and the average $\widehat{J}'$ is used as an estimate of J':

$$\widehat{J}' := \frac{1}{k} \sum_{r=1}^{k} \widehat{J}'_r.$$

For LSIF, an information criterion has also been derived [88], which is an asymptotic unbiased estimator of the error criterion J'.

4.5.3 Regularization Path Tracking

The LSIF solution $\widehat{\alpha}$ is shown to be piecewise linear with respect to the regularization parameter λ (see figure 4.4). Therefore, the *regularization path* (i.e., solutions for all λ) can be computed efficiently based on the *parametric optimization technique* [14, 44, 70].

A basic idea of regularization path tracking is to check the violation of the *Karush–Kuhn–Tucker* (KKT) conditions [27]—which are necessary and sufficient conditions for optimality of convex programs—when the regularization parameter λ is changed. A pseudo code of the regularization path tracking algorithm for LSIF is described in figure 4.5.

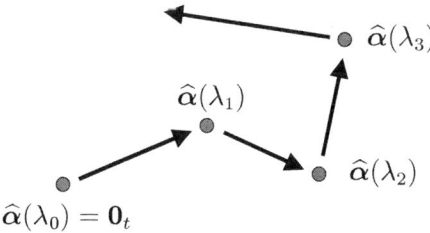

Figure 4.4
Regularization path tracking of LSIF. The solution $\widehat{\alpha}(\lambda)$ is shown to be piecewise-linear in the parameter space as a function of λ. Starting from $\lambda = \infty$, the trajectory of the solution is traced as λ is decreased to zero. When $\lambda \geq \lambda_0$ for some $\lambda_0 \geq 0$, the solution stays at the origin $\mathbf{0}_t$. When λ gets smaller than λ_0, the solution departs from the origin. As λ is further decreased, for some λ_1 such that $0 \leq \lambda_1 \leq \lambda_0$, the solution goes straight to $\widehat{\alpha}(\lambda_1)$ with a constant "speed." Then the solution path changes direction and, for some λ_2 such that $0 \leq \lambda_2 \leq \lambda_1$, the solution is headed straight for $\widehat{\alpha}(\lambda_2)$ with a constant speed as λ is further decreased. This process is repeated until λ reaches zero.

Input: $\widehat{H}$ and $\widehat{h}$ % see equations 4.9 and 4.10 for the definition
Output: entire regularization path $\widehat{\alpha}(\lambda)$ for $\lambda \geq 0$

$\tau \longleftarrow 0$;
$k \longleftarrow \mathrm{argmax}_i \{\widehat{h}_i \mid i = 1, 2, \ldots, t\}$;
$\lambda_\tau \longleftarrow \widehat{h}_k$;
$\widehat{\mathcal{A}} \longleftarrow \{1, 2, \ldots, t\} \backslash \{k\}$;
$\widehat{\alpha}(\lambda_\tau) \longleftarrow \mathbf{0}_t$;   % vector with all zeros
While $\lambda_\tau > 0$
$\quad \widehat{E} \longleftarrow \mathbf{O}_{|\widehat{\mathcal{A}}| \times t}$;   % matrix with all zeros
$\quad$ **For** $i = 1, 2, \ldots, |\widehat{\mathcal{A}}|$
$\quad \quad \widehat{E}_{i,j_i} \longleftarrow 1$; % $\widehat{\mathcal{A}} = \{j_1, j_2, \ldots, j_{|\widehat{\mathcal{A}}|} \mid j_1 < j_2 < \cdots < j_{|\widehat{\mathcal{A}}|}\}$
$\quad$ **end**
$\quad \widehat{G} \longleftarrow \begin{pmatrix} \widehat{H} & -\widehat{E}^\top \\ -\widehat{E} & \mathbf{O}_{|\widehat{\mathcal{A}}| \times |\widehat{\mathcal{A}}|} \end{pmatrix}$;
$\quad \boldsymbol{u} \longleftarrow \widehat{G}^{-1} \begin{pmatrix} \widehat{h} \\ \mathbf{0}_{|\widehat{\mathcal{A}}|} \end{pmatrix}$;
$\quad \boldsymbol{v} \longleftarrow \widehat{G}^{-1} \begin{pmatrix} \mathbf{1}_t \\ \mathbf{0}_{|\widehat{\mathcal{A}}|} \end{pmatrix}$;
$\quad$ **If** $\boldsymbol{v} \leq \mathbf{0}_{t+|\widehat{\mathcal{A}}|}$ % final interval
$\quad \quad \lambda_{\tau+1} \longleftarrow 0$;
$\quad \quad \widehat{\alpha}(\lambda_{\tau+1}) \longleftarrow (u_1, u_2, \ldots, u_t)^\top$;
$\quad$ **else** % an intermediate interval
$\quad \quad k \longleftarrow \mathrm{argmax}_i \{u_i/v_i \mid v_i > 0, \ i = 1, 2, \ldots, t + |\widehat{\mathcal{A}}|\}$;
$\quad \quad \lambda_{\tau+1} \longleftarrow \max\{0, u_k/v_k\}$;
$\quad \quad \widehat{\alpha}(\lambda_{\tau+1}) \longleftarrow (u_1, u_2, \ldots, u_t)^\top - \lambda_{\tau+1}(v_1, v_2, \ldots, v_t)^\top$;
$\quad \quad$ **If** $1 \leq k \leq t$
$\quad \quad \quad \widehat{\mathcal{A}} \longleftarrow \widehat{\mathcal{A}} \cup \{k\}$;
$\quad \quad$ **else**
$\quad \quad \quad \widehat{\mathcal{A}} \longleftarrow \widehat{\mathcal{A}} \backslash \{j_{k-t}\}$;
$\quad \quad$ **end**
$\quad$ **end**
$\quad \tau \longleftarrow \tau + 1$;
end

$\widehat{\alpha}(\lambda) \longleftarrow \begin{cases} \mathbf{0}_t & \text{if } \lambda \geq \lambda_0 \\ \frac{\lambda_{\tau+1} - \lambda}{\lambda_{\tau+1} - \lambda_\tau} \widehat{\alpha}(\lambda_\tau) + \frac{\lambda - \lambda_\tau}{\lambda_{\tau+1} - \lambda_\tau} \widehat{\alpha}(\lambda_{\tau+1}) & \text{if } \lambda_{\tau+1} \leq \lambda \leq \lambda_\tau \end{cases}$

Figure 4.5
Pseudo code for computing the entire regularization path of LSIF. The computation of $\widehat{G}^{-1}$ is sometimes unstable. For stabilization purposes, small positive diagonals may be added to $\widehat{H}$.

The pseudo code shows that a quadratic programming solver is no longer needed for obtaining the LSIF solution—just computing matrix inverses is enough. This contributes highly to saving computation time. Furthermore, the regularization path algorithm is computationally very efficient when the solution is sparse, that is, most of the elements are zero since the number of change points tends to be small for sparse solutions.

An R implementation of the entire LSIF algorithm is available from http://www.math.cm.is.nagoya-u.ac.jp/~kanamori/software/LSIF/.

4.6 Unconstrained Least-Squares Importance Fitting

LSIF combined with regularization path tracking is computationally very efficient. However, it sometimes suffers from a numerical problem, and therefore is not reliable in practice. To cope with this problem, an approximation method called *unconstrained LSIF* (uLSIF) has been introduced [88].

4.6.1 Algorithm

The approximation idea is very simple: the non-negativity constraint in the optimization problem (equation 4.11) is dropped. This results in the following unconstrained optimization problem:

$$\min_{\beta \in \mathbb{R}^t} \left[\frac{1}{2} \beta^\top \widehat{H} \beta - \widehat{h}^\top \beta + \frac{\lambda}{2} \beta^\top \beta \right]. \quad (4.12)$$

In the above, a quadratic regularization term $\lambda \beta^\top \beta / 2$ is included instead of the linear one $\lambda \mathbf{1}_t^\top \alpha$ since the linear penalty term does not work as a regularizer without the nonnegativity constraint. Equation 4.12 is an unconstrained convex quadratic program, and the solution can be analytically computed as

$$\widetilde{\beta} = (\widehat{H} + \lambda I_t)^{-1} \widehat{h},$$

where I_t is the t-dimensional identity matrix.

Since the nonnegativity constraint $\beta \geq \mathbf{0}_t$ is dropped, some of the learned parameters can be negative. To compensate for this approximation error, the solution is modified as

$$\widehat{\beta} = \max(\mathbf{0}_t, \widetilde{\beta}), \quad (4.13)$$

where the "max" operation for a pair of vectors is applied in the elementwise manner. The error caused by ignoring the nonnegativity constraint and the above rounding-up operation is theoretically investigated in [88].

An advantage of the above unconstrained formulation is that the solution can be computed just by solving a system of linear equations. Therefore, the computation is fast and stable. In addition, uLSIF has been shown to be superior in terms of condition numbers [90].

4.6.2 Analytic Computation of Leave-One-Out Cross-Validation

Another notable advantage of uLSIF is that the score of leave-one-out CV (LOOCV) can be computed analytically. Thanks to this property, the computational complexity for performing LOOCV is of the same order as computing a single solution, which is explained below.

In the current setting, two sets of samples $\{x_i^{tr}\}_{i=1}^{n_{tr}}$ and $\{x_j^{te}\}_{j=1}^{n_{te}}$ are given that generally are of different size. To explain the idea in a simple manner, we assume that $n_{tr} < n_{te}$, and x_i^{tr} and x_i^{te} ($i = 1, 2, \ldots, n_{tr}$) are held out at the same time; $\{x_j^{te}\}_{j=n_{tr}+1}^{n_{te}}$ are always used for importance estimation.

Let $\widehat{w}_i(x)$ be an estimate of the importance function obtained without x_i^{tr} and x_i^{te}. Then the LOOCV score is expressed as

$$\text{LOOCV} = \frac{1}{n_{tr}} \sum_{i=1}^{n_{tr}} \left[\frac{1}{2} (\widehat{w}_i(x_i^{tr}))^2 - \widehat{w}_i(x_i^{te}) \right]. \tag{4.14}$$

Our approach to efficiently computing the LOOCV score is to use the *Sherman–Woodbury–Morrison* formula [64] for computing matrix inverses. For an invertible square matrix A and vectors ξ and η such that $\eta^\top A^{-1} \xi \neq -1$, the Sherman–Woodbury–Morrison formula states that

$$(A + \xi \eta^\top)^{-1} = A^{-1} - \frac{A^{-1} \xi \eta^\top A^{-1}}{1 + \eta^\top A^{-1} \xi}.$$

A pseudo code of uLSIF with LOOCV-based model selection is summarized in figure 4.6.

MATLAB® and R implementations of the entire uLSIF algorithm are available from http://sugiyama-www.cs.titech.ac.jp/~sugi/software/uLSIF/ http://www.math.cm.is.nagoya-u.ac.jp/~kanamori/software/LSIF/.

4.7 Numerical Examples

In this section, we illustrate the behavior of the KLIEP method, and how it can be applied to covariate shift adaptation.

4.7. Numerical Examples

Input: $\{x_i^{tr}\}_{i=1}^{n_{tr}}$ and $\{x_j^{te}\}_{j=1}^{n_{te}}$
Output: $\widehat{w}(x)$

$t \longleftarrow \min(100, n_{te})$;
$n \longleftarrow \min(n_{tr}, n_{te})$;
Randomly choose t centers $\{c_\ell\}_{\ell=1}^{t}$ from $\{x_j^{te}\}_{j=1}^{n_{te}}$ without replacement;
For each candidate of Gaussian width σ

$$\widehat{H}_{\ell,\ell'} \longleftarrow \frac{1}{n_{tr}} \sum_{i=1}^{n_{tr}} \exp\left(-\frac{\|x_i^{tr} - c_\ell\|^2 + \|x_i^{tr} - c_{\ell'}\|^2}{2\sigma^2}\right) \text{ for } \ell, \ell' = 1, 2, \ldots, t;$$

$$\widehat{h}_\ell \longleftarrow \frac{1}{n_{te}} \sum_{j=1}^{n_{te}} \exp\left(-\frac{\|x_j^{te} - c_\ell\|^2}{2\sigma^2}\right) \text{ for } \ell = 1, 2, \ldots, t;$$

$$X_{\ell,i}^{tr} \longleftarrow \exp\left(-\frac{\|x_i^{tr} - c_\ell\|^2}{2\sigma^2}\right) \text{ for } i = 1, 2, \ldots, n \text{ and } \ell = 1, 2, \ldots, t;$$

$$X_{\ell,i}^{te} \longleftarrow \exp\left(-\frac{\|x_i^{te} - c_\ell\|^2}{2\sigma^2}\right) \text{ for } i = 1, 2, \ldots, n \text{ and } \ell = 1, 2, \ldots, t;$$

For each candidate of regularization parameter λ

$$\widehat{B} \longleftarrow \widehat{H} + \frac{\lambda(n_{tr} - 1)}{n_{tr}} I_t;$$

$$B_0 \longleftarrow \widehat{B}^{-1} \widehat{h} \mathbf{1}_n^\top + \widehat{B}^{-1} X^{tr} \operatorname{diag}\left(\frac{\widehat{h}^\top \widehat{B}^{-1} X^{tr}}{n_{tr} \mathbf{1}_n^\top - \mathbf{1}_t^\top (X^{tr} * \widehat{B}^{-1} X^{tr})}\right);$$

$$B_1 \longleftarrow \widehat{B}^{-1} X^{te} + \widehat{B}^{-1} X^{tr} \operatorname{diag}\left(\frac{\mathbf{1}_t^\top (X^{te} * \widehat{B}^{-1} X^{tr})}{n_{tr} \mathbf{1}_n^\top - \mathbf{1}_t^\top (X^{tr} * \widehat{B}^{-1} X^{tr})}\right);$$

$$B_2 \longleftarrow \max\left(\mathbf{0}_{t \times n}, \frac{n_{tr} - 1}{n_{tr}(n_{te} - 1)} (n_{te} B_0 - B_1)\right);$$

$$\operatorname{LOOCV}(\sigma, \lambda) \longleftarrow \frac{\|(X^{tr} * B_2)^\top \mathbf{1}_t\|^2}{2n} - \frac{\mathbf{1}_t^\top (X^{te} * B_2) \mathbf{1}_n}{n};$$

end
end

$(\widehat{\sigma}, \widehat{\lambda}) \longleftarrow \operatorname{argmin}_{(\sigma, \lambda)} \operatorname{LOOCV}(\sigma, \lambda);$

$$\widetilde{H}_{\ell,\ell'} \longleftarrow \frac{1}{n_{tr}} \sum_{i=1}^{n_{tr}} \exp\left(-\frac{\|x_i^{tr} - c_\ell\|^2 + \|x_i^{tr} - c_{\ell'}\|^2}{2\widehat{\sigma}^2}\right) \text{ for } \ell, \ell' = 1, 2, \ldots, t;$$

$$\widetilde{h}_\ell \longleftarrow \frac{1}{n_{te}} \sum_{j=1}^{n_{te}} \exp\left(-\frac{\|x_j^{te} - c_\ell\|^2}{2\widehat{\sigma}^2}\right) \text{ for } \ell = 1, 2, \ldots, t;$$

$\widehat{\alpha} \longleftarrow \max(\mathbf{0}_t, (\widetilde{H} + \widehat{\lambda} I_t)^{-1} \widetilde{h});$

$$\widehat{w}(x) \longleftarrow \sum_{\ell=1}^{t} \widehat{\alpha}_\ell \exp\left(-\frac{\|x - c_\ell\|^2}{2\widehat{\sigma}^2}\right);$$

Figure 4.6
Pseudo code of uLSIF with LOOCV. $B * B'$ denotes the elementwise multiplication of matrices B and B' of the same size. For n-dimensional vectors b and b', $\operatorname{diag}\left(\frac{b}{b'}\right)$ denotes the $n \times n$ diagonal matrix with i-th diagonal element b_i / b'_i.

4.7.1 Setting
Let us consider a one-dimensional toy regression problem of learning the following function:

$$f(x) = \text{sinc}(x) := \begin{cases} 1 & \text{if } x = 0, \\ \dfrac{\sin(\pi x)}{\pi x} & \text{otherwise}. \end{cases}$$

Let the training and test input densities be

$$p_{\text{tr}}(x) = N(x; 1, (1/2)^2),$$
$$p_{\text{te}}(x) = N(x; 2, (1/4)^2),$$

where $N(x; \mu, \sigma^2)$ denotes the Gaussian density with mean μ and variance σ^2. We create the training output value $\{y_i^{\text{tr}}\}_{i=1}^{n_{\text{tr}}}$ by

$$y_i^{\text{tr}} = f(x_i^{\text{tr}}) + \epsilon_i^{\text{tr}},$$

where the i.i.d. noise $\{\epsilon_i^{\text{tr}}\}_{i=1}^{n_{\text{tr}}}$ has density $N(\epsilon; 0, (1/4)^2)$. Test output values $\{y_j^{\text{te}}\}_{j=1}^{n_{\text{te}}}$ are generated in the same way. Let the number of training samples be $n_{\text{tr}} = 200$ and the number of test samples be $n_{\text{te}} = 1000$. The goal is to obtain a function $\widehat{f}(x)$ such that the generalization error is minimized.

This setting implies that we are considering a (weak) extrapolation problem (see figure 4.7, where only 100 test samples are plotted for clear visibility).

4.7.2 Importance Estimation by KLIEP
First, we illustrate the behavior of KLIEP in importance estimation, where we use only the input points $\{x_i^{\text{tr}}\}_{i=1}^{n_{\text{tr}}}$ and $\{x_j^{\text{te}}\}_{j=1}^{n_{\text{te}}}$.

Figure 4.8 depicts the true importance and its estimates by KLIEP; the Gaussian kernel model with $b = 100$ is used, and three Gaussian widths $\sigma = 0.02, 0.2, 0.8$ are tested. The graphs show that the performance of KLIEP is highly dependent on the Gaussian width; the estimated importance function $\widehat{w}(x)$ is fluctuates highly when σ is small, and is overly smoothed when σ is large. When σ is chosen appropriately, KLIEP seems to work reasonably well for this example.

Figure 4.9 depicts the values of the true J (see equation 4.5), and its estimate by fivefold CV (see equation 4.7); the means, the 25th percentiles, and the 75th percentiles over 100 trials are plotted as functions of the Gaussian width σ. This shows that CV gives a very good estimate of KL', which results in an appropriate choice of σ.

4.7. Numerical Examples

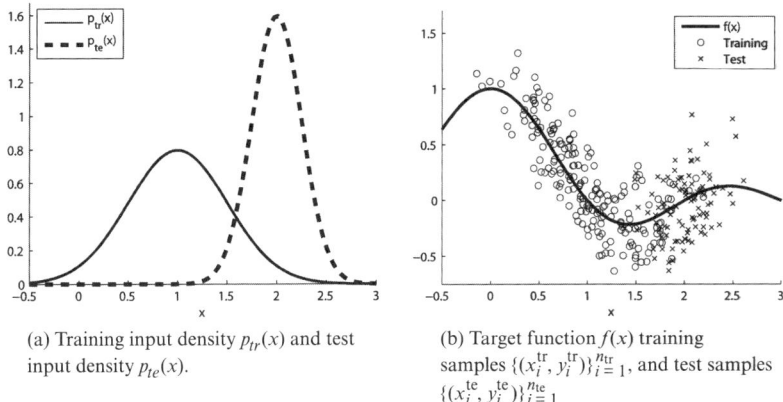

(a) Training input density $p_{tr}(x)$ and test input density $p_{te}(x)$.

(b) Target function $f(x)$ training samples $\{(x_i^{tr}, y_i^{tr})\}_{i=1}^{n_{tr}}$, and test samples $\{(x_j^{te}, y_j^{te})\}_{j=1}^{n_{te}}$

Figure 4.7
Illustrative example.

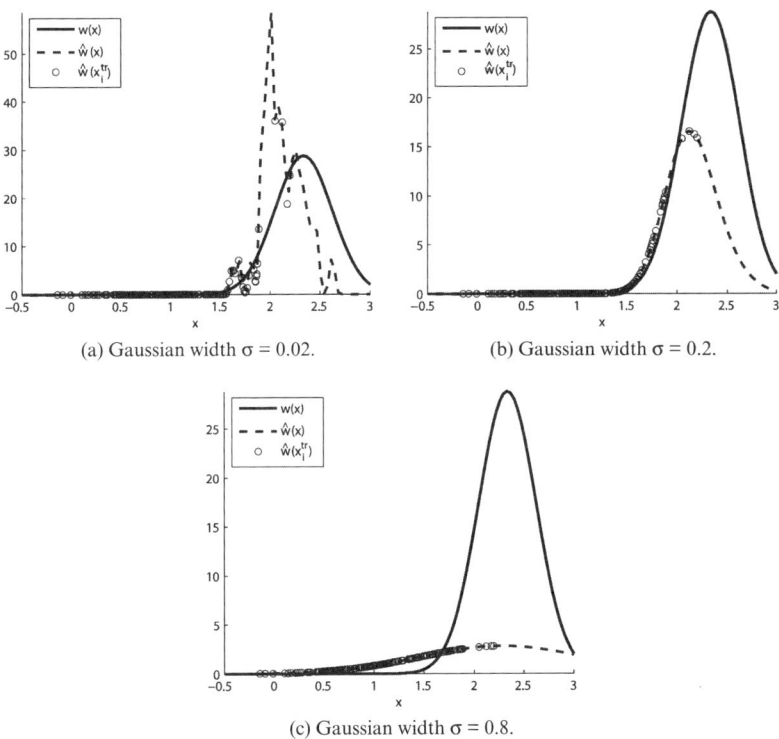

(a) Gaussian width $\sigma = 0.02$.

(b) Gaussian width $\sigma = 0.2$.

(c) Gaussian width $\sigma = 0.8$.

Figure 4.8
Results of importance estimation by KLIEP. $w(x)$ is the true importance function, and $\widehat{w}(x)$ is its estimation obtained by KLIEP.

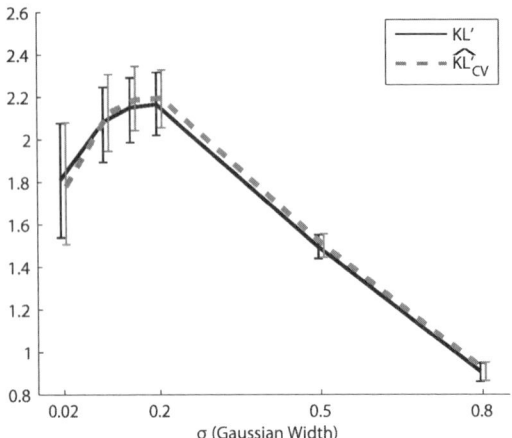

Figure 4.9
Model selection curve for KLIEP. KL' is the true score of an estimated importance (see equation 4.5), and $\widehat{KL}'_{CV}$ is its estimate by fivefold CV (see equation 4.7).

4.7.3 Covariate Shift Adaptation by IWLS and IWCV

Next, we illustrate how the estimated importance is used for covariate shift adaptation. Here we use $\{(x_i^{tr}, y_i^{tr})\}_{i=1}^{n_{tr}}$ and $\{x_j^{te}\}_{j=1}^{n_{te}}$ for learning; the test output values $\{y_j^{te}\}_{j=1}^{n_{te}}$ are used only for evaluating the generalization performance.

We use the following polynomial regression model:

$$\widehat{f}(x; \boldsymbol{\theta}) := \sum_{\ell=0}^{t} \theta_\ell x^\ell, \tag{4.15}$$

where t is the order of polynomials. The parameter vector $\boldsymbol{\theta}$ is learned by *importance-weighted least squares* (IWLS):

$$\widehat{\boldsymbol{\theta}}_{IWLS} := \underset{\boldsymbol{\theta}}{\operatorname{argmin}} \left[\sum_{i=1}^{n_{tr}} \widehat{w}(x_i^{tr}) \left(\widehat{f}(x_i^{tr}; \boldsymbol{\theta}) - y_i^{tr} \right)^2 \right].$$

IWLS is asymptotically unbiased when the true importance $w(x_i^{tr})$ is used as weights. On the other hand, ordinary LS is not asymptotically unbiased due to covariate shift, given that the model $\widehat{f}(x; \boldsymbol{\theta})$ is not correctly specified (see section 2.1.1). For the linear regression model (equation 4.15), the minimizer $\widehat{\boldsymbol{\theta}}_{IWLS}$ is given analytically by

$$\widehat{\boldsymbol{\theta}}_{IWLS} = (X^{tr\top} \widehat{W}^{tr} X^{tr})^{-1} X^{tr\top} \widehat{W}^{tr} \boldsymbol{y}^{tr},$$

4.7. Numerical Examples

where

$$X^{\text{tr}}_{i,\ell} := (x^{\text{tr}}_i)^{\ell-1},$$

$$\widehat{W}^{\text{tr}} := \text{diag}\left(\widehat{w}(x^{\text{tr}}_1), \widehat{w}(x^{\text{tr}}_2), \ldots, \widehat{w}(x^{\text{tr}}_{n_{\text{tr}}})\right),$$

$$\boldsymbol{y}^{\text{tr}} := (y^{\text{tr}}_1, y^{\text{tr}}_2, \ldots, y^{\text{tr}}_{n_{\text{tr}}})^\top.$$

$\text{diag}(a, b, \ldots, c)$ denotes the diagonal matrix with diagonal elements $a, b, \ldots, c$.

We choose the order t of polynomials based on *importance-weighted CV* (IWCV; see section 3.3). More specifically, we first divide the training samples $\{z^{\text{tr}}_i | z^{\text{tr}}_i = (x^{\text{tr}}_i, y^{\text{tr}}_i)\}^{n_{\text{tr}}}_{i=1}$ into k disjoint subsets $\{\mathcal{Z}^{\text{tr}}_i\}^k_{i=1}$. Then we learn a function $\widehat{f}_i(x)$ from $\{\mathcal{Z}^{\text{tr}}_{i'}\}_{i' \neq i}$ (i.e., without $\mathcal{Z}^{\text{tr}}_i$) by IWLS, and compute its mean test error for the remaining samples $\mathcal{Z}^{\text{tr}}_i$:

$$\widehat{\text{Gen}}_i := \frac{1}{|\mathcal{Z}^{\text{tr}}_i|} \sum_{(x,y) \in \mathcal{Z}^{\text{tr}}_i} \widehat{w}(x) \left(\widehat{f}_i(x) - y\right)^2.$$

This procedure is repeated for $i = 1, 2, \ldots, k$, and its average $\widehat{\text{Gen}}$ is used as an estimate of Gen:

$$\widehat{\text{Gen}} := \frac{1}{k} \sum_{i=1}^k \widehat{\text{Gen}}_i. \tag{4.16}$$

For model selection, we compute $\widehat{\text{Gen}}$ for all model candidates (the order $t \in \{1, 2, 3\}$ of polynomials in the current setting), and choose the one that minimizes $\widehat{\text{Gen}}$. We set the number of folds in IWCV to $k = 5$. IWCV is shown to be almost unbiased when the true importance $w(x^{\text{tr}}_i)$ is used as weights, while ordinary CV for misspecified models is highly biased due to covariate shift (see section 3.3).

Figure 4.10 depicts the functions learned by IWLS with different orders of polynomials. The results show that for all cases, the learned functions reasonably go through the test samples (note that the test *output* points are not used for obtaining the learned functions). Figure 4.11a depicts the true generalization error of IWLS and its estimate by IWCV; the means, the 25th percentiles, and the 75th percentiles over 100 runs are plotted as functions of the order of polynomials. This shows that IWCV roughly grasps the trend of the true generalization error. For comparison purposes, include the results by ordinary LS and ordinary CV in figures 4.10 and 4.11. Figure 4.10 shows that the functions obtained by ordinary LS nicely go through the training samples, but not

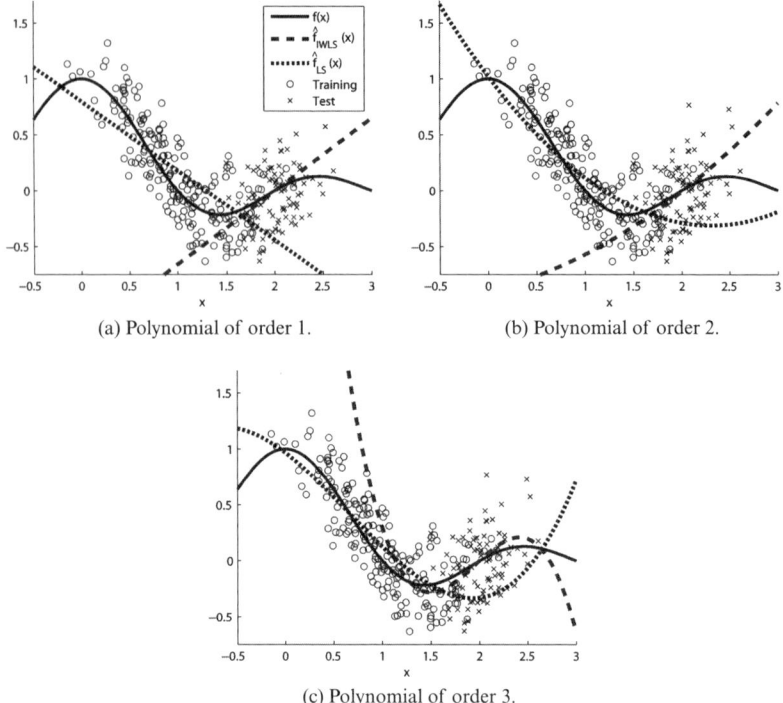

Figure 4.10
Learned functions obtained by IWLS and LS, which are denoted by $\widehat{f}_{\mathrm{IWLS}}(x)$ and $\widehat{f}_{\mathrm{LS}}(x)$, respectively.

through the test samples. Figure 4.11 shows that the scores of ordinary CV tend to be biased, implying that model selection by ordinary CV is not reliable.

Finally, we compare the generalization errors obtained by IWLS/LS and IWCV/CV, which are summarized in figure 4.12 as box plots. This shows that IWLS+IWCV tends to outperform other methods, illustrating the usefulness of the covariate shift adaptation method.

4.8 Experimental Comparison

In this section, we compare the accuracy and computational efficiency of density-ratio estimation methods.

Let the dimension of the domain be d, and

$$p_{\mathrm{tr}}(\boldsymbol{x}) = N(\boldsymbol{x}; (0, 0, \ldots, 0)^\top, \boldsymbol{I}_d),$$
$$p_{\mathrm{te}}(\boldsymbol{x}) = N(\boldsymbol{x}; (1, 0, \ldots, 0)^\top, \boldsymbol{I}_d),$$

4.8. Experimental Comparison

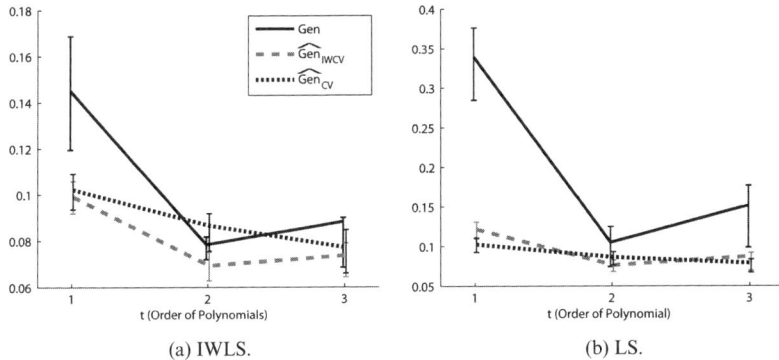

(a) IWLS.   (b) LS.

Figure 4.11
Model selection curves for IWLS/LS and IWCV/CV. Gen denotes the true generalization error of a learned function; $\widehat{\text{Gen}}_{\text{IWCV}}$ and $\widehat{\text{Gen}}_{\text{CV}}$ denote their estimates by fivefold IWCV and fivefold CV, respectively (see equation 4.16).

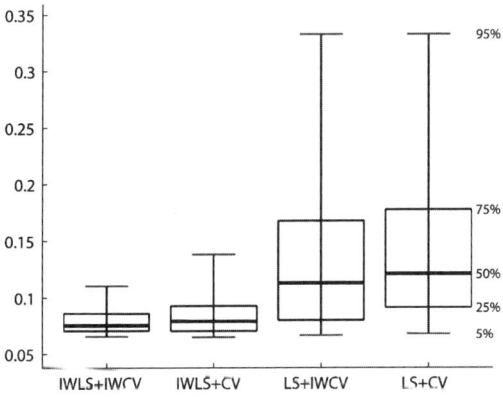

Figure 4.12
Box plots of generalization errors.

where I_d denotes the $d \times d$ identity matrix and $N(x; \mu, \Sigma)$ denotes the multi-dimensional Gaussian density with mean μ and covariance matrix Σ. The task is to estimate the importance at training points:

$$w_i = w(x_i^{\text{tr}}) = \frac{p_{\text{te}}(x_i^{\text{tr}})}{p_{\text{tr}}(x_i^{\text{tr}})} \quad \text{for } i = 1, 2, \ldots, n_{\text{tr}}.$$

We compare the following methods:

- **KDE(CV)** The Gaussian kernel (equation 4.1) is used where the kernel widths of the training and test densities are separately optimized based on fivefold CV.
- **KMM(med)** The performance of KMM is dependent on B, ϵ, and σ. We set $B = 1000$ and $\epsilon = (\sqrt{n_{\mathrm{tr}}} - 1)/\sqrt{n_{\mathrm{tr}}}$, following the original KMM paper [82], and the Gaussian width σ is set to the median distance between samples within the training set and the test set [141, 147].
- **LR(CV)** The Gaussian kernel model (equation 4.8) is used. The kernel width σ and the regularization parameter λ are chosen based on fivefold CV.
- **KLIEP(CV)** The Gaussian kernel model (equation 4.8) is used. The kernel width σ is selected based on fivefold CV.
- **uLSIF(CV)** The Gaussian kernel model (equation 4.8) is used. The kernel width σ and the regularization parameter λ are determined based on LOOCV.

All the methods are implemented using the MATLAB® environment, where the CPLEX® optimizer is used for solving quadratic programs in KMM and the *LIBLINEAR* implementation is used for LR [103].

We set the number of test points to $n_{\mathrm{te}} = 1000$, and considered the following setups for the number n_{tr} of training samples and the input dimensionality d:

(a) n_{tr} is fixed to $n_{\mathrm{tr}} = 100$, and d is changed as $d = 1, 2, \ldots, 20$

(b) d is fixed to $d = 10$, and n_{tr} is changed as $n_{\mathrm{tr}} = 50, 60, \ldots, 150$.

We ran the experiments 100 times for each d, each n_{tr}, and each method, and evaluated the quality of the importance estimates $\{\widehat{w}_i\}_{i=1}^{n_{\mathrm{tr}}}$ by the *normalized mean-squared error* (NMSE):

$$\mathrm{NMSE} := \frac{1}{n_{\mathrm{tr}}} \sum_{i=1}^{n_{\mathrm{tr}}} \left(\frac{\widehat{w}_i}{\sum_{i'=1}^{n_{\mathrm{tr}}} \widehat{w}_{i'}} - \frac{w_i}{\sum_{i'=1}^{n_{\mathrm{tr}}} w_{i'}} \right)^2.$$

For the purpose of covariate shift adaptation, the global scale of the importance values is not important. Thus, the above NMSE, evaluating only the relative magnitude among $\{\widehat{w}_i\}_{i=1}^{n_{\mathrm{tr}}}$, would be a suitable error metric for the current experiments.

NMSEs averaged over 100 trials (a) as a function of input dimensionality d and (b) as a function of the training sample size n_{tr} are plotted in log scale in

4.8. Experimental Comparison

figure 4.13. Error bars are omitted for clear visibility—instead, the best method in terms of the mean error and comparable methods based on the t-test at the significance level 1 percent are indicated by o; the methods with significant difference from the best methods are indicated by ×.

Figure 4.13a shows that the error of KDE(CV) sharply increases as the input dimensionality grows, while LR, KLIEP, and uLSIF tend to give much smaller errors than KDE. This would be an advantage of directly estimating the importance without going through density estimation. KMM tends to perform poorly, which is caused by an inappropriate choice of the Gaussian kernel width. On the other hand, model selection in LR, KLIEP, and uLSIF seems to work quite well. Figure 4.13b shows that the errors of all methods tend to decrease as the number of training samples grows. Again LR, KLIEP, and uLSIF tend to give much smaller errors than KDE and KMM.

Next, we investigate the computation time. Each method has a different model selection strategy: KMM does not involve CV; KDE and KLIEP involve CV over the kernel width; and LR and uLSIF involve CV over both the kernel width and the regularization parameter. Thus, the naive comparison of the total computation time is not so meaningful. For this reason, we first investigate the computation time of each importance estimation method after the model parameters have been determined.

The average CPU computation time over 100 trials is summarized in figure 4.14. Figure 4.14a shows that the computation times of KDE, KLIEP, and uLSIF are almost independent of the input dimensionality, while those of KMM and LR are rather dependent on the input dimensionality. Note that LR for $d \leq 3$ is slow due to a convergence problem of the LIBLINEAR package. The uLSIF is one of the fastest methods. Figure 4.14b shows that the computation times of LR, KLIEP, and uLSIF are nearly independent of the number of training samples, while those of KDE and KMM sharply increase as the number of training samples increases.

Both LR and uLSIF have high accuracy, and their computation times after model selection are comparable. Finally, we compare the entire computation times of LR and uLSIF including CV, which are summarized in figure 4.15. The Gaussian width σ and the regularization parameter λ are chosen over the 9×9 grid for both LR and uLSIF. Therefore, the comparison of the entire computation time is fair. Figures 4.15a and 4.15b show that uLSIF is approximately five times faster than LR.

Overall, uLSIF is shown to be comparable to the best existing method (LR) in terms of accuracy, but is computationally more efficient than LR.

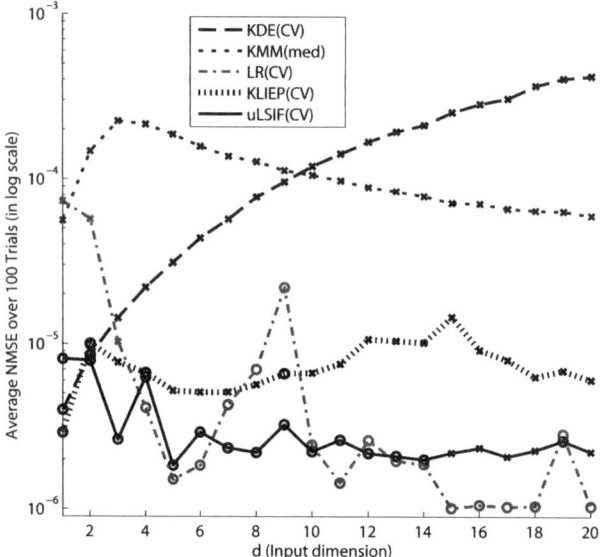

(a) When input dimensionality is changed.

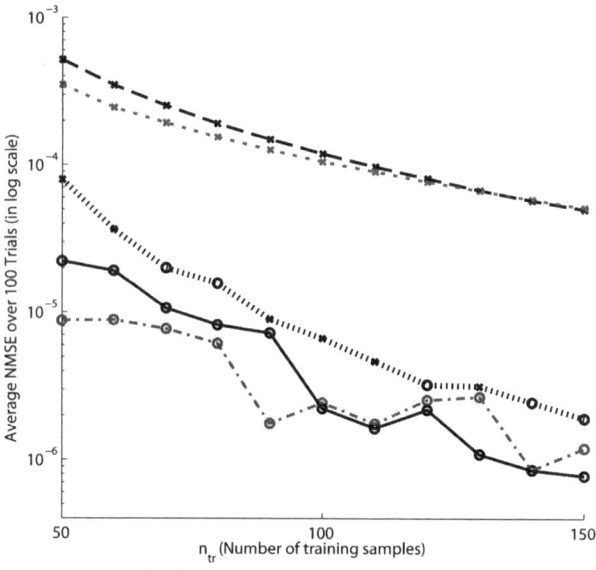

(b) When training sample size is changed.

Figure 4.13
NMSEs averaged over 100 trials in log scale for the artificial data set. Error bars are omitted for clear visibility. Instead, the best method in terms of the mean error and comparable methods based on the *t-test* at the significance level 1 percent are indicated by ∘; the methods with significant difference from the best methods are indicated by ×.

4.8. Experimental Comparison

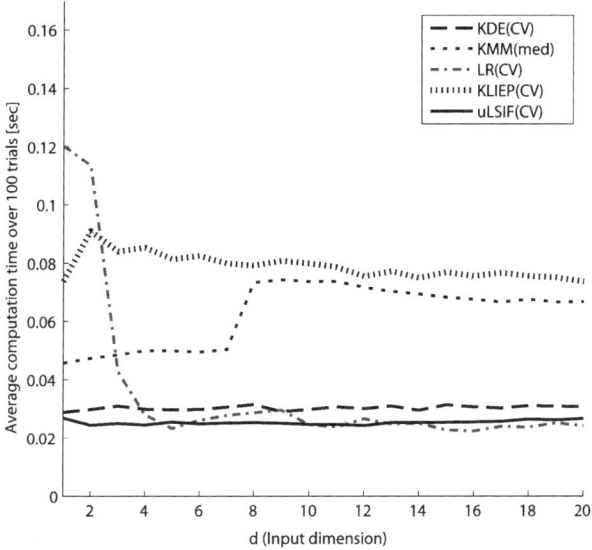

(a) When input dimensionality is changed.

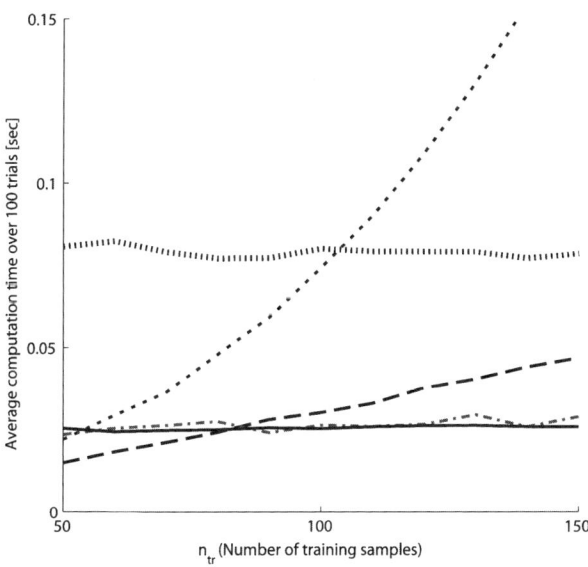

(b) When training sample size is changed.

Figure 4.14
Average computation time (after model selection) over 100 trials for the artificial data set.

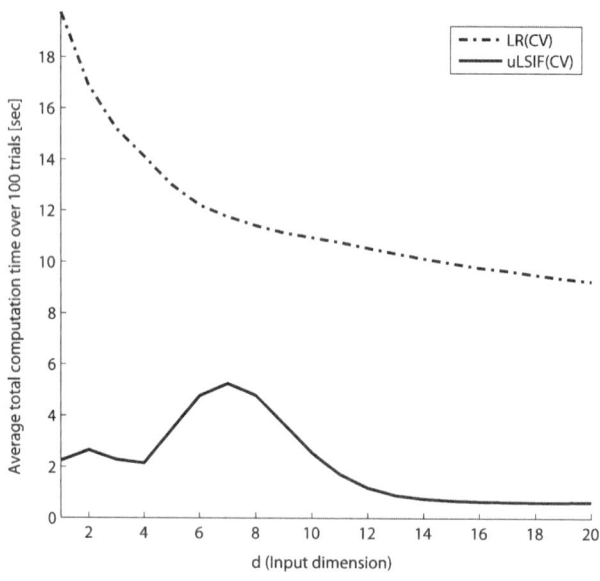

(a) When input dimensionality is changed.

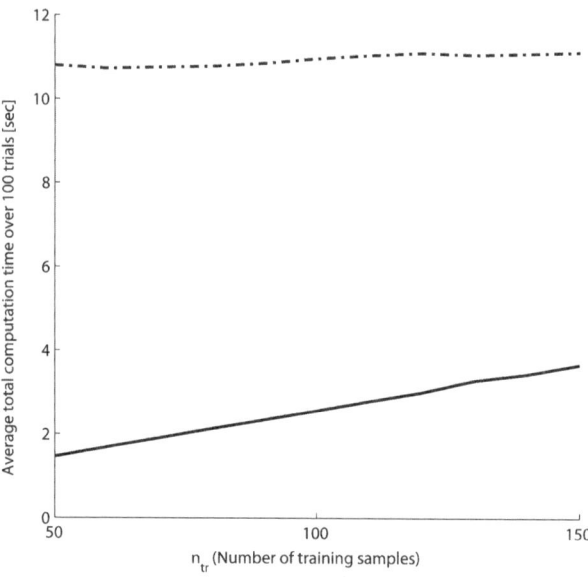

(b) When training sample size is changed.

Figure 4.15
Average computation time over 100 trials for the artificial data set (including model selection of the Gaussian width σ and the regularization parameter λ over the 9×9 grid).

4.9 Summary

In this chapter, we have shown methods of importance estimation that can avoid solving a substantially more difficult task of density estimation. Table 4.1 summarizes properties of the importance estimation methods.

Kernel density estimation (KDE; section 4.1) is computationally very efficient since no optimization is involved, and model selection is possible by cross-validation (CV). However, KDE may suffer from the curse of dimensionality due to the difficulty of density estimation in high dimensions.

Kernel mean matching (KMM; section 4.2) may potentially work better by directly estimating the importance. However, since objective model selection methods are missing for KMM, model parameters such as the Gaussian width need to be determined by hand. This is highly unreliable unless we have strong prior knowledge. Furthermore, the computation of KMM is rather demanding since a quadratic programming problem has to be solved.

Logistic regression (LR; section 4.3) and the Kullback–Leibler importance estimation procedure (KLIEP; section 4.4) also do not involve density estimation. However, in contrast to KMM, LR and KLIEP are equipped with CV for model selection, which is a significant advantage over KMM. Nevertheless, LR and KLIEP are computationally rather expensive since nonlinear optimization problems have to be solved.

Least-squares importance fitting (LSIF; section 4.5) is qualitatively similar to LR and KLIEP, that is, it can avoid density estimation, model selection is possible, and nonlinear optimization is involved. LSIF is more advantageous than LR and KLIEP in that it is equipped with a regularization path tracking algorithm. Thanks to this, model selection for LSIF is computationally much more efficient than for LR and KLIEP. However, the regularization path tracking algorithm tends to be numerically unstable.

Table 4.1
Importance estimation methods

Methods	Density Estimation	Model Selection	Optimization	Out-of-sample Prediction
KDE	Necessary	Available	Analytic	Possible
KMM	Not necessary	Not available	Convex QP	Not possible
LR	Not necessary	Available	Convex non-linear	Possible
KLIEP	Not necessary	Available	Convex non-linear	Possible
LSIF	Not necessary	Available	Convex QP	Possible
uLSIF	Not necessary	Available	Analytic	Possible

QP, quadratic program.

Unconstrained LSIF (uLSIF; section 4.6) exhibits good properties of other methods (e.g., no density estimation is involved and a built-in model selection method is available). In addition to these properties, the solution of uLSIF can be computed analytically by solving a system of linear equations. Therefore, uLSIF is computationally very efficient and numerically stable. Furthermore, thanks to the availability of the closed-form solution, the LOOCV score of uLSIF can be computed analytically without repeating holdout loops, which highly contributes to reducing the computation time in the model selection phase.

Consequently, uLSIF is a preferable method for importance estimation.

5 Direct Density-Ratio Estimation with Dimensionality Reduction

As shown in chapter 5, various methods have been developed for directly estimating the density ratio without going through density estimation. However, even these methods can perform rather poorly when the dimensionality of the data domain is high. In this chapter, a dimensionality reduction scheme for density-ratio estimation, called *direct density-ratio estimation with dimensionality reduction* (D^3; pronounced as "D-cube") [158], is introduced.

5.1 Density Difference in Hetero-Distributional Subspace

The basic assumption behind D^3 is that the densities $p_{tr}(x)$ and $p_{te}(x)$ are different not in the entire space, but only in some *subspace*. This assumption can be mathematically formulated with the following linear mixing model.

Let $\{u_i^{tr}\}_{i=1}^{n_{tr}}$ be i.i.d. samples drawn from an m-dimensional distribution with density[1] $p_{tr}(u)$, where m is in $\{1, 2, \ldots, d\}$. We assume $p_{tr}(u) > 0$ for all u. Let $\{u_j^{te}\}_{j=1}^{n_{te}}$ be i.i.d. samples drawn from another m-dimensional distribution with density $p_{te}(u)$. Let $\{v_i^{tr}\}_{i=1}^{n_{tr}}$ and $\{v_j^{te}\}_{j=1}^{n_{te}}$ be i.i.d. samples drawn from a $(d-m)$-dimensional distribution with density $p(v)$. We assume $p(v) > 0$ for all v. Let A be a $d \times m$ matrix and B be a $d \times (d-m)$ matrix such that the column vectors of A and B span the entire space. Based on these quantities, we consider the case where the samples $\{x_i^{tr}\}_{i=1}^{n_{tr}}$ and $\{x_j^{te}\}_{j=1}^{n_{te}}$ are generated as

$$x_i^{tr} = Au_i^{tr} + Bv_i^{tr},$$
$$x_j^{te} = Au_j^{te} + Bv_j^{te}.$$

---

1. With abuse of notation, we use $p_{tr}(u)$ and $p_{te}(u)$, which are different from $p_{tr}(x)$ and $p_{te}(x)$, for simplicity.

Thus, $p_{\mathrm{tr}}(x)$ and $p_{\mathrm{te}}(x)$ are expressed as

$$p_{\mathrm{tr}}(x) = c\, p_{\mathrm{tr}}(u)\, p(v),$$
$$p_{\mathrm{te}}(x) = c\, p_{\mathrm{te}}(u)\, p(v),$$

where c is the *Jacobian* between the observation x and (u, v). We call $\mathcal{R}(A)$ and $\mathcal{R}(B)$ the *hetero-distributional subspace* and the *homo-distributional subspace*, respectively, where $\mathcal{R}(\cdot)$ denotes the range of a matrix. Note that $\mathcal{R}(A)$ and $\mathcal{R}(B)$ are not generally orthogonal to one another (see figure 5.1).

Under the above decomposability assumption with independence of u and v, the density ratio of $p_{\mathrm{te}}(x)$ and $p_{\mathrm{tr}}(x)$ can be simplified as

$$w(x) = \frac{p_{\mathrm{te}}(x)}{p_{\mathrm{tr}}(x)} = \frac{c\, p_{\mathrm{te}}(u)\, p(v)}{c\, p_{\mathrm{tr}}(u)\, p(v)} = \frac{p_{\mathrm{te}}(u)}{p_{\mathrm{tr}}(u)} = w(u). \tag{5.1}$$

This means that the density ratio does not have to be estimated in the entire d-dimensional space, but only in the heterodistributional subspace of dimension m ($\leq d$). Now we want to extract the hetero-distributional components u_i^{tr} and u_j^{te} from the original high-dimensional samples x_i^{tr} and x_j^{te}. This allows us to estimate the density ratio only in $\mathcal{R}(A)$ via equation 5.1. As illustrated in figure 5.1, the *oblique* projection of x_i^{tr} and x_j^{te} onto $\mathcal{R}(A)$ along $\mathcal{R}(B)$ gives u_i^{tr} and u_j^{te}.

5.2 Characterization of Hetero-Distributional Subspace

Let us denote the oblique projection matrix onto $\mathcal{R}(A)$ along $\mathcal{R}(B)$ by $P_{\mathcal{R}(A),\mathcal{R}(B)}$. In order to characterize the oblique projection matrix $P_{\mathcal{R}(A),\mathcal{R}(B)}$, let us consider matrices U and V whose rows consist of *dual* bases for the column vectors of A and B, respectively. More specifically, U is an $m \times d$ matrix and V is a $(d-m) \times d$ matrix such that they are *bi-orthogonal* to one another:

$$UB = O_{m \times (d-m)},$$
$$VA = O_{(d-m) \times m},$$

where $O_{m \times m'}$ denotes the $m \times m'$ matrix with all zeros. Thus, $\mathcal{R}(B)$ and $\mathcal{R}(U^\top)$ are orthogonal to one another, and $\mathcal{R}(A)$ and $\mathcal{R}(V^\top)$ are orthogonal to one another, where $^\top$ denotes the transpose. When $\mathcal{R}(A)$ and $\mathcal{R}(B)$ are orthogonal to one another, $\mathcal{R}(U^\top)$ agrees with $\mathcal{R}(A)$ and $\mathcal{R}(V^\top)$ agrees with $\mathcal{R}(B)$; however, in general they are different, as illustrated in figure 5.1.

5.2. Characterization of Hetero-Distributional Subspace

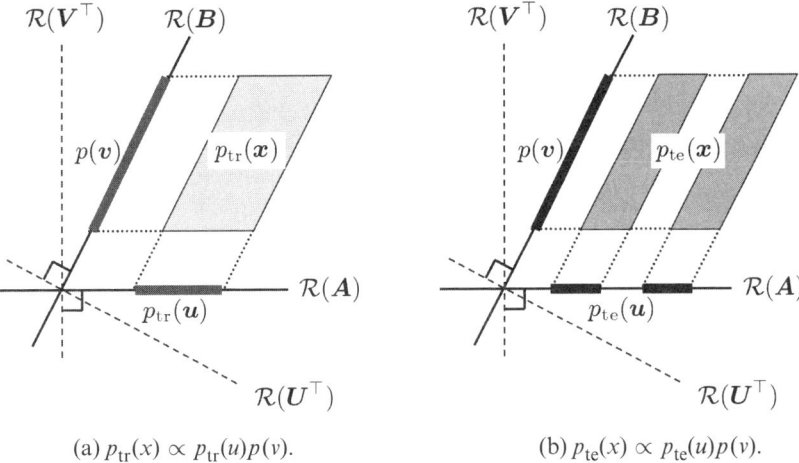

(a) $p_{\mathrm{tr}}(x) \propto p_{\mathrm{tr}}(u)p(v)$. (b) $p_{\mathrm{te}}(x) \propto p_{\mathrm{te}}(u)p(v)$.

Figure 5.1
A schematic picture of the hetero-distributional subspace for $d = 2$ and $m = 1$. Let $A \propto (1, 0)^\top$ and $B \propto (1, 2)^\top$. Then $U \propto (2, -1)$ and $V \propto (0, 1)$. $\mathcal{R}(A)$ and $\mathcal{R}(B)$ are called the hetero-distributional subspace and the homo-distributional subspace, respectively. If a data point x is projected onto $\mathcal{R}(A)$ along $\mathcal{R}(B)$, the homo-distributional component v can be eliminated and the hetero-distributional component u can be extracted.

The relation between A and B and the relation between U and V can be characterized in terms of the covariance matrix Σ (of either $p_{\mathrm{tr}}(x)$ or $p_{\mathrm{te}}(x)$) as

$$A^\top \Sigma^{-1} B = O_{(d-m)\times m}, \tag{5.2}$$
$$U \Sigma V^\top = O_{m \times (d-m)}. \tag{5.3}$$

These orthogonality relations in terms of Σ follow from the statistical independence between the components in $\mathcal{R}(A)$ and $\mathcal{R}(B)$—more specifically, equation 5.2 follows from the fact that the *sphering* operation (transforming samples x by $x \leftarrow \Sigma^{-1/2} x$ in advance) orthogonalizes independent components u and v [84], and equation 5.3 is its dual expression [92]. After sphering, the covariance matrix becomes identity, and consequently all the discussions become simpler. However, estimating the covariance matrix from samples can be erroneous in high-dimensional problems, and taking its inverse further magnifies the estimation error. For this reason, we decided to deal directly with nonorthogonal A and B below.

For normalization purposes, we further assume that

$$UA = I_m,$$
$$VB = I_{d-m},$$

where I_m denotes the m-dimensional identity matrix. Then the oblique projection matrices $P_{\mathcal{R}(A),\mathcal{R}(B)}$ and $P_{\mathcal{R}(B),\mathcal{R}(A)}$ can be expressed as

$$P_{\mathcal{R}(A),\mathcal{R}(B)} = AU,$$

$$P_{\mathcal{R}(B),\mathcal{R}(A)} = BV,$$

which can be confirmed by the facts that $P^2_{\mathcal{R}(A),\mathcal{R}(B)} = P_{\mathcal{R}(A),\mathcal{R}(B)}$ (*idempotence*); the null space of $P_{\mathcal{R}(A),\mathcal{R}(B)}$ is $\mathcal{R}(B)$; and the range of $P_{\mathcal{R}(A),\mathcal{R}(B)}$ is $\mathcal{R}(A)$; the same is true for $P_{\mathcal{R}(B),\mathcal{R}(A)}$. The above expressions of $P_{\mathcal{R}(A),\mathcal{R}(B)}$ and $P_{\mathcal{R}(B),\mathcal{R}(A)}$ imply that U expresses projected images in an m-dimensional coordinate system within $\mathcal{R}(A)$, while V expresses projected images in a $(d - m)$-dimensional coordinate system within $\mathcal{R}(B)$. We call U and V the hetero-distributional mapping and the homo-distributional mapping, respectively.

Now u_i^{tr}, u_j^{te}, v_i^{tr}, and v_j^{te} are expressed as

$$u_i^{tr} = Ux_i^{tr}, \quad u_j^{te} = Ux_j^{te},$$

$$v_i^{tr} = Vx_i^{tr}, \quad v_j^{te} = Vx_j^{te}.$$

Thus, if the hetero-distributional mapping U is estimated, estimation of the density ratio $w(x)$ can be carried out in a low-dimensional hetero-distributional subspace via equation 5.1.

The above framework is called the *direct density-ratio estimation with dimensionality reduction* (D^3) [158]. For the time being, we assume that the dimension m of the hetero-distributional subspace is known; we show how m is estimated from data in section 5.5.

5.3 Identifying Hetero-Distributional Subspace by Supervised Dimensionality Reduction

In this section, we explain how the hetero-distributional subspace is estimated.

5.3.1 Basic Idea

In order to estimate the hetero-distributional subspace, we need a criterion that reflects the degree of distributional difference in a subspace. A key observation in this context is that the existence of distributional difference can be checked to determine whether samples from the two distributions are separated from one another. That is, if samples of one distribution can be distinguished from the samples of the other distribution, one may conclude that two distributions

5.3. Identifying Hetero-Distributional Subspace

are different; otherwise, distributions may be similar. We employ this idea for finding the hetero-distributional subspace.

Let us denote the samples projected onto the hetero-distributional subspace by

$$\{u_i^{tr} \mid u_i^{tr} = Ux_i^{tr}\}_{i=1}^{n_{tr}},$$
$$\{u_j^{te} \mid u_j^{te} = Ux_j^{te}\}_{j=1}^{n_{te}}.$$

Then our goal is to find the matrix U such that $\{u_i^{tr}\}_{i=1}^{n_{tr}}$ and $\{u_j^{te}\}_{j=1}^{n_{te}}$ are maximally separated from one another. For that purpose, we may use *any* supervised dimensionality reduction methods.

Among supervised dimensionality reduction methods (e.g., [72, 73, 56, 63, 62]), we decided to use *local Fisher discriminant analysis* (LFDA; [154]), which is an extension of classical *Fisher discriminant analysis* (FDA; [50]) for multimodally distributed data. LFDA has useful properties, in practice; for instance, there is no limitation on the dimension of the reduced subspace: (FDA is limited to one-dimensional projection for two-class problems [57]); it works well even when data have multimodal structure such as separate clusters; it is robust against outliers; its solution can be analytically computed using eigenvalue decomposition as stable and efficient as the original FDA; and its experimental performance has been shown to be better than other supervised learning methods.

Below, we briefly review technical details of LFDA, showing how to use it for hetero-distributional subspace search. To simplify the notation, we consider a set of binary-labeled training samples

$$\{(x_k, y_k) \mid x_k \in \mathbb{R}^d, y_k \in \{+1, -1\}\}_{k=1}^n,$$

and reduce the dimensionality of x_k, using an $m \times d$ transformation matrix T, as

$$u_k = Tx_k.$$

Effectively, the training samples $\{(x_k, y_k)\}_{k=1}^n$ correspond to the following setup: for $n = n_{tr} + n_{te}$,

$$\{x_k\}_{k=1}^n = \{x_i^{tr}\}_{i=1}^{n_{tr}} \cup \{x_j^{te}\}_{j=1}^{n_{te}},$$

$$y_k = \begin{cases} +1 & \text{if } x_k \in \{x_i^{tr}\}_{i=1}^{n_{tr}}, \\ -1 & \text{if } x_k \in \{x_j^{te}\}_{j=1}^{n_{te}}. \end{cases}$$

5.3.2 Fisher Discriminant Analysis

Since LFDA is an extension of FDA [50], we first briefly review the original FDA (see also section 2.3.1).

Let n_+ and n_- be the numbers of samples in class $+1$ and class -1, respectively. Let $\boldsymbol{\mu}$, $\boldsymbol{\mu}_+$, and $\boldsymbol{\mu}_-$ be the means of $\{\boldsymbol{x}_k\}_{k=1}^n$, $\{\boldsymbol{x}_k | y_k = +1\}_{k=1}^n$, and $\{\boldsymbol{x}_k | y_k = -1\}_{k=1}^n$, respectively:

$$\boldsymbol{\mu} := \frac{1}{n} \sum_{k=1}^n \boldsymbol{x}_k,$$

$$\boldsymbol{\mu}_+ := \frac{1}{n_+} \sum_{k: y_k = +1} \boldsymbol{x}_k,$$

$$\boldsymbol{\mu}_- := \frac{1}{n_-} \sum_{k: y_k = -1} \boldsymbol{x}_k.$$

Let $\boldsymbol{S}^b$ and $\boldsymbol{S}^w$ be the *between-class scatter matrix* and the *within-class scatter matrix*, respectively, defined as

$$\boldsymbol{S}^b := n_+ (\boldsymbol{\mu}_+ - \boldsymbol{\mu})(\boldsymbol{\mu}_+ - \boldsymbol{\mu})^\top + n_- (\boldsymbol{\mu}_- - \boldsymbol{\mu})(\boldsymbol{\mu}_- - \boldsymbol{\mu})^\top,$$

$$\boldsymbol{S}^w := \sum_{k: y_k = +1} (\boldsymbol{x}_k - \boldsymbol{\mu}_+)(\boldsymbol{x}_k - \boldsymbol{\mu}_+)^\top + \sum_{k: y_k = -1} (\boldsymbol{x}_k - \boldsymbol{\mu}_-)(\boldsymbol{x}_k - \boldsymbol{\mu}_-)^\top.$$

The FDA transformation matrix $\boldsymbol{T}_{\text{FDA}}$ is defined as

$$\boldsymbol{T}_{\text{FDA}} := \underset{\boldsymbol{T} \in \mathbb{R}^{m \times d}}{\operatorname{argmax}} \left[\operatorname{tr}(\boldsymbol{T} \boldsymbol{S}^b \boldsymbol{T}^\top (\boldsymbol{T} \boldsymbol{S}^w \boldsymbol{T}^\top)^{-1}) \right].$$

That is, FDA seeks a transformation matrix $\boldsymbol{T}$ with large between-class scatter and small within-class scatter in the embedding space $\mathbb{R}^m$. In the above formulation, we implicitly assume that $\boldsymbol{S}^w$ is full-rank and $\boldsymbol{T}$ has rank m so that the inverse of $\boldsymbol{T} \boldsymbol{S}^w \boldsymbol{T}^\top$ exists.

Let $\{\boldsymbol{\psi}_l\}_{l=1}^d$ be the generalized eigenvectors associated with the generalized eigenvalues $\{\eta_l\}_{l=1}^d$ of the following generalized eigenvalue problem [57]:

$$\boldsymbol{S}^b \boldsymbol{\psi} = \eta \boldsymbol{S}^w \boldsymbol{\psi}.$$

We assume that the generalized eigenvalues are sorted as

$$\eta_1 \geq \eta_2 \geq \cdots \geq \eta_d.$$

5.3. Identifying Hetero-Distributional Subspace

Then a solution T_{FDA} is analytically given as follows (e.g., [42]):

$$T_{\text{FDA}} = (\boldsymbol{\psi}_1|\boldsymbol{\psi}_2|\cdots|\boldsymbol{\psi}_m)^\top.$$

FDA works very well if samples in each class are Gaussian with common covariance structure. However, it tends to give undesired results if samples in a class form several separate clusters or there are outliers. Furthermore, the between-class scatter matrix S^{b} is known to have rank 1 in the current setup (see, e.g., [57]), implying that we can obtain only one meaningful feature $\boldsymbol{\psi}_1$ through the FDA criterion; the remaining features $\{\boldsymbol{\psi}_l\}_{l=2}^d$ found by FDA are arbitrary in the null space of S^{b}. This is an essential limitation of FDA in dimensionality reduction.

5.3.3 Local Fisher Discriminant Analysis

In order to overcome the weaknesses of FDA explained above, LFDA has been introduced [154]. Here, we explain the main idea of LFDA briefly.

The scatter matrices S^{b} and S^{w} in the original FDA can be expressed in the *pairwise form* as follows [154]:

$$S^{\text{b}} = \frac{1}{2} \sum_{k,k'=1}^n W^{\text{b}}_{k,k'}(\boldsymbol{x}_k - \boldsymbol{x}_{k'})(\boldsymbol{x}_k - \boldsymbol{x}_{k'})^\top,$$

$$S^{\text{w}} = \frac{1}{2} \sum_{k,k'=1}^n W^{\text{w}}_{k,k'}(\boldsymbol{x}_k - \boldsymbol{x}_{k'})(\boldsymbol{x}_k - \boldsymbol{x}_{k'})^\top,$$

where

$$W^{\text{b}}_{k,k'} := \begin{cases} 1/n - 1/n_+ & \text{if } y_k = y_{k'} = +1, \\ 1/n - 1/n_- & \text{if } y_k = y_{k'} = -1, \\ 1/n & \text{if } y_k \neq y_{k'}, \end{cases}$$

$$W^{\text{w}}_{k,k'} := \begin{cases} 1/n_+ & \text{if } y_k = y_{k'} = +1, \\ 1/n_- & \text{if } y_k = y_{k'} = -1, \\ 0 & \text{if } y_k \neq y_{k'}. \end{cases}$$

Note that $(1/n - 1/n_+)$ and $(1/n - 1/n_-)$ included in the definition of W^{b} are negative values.

Based on the above pairwise expression, let us define the *local* between-class scatter matrix S^{lb} and the *local* within-class scatter matrix S^{lw} as

$$S^{\text{lb}} := \frac{1}{2} \sum_{k,k'=1}^{n} W_{k,k'}^{\text{lb}} (x_k - x_{k'})(x_k - x_{k'})^\top,$$

$$S^{\text{lw}} := \frac{1}{2} \sum_{k,k'=1}^{n} W_{k,k'}^{\text{lw}} (x_k - x_{k'})(x_k - x_{k'})^\top,$$

where

$$W_{k,k'}^{\text{lb}} := \begin{cases} A_{k,k'}(1/n - 1/n_+) & \text{if } y_k = y_{k'} = +1, \\ A_{k,k'}(1/n - 1/n_-) & \text{if } y_k = y_{k'} = -1, \\ 1/n & \text{if } y_k \neq y_{k'}, \end{cases}$$

$$W_{k,k'}^{\text{lw}} := \begin{cases} A_{k,k'}/n_+ & \text{if } y_k = y_{k'} = +1, \\ A_{k,k'}/n_- & \text{if } y_k = y_{k'} = -1, \\ 0 & \text{if } y_k \neq y_{k'}. \end{cases}$$

$A_{k,k'}$ is the affinity value between x_k and $x_{k'}$ (e.g., as defined based on the *local scaling heuristic* [208]):

$$A_{k,k'} := \exp\left(-\frac{\|x_k - x_{k'}\|^2}{\tau_k \tau_{k'}}\right).$$

τ_k is the local scaling factor around x_k defined by

$$\tau_k := \|x_k - x_k^{(K)}\|,$$

where $x_k^{(K)}$ denotes the K-th nearest neighbor of x_k. A heuristic choice of $K=7$ was shown to be useful through extensive simulations [208, 154]. Note that the local scaling factors are computed in a classwise manner in LFDA (see the pseudo code of LFDA in figure 5.2).

Based on the local scatter matrices S^{lb} and S^{lw}, the LFDA transformation matrix T_{LFDA} is defined as

$$T_{\text{LFDA}} := \underset{T \in \mathbb{R}^{m \times d}}{\text{argmax}} \left[\text{tr}(T S^{\text{lb}} T^\top (T S^{\text{lw}} T^\top)^{-1}) \right].$$

5.3. Identifying Hetero-Distributional Subspace

Input: Two sets of samples $\{x_i^{\text{tr}}\}_{i=1}^{n_{\text{tr}}}$ and $\{x_j^{\text{te}}\}_{j=1}^{n_{\text{te}}}$ on $\mathbb{R}^d$
Dimensionality of embedding space m $(1 \le m \le d)$
Output: $m \times d$ transformation matrix T_{LFDA}

$\widetilde{x}_i^{\text{tr}} \longleftarrow$ 7th nearest neighbor of x_i^{tr} among $\{x_{i'}^{\text{tr}}\}_{i'=1}^{n_{\text{tr}}}$
     for $i = 1, 2, \ldots, n_{\text{tr}}$;
$\widetilde{x}_j^{\text{te}} \longleftarrow$ 7th nearest neighbor of x_j^{te} among $\{x_{j'}^{\text{te}}\}_{j'=1}^{n_{\text{te}}}$
     for $j = 1, 2, \ldots, n_{\text{te}}$;
$\tau_i^{\text{tr}} \longleftarrow \|x_i^{\text{tr}} - \widetilde{x}_i^{\text{tr}}\|$ for $i = 1, 2, \ldots, n_{\text{tr}}$;
$\tau_j^{\text{te}} \longleftarrow \|x_j^{\text{te}} - \widetilde{x}_j^{\text{te}}\|$ for $j = 1, 2, \ldots, n_{\text{te}}$;
$A_{i,i'}^{\text{tr}} \longleftarrow \exp\left(-\dfrac{\|x_i^{\text{tr}} - x_{i'}^{\text{tr}}\|^2}{\tau_i^{\text{tr}} \tau_{i'}^{\text{tr}}}\right)$ for $i, i' = 1, 2, \ldots, n_{\text{tr}}$;
$A_{j,j'}^{\text{te}} \longleftarrow \exp\left(-\dfrac{\|x_j^{\text{te}} - x_{j'}^{\text{te}}\|^2}{\tau_j^{\text{te}} \tau_{j'}^{\text{te}}}\right)$ for $j, j' = 1, 2, \ldots, n_{\text{te}}$;
$X^{\text{tr}} \longleftarrow (x_1^{\text{tr}}|x_2^{\text{tr}}|\cdots|x_{n_{\text{tr}}}^{\text{tr}})$;
$X^{\text{te}} \longleftarrow (x_1^{\text{te}}|x_2^{\text{te}}|\cdots|x_{n_{\text{te}}}^{\text{te}})$;
$G^{\text{tr}} \longleftarrow X^{\text{tr}} \operatorname{diag}(A^{\text{tr}} \mathbf{1}_{n_{\text{tr}}}) X^{\text{tr}\top} - X^{\text{tr}} A^{\text{tr}} X^{\text{tr}\top}$;
$G^{\text{te}} \longleftarrow X^{\text{te}} \operatorname{diag}(A^{\text{te}} \mathbf{1}_{n_{\text{te}}}) X^{\text{te}\top} - X^{\text{te}} A^{\text{te}} X^{\text{te}\top}$;
$S^{\text{lw}} \longleftarrow \dfrac{1}{n_{\text{tr}}} G^{\text{tr}} + \dfrac{1}{n_{\text{te}}} G^{\text{te}}$;
$n \longleftarrow n_{\text{tr}} + n_{\text{te}}$;
$S^{\text{lb}} \longleftarrow \left(\dfrac{1}{n} - \dfrac{1}{n_{\text{tr}}}\right) G^{\text{tr}} + \left(\dfrac{1}{n} - \dfrac{1}{n_{\text{te}}}\right) G^{\text{te}} + \dfrac{n_{\text{te}}}{n} X^{\text{tr}} X^{\text{tr}\top} + \dfrac{n_{\text{tr}}}{n} X^{\text{te}} X^{\text{te}\top}$
     $- \dfrac{1}{n} X^{\text{tr}} \mathbf{1}_{n_{\text{tr}}} (X^{\text{te}} \mathbf{1}_{n_{\text{te}}})^\top - \dfrac{1}{n} X^{\text{te}} \mathbf{1}_{n_{\text{te}}} (X^{\text{tr}} \mathbf{1}_{n_{\text{tr}}})^\top$;
$\{\eta_l, \psi_l\}_{l=1}^m \longleftarrow$ generalized eigenvalues and eigenvectors of
     $S^{\text{lb}} \psi = \eta S^{\text{lw}} \psi;$ % $\eta_1 \ge \eta_2 \ge \cdots \ge \eta_d$
$\{\widetilde{\psi}_l\}_{l=1}^m \longleftarrow$ orthonormal basis of $\{\psi_l\}_{l=1}^m$;
     % $\operatorname{span}(\{\widetilde{\psi}_l\}_{l=1}^{m'}) = \operatorname{span}(\{\psi_l\}_{l=1}^{m'})$ for $m' = 1, 2, \ldots, m$
$T_{\text{LFDA}} \longleftarrow (\widetilde{\psi}_1 | \widetilde{\psi}_2 | \cdots | \widetilde{\psi}_m)^\top$;

Figure 5.2
Pseudo code of LFDA. $\mathbf{1}_n$ denotes the n-dimensional vectors with all ones, and $\operatorname{diag}(b)$ denotes the diagonal matrix with diagonal elements specified by a vector b.

Recalling that $(1/n - 1/n_+)$ and $(1/n - 1/n_-)$ included in the definition of W^{lb} are negative values, the definitions of S^{lb} and S^{lw} imply that LFDA seeks a transformation matrix T such that nearby data pairs in the same class are made close and the data pairs in different classes are made apart; far apart data pairs in the same class are not forced to be close.

By the localization effect brought by the introduction of the affinity matrix, LFDA can overcome the weakness of the original FDA against clustered data and outliers. When $A_{k,k'} = 1$ for all k, k' (i.e., no locality), S^{lw} and S^{lb} are reduced to S^{w} and S^{b}. Thus, LFDA can be regarded as a natural localized variant of FDA. The between-class scatter matrix S^b in the original FDA had only rank 1, whereas its local counterpart S^{lb} in LFDA usually has full rank with no multiplicity in eigenvalues (given $n \geq d$). Therefore, LFDA can be applied to dimensionality reduction into *any* dimensional spaces, which is a significant advantage over the original FDA.

A solution T_{LFDA} can be computed in the same way as the original FDA. Namely, the LFDA solution is given as

$$T_{\text{LFDA}} = (\psi_1 | \psi_2 | \cdots | \psi_m)^\top,$$

where $\{\psi_l\}_{l=1}^d$ are the generalized eigenvectors associated with the generalized eigenvalues $\eta_1 \geq \eta_2 \geq \cdots \geq \eta_d$ of the following generalized eigenvalue problem:

$$S^{lb} \psi = \eta S^{lw} \psi. \tag{5.4}$$

Since the LFDA solution can be computed in the same way as the original FDA solution, LFDA is computationally as efficient as the original FDA. A pseudo code of LFDA is summarized in figure 5.2.

A MATLAB® implementation of LFDA is available from http://sugiyama-www.cs.titech.ac.jp/~sugi/software/LFDA/.

5.4 Using LFDA for Finding Hetero-Distributional Subspace

Finally, we show how to obtain an estimate of the transformation matrix U needed in the density-ratio estimation procedure (see section 5.3) from the LFDA transformation matrix T_{LFDA}.

First, an orthonormal basis $\{\widetilde{\psi}_l\}_{l=1}^m$ of the LFDA subspace is computed from the generalized eigenvectors $\{\psi_l\}_{l=1}^m$ so that the span of $\{\widetilde{\psi}_l\}_{l=1}^{m'}$ agrees with the span of $\{\psi_l\}_{l=1}^{m'}$ for all m' ($1 \leq m' \leq m$). This can be carried out in a straightforward way, for instance, by the *Gram–Schmidt orthonormalization* (see, e.g., [5]). Then an estimate $\widehat{U}$ is given as

$$\widehat{U} := (\widetilde{\psi}_1 | \widetilde{\psi}_2 | \cdots | \widetilde{\psi}_m)^\top,$$

and the samples are transformed as

$$\widehat{u}_i^{\text{tr}} := \widehat{U} x_i^{\text{tr}} \text{ for } i = 1, 2, \ldots, n_{\text{tr}},$$
$$\widehat{u}_j^{\text{te}} := \widehat{U} x_j^{\text{te}} \text{ for } j = 1, 2, \ldots, n_{\text{te}}.$$

The above expression of $\widehat{U}$ implies another useful advantage of LFDA. In density-ratio estimation, one needs the LFDA solution for each reduced

5.6. Numerical Examples

dimensionality $m = 1, 2, \ldots, d$ (see section 5.5). However, we do not actually have to compute the LFDA solution for each m, but only to solve the generalized eigenvalue problem (equation 5.4) once for $m = d$ and compute the orthonormal basis $\{\widetilde{\boldsymbol{\psi}}_l\}_{l=1}^d$; the solution for $m < d$ can be obtained by simply taking the first m basis vectors $\{\widetilde{\boldsymbol{\psi}}_l\}_{l=1}^m$.

5.5 Density-Ratio Estimation in the Hetero-Distributional Subspace

Given that the hetero-distributional subspace has been successfully identified by the above procedure, the next step is to estimate the density ratio within the subspace. Since the direct importance estimator *unconstrained least-squares importance fitting* (uLSIF; [88]) explained in section 4.6 was shown to be accurate and computationally very efficient, it would be advantageous to combine LFDA with uLSIF.

So far, we have explained how the dimensionality reduction idea can be incorporated into density-ratio estimation, when the dimension m of the hetero-distributional subspace is known in advance. Here we address how the dimension m is estimated from samples, which results in a practical procedure.

For dimensionality selection, the CV score of the uLSIF algorithm can be utilized. In particular, uLSIF allows one to compute the leave-one-out CV (LOOCV) score analytically (see section 4.6.2):

$$\text{LOOCV} = \frac{1}{\min(n_{\text{tr}}, n_{\text{te}})} \sum_{i=1}^{\min(n_{\text{tr}}, n_{\text{te}})} \left[\frac{1}{2} (\widehat{w}_i(\widehat{\boldsymbol{u}}_i^{\text{tr}}))^2 - \widehat{w}_i(\widehat{\boldsymbol{u}}_i^{\text{te}}) \right],$$

where $\widehat{w}_i(\boldsymbol{u})$ is a density-ratio estimate obtained without $\widehat{\boldsymbol{u}}_i^{\text{tr}}$ and $\widehat{\boldsymbol{u}}_i^{\text{te}}$. Thus, the above LOOCV score is computed as a function of m, and the one that minimizes the LOOCV score is chosen.

The pseudo code of the entire algorithm is summarized in figure 5.3.

5.6 Numerical Examples

In this section, we illustrate how the D^3 algorithm behaves.

5.6.1 Illustrative Example

Let the input domain be $\mathbb{R}^2$ (i.e., $d = 2$), and the denominator and numerator densities be set to

$$p_{\text{tr}}(\boldsymbol{x}) = N\left(\boldsymbol{x}; \begin{bmatrix} 0 \\ 0 \end{bmatrix}, \begin{bmatrix} 4 & 0 \\ 0 & 1 \end{bmatrix}\right),$$

> **Input:** Two sets of samples $\{\boldsymbol{x}_i^{\mathrm{tr}}\}_{i=1}^{n_{\mathrm{tr}}}$ and $\{\boldsymbol{x}_j^{\mathrm{te}}\}_{j=1}^{n_{\mathrm{te}}}$ on $\mathbb{R}^d$
> **Output:** Density-ratio estimate $\widehat{w}(\boldsymbol{x})$
>
> Obtain orthonormal basis $\{\widetilde{\boldsymbol{\psi}}_l\}_{l=1}^d$ using LFDA
> with $\{\boldsymbol{x}_i^{\mathrm{tr}}\}_{i=1}^{n_{\mathrm{tr}}}$ and $\{\boldsymbol{x}_j^{\mathrm{te}}\}_{j=1}^{n_{\mathrm{te}}}$;
> **For** each reduced dimension $m = 1, 2, \ldots, d$
>   Form projection matrix: $\widehat{\boldsymbol{U}}_m = (\widetilde{\boldsymbol{\psi}}_1 | \widetilde{\boldsymbol{\psi}}_2 | \cdots | \widetilde{\boldsymbol{\psi}}_m)^\top$;
>   Project samples: $\{\widehat{\boldsymbol{u}}_{i,m}^{\mathrm{tr}} \mid \widehat{\boldsymbol{u}}_{i,m}^{\mathrm{tr}} = \widehat{\boldsymbol{U}}_m \boldsymbol{x}_i^{\mathrm{tr}}\}_{i=1}^{n_{\mathrm{tr}}}$ and
> $\{\widehat{\boldsymbol{u}}_{j,m}^{\mathrm{te}} \mid \widehat{\boldsymbol{u}}_{j,m}^{\mathrm{te}} = \widehat{\boldsymbol{U}}_m \boldsymbol{x}_j^{\mathrm{te}}\}_{j=1}^{n_{\mathrm{te}}}$;
>   **For** each candidate of Gaussian width σ
>   **For** each candidate of regularization parameter λ
>   Compute LOOCV score $\mathrm{LOOCV}(m, \sigma, \lambda)$ using
> $\{\widehat{\boldsymbol{u}}_{i,m}^{\mathrm{tr}}\}_{i=1}^{n_{\mathrm{tr}}}$ and $\{\widehat{\boldsymbol{u}}_{j,m}^{\mathrm{te}}\}_{j=1}^{n_{\mathrm{te}}}$;
>   **end**
>   **end**
> **end**
> Choose the best model: $(\widehat{m}, \widehat{\sigma}, \widehat{\lambda}) \leftarrow \mathrm{argmin}_{(m,\sigma,\lambda)} \mathrm{LOOCV}(m, \sigma, \lambda)$;
> Estimate density ratio from $\{\widehat{\boldsymbol{u}}_{i,\widehat{m}}^{\mathrm{tr}}\}_{i=1}^{n_{\mathrm{tr}}}$ and $\{\widehat{\boldsymbol{u}}_{j,\widehat{m}}^{\mathrm{te}}\}_{j=1}^{n_{\mathrm{te}}}$ using uLSIF
> with $(\widehat{\sigma}, \widehat{\lambda})$;

Figure 5.3
Pseudo code of direct density-ratio estimation with dimensionality reduction (D³).

$$p_{\mathrm{te}}(\boldsymbol{x}) = \frac{1}{2} N\left(\boldsymbol{x}; \begin{bmatrix} -3 \\ 0 \end{bmatrix}, \begin{bmatrix} 1 & 0 \\ 0 & 1 \end{bmatrix}\right) + \frac{1}{2} N\left(\boldsymbol{x}; \begin{bmatrix} 3 \\ 0 \end{bmatrix}, \begin{bmatrix} 1 & 0 \\ 0 & 1 \end{bmatrix}\right),$$

where $N(\boldsymbol{x}; \boldsymbol{\mu}, \boldsymbol{\Sigma})$ denotes the multivariate Gaussian density with mean $\boldsymbol{\mu}$ and covariance matrix $\boldsymbol{\Sigma}$. The profiles of the above densities and their ratios are illustrated in figures 5.4 and 5.7a, respectively. We sample $n_{\mathrm{tr}} = 100$ points from $p_{\mathrm{tr}}(\boldsymbol{x})$ and $n_{\mathrm{te}} = 100$ points from $p_{\mathrm{te}}(\boldsymbol{x})$; the samples are illustrated in figure 5.5. In this data set, the distributions are different only in the one-dimensional subspace spanned by $(1, 0)^\top$, that is, the true dimensionality of the hetero-distributional subspace is $m = 1$. The true hetero-distributional subspace is depicted by the solid line in figure 5.5.

The dotted line in figure 5.5 depicts the hetero-distributional subspace estimated by LFDA with reduced dimensionality 1; when the reduced dimensionality is 2, LFDA gives the entire space. This shows that for reduced dimensionality 1, LFDA gives a very good estimate of the true hetero-distributional subspace.

Next, we choose reduced dimensionality m as well as the Gaussian width σ and the regularization parameter λ in uLSIF. Figure 5.6 depicts the LOOCV

5.6. Numerical Examples

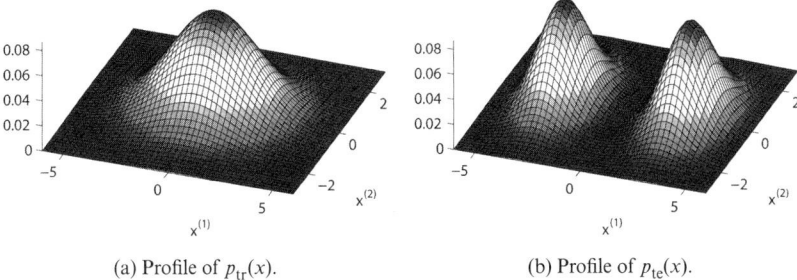

(a) Profile of $p_{\mathrm{tr}}(x)$. (b) Profile of $p_{\mathrm{te}}(x)$.

Figure 5.4
Two-dimensional toy data set.

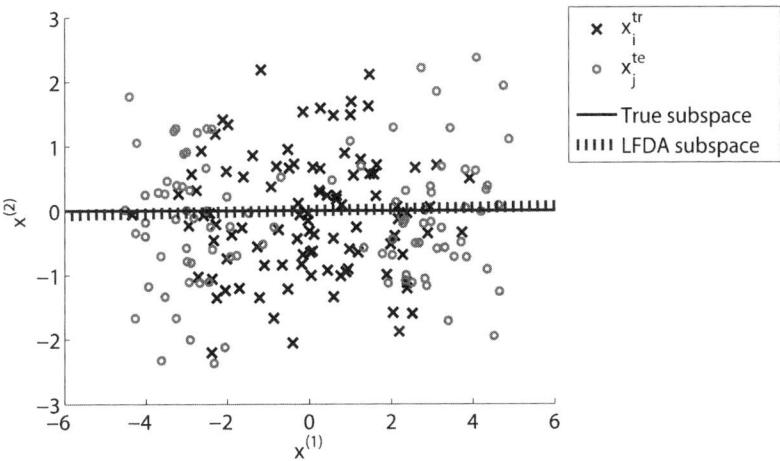

Figure 5.5
Samples and the hetero-distributional subspace of two-dimensional toy data set. The LFDA estimate of the hetero-distributional subspace is spanned by $(1.00, 0.01)^\top$, which is very close to the true hetero-distributional subspace spanned by $(1, 0)^\top$.

score of uLSIF, showing that

$$(\widehat{m}, \widehat{\sigma}, \widehat{\lambda}) = (1, 1, 10^{-0.5})$$

is the minimizer.

Finally, the density ratio is estimated by uLSIF. Figure 5.7 depicts the true density ratio, its estimate by uLSIF without dimensionality reduction, and its estimate by uLSIF with dimensionality reduction by LFDA. For uLSIF without

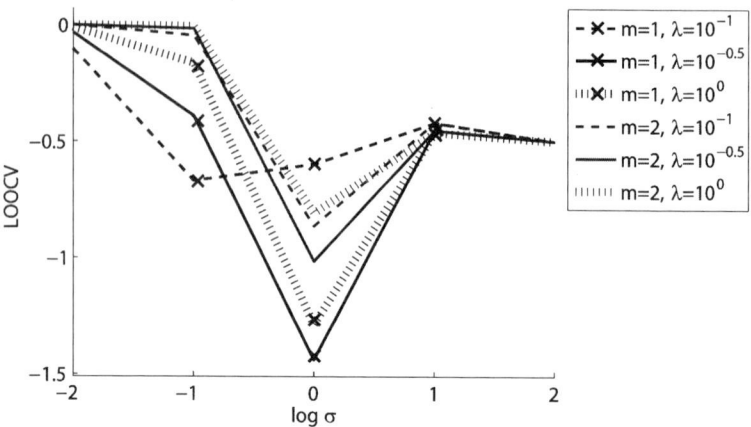

Figure 5.6
LOOCV score of uLSIF for two-dimensional toy data set.

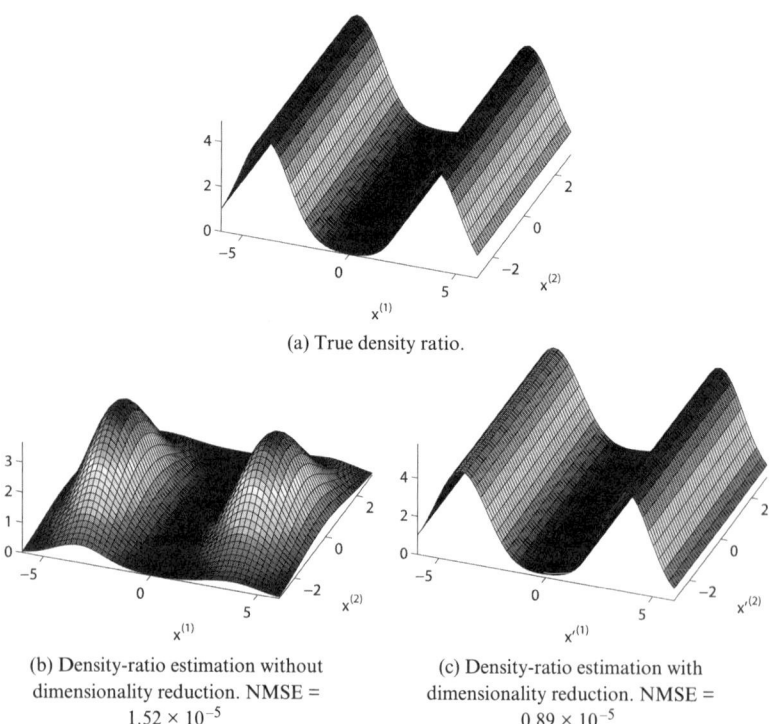

Figure 5.7
True and estimated density ratio functions. $x'^{(1)}$ and $x'^{(2)}$ in (c) denote the LFDA solution, that is, $x'^{(1)} = 1.00x^{(1)} + 0.01x^{(2)}$ and $x'^{(2)} = -0.01x^{(1)} + 1.00x^{(2)}$, respectively.

5.6. Numerical Examples

dimensionality reduction,

$$(\widehat{\sigma}, \widehat{\lambda}) = (1, 10^{-0.5})$$

is chosen by LOOCV (see figure 5.6 with $m = 2$). This shows that when dimensionality reduction is not performed, independence between the density ratio $w(x)$ and the second input element $x^{(2)}$ (figure 5.7a) is not incorporated, and the estimated density ratio has Gaussian-tail structure along $x^{(2)}$ (figure 5.7b). On the other hand, when dimensionality reduction is carried out, independence between the density ratio function $w(x)$ and the second input element $x^{(2)}$ can be successfully captured, and consequently a more accurate estimator is obtained (figure 5.7c).

The accuracy of an estimated density ratio is measured by the *normalized mean-squared error* (NMSE):

$$\text{NMSE} := \sum_{i=1}^{n_{tr}} \left(\frac{\widehat{w}(x_i^{tr})}{\sum_{i'=1}^{n_{tr}} \widehat{w}(x_{i'}^{tr})} - \frac{w(x_i^{tr})}{\sum_{i'=1}^{n_{tr}} w(x_{i'}^{tr})} \right)^2. \tag{5.5}$$

By dimensionality reduction, NMSE is reduced from 1.52×10^{-5} to 0.89×10^{-5}. Thus, we gain a 41.5 percent reduction in NMSE.

5.6.2 Performance Comparison Using Artificial Data Sets

Here, we investigate the performance of the D^3 algorithm using six artificial data sets. The input domain of the data sets is d-dimensional ($d \geq 2$), and the true dimensionality of the hetero-distributional subspace is $m = 1$ or 2. The homo-distributional component of the data sets is the $(d - m)$-dimensional Gaussian distribution with mean zero and covariance identity. The hetero-distributional component of each data set is given as follows:

(a) Data set 1 (shifting, $m = 1$):

$$u^{tr} \sim N\left(\begin{bmatrix} 0 \\ 0 \end{bmatrix}, \begin{bmatrix} 1 & 0 \\ 0 & 1 \end{bmatrix}\right),$$

$$u^{te} \sim N\left(\begin{bmatrix} 3 \\ 0 \end{bmatrix}, \begin{bmatrix} 1 & 0 \\ 0 & 1 \end{bmatrix}\right).$$

(b) Data set 2 (shrinking, $m = 2$):

$$u^{tr} \sim N\left(\begin{bmatrix} 0 \\ 0 \end{bmatrix}, \begin{bmatrix} 4 & 0 \\ 0 & 4 \end{bmatrix}\right),$$

$$u^{te} \sim N\left(\begin{bmatrix} 0 \\ 0 \end{bmatrix}, \begin{bmatrix} 1/4 & 0 \\ 0 & 1/4 \end{bmatrix}\right).$$

(c) Data set 3 (magnifying, $m=2$):

$$u^{\text{tr}} \sim N\left(\begin{bmatrix}0\\0\end{bmatrix}, \begin{bmatrix}1/4 & 0\\0 & 1/4\end{bmatrix}\right),$$

$$u^{\text{te}} \sim N\left(\begin{bmatrix}0\\0\end{bmatrix}, \begin{bmatrix}4 & 0\\0 & 4\end{bmatrix}\right).$$

(d) Data set 4 (rotating, $m=2$):

$$u^{\text{tr}} \sim N\left(\begin{bmatrix}1\\0\end{bmatrix}, \begin{bmatrix}4 & 0\\0 & 1\end{bmatrix}\right),$$

$$u^{\text{te}} \sim N\left(\begin{bmatrix}1/\sqrt{2}\\1/\sqrt{2}\end{bmatrix}, \begin{bmatrix}5/2 & 3/2\\3/2 & 5/2\end{bmatrix}\right).$$

(e) Data set 5 (one-dimensional splitting, $m=1$):

$$u^{\text{tr}} \sim N\left(\begin{bmatrix}0\\0\end{bmatrix}, \begin{bmatrix}1 & 0\\0 & 1\end{bmatrix}\right),$$

$$u^{\text{te}} \sim \frac{1}{2}N\left(\begin{bmatrix}2\\0\end{bmatrix}, \begin{bmatrix}1/4 & 0\\0 & 1/4\end{bmatrix}\right) + \frac{1}{2}N\left(\begin{bmatrix}2\\0\end{bmatrix}, \begin{bmatrix}1/4 & 0\\0 & 1/4\end{bmatrix}\right).$$

(f) Data set 6 (two-dimensional splitting, $m=2$):

$$u^{\text{tr}} \sim N\left(\begin{bmatrix}0\\0\end{bmatrix}, \begin{bmatrix}1 & 0\\0 & 1\end{bmatrix}\right),$$

$$u^{\text{te}} \sim \frac{1}{4}N\left(\begin{bmatrix}2\\0\end{bmatrix}, \begin{bmatrix}1/4 & 0\\0 & 1/4\end{bmatrix}\right) + \frac{1}{4}N\left(\begin{bmatrix}-2\\0\end{bmatrix}, \begin{bmatrix}1/4 & 0\\0 & 1/4\end{bmatrix}\right)$$
$$+ \frac{1}{4}N\left(\begin{bmatrix}0\\2\end{bmatrix}, \begin{bmatrix}1/4 & 0\\0 & 1/4\end{bmatrix}\right) + \frac{1}{4}N\left(\begin{bmatrix}0\\-2\end{bmatrix}, \begin{bmatrix}1/4 & 0\\0 & 1/4\end{bmatrix}\right).$$

The number of samples is set to $n_{\text{tr}}=200$ and $n_{\text{te}}=1000$ for all the data sets. Examples of realized samples are illustrated in figure 5.8. For each dimensionality $d=2,3,\ldots,10$, the density ratio is estimated using uLSIF with/without dimensionality reduction. This experiment is repeated 100 times for each d with different random seed.

Figure 5.9 depicts choice of the dimensionality of the hetero-distributional subspace by LOOCV for each d. This shows that for data sets 1, 2, 4, and

5.6. Numerical Examples

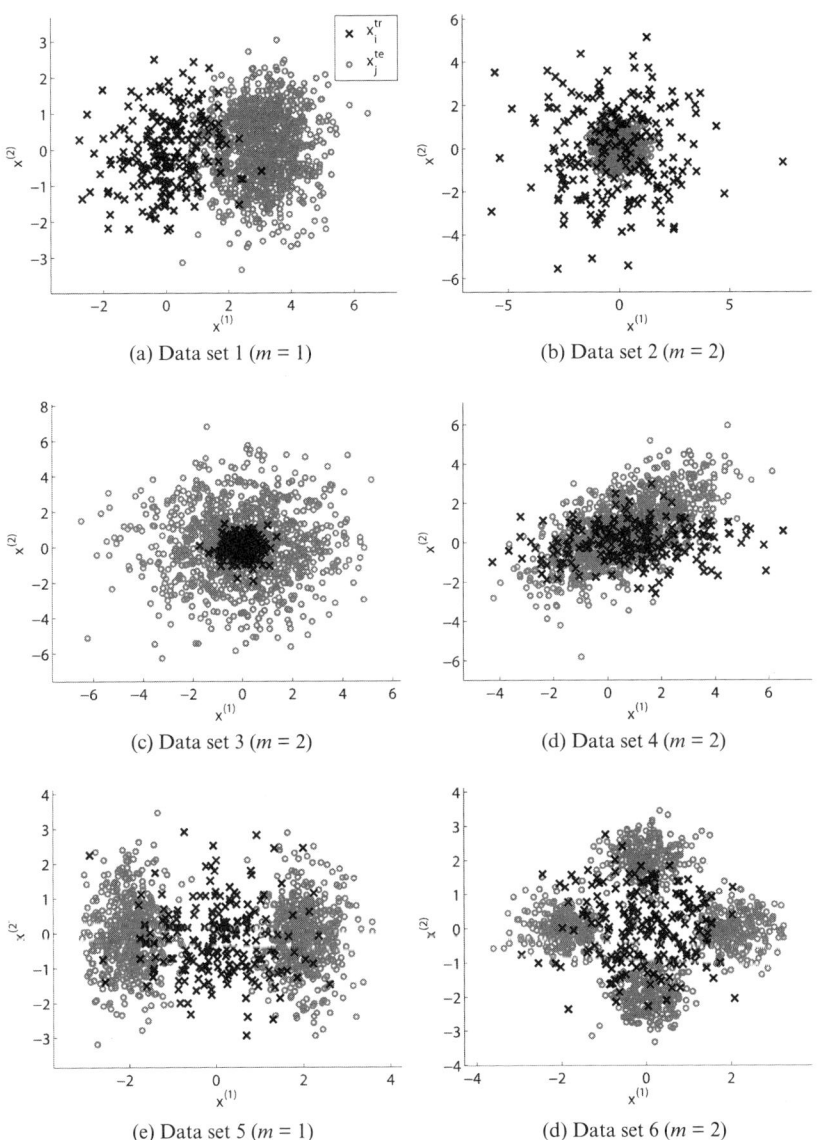

Figure 5.8
Artificial data sets.

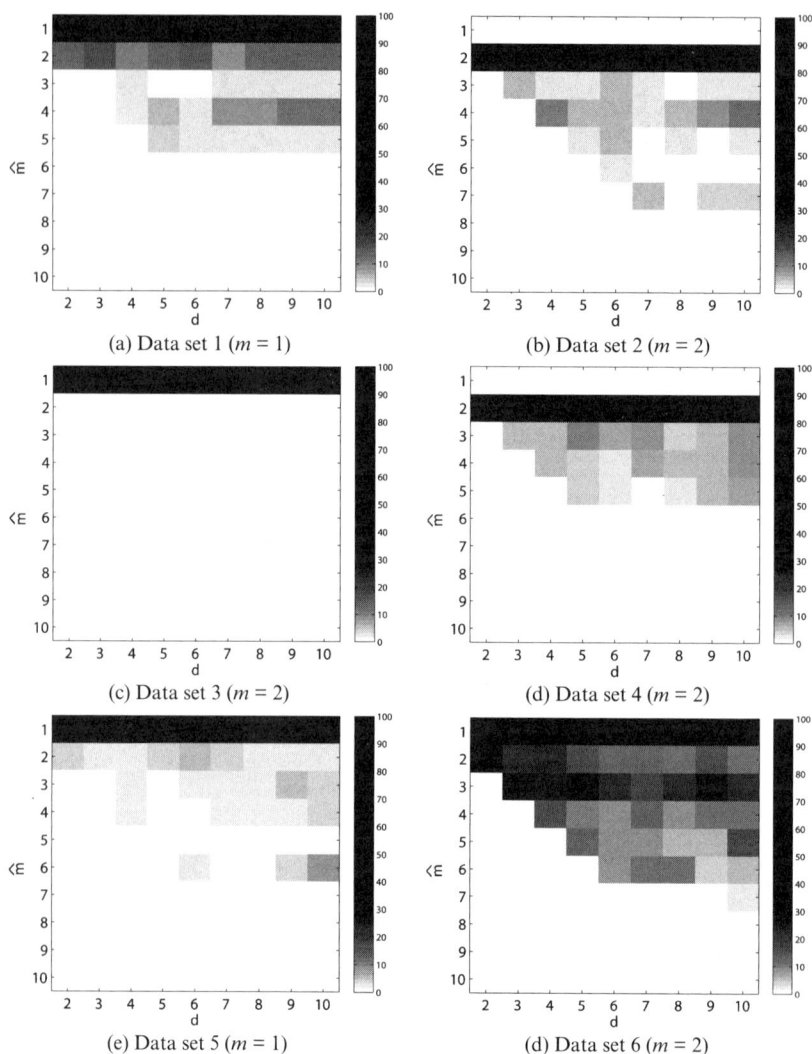

Figure 5.9
Dimension choice of the hetero-distributional subspace by LOOCV over 100 runs.

5, dimensionality choice by LOOCV works well. For data set 3, $\widehat{m} = 1$ is always chosen although the true dimensionality is $m = 2$. For data set 6, dimensionality choice is rather unstable, but it still works reasonably well.

Figure 5.10 depicts the value of NMSE (see equation 5.5) averaged over 100 trials. For each d, the t-test (see, e.g., [78]) at the significance level 5 percent is performed, and the best method as well as the comparable method in terms of mean NMSE are indicated by ×. (In other words, the method without the symbol × is significantly worse than the other method.) This shows that mean NMSE of the baseline method (no dimensionality reduction) tends to grow rapidly as the dimensionality d increases. On the other hand, increase of mean NMSE of the D^3 algorithm is much smaller than that of the baseline method. Consequently, mean NMSE of D^3 is much smaller than that of the baseline method when the input dimensionality d is large. The difference of mean NMSE is statistically significant for the data sets 1, 2, 5, and 6.

The above experiments show that the dimensionality reduction scheme is useful in high-dimensional density-ratio estimation.

5.7 Summary

The direct importance estimators explained in chapter 4 tend to perform better than naively taking the ratio of density estimators. However, in high-dimensional problems, there is still room for further improvement in terms of estimation accuracy. In this chapter, we have explained how *dimensionality reduction* can be incorporated into direct importance estimation. The basic idea was to perform importance estimation only in a subspace where two densities are significantly different. We called this framework *direct density-ratio estimation with dimensionality reduction* (D^3).

Finding such a subspace, which we called the *hetero-distributional subspace*, is a key challenge in this context. We explained that the hetero-distributional subspace can be identified by finding a subspace in which training and test samples are maximally separated. We showed that the accuracy of the *unconstrained least-squares importance fitting* (uLSIF; [88]) algorithm can be improved by combining uLSIF with a supervised dimensionality reduction method called *local Fisher discriminant analysis* (LFDA; [154]).

We chose LFDA because it was shown to be superior in terms of both accuracy and computational efficiency. On the other hand, supervised dimensionality reduction is one of the most active research topics, and better methods will be developed in the future. The framework of D^3 allows one to use *any* supervised dimensionality reduction method for importance estimation. Thus, if better methods of supervised dimensionality reduction are developed in the

5 Direct Density-Ratio Estimation with Dimensionality Reduction

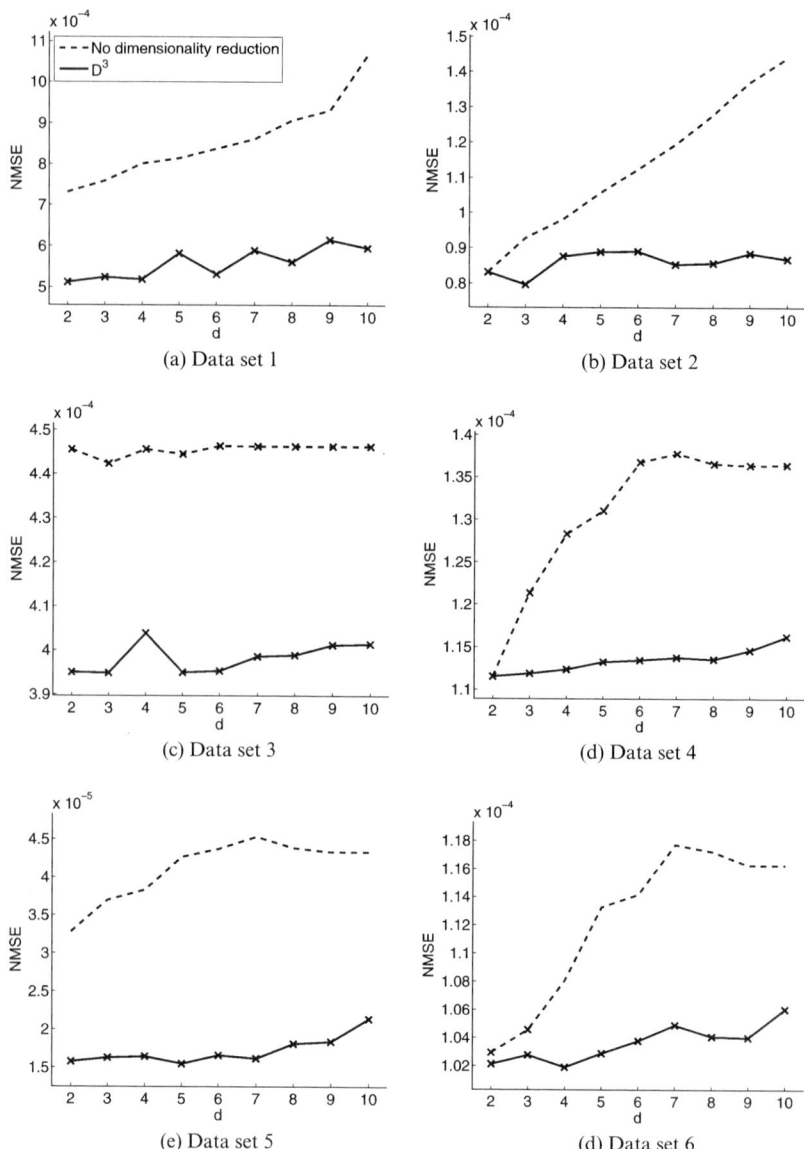

Figure 5.10
Mean NMSE of the estimated density-ratio functions over 100 runs. For each d, the t-test at the significance level 5 percent is performed and the best method as well as the comparable method in terms of mean NMSE, are indicated by $\times$.

5.7. Summary

future, the new dimensionality reduction methods can be incorporated into the direct importance estimation framework.

The D^3 formulation explained in this chapter assumes that the components inside and outside the hetero-distributional subspace are statistically independent. A possible generalization of this framework is to weaken this condition, for example, by following the line of [173].

We focused on a linear hetero-distributional subspace. Another possible generalization of D^3 would be to consider a nonlinear hetero-distributional manifold. Using a kernelized version of LFDA [154] is one possibility. Another possibility is to use a *mixture of probabilistic principal component analyzers* in importance estimation [205].

6 Relation to Sample Selection Bias

One of the most famous works on learning under changing environment is Heckman's method for coping with *sample selection bias* [76, 77]. Sample selection bias has been proposed and extensively studied in econometrics and sociology, and Heckman received the Nobel Prize for economics in 2000.

Sample selection bias indicates the situation where the training data set consists of nonrandomly selected (i.e., biased) samples. Data samples collected through Internet surveys typically suffer from sample selection bias—samples corresponding to those who do not have access to the Internet are completely missing. Since the number of conservative people, such as the elderly, is less than reality in the Internet surveys, rather progressive conclusions tend to be drawn.

Heckman introduced a sample selection model in his seminal papers [76, 77], which characterized the selection bias based on parametric assumptions. Then he proposed a two-step procedure for correcting sample selection bias. In this chapter, we briefly explain Heckman's model and his two-step procedure, and discuss its relation to the covariate shift approach.

6.1 Heckman's Sample Selection Model

In order to deal with sample selection bias, Heckman considered a linear regression model specifying the selection process, in addition to the regression model that characterizes the target behavioral relationship for the entire population. The sign of the latent response variable of this regression model determines whether each sample is observed or not. The key assumption in this model is that error terms of the two regression models are correlated to one another, causing nonrandom sample selection (see figure 6.1).

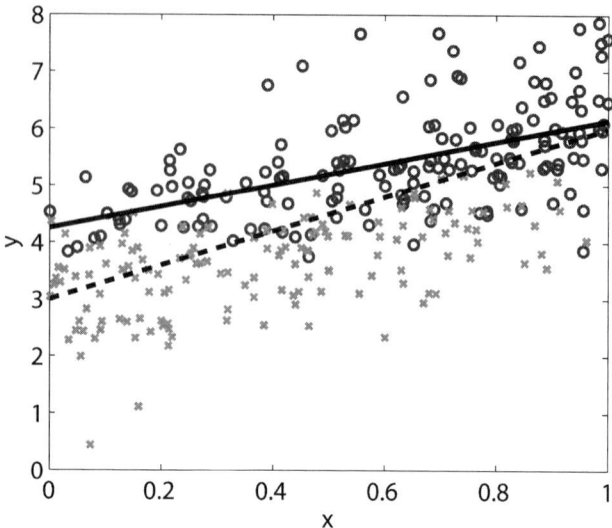

Figure 6.1
A numerical example of sample selection bias. This data set was generated according to Heckman's model. The circles denote observed samples, and the crosses are missing samples. Because of large positive correlation between the error terms ($\rho = 0.9$), we can see that only the samples with higher responses y are observed when the covariate x is small. Thus, the OLS estimator (solid line) computed from the observed samples is significantly biased from the true populational regressor (dotted line).

Let Y_1^* be the target quantity on which we want to make inference. Heckman assumed a linear regression model

$$Y_1^* = x^\top \beta + U_1, \tag{6.1}$$

where x is a covariate and U_1 is an error term. However, Y_1^* is not always observed. Samples are selected depending on another random variable Y_2^*; the variable Y_1^* is observable only if $Y_2^* > 0$. Let Y be the observed response variable, that is,

$$Y = \begin{cases} Y_1^* & \text{if } Y_2^* > 0, \\ \text{missing value} & \text{if } Y_2^* \leq 0. \end{cases} \tag{6.2}$$

The variable Y_2^* obeys another linear regression model,

$$Y_2^* = z^\top \gamma + U_2, \tag{6.3}$$

6.1. Heckman's Sample Selection Model

where z is a covariate and U_2 is an error term. Note that the covariates x in equation 6.1 and z in equation 6.3 can contain common components.

In Heckman's papers [76, 77], the error terms U_1 and U_2 are assumed to be jointly bivariate-normally distributed with mean zero and covariance matrix Σ, conditioned on x and z. Since only the sign of the latent variable Y_2^* matters later, we can fix the variance of U_2 at 1 without loss of generality. We denote the variance of U_1 and the covariance between U_1 and U_2 by σ^2 and ρ, respectively:

$$\Sigma = \mathrm{Var}\left(\begin{bmatrix} U_1 \\ U_2 \end{bmatrix}\right) = \begin{bmatrix} \sigma^2 & \rho\sigma \\ \rho\sigma & 1 \end{bmatrix}.$$

If there is no correlation between U_1 and U_2 ($\rho = 0$), the selection process (equation 6.3) is independent of the regression model (equation 6.1) of interest. This situation is called *missing at random* (see [104]). On the other hand, if the error terms are correlated ($\rho \neq 0$), the selection process makes the distribution of Y different from that of Y_1^*. For example, the expectation of the observation Y has some bias from that of Y_1^* (i.e., $x^\top \beta$).

Figure 6.2 illustrates the sample selection bias for different selection probabilities when the correlation ρ is nonzero. If the mean of Y_2^*, $z^\top \gamma$, is large in the positive direction, most of the samples are observed and the selection bias

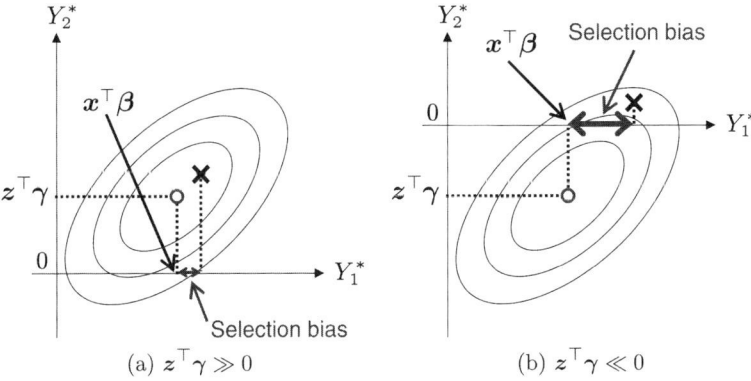

Figure 6.2
Sample selection biases for different selection probabilities in Heckman's model (when the correlation ρ is nonzero). The symbol ∘ denotes the mean of Y_1^* for all samples, while the symbol × denotes the mean of Y_1^* only for $Y_2^* > 0$. (a) If $z^\top \gamma$ is large in the positive direction, most of the samples are observed and the selection bias is small. (b) If $z^\top \gamma$ is large in the negative direction, only a small portion of samples can be observed and the sample selection bias becomes large.

is small (see figure 6.2a). On the other hand, if $z^\top \gamma$ is large in the negative direction, only a small portion of samples can be observed and the sample selection bias becomes large (see figure 6.2b).

As illustrated in figure 6.3, the bias becomes positive in positively correlated cases ($\rho > 0$) and negative in negatively correlated cases ($\rho < 0$). Indeed, the conditional expectation of the observation Y, given x, can be expressed as

$$\mathbb{E}[Y|x, z] = \mathbb{E}[Y_1^*|x, z, Y_2^* > 0]$$
$$= x^\top \beta + \mathbb{E}[U_1|U_2 > -z^\top \gamma], \qquad (6.4)$$

where the second term is the selection bias from the conditional expectation $\mathbb{E}[Y_1^*|x] = x^\top \beta$ of the latent variable Y_2^*. Heckman calculated the second term in equation 6.4 explicitly, as explained below.

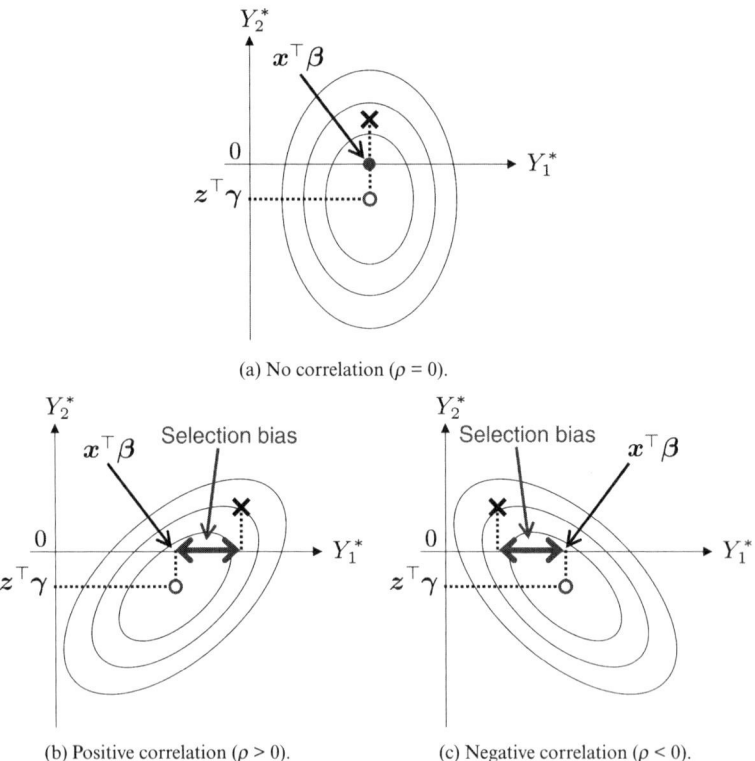

Figure 6.3
Sample selection bias corresponding to no, positive, and negative correlation ρ. When $\rho \neq 0$, the conditional mean of the observed area ($Y_2^* \geq 0$) differs from the unconditional average $x^\top \beta$. In Heckman's model, this gap (which is the sample selection bias) can be calculated explicitly.

6.2 Distributional Change and Sample Selection Bias

As defined in equation 6.1, the conditional density of the latent variable Y_1^*, given x, is Gaussian:

$$p^*(y|x; \boldsymbol{\beta}, \sigma) = \frac{1}{\sigma} \phi\left(\frac{y - x^\top \boldsymbol{\beta}}{\sigma}\right), \tag{6.5}$$

where ϕ denotes the density function of the standard Gaussian distribution $N(0, 1)$. Thanks to the Gaussian assumption of the error terms U_1 and U_2, we can also characterize the conditional distribution of the observation Y explicitly.

Let D be an indicator variable taking the value 1 if Y is observed, and 0 if not, that is,

$$D = I(Y_2^* > 0),$$

where $I(\cdot)$ is the indicator function. The assumption is that in the selection process (equation 6.3), we cannot observe the value of Y_2^*; we can observe only D (i.e., the sign of Y_2^*). The conditional probability of $D = 1$ can be expressed as

$$\begin{aligned} P(D=1|x, z; \boldsymbol{\gamma}) &= P(Y_2^* > 0|x, z; \boldsymbol{\gamma}) \\ &= \Phi(z^\top \boldsymbol{\gamma}), \end{aligned} \tag{6.6}$$

where Φ is the cumulative distribution function of the standard Gaussian (i.e., the *error function*). This binary-response distribution is called the *probit model* in statistics.

By the definition of the indicator D and the selection process (equation 6.3), the conditional distribution of the observation y given $D = 1$, x, and z is rewritten as

$$\begin{aligned} P_o(y|x, z) &= P(Y \leq y | D=1, x, z) \\ &= \frac{P(Y \leq y, \ D=1|x, z)}{P(D=1|x, z)} \\ &= \frac{P(Y_1^* \leq y, \ Y_2^* > 0|x, z)}{P(D=1|x, z)}. \end{aligned} \tag{6.7}$$

From equation 6.6, the denominator of equation 6.7 is expressed by the error function Φ.

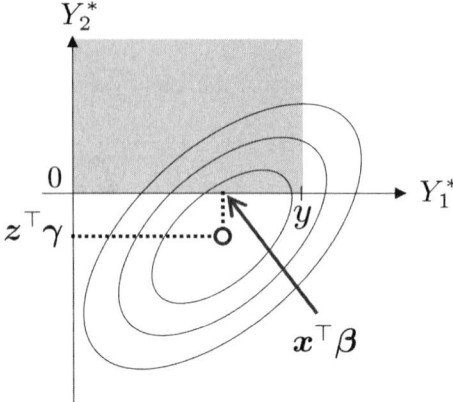

Figure 6.4
In order to compute the distribution function of the observable Y in equation 6.7, the shaded area of the bivariate Gaussian distribution should be integrated.

In order to calculate the numerator of equation 6.7, we need to integrate the correlated Gaussian distribution over the region illustrated in figure 6.4 for each fixed y. To this end, the error term U_1 is decomposed into two terms:

$$U_1 = \sigma\sqrt{1-\rho^2}\,\tilde{U}_1 + \rho\sigma U_2,$$

where $\tilde{U}_1$ is independent of U_2. Although the resulting formula still contains a single integral, by taking the partial derivative with respect to y, the conditional density p_o can be expressed using the density ϕ of the Gaussian and the error function Φ as shown below.

$$\begin{aligned} p_o(y|x,z;\boldsymbol{\beta},\boldsymbol{\gamma},\rho,\sigma) &= \frac{\partial}{\partial y}P_o(y|x,z) \\ &= \frac{1}{\sigma\Phi(z^\top\boldsymbol{\gamma})}\phi\left(\frac{y-x^\top\boldsymbol{\beta}}{\sigma}\right)\Phi\left(\frac{\rho(y-x^\top\boldsymbol{\beta})/\sigma + z^\top\boldsymbol{\gamma}}{\sqrt{(1-\rho^2)}}\right). \end{aligned} \qquad (6.8)$$

Note that if the selection process (equation 6.3) is independent of Y_1^* ($\rho = 0$), this conditional density results in that of Y_1^* (see equation 6.5). The detailed derivation can be found in [19].

Figure 6.5 shows the conditional density function (equation 6.8) for different sample selection thresholds when $\rho = 0.5$ and $\rho = -0.5$. Here, we took the standard Gaussian $N(0,1)$ for the distribution of Y_1^*, that is, the other parameters are set to $x^\top\boldsymbol{\beta} = 0$ and $\sigma = 1$. The smaller the mean $z^\top\boldsymbol{\gamma}$ of Y_2^* is, the larger the shift is from the unconditional distribution. In other words, we suffer

6.3. The Two-Step Algorithm

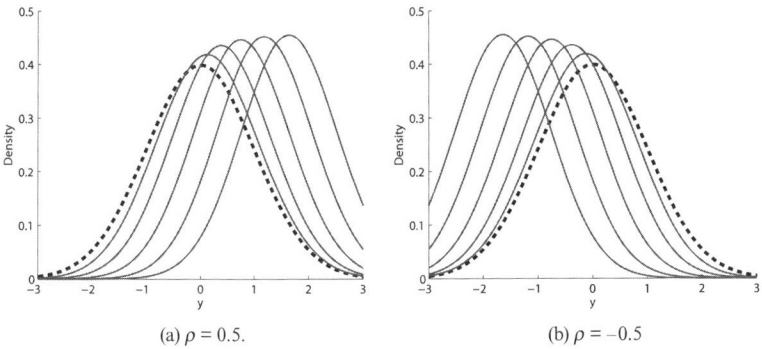

(a) $\rho = 0.5$. (b) $\rho = -0.5$

Figure 6.5
Conditional density functions for $\rho = 0.5$ and $\rho = -0.5$ ($x^\top \beta = 0$ and $\sigma = 1$), denoted by the solid lines. The selection thresholds are set to $z^\top \gamma = -3, -2, -1, 0, 1$ from closest to farthest. The dashed line denotes the Gaussian density when $\rho = 0$.

from larger selection bias when the threshold is relatively higher, and therefore a small portion of the entire population is observed (see figure 6.2).

The conditional expectation and variance of Y can be calculated from the moment generating function. As in the previous calculation, the resulting formula contains a single integral, but its derivative at the origin can be written explicitly with the Gaussian density ϕ and the error function Φ as follows.

$$\mathbb{E}[Y|D=1, x, z] = x^\top \beta + \rho\sigma \frac{\phi(z^\top \gamma)}{\Phi(z^\top \gamma)},$$

$$\mathrm{Var}[Y|D=1, x, z] = \sigma^2 - \rho^2\sigma^2 \left(z^\top \gamma + \frac{\phi(z^\top \gamma)}{\Phi(z^\top \gamma)} \right) \frac{\phi(z^\top \gamma)}{\Phi(z^\top \gamma)}. \quad (6.9)$$

The function $\lambda(t) = \phi(t)/\Phi(-t)$ is often called the *inverse Mills ratio*, and is also known as the *hazard ratio* in survival data analysis. As plotted in figure 6.6, it is a monotonically increasing function of t, and can be approximated by a linear function for a wide range of its argument.

6.3 The Two-Step Algorithm

Based on the theoretical development in the previous section, Heckman [76,77] treated sample selection bias as an ordinary model specification error or "omitted variable" bias. More specifically, he reformulated the linear regression

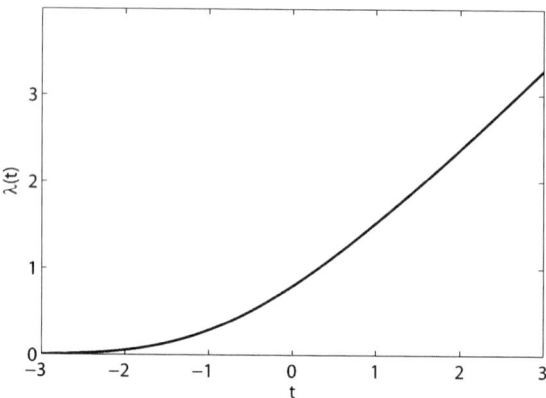

Figure 6.6
Hazard ratio.

model (equation 6.1) as

$$Y = \mathbb{E}[Y|D=1, x, z] + V \qquad (6.10)$$
$$= x^\top \beta + \rho\sigma\lambda(-z^\top \gamma) + V,$$

where V has mean 0 conditioned on being observable, that is,

$$\mathbb{E}[V|D=1, x, z] = 0.$$

If the hazard ratio term were available or, equivalently, the parameter γ of the selection process (equation 6.3) were known, it would become just a linear regression problem with the extended covariates $[x, \lambda(-z^\top \gamma)]$, and then ordinary least squares (OLS) would give a consistent estimator of the regression parameters β and $\rho\sigma$. However, we need to estimate the parameter γ from the data as well.

In [77], Heckman considers a situation where the covariate z in the selection process can be observed in any case, that is, regardless of whether Y_1^* is observed or not. Then, it is possible to estimate the regression parameter γ from the input–output pairs of (z, D) by *probit analysis* [114], which is the first step of Heckman's algorithm. More specifically, the regression parameter γ is determined as

$$\widehat{\gamma} := \underset{\gamma}{\operatorname{argmax}} \left[\sum_{i=1}^{n_0} \log \Phi(z_i^\top \gamma) + \sum_{i=n_0+1}^{n} \log\{1 - \Phi(z_i^\top \gamma)\} \right]. \qquad (6.11)$$

6.3. The Two-Step Algorithm

Input: observed samples $\{x_i, z_i, y_i\}_{i=1}^{n_o}$ and missing samples $\{z_i\}_{i=n_o+1}^{n}$

Output: parameter estimates $(\widehat{\beta}, \widehat{\gamma}, \widehat{\sigma}, \widehat{\rho})$

1. Fit the selection model (i.e., estimate γ) by probit analysis (equation 6.11) from all input-output pairs $\{z_i, 1\}_{i=1}^{n_o}$ and $\{z_i, 0\}_{i=n_o+1}^{n}$.

2. Calculate the estimates of the hazard ratio by plugging in $\widehat{\gamma}$ for the observed samples:
$$\widehat{\lambda}_i = \lambda(-z_i^\top \widehat{\gamma}) = \frac{\phi(z_i^\top \widehat{\gamma})}{\Phi(z_i^\top \widehat{\gamma})}, \quad i = 1, \ldots, n_o.$$

3. Estimate the parameters β and $\rho\sigma$ in the modified linear regression model (equation 6.10) by the ordinary least squares (OLS) based on the extended covariates $\{x_i, \widehat{\lambda}_i\}_{i=1}^{n_o}$ and the observed responses $\{y_i\}_{i=1}^{n_o}$. The estimators $\widehat{\beta}$ and $\widehat{\rho\sigma}$ are consistent estimators of β and $\rho\sigma$, respectively.

4. Estimate the parameters $\widehat{\sigma}^2$ and $\widehat{\rho}$ from the residuals
$$\{\widehat{v}_i = y_i - x_i^\top \widehat{\beta} - \widehat{\rho\sigma}\widehat{\lambda}_i\}_{i=1}^{n_o},$$
as follows (See the conditional variance, equation 6.9:
$$\widehat{\sigma}^2 = \frac{1}{n_o}\sum_{i=1}^{n_o} \widehat{v}_i^2 + \frac{\widehat{\rho\sigma}^2}{n_o}\sum_{i=1}^{n_o}(z_i^\top \widehat{\gamma}\widehat{\lambda}_i + \widehat{\lambda}_i^2),$$
$$\widehat{\rho} = \frac{\widehat{\rho\sigma}}{\widehat{\sigma}}.$$

Figure 6.7
Pseudo code of Heckman's two-step algorithm. Step 4 is not necessary if we are interested only in prediction.

Since the probit estimator $\widehat{\gamma}$ is consistent, the plug-in hazard ratio $\lambda(-z^\top \widehat{\gamma})$ can be used as the extra covariate in the second OLS step. This is the core idea of Heckman's two-step algorithm. A pseudo code of Heckman's two-step procedure is summarized in figure 6.7.

Heckman considered his estimator to be useful for providing good initial values for more efficient methods or for exploratory analysis. Nevertheless, it has become a standard way to obtain final results for the sample selection model. However, there are several criticisms of Heckman's two-step algorithm [126], such as statistical inefficiency, collinearity, and the restrictive Gaussian-noise assumption.

At first, Heckman's estimator is statistically less efficient. Because the modified regression problem (equation 6.11) has the heterogeneous variance as in equation 6.9, the *general least squares* (GLS) [41] may be used as an alternative to OLS, which minimizes the squared error weighted according to the inverse of the noise variance at each sample point. However, GLS is not an efficient estimator—an efficient estimator can be obtained by the *maximum likelihood estimator* (MLE), which maximizes the following log-likelihood function:

$$\log \mathcal{L}(\boldsymbol{\beta}, \boldsymbol{\gamma}, \rho, \sigma) = \sum_{i=1}^{n_o} \log p_o(y_i|\boldsymbol{x}_i, \boldsymbol{z}_i; \boldsymbol{\beta}, \boldsymbol{\gamma}, \rho, \sigma) + \sum_{i=1}^{n_o} \log \Phi(\boldsymbol{z}_i^\top \boldsymbol{\gamma})$$
$$+ \sum_{i=n_o+1}^{n} \log \left\{ 1 - \Phi(\boldsymbol{z}_i^\top \boldsymbol{\gamma}) \right\},$$

where we assume that we are given n_o input–output pairs $\{\boldsymbol{x}_i, \boldsymbol{z}_i, y_i\}_{i=1}^{n_o}$ for observed samples and $(n - n_o)$ input-only samples (i.e., covariates) $\{\boldsymbol{z}_i\}_{i=n_o+1}^{n}$ for missing samples. For computing the MLE solution, gradient ascent or quasi-Newton iterations are usually employed, and Heckman's two-step estimator can be used as an initial value since it is computationally very efficient and widely available in standard software toolboxes.

The second criticism is that collinearity problems (two variables are highly correlated to one another) can occur rather frequently. For example, if all the covariates in z are included in x, the extra covariate $\lambda(-\boldsymbol{z}^\top \widehat{\boldsymbol{\gamma}})$ in the second step can be collinear with the other covariates in x, because the hazard ratio $\lambda(t)$ is an approximately linear function over a wide range of its argument. In other words, in order to let Heckman's algorithm work in practice, we need variables in z which are good predictors of Y_2^* and do not appear in x. Unfortunately, it is often very difficult to find such variables in practice.

Finally, Heckman's procedure relies heavily on the Gaussian assumptions for the error terms in equations 6.1 and 6.3. Instead, some authors have proposed semiparametric or nonparametric procedures with milder distributional assumptions. See [119, 126] for details.

6.4 Relation to Covariate Shift Approach

In this section, we discuss similarities and differences between Heckman's approach and the covariate shift approach. For ease of comparison, we consider the case where the covariates z and x in the sample selection model coincide. Note that the distribution of the entire population in Heckman's formulation

6.4. Relation to Covariate Shift Approach

corresponds to the test distribution in the covariate shift formulation, and that of observed samples corresponds to the training distribution:

Covariate shift		Heckman's model
$p_{te}(x, y)$	$\iff$	$p(x, y)$
$p_{tr}(x, y)$	$\iff$	$p(x, y \mid D = 1)$.

Although Heckman did not specify the probability distribution for the covariates x, we will proceed as if they were generated from a probability distribution.

One of the major differences is that in Heckman's model, the conditional distribution $p(y \mid x, D = 1)$ of observed samples changes from its populational counterpart $p(y \mid x)$ in addition to a change in covariate distributions. In this sense, the sample selection model deals with more general distribution changes—it is reduced to covariate shift (i.e., the conditional distribution does not change) only if the selection process is independent of the behavioral model ($\rho = 0$ and no selection bias). On the other hand, in Heckman's model the distributional change including the selection bias is computed under a very strong assumption of linear regression models with bivariate Gaussian error terms. When this assumption is not fulfilled, there is no guarantee that the selection bias can be captured reasonably. In machine learning applications, we rarely expect that statistical models at hand are correctly specified and noise is purely Gaussian. Thus, Heckman's model is too restrictive to be used in real-world machine learning applications.

Another major difference between Heckman's approach and the covariate shift approach is the way the sample selection bias is reduced. As explained in chapters 2 and 3, covariate shift adaptation is carried out via importance weighting, which substantially increases the estimation variance. On the other hand, Heckman's correction compensates directly for the selection bias in order to make the estimator consistent, which does not increase the estimation variance. However, the price we have to pay for the "free" bias reduction is that Heckman's procedure is not at all robust against model misspecification. The bias caused by model misspecification can be corrected by postbias subtraction, but this is a hard task in general (e.g., bootstrap bias estimates are not accurate; see [45]). On the other hand, in covariate shift adaptation, importance weighting guarantees to asymptotically minimize the bias for misspecified models.[1] Since the increase of variance caused by importance

---

1. Note that when the model is correctly specified, no importance weighting is needed (see chapter 2).

weighting can be controlled by *regularization* with model selection, the covariate shift approach would be more useful for machine learning applications where correctly specified models are not available.

Finally, in covariate shift adaptation, the importance weight $w(x) = p_{te}(x)/p_{tr}(x)$ is estimated in an nonparametric way over the multidimensional input space (see chapter 4). If we compute the importance weight between the joint distributions[2] of (x, y) for Heckman's model, we get

$$w(x, y) := \frac{p(x, y)}{p(x, y | D = 1)}$$
$$\propto \frac{p(y|x)}{p(y|x, D=1)P(D=1|x)}$$
$$= \left\{ \Phi \left(\frac{\rho(y - x^\top \beta)/\sigma + x^\top \gamma}{\sqrt{(1-\rho^2)}} \right) \right\}^{-1}.$$

Due to the linear and Gaussian assumptions, this importance weight has a fixed functional form specified by the error function Φ and depends only on the one-dimensional projection $x^\top(\gamma - \frac{\rho}{\sigma}\beta)$ of the input and the response variable y. Especially if the selection process is independent of the behavioral model ($\rho = 0$, when only the covariate density changes), the importance weight is reduced to

$$w(x) \propto \left\{ \Phi(x^\top \gamma) \right\}^{-1}.$$

In this respect, the covariate shift approach covers more flexible changes of distributions than Heckman's sample selection model.

---

2. Such a joint importance weight can be used for multitask learning [16].

7 Applications of Covariate Shift Adaptation

In this chapter, we show applications of covariate shift adaptation techniques to real-world problems: the brain–computer interface in section 7.1, speaker identification in section 7.2, natural language processing in section 7.3, face-based age prediction in section 7.4, and human activity recognition from accelerometric data in section 7.5. In section 7.6, covariate shift adaptation techniques are employed for efficient sample reuse in the framework of reinforcement learning.

7.1 Brain–Computer Interface

In this section, importance-weighting methods are applied to *brain–computer interfaces* (BCIs), which have attracted a great deal of attention in biomedical engineering and machine learning [160, 102].

7.1.1 Background

A BCI system allows direct communication from human to machine [201, 40]. Cerebral electric activity is recorded via the *electroencephalogram* (EEG): electrodes attached to the scalp measure the electric signals of the brain. These signals are amplified and transmitted to the computer, which translates them into device control commands. The crucial requirement for the successful functioning of BCI is that the electric activity on the scalp surface already reflects, for instances, motor intentions, such as the neural correlate of preparation for hand or foot movements. A BCI system based on motor imagery can detect the motor-related EEG changes and uses this information, for example, to perform a choice between two alternatives: the detection of the preparation to move the left hand leads to the choice of the first control command, whereas the right hand intention would lead to the second command. By this means, it is possible to operate devices which are connected to the computer (see figure 7.1).

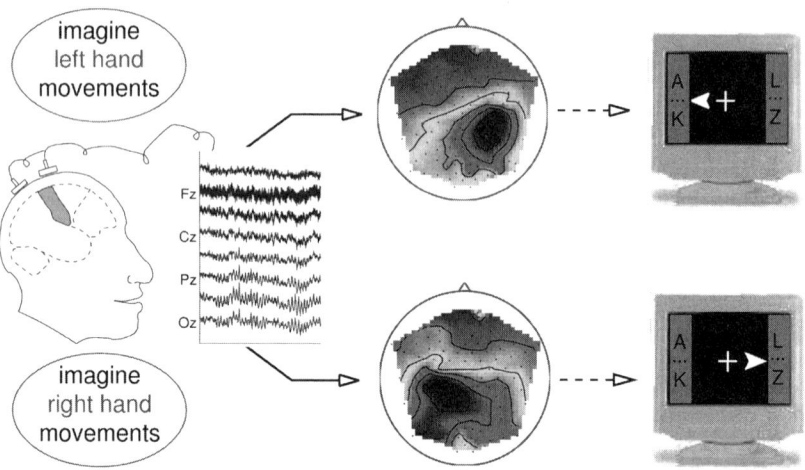

Figure 7.1
Illustration of BCI system.

For classification of appropriately preprocessed EEG signals [130,122,101], the *Fisher discriminant analysis* (FDA) [50] has been shown to work well [201, 39, 8]. On the other hand, strong non-stationarity effects have often been observed in brain signals between training and test sessions [194, 116, 143], which could be regarded as an example of covariate shift. This indicates that employing importance-weighting methods could further improve the BCI recognition accuracy.

Here, *adaptive importance-weighted FDA* (AIWFDA; see section 2.3.1) is employed for coping with the non-stationarity. AIWFDA is tested on 14 data sets obtained from 5 different subjects (see table 7.1 for specification), where the task is binary classification of EEG signals.

7.1.2 Experimental Setup

Here, how the data samples are gathered and preprocessed in the BCI experiments is briefly described. Further details are given in [23, 22].

The data in this study were recorded in a series of online BCI experiments in which the *event-related desynchronization* [122] was used to discriminate between various mental states. During imagined hand or foot movement, the spectral power in the frequency band between 8 Hz and 35 Hz is known to decrease in the EEG signals of the corresponding motor cortices. The data acquired from 128 EEG channels at a rate of 1000 Hz were downsampled to 100 Hz and band-pass filtered to specifically selected frequency bands. The

7.1. Brain–Computer Interface

Table 7.1
Specification of BCI data

Subject	Session ID	Dim. of Samples	# of Training Samples	# of Unlabeled Samples	# of Test Samples
1	1	3	280	112	112
1	2	3	280	120	120
1	3	3	280	35	35
2	1	3	280	113	112
2	2	3	280	112	112
2	3	3	280	35	35
3	1	3	280	91	91
3	2	3	280	112	112
3	3	3	280	30	30
4	1	6	280	112	112
4	2	6	280	126	126
4	3	6	280	35	35
5	1	2	280	112	112
5	2	2	280	112	112

common spatial patterns (CSP) algorithm [130], a spatial filter that maximizes the band power in one class while minimizing it for the other class, was applied and the data were projected onto three to six channels. The features were finally extracted by calculating the log-variance over a window one second long.

The experiments consisted of an initial training period and three test periods. During the training period, the letters (L), (R), or (F) were displayed on the screen to instruct the subjects to imagine left hand, right hand, or foot movements. Then a classifier was trained on the two classes with the best discriminability. This classifier was then used in test periods. In each test period, a cursor could be controlled horizontally by the subjects, using the classifier output. One of the targets on the left and right sides of the computer screen was highlighted to indicate that the subjects should then try to select this target with the cursor. The experiments were carried out with five subjects. Note that the third test period for the fifth subject is missing. So there was a total of 14 test sets (see table 7.1 for specification).

In the evaluation below, the misclassification rates of the classifiers are reported. Note that the classifier output was not directly translated into the position of a cursor on the monitor, but underwent some postprocessing steps (averaging, scaling, and biasing). Therefore, a wrong classification did not necessarily result in the wrong target being selected. Since the time window chosen for this evaluation is at the beginning of the trial, a better classification accuracy on this data will lead to a shortened trial length, and therefore to a higher bit rate (see [23] for details).

Training samples and unlabeled/test samples were gathered in different recording sessions, so the non-stationarity in brain signals may have changed the distributions. On the other hand, the unlabeled samples and test samples were gathered in the same recording session; more precisely, the unlabeled samples were gathered in the first half of the session and the test samples (with labels) were collected in the latter half. Therefore, unlabeled samples may have contained some information on the test input distribution. However, input distributions of unlabeled and test samples are not necessarily identical since the non-stationarity in brain signals can cause a small change in distributions even within the same session. Thus, this setting realistically renders the classifier update in online BCI systems.

$p_{tr}(x)$ and $p_{te}(x)$ were estimated by maximum likelihood fitting of the multidimensional Gaussian density with full covariance matrix. $p_{tr}(x)$ was estimated using training samples, and $p_{te}(x)$ was estimated using unlabeled samples.

7.1.3 Experimental Results

Table 7.2 describes the misclassification rates of test samples by FDA (corresponding to AIWFDA with *flattening parameter* $\lambda = 0$), AIWFDA with λ chosen based on tenfold IWCV or tenfold CV, and AIWFDA with optimal λ (i.e., for each case, λ is determined so that the misclassification rate is minimized). The value of flattening parameter λ was selected from $\{0, 0.1, 0.2, \ldots, 1.0\}$; chosen flattening parameter values are also in the table. Table 7.2 also contains the *Kullback–Leibler (KL) divergence* [97] from the estimated training input distribution to the estimated test input distribution. Since we wanted to have an accurate estimate of the KL divergence, we used test samples for estimating the test input distribution when computing the KL divergence (only unlabeled samples were used when the test input distribution is estimated for AIWFDA and IWCV). The KL values may be interpreted as the level of covariate shift.

First, FDA is compared with OPT (AIWFDA with optimal λ). The table shows that OPT outperforms FDA in 8 out of 14 cases. This implies that the non-stationarity in the brain signals can be modeled well by covariate shift, which motivates us to employ AIWFDA in BCI. Within each subject, it can be

7.1. Brain–Computer Interface

Table 7.2
Misclassification rates for BCI data

Subject	Trial	OPT	FDA	IWCV	CV	KL
1	1	* 8.7 (0.5)	9.3 (0)	− 10.0 (0.9)	10.0 (0.9)	0.76
1	2	* 6.2 (0.3)	8.8 (0)	8.8 (0)	8.8 (0)	1.11
1	3	4.3 (0)	4.3 (0)	4.3 (0)	4.3 (0)	0.69
2	1	40.0 (0)	40.0 (0)	° 40.0 (0)	41.3 (0.7)	0.97
2	2	* 38.7 (0.1)	39.3 (0)	^+_o 38.7 (0.2)	39.3 (0)	1.05
2	3	25.5 (0)	25.5 (0)	25.5 (0)	25.5 (0)	0.43
3	1	* 34.4 (0.2)	36.9 (0)	+ 34.4 (0.2)	34.4 (0.2)	2.63
3	2	* 18.0 (0.4)	21.3 (0)	+ 19.3 (0.6)	19.3 (0.9)	2.88
3	3	* 15.0 (0.6)	22.5 (0)	+ 17.5 (0.3)	17.5 (0.4)	1.25
4	1	20.0 (0.2)	21.3 (0)	21.3 (0)	21.3 (0)	9.23
4	2	2.4 (0)	2.4 (0)	2.4 (0)	2.4 (0)	5.58
4	3	6.4 (0)	6.4 (0)	6.4 (0)	6.4 (0)	1.83
5	1	21.3 (0)	21.3 (0)	21.3 (0)	21.3 (0)	0.79
5	2	* 13.3 (0.5)	15.3 (0)	^+_o 14.0 (0.1)	15.3 (0)	2.01

All values are in percent. IWCV or CV refers to AIWFDA with λ chosen by ten fold IWCV or ten fold CV. OPT refers to AIWFDA with optimal λ. Values of chosen λ are in parentheses (FDA is denoted as $\lambda = 0$). ∗ in the table indicates the case where OPT is better than FDA. + is the case where IWCV outperforms FDA, and − is the opposite case where FDA outperforms IWCV. ◦ denotes the case where IWCV outperforms CV. KL refers to the Kullback–Leibler divergence between (estimated) training and test input distributions.

observed that OPT outperforms FDA when the KL divergence is large, but they are comparable to one another when the KL divergence is small. This agrees well with the theory that AIWFDA corrects the bias caused by covariate shift, and AIWFDA is reduced to plain FDA in the absence of covariate shift. Next, IWCV (applied to AIWFDA) is compared with FDA. IWCV outperforms FDA in five cases, whereas the opposite case occurs only once. Therefore, IWCV combined with AIWFDA certainly contributes to improving the classification accuracy in BCI. The table also shows that within each subject, IWCV tends to outperform FDA when the KL divergence is large. Finally, IWCV is compared with CV (applied to AIWFDA). IWCV outperforms CV in three cases, and the opposite case does not occur. This substantiates the effectiveness of IWCV as a model selection criterion in BCI. IWCV tends to outperform CV when the KL divergence is large within each subject.

The above results showed that non-stationarity in brain signals can be successfully compensated for by IWCV combined with AIWFDA, which certainly contributes to improving the recognition accuracy of BCI.

7.2 Speaker Identification

In this section, we describe an application of covariate shift adaptation techniques to *speaker identification* [204].

7.2.1 Background

Speaker identification methods are widely used in real-world situations such as controlling access to information service systems, speaker detection in speech dialogue, and speaker indexing problems with large audio archives [133]. Recently, the speaker identification and indexing problems have attracted a great deal of attention.

Popular methods of text-independent speaker identification are based on the *Gaussian mixture model* [132] or kernel methods such as the *support vector machine* [29, 110]. In these supervised learning methods, it is implicitly assumed that training and test data follow the same probability distribution. However, since speech features vary over time due to session-dependent variation, the recording environment change, and physical conditions/emotions, the training and test distributions are not necessarily the same in practice. In a paper by Furui [59], the influence of the session-dependent variation of voice quality in speaker identification problems is investigated, and the identification performance is to decrease significantly over three months—the major cause for the performance degradation is the characteristic variations of the voice source.

To alleviate the influence of session-dependent variation, it is popular to use several sessions of speaker utterance samples [111, 113] or to use *cepstral mean normalization* [58]. However, gathering several sessions of speaker utterance data and assigning the speaker ID to the collected data are expensive in both time and cost, and therefore not realistic in practice. Moreover, it is not possible to perfectly remove the session-dependent variation by cepstral mean normalization alone.

A more practical and effective setup is *semisupervised learning* [30], where unlabeled samples are additionally given from the testing environment. In semisupervised learning, it is required that the probability distributions of training and test are related to each other in some sense; otherwise, we may not be able to learn anything about the test probability distribution from the training samples. Below, the semisupervised speaker identification problem is formulated as a covariate shift adaptation problem [204].

7.2.2 Formulation

Here, the speaker identification problem is formulated.

7.2. Speaker Identification

An utterance feature X pronounced by a speaker is expressed as a set of N *mel-frequency cepstrum coefficients* (MFCC) [129], which are vectors of d dimensions:

$$X = [x_1, x_2, \ldots, x_N] \in \mathbb{R}^{d \times N}.$$

For training, we are given n_{tr} labeled utterance samples

$$\mathcal{Z}^{\text{tr}} = \{X_i^{\text{tr}}, y_i^{\text{tr}}\}_{i=1}^{n_{\text{tr}}},$$

where

$$y_i^{\text{tr}} \in \{1, 2, \ldots, C\}$$

denotes the index of the speaker who pronounces X_i^{tr}.

The goal of speaker identification is to predict the speaker index of a test utterance sample X^{te} based on the training samples. The speaker index c of a test sample X^{te} is predicted based on the *Bayes decision rule*:

$$p(y = c | X^{\text{te}}) > p(y = c' | X^{\text{te}}) \quad \forall c' \neq c.$$

For approximating the class-posterior probability, the following *logistic model* $\widehat{p}(y = c | X)$ is used:

$$\widehat{p}(y = c | X) = \frac{\exp\{\widehat{f}_c(X)\}}{\sum_{c'=1}^{C} \exp\{\widehat{f}_{c'}(X)\}},$$

where $\widehat{f}_c(X)$ is a discriminant function corresponding to the speaker c.

The following *kernel model* is used as the discriminant function [113]:

$$\widehat{f}_c(X) = \sum_{\ell=1}^{n_{\text{tr}}} \theta_{c,\ell} \mathcal{K}(X, X_\ell^{\text{tr}}), \quad c = 1, 2, \ldots, C,$$

where $\{\theta_{c,\ell}\}_{\ell=1}^{n_{\text{tr}}}$ are parameters corresponding to speaker c and $\mathcal{K}(X, X')$ is a kernel function. The *sequence kernel* [110] is used as the kernel function here because it allows us to handle features of different size; for two utterance samples $X = [x_1, x_2, \ldots, x_N] \in \mathbb{R}^{d \times N}$ and $X' = [x'_1, x'_2, \ldots, x'_{N'}] \in \mathbb{R}^{d \times N'}$ (generally $N \neq N'$), the sequence kernel is defined as

$$\mathcal{K}(X, X') = \frac{1}{NN'} \sum_{i=1}^{N} \sum_{i'=1}^{N'} K(x_i, x'_{i'}),$$

where $K(x, x')$ is a vectorial kernel. We use the *Gaussian kernel* here:

$$K(x, x') = \exp\left(\frac{-\|x - x'\|^2}{2\sigma^2}\right).$$

The parameters $\{\theta_{c,\ell}\}_{\ell=1}^{n_{\mathrm{tr}}}$ are learned so that the following negative penalized log-likelihood is minimized:

$$\widehat{\boldsymbol{\theta}}_\gamma = \underset{\boldsymbol{\theta}}{\mathrm{argmin}} \left[-\sum_{i=1}^{n_{\mathrm{tr}}} \log \widehat{p}(y = y_i^{\mathrm{tr}} | X_i^{\mathrm{tr}}) + \lambda \sum_{c=1}^{C} \sum_{\ell=1}^{n_{\mathrm{tr}}} \theta_{c,\ell}^2 \right],$$

where $\lambda \ (\geq 0)$ is the regularization parameter.

In practical speaker identification tasks, speech features are not stationary due to time-dependent voice variation, change in the recording environment, and physical conditions/emotion. Thus, the training and test feature distributions are not generally the same. Here, we deal with such changing environment via the covariate shift model, and employ *importance-weighted logistic regression* (IWLR; see section 2.3.2) with the sequence kernel. The tuning parameters in kernel logistic regression are chosen by *importance-weighted cross-validation* (IWCV; see section 3.3), where the importance weights are learned by the *Kullback–Leibler importance-estimation procedure* (KLIEP; see section 4.4) with the sequence kernel.

7.2.3 Experimental Results

Training and test samples were collected from ten male speakers, and two types of experiments were conducted: *text-dependent* and *text-independent* speaker identification. In text-dependent speaker identification, the training and test sentences were common to all speakers. In text-independent speaker identification, the training sentences were common to all speakers, but the test sentences were different from training sentences.

The *NTT data set* [112] was used here. Each speaker uttered several Japanese sentences for text-dependent and text-independent speaker identification evaluation. The following three sentences were used as training and test samples in the text-dependent speaker identification experiments (Japanese sentences written using the Hepburn system of romanization):

- seno takasawa hyakunanajusseNchi hodode mega ookiku yaya futotteiru,
- oogoeo dashisugite kasuregoeni natte shimau,
- tashizaN hikizaNwa dekinakutemo eha kakeru.

7.2. Speaker Identification

In the text-independent speaker identification experiments, the same three sentences were used as training samples:

. seno takasawa hyakunanajusseNchi hodode mega ookiku yaya futotteiru,

. oogoeo dashisugite kasuregoeni natte shimau,

. tashizaN hikizaNwa dekinakutemo eha kakeru.

The following five sentences were used as test samples:

. tobujiyuuwo eru kotowa jiNruino yume datta,

. hajimete ruuburubijutsukaNe haittanowa juuyoneNmaeno kotoda,

. jibuNno jitsuryokuwa jibuNga ichibaN yoku shitteiru hazuda,

. koremade shouneNyakyuu mamasaN bareenado chiikisupootsuo sasae shimiNni micchakushite kitanowamusuuno boraNtiadatta,

. giNzakeno tamagoo yunyuushite fukasase kaichuude sodateru youshokumo hajimatteiru.

The utterance samples for training were recorded in 1990/12, and the utterance samples for testing were recorded in 1991/3, 1991/6, and 1991/9, respectively. Since the recording times between training and test utterance samples are different, the voice quality variation is expected to be included. Thus, this target speaker identification problem is a challenging task.

The total duration of the training sentences is about 9 seconds. The durations of the test sentences for text-dependent and text-independent speaker identification are 9 seconds and 24 seconds, respectively. There are approximately ten vowels in the sentences for every 1.5 seconds.

The input utterance is sampled at 16 kHz. A feature vector consists of 26 components: 12 mel-frequency cepstrum coefficients, the normalized log energy, and their first derivatives. Feature vectors are derived at every 10 milliseconds over the 25.6-millisecond Hamming-windowed speech segment, and cepstral mean normalization is applied over the features to remove channel effects. Each utterance is divided into 300-millisecond disjoint segments, each of which corresponds to a set of features of size 26×30. Thus, the training set is given as

$$\mathcal{X}^{tr} = \{\boldsymbol{X}_i^{tr}\}_{i=1}^{411}$$

for text-independent and text-dependent speaker identification evaluation. For text-independent speaker identification, the sets of test samples for 1991/3, 1991/6, and 1991/9 are given as

$\mathcal{X}_1^{\text{te1}} = \{X_i^{\text{te1}}\}_{i=1}^{907}$, $\mathcal{X}_1^{\text{te2}} = \{X_i^{\text{te2}}\}_{i=1}^{919}$, and $\mathcal{X}_1^{\text{te3}} = \{X_i^{\text{te3}}\}_{i=1}^{906}$.

For text-dependent speaker identification, the sets of test data are given as

$\mathcal{X}_2^{\text{te1}} = \{X_i^{\text{te1}}\}_{i=1}^{407}$, $\mathcal{X}_2^{\text{te2}} = \{X_i^{\text{te2}}\}_{i=1}^{407}$, and $\mathcal{X}_2^{\text{te3}} = \{X_i^{\text{te3}}\}_{i=1}^{412}$.

In the above, we assume that samples are sorted according to time, with the index $i = 1$ being the first sample.

The speaker identification rate was computed at every 1.5 seconds, 3.0 seconds, and 4.5 seconds, and the speaker was identified based on the average posterior probability

$$\widehat{p}(y|X_t^{\text{te}}) = \frac{1}{m} \sum_{i=1}^{m} \widehat{p}(y|X_{t-i+1}^{\text{te}}),$$

where $m = 5$, 10, and 15 for 1.5 seconds, 3.0 seconds, and 4.5 seconds, respectively.

Here, the product-of-Gaussian model (PoG) [81], plain logistic regression (LR) with the sequence kernel, and importance-weighted logistic regression (IWLR) with the sequence kernel were tested, and the speaker identification rates were compared with the data taken in 1991/3, 1991/6, and 1991/9. For PoG and LR training, we used the 1990/12 data set (inputs $\mathcal{X}^{\text{tr}}$ and their labels).

For PoG training, the means, diagonal covariance matrices, and mixing coefficients were initialized by the results of *k-means clustering* on all training sentences for all speakers; then these parameters were estimated via the *EM algorithm* [38, 21] for each speaker. The number of components, b, was determined by fivefold cross-validation. In the test phase of PoG, the probability for the speaker c was computed as

$$\widehat{p}_c(X_t^{\text{te}}) = \prod_{i=1}^{m} \prod_{j=1}^{N} q_c(x_{t-i+1,j}^{\text{te}}),$$

where $X_t^{\text{te}} = [x_{t,1}^{\text{te}}, x_{t,2}^{\text{te}}, \ldots, x_{t,N}^{\text{te}}]$ and $q_c(x)$ was a PoG for the speaker c. In the current setup, $N = 30$ and $m = 5$, 10, and 15 (which correspond to 1.5 seconds, 3.0 seconds, and 4.5 seconds, respectively).

For IWLR training, unlabeled samples $\mathcal{X}^{\text{te1}}$, $\mathcal{X}^{\text{te2}}$, and $\mathcal{X}^{\text{te3}}$ in addition to the training inputs $\mathcal{X}^{\text{tr}}$ and their labels (i.e., semisupervised) were used. We first estimated the importance weight from the training and test data set pairs ($\mathcal{X}^{\text{tr}}$, $\mathcal{X}^{\text{te1}}$), ($\mathcal{X}^{\text{tr}}$, $\mathcal{X}^{\text{te2}}$), or ($\mathcal{X}^{\text{tr}}$, $\mathcal{X}^{\text{te3}}$) by KLIEP with fivefold CV (see section 4.4),

7.2. Speaker Identification

and we used fivefold IWCV (see section 3.3) to decide the Gaussian kernel width σ and regularization parameter λ.

In practice, the k-fold CV and k-fold IWCV scores can be strongly affected by the way the data samples are split into k disjoint subsets (we used $k = 5$). This phenomenon is due to the non-i.i.d. nature of the mel-frequency cepstrum coefficient features, which is different from the theory. To obtain reliable experimental results, the CV procedure was repeated 50 times with different random data splits, and the highest score was used for model selection.

Table 7.3 shows the text-independent speaker identification rates in percent for 1991/3, 1991/6, and 1991/9. IWLR refers to IWLR with σ and λ chosen by fivefold IWCV, LR refers to LR with σ and λ chosen by fivefold CV, and PoG refers to PoG with the number of mixtures b chosen by fivefold CV. The chosen values of these hyperparameters are described in parentheses. DoDC (degree of distribution change) refers to the standard deviation of estimated importance weights $\{w(\boldsymbol{X}_i^{\text{tr}})\}_{i=1}^{n_{\text{tr}}}$; the smaller the standard deviation is, the "flatter" the importance weights are. Flat importance weights imply that

Table 7.3
Correct classification rates for text-independent speaker identification

1991/3 (DoDC=0.34)	IWLR ($\sigma = 1.4, \lambda = 10^{-4}$)	LR ($\sigma = 1.0, \lambda = 10^{-2}$)	PoG ($b = 16$)
1.5 sec.	**91.0**	88.2	89.7
3.0 sec.	**95.0**	92.9	94.4
4.5 sec.	**97.7**	96.1	94.6
1991/6 (DoDC=0.37)	IWLR ($\sigma = 1.3, \lambda = 10^{-4}$)	LR ($\sigma = 1.0, \lambda = 10^{-2}$)	PoG ($b = 16$)
1.5 sec.	**91.0**	87.7	90.2
3.0 sec.	**95.3**	91.1	94.0
4.5 sec.	**97.4**	93.4	96.1
1991/9 (DoDC=0.35)	IWLR ($\sigma = 1.2, \lambda = 10^{-4}$)	LR ($\sigma = 1.0, \lambda = 10^{-2}$)	PoG ($b = 16$)
1.5 sec.	**94.8**	91.7	92.1
3.0 sec.	**97.9**	96.3	95.0
4.5 sec.	**98.8**	98.3	95.8

All values are in percent. IWLR refers to IWLR with (σ, λ) chosen by fivefold IWCV, LR refers to LR with (σ, λ) chosen by fivefold CV, and PoG refers to PoG with the number of components b chosen by fivefold CV. The chosen values of these hyperparameters are described in parentheses. DoDC refers to the standard deviation of estimated importance weights $\{w(\boldsymbol{X}_i^{\text{tr}})\}_{i=1}^{n_{\text{tr}}}$, which roughly indicates the degree of distribution change.

there is no significant distribution change between the training and test phases. Thus, the standard deviation of estimated importance weights may be regarded as a rough indicator of the degree of distribution change.

As can be seen from the table, IWLR+IWCV outperforms PoG+CV and LR+CV for all sessions. This result implies that importance weighting is useful in coping with the influence of non-stationarity in practical speaker identification such as utterance variation, change in the the recording environment, physical conditions/emotions.

Table 7.4 summarizes the text-dependent speaker identification rates in percent for 1991/3, 1991/6, and 1991/9, showing that IWLR+IWCV and LR+CV slightly outperform PoG and are highly comparable to each other. The result that IWLR+IWCV and LR+CV are comparable in this experiment is a reasonable consequence since the standard deviation of estimated importance weights is very small in all three cases—implying that there is no significant distribution change, and therefore no adaptation is necessary. This result indicates that

Table 7.4
Correct classification rates for text-dependent speaker identification

1991/3 (DoDC=0.05)	IWLR ($\sigma = 1.2, \lambda = 10^{-4}$)	LR ($\sigma = 1.0, \lambda = 10^{-2}$)	PoG ($b = 16$)
1.5 sec.	**100.0**	98.9	96.8
3.0 sec.	**100.0**	100.0	97.7
4.5 sec.	**100.0**	100.0	97.9
1991/6 (DoDC=0.05)	IWLR ($\sigma = 1.2, \lambda = 10^{-4}$)	LR ($\sigma = 1.0, \lambda = 10^{-2}$)	PoG ($b = 16$)
1.5 sec.	97.5	96.2	**97.8**
3.0 sec.	97.5	97.2	**98.1**
4.5 sec.	**98.9**	97.4	98.3
1991/9 (DoDC=0.05)	IWLR ($\sigma = 1.2, \lambda = 10^{-4}$)	LR ($\sigma = 1.0, \lambda = 10^{-2}$)	PoG ($b = 16$)
1.5 sec.	**100.0**	**100.0**	98.2
3.0 sec.	**100.0**	**100.0**	98.4
4.5 sec.	**100.0**	**100.0**	98.5

All values are in percent. IWLR refers to IWLR with (σ, λ) chosen by fivefold IWCV, LR refers to LR with (σ, λ) chosen by fivefold CV, and PoG refers to PoG with the number of components b chosen by fivefold CV. The chosen values of these hyperparameters are described in parentheses. DoDC refers to the standard deviation of estimated importance weights $\{w(X_i^{\text{tr}})\}_{i=1}^{n_{\text{tr}}}$, which roughly indicates the degree of distribution change.

the proposed method does not degrade the accuracy when there is no significant distribution change.

Overall, the importance-weighting method tends to improve the performance when a significant distribution change exists. It also tends to maintain the good performance of the baseline method when no distribution change exists. Thus, the importance-weighting method is a promising approach to handling session-dependent variation in practical speaker identification.

7.3 Natural Language Processing

In this section, importance-weighting methods are applied to a domain adaptation task in *natural language processing* (NLP).

7.3.1 Formulation

A standard way to train an NLP system is to use data collected from the target domain in which the system is operated. In practice, though, collecting data from the target domain is often costly, so it is desirable to (re)use data obtained from other domains. However, due to the difference in vocabulary and writing style, a naive use of the data obtained from other domains results in serious performance degradation. For this reason, *domain adaptation* is one of the most important challenges in NLP [24, 86, 36].

Here, domain adaptation experiments are conducted for a Japanese word segmentation task. It is not trivial to detect word boundaries for nonsegmented languages such as Japanese or Chinese. In the word segmentation task,

$$X = (x_1, x_2, \ldots, x_T)$$

represents a sequence of features at character boundaries of a sentence, and

$$y = (y_1, y_2, \ldots, y_T)$$

is a sequence of the corresponding labels, which specify whether the current position is a word boundary. It would be reasonable to consider the domain adaptation task of word segmentation as a covariate shift adaptation problem since a word segmentation policy, $p(y|X)$, rarely changes across domains in the same language, but the distribution of characters, $p(X)$, tends to vary over different domains.

The goal of the experiments here is to adapt a word segmentation system from a daily conversation domain to a medical domain [187]. One of the characteristics of the NLP tasks is their high dimensionality. The total number of distinct features is about $d = 300,000$ in this data set. $n_{tr} = 13,000$ labeled (i.e., word-segmented) sentences from the source domain, and $n_{\text{te}} = 53{,}834$ unlabeled (i.e., unsegmented) sentences from the target domain are used for learning. In addition, 1000 labeled sentences from the target domain are used for the evaluation of the domain adaptation performance.

As a word segmentation model, *conditional random fields* (CRFs) are used, which are generalizations of the logistic regression models (see section 2.3.2) for structured prediction [98]. The CRFs model the conditional probability $p(y|X; \theta)$ of output structure y, given an input X:

$$p(y|X; \theta) = \frac{\exp\{\theta^\top \varphi(X, y)\}}{\sum_{y'} \exp\{\theta^\top \varphi(X, y')\}},$$

where $\varphi(X, y)$ is a basis function mapping (X, y) to a b-dimensional feature vector,[1] and b is the dimension of the parameter vector θ. Although the conventional CRF learning algorithm minimizes the regularized negative log-likelihood, an *importance-weighted CRF* (IWCRF) training algorithm is used here for covariate shift adaptation:

$$\widehat{\theta}_{\text{IWCRF}} := \underset{\theta}{\operatorname{argmin}} \left[-\sum_{i=1}^{n_{\text{tr}}} w(X_i^{\text{tr}}) \log p(y_i^{\text{tr}} | X_i^{\text{tr}}; \theta) + \lambda \|\theta\|^2 \right].$$

The *Kullback–Leibler importance estimation procedure* (KLIEP; see section 4.4) for *log-linear models* is used to estimate the importance weight $w(X)$.

$$\widehat{w}(X) = \frac{\exp\left(\alpha^\top \psi(X)\right)}{\frac{1}{n_{\text{tr}}} \sum_{i=1}^{n_{\text{tr}}} \exp\left(\alpha^\top \psi(X_i^{\text{tr}})\right)},$$

where the basis function $\psi(X)$ is set to the average value of features for CRFs in a sentence:

$$\psi(X) = \frac{1}{T} \sum_{t=1}^{T} x_t.$$

Since KLIEP for log-linear models is computationally more efficient than KLIEP for linear models when the number of test samples is large (see section 4.4), we chose the log-linear model here.

---

1. Its definition is omitted here. See [187] for details.

7.3. Natural Language Processing

7.3.2 Experimental Results

The performance is evaluated by the *F-measure*,

$$F = \frac{2 \times R \times P}{R + P},$$

where R and P denote recall and precision defined by

$$R = \frac{\text{\# of correct words}}{\text{\# of words in test data}} \times 100,$$

$$P = \frac{\text{\# of correct words}}{\text{\# of words in system output}} \times 100.$$

The hyperparameter of IWCRF is optimized based on an *importance-weighted F-measure* (IWF) for separate validation data in which the number of correct words is weighted according to the importance of the sentence that these words belong to:

$$\text{IWF}(D) = \frac{2 \times \text{IWR}(D) \times \text{IWP}(D)}{\text{IWR}(D) + \text{IWP}(D)}$$

for the validation set D, where

$$\text{IWR}(D) = \frac{\sum_{(X,y) \in D} w(X) \sum_{t=1}^{T} [\widehat{y}_t = y_t]}{T \sum_{(X,y) \in D} w(X)} \times 100,$$

$$\text{IWP}(D) = \frac{\sum_{(X,y) \in D} w(X) \sum_{t=1}^{T} [\widehat{y}_t = y_t]}{T \sum_{(X,y) \in D} w(X)} \times 100,$$

and

$$\widehat{y} = (\widehat{y}_1, \widehat{y}_2, \ldots, \widehat{y}_T)^\top = \underset{y}{\arg\max}\, p(y|X; \boldsymbol{\theta}).$$

Ten percent of the training data is used as the validation set D.

The performances of CRF, IWCRF, and CRF' (a CRF trained with additional 1000 labeled manual word segmentation samples an from the target domain [187]) are compared. For importance estimation, log-linear KLIEP and the logistic regression (LR) approach (see section 4.3) are tested, and fivefold cross-validation is used to find the optimal Gaussian width σ in the LR model.

Table 7.5 summarizes the performance, showing that IWCRF+KLIEP significantly outperforms CRF. CRF', which used additional labeled samples in the target domain and thus was highly expensive, tends to perform better

Table 7.5
Word segmentation performance in the target domain

	F	R	P
CRF	92.30	90.58	94.08
IWCRF+KLIEP	**94.46**	**94.32**	94.59
IWCRF+LR	93.68	94.30	93.07
CRF′	94.43	93.49	**95.39**

CRF′ indicates the performance of a CRF′ trained with additional 1000 manual word segmentation samples in the target domain.

than CRF, as expected. A notable fact is that IWCRF+KLIEP, which does not require expensive labeled samples in the target domain, is on par with CRF′. Empirically, the covariate shift adaptation technique seems to improve the coverage (R) in the target domain. Compared with LR, KLIEP seems to perform better in this experiment. Since it is easy to obtain a large amount of unlabeled text data in NLP tasks, domain adaptation by importance weighting is a promising approach in NLP.

7.4 Perceived Age Prediction from Face Images

In this section, covariate shift adaptation techniques are applied to perceived age prediction from face images [188].

7.4.1 Background

Recently, demographic analysis in public places such as shopping malls and stations has been attracting a great deal of attention. Such information is useful for various purposes such as designing effective marketing strategies and targeting advertisements based on prospective customers' genders and ages. For this reason, a number of approaches have been explored for age estimation from face images [61, 54, 65]. Several databases are now publicly available [49, 123, 134].

The accuracy of age prediction systems is significantly influenced by the type of camera, the camera calibration, and lighting variations. The publicly available databases were collected mainly in semicontrolled environments such as a studio with appropriate illumination. However, in real-world environments, lighting conditions vary considerabley: strong sunlight may be cast on the sides of faces, or there is not enough light. For this reason, training and test data tend to have different distributions. Here, covariate shift adaptation techniques are employed to alleviate changes in lighting conditions.

7.4.2 Formulation

Let us consider a regression problem of estimating the age y of subject x (x corresponds to a face-feature vector). Here, age estimation is performed not on the basis of subjects' real ages, but on their *perceived* ages. Thus, the "true" age of a subject is defined as the average perceived age evaluated by those who observed the subject's face images (the number is rounded to the nearest integer).

Suppose training samples $\{(x_i^{tr}, y_i^{tr})\}_{i=1}^{n_{tr}}$ are given. We use the following kernel model for age estimation (see section 1.3.5.3).

$$\widehat{f}(x; \theta) = \sum_{\ell=1}^{n_{tr}} \theta_\ell K(x, x_\ell),$$

where $\theta = (\theta_1, \theta_2, \ldots, \theta_{n_{tr}})^\top$ are parameters and $K(\cdot, \cdot)$ is a kernel function. Here the Gaussian kernel is used:

$$K(x, x') = \exp\left(-\frac{\|x - x'\|^2}{2\sigma^2}\right),$$

where σ (> 0) denotes the Gaussian width. Under the covariate shift formulation, the parameter θ may be learned by *regularized importance-weighted least squares* (see section 2.2.1):

$$\min_\theta \left[\frac{1}{n_{tr}} \sum_{i=1}^{n_{tr}} \frac{p_{te}(x_i^{tr})}{p_{tr}(x_i^{tr})} \left(\widehat{f}(x_i^{tr}; \theta) - y_i^{tr}\right)^2 + \lambda \sum_{\ell=1}^{n_{tr}} \theta_\ell^2 \right],$$

where λ (≥ 0) is the regularization parameter.

7.4.3 Incorporating Characteristics of Human Age Perception

Human age perception is known to have heterogeneous characteristics. For example, it is rare to misjudge the age of a 5-year-old child as 15 years, but the age of a 35-year-old person is often misjudged as 45 years. A paper by Ueki et al. [189] quantified this phenomenon by carrying out a large-scale questionnaire survey: each of 72 volunteers was asked to give age labels y to approximately 1000 face images.

Figure 7.2 depicts the relation between subjects' perceived ages and its standard deviation. The standard deviation is approximately 2 (years) when the true age is less than 15. It increases and goes beyond 6 as the true age increases from 15 to 35. Then the standard deviation decreases to around 5 as the true age increases from 35 to 70. This graph shows that the perceived age deviation

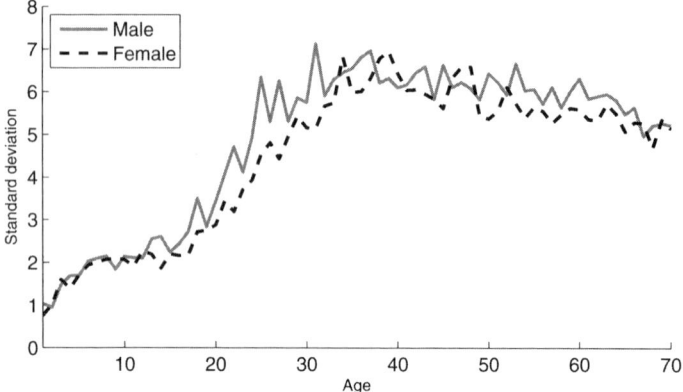

Figure 7.2
The relation between subjects' perceived ages (horizontal axis) and its standard deviation (vertical axis).

tends to be small in younger age brackets and large in older age groups. This agress well with our intuition concerning the human growth process.

In order to match characteristics of age prediction systems to those of human age perception, the goodness-of-fit term in the training criterion is weighted according to the inverse variance of the perceived age:

$$\widehat{\boldsymbol{\theta}} := \underset{\boldsymbol{\theta}}{\operatorname{argmin}} \left[\frac{1}{n_{\text{tr}}} \sum_{i=1}^{n_{\text{tr}}} \frac{p_{\text{te}}(\boldsymbol{x}_i^{\text{tr}})}{p_{\text{tr}}(\boldsymbol{x}_i^{\text{tr}})} \frac{1}{\zeta^2(y_i^{\text{tr}})} \left(\widehat{f}(\boldsymbol{x}_i^{\text{tr}}; \boldsymbol{\theta}) - y_i^{\text{tr}} \right)^2 + \lambda \sum_{\ell=1}^{n_{\text{tr}}} \theta_\ell^2 \right],$$

where $\zeta(y)$ is the standard deviation of the perceived age at y (i.e., the values in figure 7.2). The solution $\widehat{\boldsymbol{\theta}}$ is given analytically by

$$\widehat{\boldsymbol{\theta}} = (\boldsymbol{K}^{\text{tr}} \boldsymbol{W} \boldsymbol{K}^{\text{tr}} + \lambda \boldsymbol{I}_{n_{\text{tr}}})^{-1} \boldsymbol{K}^{\text{tr}} \boldsymbol{W} \boldsymbol{y}^{\text{tr}},$$

where $\boldsymbol{K}^{\text{tr}}$ is the $n_{\text{tr}} \times n_{\text{tr}}$ matrix with the (i, i')-th element

$$K_{i,i'}^{\text{tr}} = K(\boldsymbol{x}_i^{\text{tr}}, \boldsymbol{x}_{i'}^{\text{tr}}),$$

$\boldsymbol{W}$ is the diagonal matrix with the i-th diagonal element

$$W_{i,i} = \frac{p_{\text{te}}(\boldsymbol{x}_i^{\text{tr}})}{p_{\text{tr}}(\boldsymbol{x}_i^{\text{tr}})} \frac{1}{\zeta^2(y_i^{\text{tr}})},$$

7.4. Perceived Age Prediction from Face Images

$I_{n_{\text{tr}}}$ is the n_{tr}-dimensional identity matrix, and

$$\boldsymbol{y}^{\text{tr}} = (y_1^{\text{tr}}, y_2^{\text{tr}}, \ldots, y_{n_{\text{tr}}}^{\text{tr}})^\top.$$

7.4.4 Experimental Results

The face images recorded under 17 different lighting conditions were used for experiments: for instance, average illuminance from above is approximately 1000 lux and 500 lux from the front in the standard lighting condition; 250 lux from above and 125 lux from the front in the dark setting; and 190 lux from the subject's right and 750 lux from his left in another setting (see figure 7.3). Images were recorded as movies with the camera at a negative elevation angle of 15 degrees. The number of subjects was approximately 500 (250 of each gender). A face detector was used for localizing the eye pupils, and then the image was rescaled to 64 × 64 pixels. The number of face images in each environment was about 2500 (5 face images × 500 subjects). As preprocessing, a feature extractor based on convolutional neural networks [184] was used to extract 100 dimensional features from 64 × 64 face images. Learning for male/female data was performed separately, assuming that gender classification had been correctly carried out in advance.

The 250 subjects of each gender were split into the training set (200 subjects) and the test set (50 subjects). For the test samples $\{(\boldsymbol{x}_j^{\text{te}}, y_j^{\text{te}})\}_{j=1}^{n_{\text{te}}}$ corresponding to the environment with strong light from a side, the following *age-weighted mean-square error* (AWMSE) was calculated as a performance measure for a learned parameter $\widehat{\boldsymbol{\theta}}$:

$$\text{AWMSE} = \frac{1}{n_{\text{te}}} \sum_{j=1}^{n_{\text{te}}} \frac{1}{\zeta^2(y_j^{\text{te}})} \left(y_j^{\text{te}} - \widehat{f}(\boldsymbol{x}_j^{\text{te}}; \widehat{\boldsymbol{\theta}})\right)^2. \tag{7.1}$$

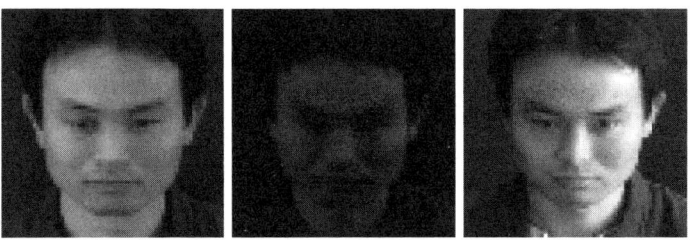

Figure 7.3
Examples of face images under different lighting conditions. Left: standard lighting; middle: dark; right: strong light from the subjects right-hand side.

The training set and the test set were shuffled five times in such a way that each subject was selected as a test sample once. The final performance was evaluated based on the average AWMSE over the five trials.

The performances of the following three methods were compared:

. IW Training samples were taken from all 17 lighting conditions. The importance weights were estimated by the *Kullback–Leibler importance estimation procedure* (KLIEP; see section 4.4), using the training samples and additional unlabeled test samples; the Gaussian width included in KLIEP was determined based on twofold likelihood cross-validation. The importance weights for training samples estimated by KLIEP were averaged over samples in each lighting condition, and the average importance weights were used in the training of regression models. This had the effect of smoothing the importance weights. The Gaussian width σ and the regularization parameter λ were determined based on fourfold importance-weighted cross-validation (IWCV; see section 3.3) over AWMSE; that is, the training set was further divided into a training part (150 subjects) and a validation part (50 subjects).

. NIW Training samples were taken from all 17 lighting conditions. No importance weight was incorporated in the training criterion (the age weights were included). The Gaussian width σ and the regularization parameter λ were determined based on fourfold cross-validation over AWMSE.

. NIW′ Only training samples taken the standard lighting condition were used. Other setups were the same as NIW.

Table 7.6 summarizes the experimental results, showing that for both male and female data, IW is better than NIW, and NIW is better than NIW′. This illustrates that the covariate shift adaptation techniques are useful for alleviating the influence of changes in lighting conditions.

Table 7.6
The age prediction performance measured by AWMSE

	Male	Female
IW	2.54	3.90
NIW	2.64	4.40
NIW′	2.83	6.51

See equation 7.1.

7.5 Human Activity Recognition from Accelerometric Data

In this section, covariate shift adaptation techniques are applied to accelerometer-based human activity recognition [68].

7.5.1 Background

Human activity recognition from accelerometric data (e.g., obtained by a smart phone) has been gathering a great deal of attention recently [11, 15, 75], since it can be used for purposes such as remote health care [60, 152, 100] and worker behavior monitoring [207]. To construct a good classifier for activity recognition, users are required to prepare accelerometric data with activity labels for types of actions such as walking, running, and bicycle riding. However, since gathering labeled data is costly, this initial data collection phase prevents new users from using the activity recognition system. Thus, overcoming such a new user problem is an important challenge for making the human activity recognition system useful in practical ways.

Since unlabeled data are relatively easy to gather, we can typically use labeled data obtained from existing users and unlabeled data obtained from a new user for developing the new user's activity classifier. Such a situation is commonly called *semisupervised learning*, and various learning methods that utilize unlabeled samples have been proposed [30]. However, semisupervised learning methods tend to perform poorly if unlabeled test data have a significantly different distribution than the labeled training data. Unfortunately, this is a typical situation in human activity recognition since motion patterns (and thus distributions of motion data) depend heavily on users.

In this section, we apply an importance-weighted variant of a probabilistic classification algorithm called *least-squares probabilistic classifier* (LSPC) [155] to real-world human activity recognition.

7.5.2 Importance-Weighted Least-Squares Probabilistic Classifier

Here, we describe a covariate shift adaptation method called the *importance-weighted least-squares probabilistic classifier* (IWLSPC) [68].

Let us consider a problem of classifying an accelerometric sample x ($\in \mathbb{R}^d$) into activity class y ($\in \{1, 2, \ldots, c\}$), where d is the input dimensionality and c denotes the number of classes. IWLSPC estimates the class-posterior probability $p(y|x)$ from training input–output samples $\{(x_i^{\text{tr}}, y_i^{\text{tr}})\}_{i=1}^{n_{\text{tr}}}$ and test input-only samples $\{x_j^{\text{te}}\}_{j=1}^{n_{\text{te}}}$ under covariate shift. In the context of human activity recognition, the labeled training samples $\{(x_i^{\text{tr}}, y_i^{\text{tr}})\}_{i=1}^{n_{\text{tr}}}$ correspond to the data obtained from existing users, and the unlabeled test input samples $\{x_j^{\text{te}}\}_{j=1}^{n_{\text{te}}}$ correspond to the data obtained from a new user.

Let us model the class-posterior probability $p(y|x)$ by

$$\widehat{p}(y|x;\boldsymbol{\theta}_y) = \sum_{\ell=1}^{n_{\text{te}}} \theta_{y,\ell} K(x, x_\ell^{\text{te}}),$$

where $\boldsymbol{\theta}_y = (\theta_{y,1}, \theta_{y,2}, \ldots, \theta_{y,n_{\text{te}}})^\top$ is the parameter vector and $K(x, x')$ is a kernel function. We focus on the Gaussian kernel here:

$$K(x, x') = \exp\left(-\frac{\|x - x'\|^2}{2\sigma^2}\right),$$

where σ denotes the Gaussian kernel width. We determine the parameter $\boldsymbol{\theta}_y$ so that the following squared error J_y is minimized:

$$\begin{aligned} J_y(\boldsymbol{\theta}_y) &= \frac{1}{2} \int \left(\widehat{p}(y|x;\boldsymbol{\theta}_y) - p(y|x)\right)^2 p_{\text{te}}(x) dx \\ &= \frac{1}{2} \int \widehat{p}(y|x;\boldsymbol{\theta}_y)^2 p_{\text{te}}(x) dx - \int \widehat{p}(y|x;\boldsymbol{\theta}_y) p(y|x) p_{\text{te}}(x) dx + C \\ &= \frac{1}{2} \boldsymbol{\theta}_y^\top Q \boldsymbol{\theta}_y - q_y^\top \boldsymbol{\theta}_y + C, \end{aligned}$$

where C is a constant independent of the parameter $\boldsymbol{\theta}_y$, and Q is the $n_{\text{te}} \times n_{\text{te}}$ matrix, and $q_y = (q_{y,1}, \ldots, q_{y,n_{\text{te}}})^\top$ is the n_{te}-dimensional vector defined as

$$Q_{\ell,\ell'} := \int K(x, x_\ell^{\text{te}}) K(x, x_{\ell'}^{\text{te}}) p_{\text{te}}(x) dx,$$

$$q_{y,\ell} := \int K(x, x_\ell^{\text{te}}) p(y|x) p_{\text{te}}(x) dx.$$

Here, we approximate Q and q_y using the adaptive importance sampling technique (see section 2.1.2) as follows. First, using the importance weight defined as

$$w(x) := \frac{p_{\text{te}}(x)}{p_{\text{tr}}(x)},$$

we express Q and q_y in terms of the training distribution as

$$Q_{\ell,\ell'} = \int K(x, x_\ell^{\text{te}}) K(x, x_{\ell'}^{\text{te}}) p_{\text{tr}}(x) w(x) dx,$$

7.5. Human Activity Recognition from Accelerometric Data

$$q_{y,\ell} = \int K(\boldsymbol{x}, \boldsymbol{x}_\ell^{\text{te}}) p(y|\boldsymbol{x}) p_{\text{tr}}(\boldsymbol{x}) w(\boldsymbol{x}) d\boldsymbol{x}$$

$$= p(y) \int K(\boldsymbol{x}, \boldsymbol{x}_\ell^{\text{te}}) p_{\text{tr}}(\boldsymbol{x}|y) w(\boldsymbol{x}) d\boldsymbol{x},$$

where $p_{\text{tr}}(\boldsymbol{x}|y)$ denotes the training input density for class y. Then, based on the above expressions, $\boldsymbol{Q}$ and $\boldsymbol{q}_y$ are approximated using the training samples $\{(\boldsymbol{x}_i^{\text{tr}}, y_i^{\text{tr}})\}_{i=1}^{n_{\text{tr}}}$ as follows[2]:

$$\widehat{Q}_{\ell,\ell'} := \frac{1}{n_{\text{tr}}} \sum_{i=1}^{n_{\text{tr}}} K(\boldsymbol{x}_i^{\text{tr}}, \boldsymbol{x}_\ell^{\text{te}}) K(\boldsymbol{x}_i^{\text{tr}}, \boldsymbol{x}_{\ell'}^{\text{te}}) w(\boldsymbol{x}_i^{\text{tr}})^\nu,$$

$$\widehat{q}_{y,\ell} := \frac{1}{n_{\text{tr}}} \sum_{i: y_i^{\text{tr}} = y} K(\boldsymbol{x}_i^{\text{tr}}, \boldsymbol{x}_\ell^{\text{te}}) w(\boldsymbol{x}_i^{\text{tr}})^\nu,$$

where the class-prior probability $p(y)$ is approximated by $n_{\text{tr}}^{(y)}/n_{\text{tr}}$, and $n_{\text{tr}}^{(y)}$ denotes the number of training samples with label y. Also, ν ($0 \leq \nu \leq 1$) denotes the *flattening parameter*, which controls the bias-variance trade-off in importance sampling (see section 2.1.2).

Consequently, we arrive at the following optimization problem:

$$\widehat{\boldsymbol{\theta}}_y = \arg\min_{\boldsymbol{\theta}_y} \left[\frac{1}{2} \boldsymbol{\theta}_y^\top \widehat{\boldsymbol{Q}} \boldsymbol{\theta}_y - \widehat{\boldsymbol{q}}_y^\top \boldsymbol{\theta}_y + \frac{\lambda}{2} \boldsymbol{\theta}_y^\top \boldsymbol{\theta}_y \right],$$

where $\frac{\lambda}{2} \boldsymbol{\theta}_y^\top \boldsymbol{\theta}_y$ is a regularization term to avoid overfitting and λ (≥ 0) denotes the regularization parameter. Then, the IWLSPC solution is given analytically as

$$\widehat{\boldsymbol{\theta}}_y = (\widehat{\boldsymbol{Q}} + \lambda \boldsymbol{I}_{n_{\text{te}}})^{-1} \widehat{\boldsymbol{q}}_y,$$

where $\boldsymbol{I}_{n_{\text{te}}}$ denotes the n_{te}-dimensional identity matrix. Since the class-posterior probability is nonnegative by definition, we modify the solution as

[2]. When $\nu = 1$, $\boldsymbol{Q}$ may be approximated directly by using the test input samples $\{\boldsymbol{x}_j^{\text{te}}\}_{j=1}^{n_{\text{te}}}$ as

$$\widehat{Q}_{\ell,\ell'} := \frac{1}{n_{\text{te}}} \sum_{j=1}^{n_{\text{te}}} K(\boldsymbol{x}_j^{\text{te}}, \boldsymbol{x}_\ell^{\text{te}}) K(\boldsymbol{x}_j^{\text{te}}, \boldsymbol{x}_{\ell'}^{\text{te}}).$$

follows [206]:

$$\widehat{p}(y|x) = \frac{1}{Z} \max\left(0, \sum_{\ell=1}^{n_{\text{te}}} \widehat{\theta}_{y,\ell} K(x, x_\ell^{\text{te}})\right),$$

if $Z = \sum_{y=1}^{c} \max\left(0, \sum_{\ell=1}^{n_{\text{te}}} \widehat{\theta}_{y,\ell} K(x, x_\ell^{\text{te}})\right) > 0$; otherwise, $\widehat{p}(y|x) = 1/c$, where c denotes the number of classes.

The learned class-posterior probability $\widehat{p}(y|x)$ allows us to predict the class label $\widehat{y}$ of a new sample x with *confidence* $\widehat{p}(\widehat{y}|x)$ as

$$\widehat{y} = \arg\max_{y} \widehat{p}(y|x).$$

In practice, the importance $w(x)$ can be estimated by the methods described in chapter 4, and the tuning parameters such as the regularization parameter λ, the Gaussian kernel width σ, and the flattening parameter ν may be chosen based on importance-weighted cross-validation (IWCV; see section 3.3).

An importance-weighted variant of *kernel logistic regression* (IWKLR; see section 2.3.2) also can be used for estimating the class-posterior probability under covariate shift [204]. However, training a large-scale IWKLR model is computationally challenging since it requires numerical optimization of the all-class parameter of dimension $c \times n_{\text{te}}$. On the other hand, IWLSPC optimizes the classwise parameter θ_y of dimension n_{te} separately c times in an analytic form.

7.5.3 Experimental Results

Here, we apply IWLSPC to real-world human activity recognition.

We use three-axis accelerometric data collected by *iPodTouch*.[3] In the data collection procedure, subjects were asked to perform a specific task such as walking, running, or bicycle riding. The duration of each task was arbitrary, and the sampling rate was 20 Hz with small variations. An example of three-axis accelerometric data for walking is plotted in figure 7.4.

To extract features from the accelerometric data, each data stream was segmented in a sliding window manner with a width of five seconds and a sliding step of one second. Depending on subjects, the position and orientation of iPodTouch was arbitrary—held in the hand or kept in a pocket or a bag. For this reason, we decided to take the ℓ_2-norm of the three-dimensional acceleration vector at each time step, and computed the following

---

3. The data set is available from http://alkan.mns.kyutech.ac.jp/web/data.html.

7.5. Human Activity Recognition from Accelerometric Data

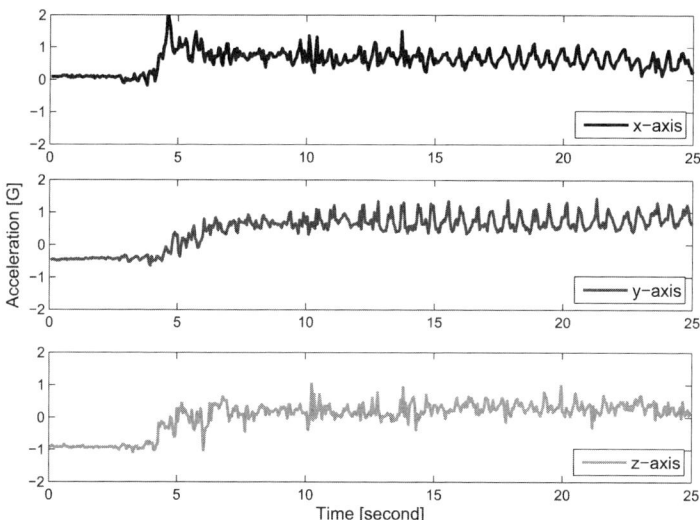

Figure 7.4
Example of three-axis accelerometric data for walking.

five orientation-invariant features from each window: mean, standard deviation, fluctuation of amplitude, average energy, and frequency-domain entropy [11, 15].

Let us consider a situation where two new users want to use the activity recognition system. Since they do not want to label their accelerometric data, only unlabeled test samples are available from the new users. Labeled data obtained from 20 existing users are available for training the new users' classifiers. Each existing user has at most 100 labeled samples for each action.

We compared the performance of the following six classification methods.

- **LapRLS[4]+IWCV** A semisupervised learning method called *Laplacian regularized least squares* (LapRLS) [30] with the Gaussian kernel as basis functions. Hyperparameters are selected by IWCV.

---

4. Laplacian regularized least squares (LapRLS) is a standard semisupervised learning method which tries to impose smoothness over nonlinear data manifold [30]. Let us consider a binary classification problem where $y \in \{+1, -1\}$. LapRLS uses a kernel model for class prediction:

$$k(\boldsymbol{x}; \boldsymbol{\theta}) := \sum_{\ell=1}^{n_{\text{te}}} \theta_\ell K(\boldsymbol{x}, \boldsymbol{x}_\ell^{\text{te}}).$$

- **LapRLS+CV** LapRLS with hyperparameters chosen by ordinary CV (i.e., no importance weighting).
- **IWKLR+IWCV** An adaptive and regularized variant of IWKLR (see section 2.3.2) with the Gaussian kernel as basis functions. The hyperparameters are selected by IWCV. A MATLAB implementation of a *limited memory BFGS (Broyden–Fletcher–Goldfarb–Shanno) quasi-Newton method* included in the *minFunc* package [140] was used for optimization.
- **KLR+CV** IWKLR+IWCV without importance weighting.
- **IWLSPC+IWCV** The probabilistic classification method described in section 7.5.2. The hyperparameters are chosen by IWCV.
- **LSPC+CV**: IWLSPC+IWCV without importance weighting.

The uLSIF method (see section 4.6) was used for importance estimation. For stabilization purposes, estimated importance weights were averaged in a userwise manner in IWCV.

The experiments were repeated 50 times with different sample choices. Table 7.7 shows the experimental results for each new user (specified by u1 and u2) in three binary classification tasks: walk vs. run, walk vs. riding a bicycle, walk vs. taking a train. The table shows that IWKLR+IWCV and IWLSPC+IWCV compare favorably with other methods in terms of classification accuracy. Table 7.8 depicts the computation time for training

---

The parameter θ is determined as

$$\min_{\theta} \left[\frac{1}{n_{\mathrm{tr}}} \sum_{i=1}^{n_{\mathrm{tr}}} \left(k(x_i^{\mathrm{tr}}; \theta) - y_i^{\mathrm{tr}} \right)^2 + \lambda \theta^\top \theta + \eta \sum_{i,i'=1}^{n} L_{i,i'} k(x_i; \theta) k(x_{i'}; \theta) \right],$$

where the first term is the goodness of fit, the second term is the ℓ_2-regularizer to avoid overfitting, and the third term is the Laplacian regularizer to impose smoothness over data manifold. $n := n_{\mathrm{tr}} + n_{\mathrm{te}}$, $L := D - W$ is an $n \times n$ graph Laplacian matrix, W is an affinity matrix defined by

$$W_{i,i'} := \exp\left(-\frac{\|x_i - x_{i'}\|^2}{2\tau^2} \right),$$

$(x_1, \ldots, x_n) := (x_1^{\mathrm{tr}}, \ldots, x_{n_{\mathrm{tr}}}^{\mathrm{tr}}, x_1^{\mathrm{te}}, \ldots, x_{n_{\mathrm{te}}}^{\mathrm{te}})$, τ is an affinity-controlling parameter, and D is the diagonal matrix given by $D_{i,i} := \sum_{i'=1}^{n} W_{i,i'}$.

The solution of LapRLS can be analytically computed since the optimization problem is an unconstrained quadratic program. However, covariate shift is not taken into account in LapRLS, and thus it will not perform well if training and test distributions are significantly different.

7.5. Human Activity Recognition from Accelerometric Data

Table 7.7
Mean misclassification rates [%] and standard deviation (in parentheses) Averaged over 50 trials for each new user (specified by u1 and u2) in Human Activity Recognition

Walk vs.	LapRLS + CV	LapRLS + IWCV	KLR + CV	IWKLR + IWCV	LSPC + CV	IWLSPC + IWCV
Run (u1)	21.2(4.7)	11.4(4.0)	15.0(6.6)	**9.0**(0.5)	13.3(3.9)	**9.0**(0.4)
Bicycle (u1)	9.9(1.1)	12.6(1.3)	**9.5**(0.7)	**8.7**(4.6)	**9.7**(0.7)	**8.7**(5.0)
Train (u1)	2.2(0.2)	2.2(0.2)	**1.4**(0.4)	**1.2**(1.5)	1.5(0.4)	**1.1**(1.5)
Run (u2)	24.7(5.0)	**20.6**(9.7)	25.6(1.3)	**22.4**(6.1)	25.6(0.8)	**21.9**(5.9)
Bicycle (u2)	13.0(1.5)	14.0(2.1)	11.1(1.8)	11.0(1.7)	**10.9**(1.8)	**10.4**(1.7)
Train (u2)	3.9(1.3)	3.7(1.1)	3.6(0.6)	**2.9**(0.7)	3.5(0.5)	**3.1**(0.5)

A number in boldface indicates that the method is the best or comparable to the best in terms of the mean misclassification rate by the t-test at the significance level 5 percent.

Table 7.8
Mean computation time (sec) and standard deviation (in parentheses) averaged over 50 trials for each new user (specified by u1 and u2) in Human Activity Recognition

Walk vs.	LapRLS + CV	LapRLS + IWCV	KLR + CV	IWKLR + IWCV	LSPC + CV	IWLSPC + IWCV
Run (u1)	14.1(0.7)	14.5(0.8)	86.8(16.2)	78.8(23.2)	7.3(1.1)	**6.6**(1.3)
Bicycle (u1)	38.8(4.8)	52.8(8.1)	38.8(4.8)	52.8(8.1)	4.2(0.8)	**3.7**(0.8)
Train (u1)	5.5(0.6)	5.4(0.6)	19.8(7.3)	30.9(6.0)	**3.9**(0.8)	4.0(0.8)
Run (u2)	12.6(2.1)	12.1(2.2)	70.1(12.9)	128.5(51.7)	**8.2**(1.3)	**7.8**(1.5)
Bicycle (u2)	16.8(7.0)	27.2(5.6)	16.8(7.0)	27.2(5.6)	3.7(0.8)	**3.1**(0.9)
Train (u2)	5.6(0.7)	5.6(0.6)	24.9(10.8)	29.4(10.3)	**4.1**(0.8)	**3.9**(0.8)

A number in boldface indicates that the method is the best or comparable to the best in terms of the mean computation time by the t-test at the significance level 5 percent.

classifiers, showing that the LSPC-based methods are computationally much more efficient than the KLR-based methods.

Figure 7.5 depicts the mean misclassification rate for various *coverage* levels, which is the ratio of test sample size used for evaluating the misclassification rate. For example, the coverage 0.8 means that 80 percent of test samples with high confidence level (obtained by an estimated class-posterior probability) are used for evaluating the misclassification rate. This renders a realistic situation where prediction with low confidence level is rejected; if the prediction is rejected, the prediction obtained in the previous time step will be inherited since an action usually continues for a certain duration. The

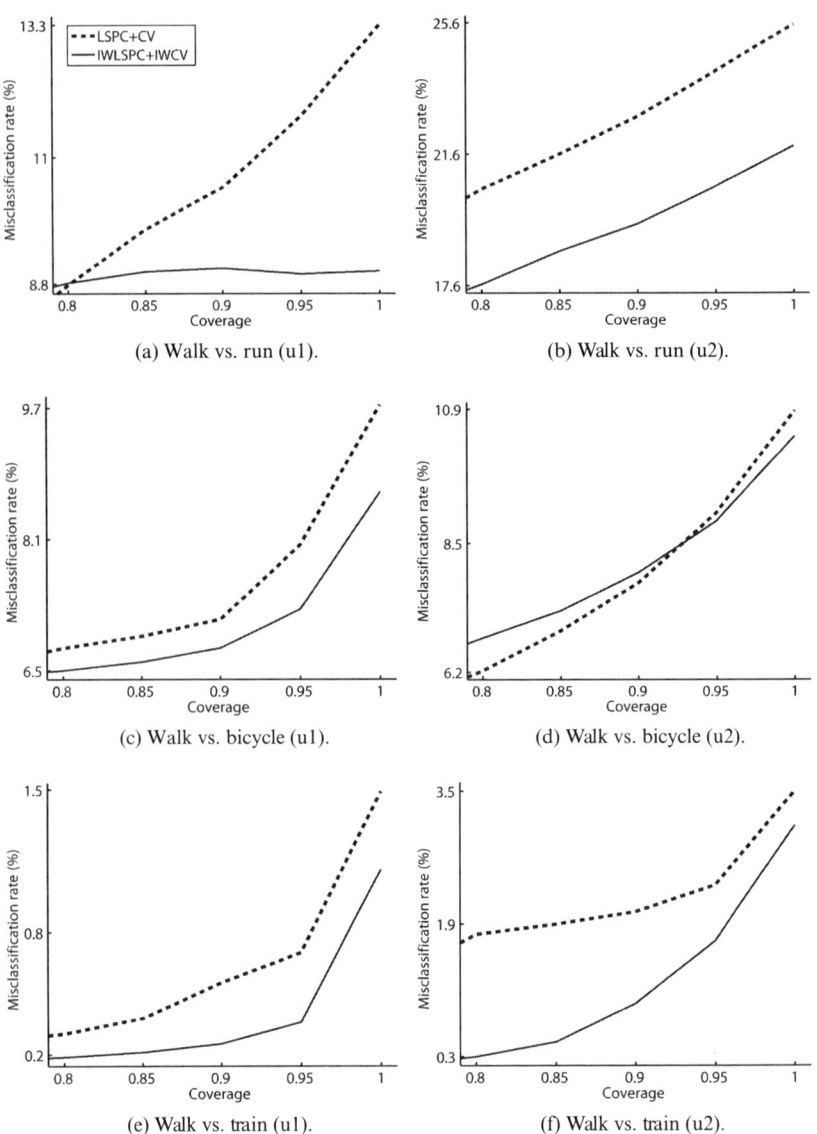

Figure 7.5
Misclassification rate as a function of coverage for each new user (specified by u1 and u2) in human activity recognition.

graphs show that for most of the coverage level, IWLSPC+IWCV outperforms LSPC+CV. The misclassification rates of IWLSPC+IWCV and LSPC+CV tend to decrease as the coverage level decreases, implying that the confidence estimation by (IW)LSPC is reliable since erroneous prediction can be successfully rejected.

7.6 Sample Reuse in Reinforcement Learning

Reinforcement learning (RL) [174] is a framework which allows a robot agent to act optimally in an unknown environment through interaction. Because of its usefulness and generality, reinforcement learning is gathering a great deal of attention in the machine learning, artificial intelligence, and robotics communities. In this section, we show that covariate shift adaptation techniques can be successfully employed in the reinforcement learning scenario [66].

7.6.1 Markov Decision Problems

Let us consider a *Markov decision problem* (MDP) specified by

$(\mathcal{S}, \mathcal{A}, p_\mathrm{I}, p_\mathrm{T}, R, \gamma)$,

where

- $\mathcal{S}$ is a set of states,
- $\mathcal{A}$ is a set of actions,
- $p_\mathrm{I}(s) \in [0, 1]$ is the initial-state probability density, $p_\mathrm{T}(s'|s, a) \in [0, 1]$ is the transition probability density from state s to state s' when action a is taken,
- $R(s, a, s') \in \mathbb{R}$ is a reward for transition from s to s' by taking action a,
- $\gamma \in (0, 1]$ is the discount factor for future rewards.

Let $\pi(a|s) \in [0, 1]$ be a stochastic policy of the agent, which is the conditional probability density of taking action a given state s. The state-action value function $Q^\pi(s, a) \in \mathbb{R}$ for policy π is the expected discounted sum of rewards the agent will receive when taking action a in state s and following policy π thereafter. That is,

$$Q^\pi(s, a) := \mathbb{E}_{\pi, p_\mathrm{T}} \left[\sum_{n=1}^\infty \gamma^{n-1} R(s_n, a_n, s_{n+1}) \,\Big|\, s_1 = s, a_1 = a \right],$$

where $\mathbb{E}_{\pi, p_\mathrm{T}}$ denotes the expectation over $\{s_n, a_n\}_{n=1}^\infty$ following $\pi(a_n|s_n)$ and $p_\mathrm{T}(s_{n+1}|s_n, a_n)$.

The goal of reinforcement learning is to obtain the policy which maximizes the sum of future rewards. Then the optimal policy can be expressed as follows[5]:

$$\pi^*(a|s) = \delta(a - \underset{a'}{\operatorname{argmax}}\, Q^*(s, a')),$$

where $\delta(\cdot)$ is the *Dirac delta function* and $Q^*(s, a)$ is the optimal state-action value function defined by

$$Q^*(s, a) := \max_\pi Q^\pi(s, a).$$

$Q^\pi(s, a)$ can be expressed as the following recurrent form, called the *Bellman equation* [174]:

$$Q^\pi(s, a) = R(s, a) + \gamma \, \underset{p_T(s'|s,a)}{\mathbb{E}} \, \underset{\pi(a'|s')}{\mathbb{E}} \left[Q^\pi(s', a') \right], \; \forall s \in \mathcal{S}, \forall a \in \mathcal{A}, \quad (7.2)$$

where $R(s, a)$ is the expected reward function when the agent takes action a in state s:

$$R(s, a) := \underset{p_T(s'|s,a)}{\mathbb{E}} \left[R(s, a, s') \right].$$

$\mathbb{E}_{p_T(s'|s,a)}$ denotes the conditional expectation of s' over $p_T(s'|s, a)$, given s and a. $\mathbb{E}_{\pi(a'|s')}$ denotes the conditional expectation of a' over $\pi(a'|s')$, given s'.

7.6.2 Policy Iteration

The computation of the value function $Q^\pi(s, a)$ is called *policy evaluation*. With $Q^\pi(s, a)$, one can find a better policy $\pi'(a|s)$ by means of

$$\pi'(a|s) = \delta(a - \underset{a'}{\operatorname{argmax}}\, Q^\pi(s, a')).$$

This is called (greedy) *policy improvement*. It is known that repeating policy evaluation and policy improvement results in the optimal policy $\pi^*(a|s)$ [174]. This entire process is called *policy iteration*:

$$\pi_1 \overset{E}{\to} Q^{\pi_1} \overset{I}{\to} \pi_2 \overset{E}{\to} Q^{\pi_2} \overset{I}{\to} \pi_3 \overset{E}{\to} \cdots \overset{I}{\to} \pi^*,$$

---

5. We assume that given state s, there is only one action maximizing the optimal value function $Q^*(s, a)$.

where π_1 is an initial policy. E and I indicate the policy evaluation and policy improvement steps, respectively. For technical reasons, we assume that all policies are strictly positive (i.e., all actions have nonzero probability densities). In order to guarantee this, *explorative* policy improvement strategies such as the *Gibbs policy* and the *ϵ-greedy policy* are used here. In the case of the Gibbs policy,

$$\pi'(a|s) = \frac{\exp(Q^\pi(s,a)/\tau)}{\int_\mathcal{A} \exp(Q^\pi(s,a')/\tau)\,da'}, \tag{7.3}$$

where τ is a positive parameter which determines the randomness of the new policy π'. In the case of the ϵ-greedy policy,

$$\pi'(a|s) = \begin{cases} 1 - \epsilon + \epsilon/|\mathcal{A}| & \text{if } a = a^*, \\ \epsilon/|\mathcal{A}| & \text{otherwise,} \end{cases} \tag{7.4}$$

where

$$a^* = \underset{a}{\operatorname{argmax}}\, Q^\pi(s,a)$$

and $\epsilon \in (0,1]$ determines how stochastic the new policy π' is.

7.6.3 Value Function Approximation

Although policy iteration is guaranteed to produce the optimal policy, it is often computationally intractable since the number of state-action pairs $|\mathcal{S}| \times |\mathcal{A}|$ is very large; $|\mathcal{S}|$ or $|\mathcal{A}|$ can even become infinite when the state space or action space is continuous. To overcome this problem, the state-action value function $Q^\pi(s,a)$ is approximated using the following linear model [174, 124, 99]:

$$\widehat{Q}^\pi(s,a;\boldsymbol{\theta}) := \sum_{b=1}^B \theta_b \phi_b(s,a) = \boldsymbol{\theta}^\top \boldsymbol{\phi}(s,a),$$

where

$$\boldsymbol{\phi}(s,a) = (\phi_1(s,a), \phi_2(s,a), \ldots, \phi_B(s,a))^\top$$

are the fixed basis functions, $\top$ denotes the transpose, B is the number of basis functions, and

$$\boldsymbol{\theta} = (\theta_1, \theta_2, \ldots, \theta_B)^\top$$

are model parameters. Note that B is usually chosen to be much smaller than $|\mathcal{S}| \times |\mathcal{A}|$.

For N-step transitions, the ideal way to learn the parameters $\boldsymbol{\theta}$ is to minimize the approximation error of the state-action value function $Q^\pi(s,a)$:

$$\min_{\boldsymbol{\theta}} \; \mathbb{E}_{p_1,\pi,p_T}\left[\frac{1}{N}\sum_{n=1}^{N}\left(\widehat{Q}^\pi(s_n,a_n;\boldsymbol{\theta}) - Q^\pi(s_n,a_n)\right)^2\right],$$

where $\mathbb{E}_{p_1,\pi,p_T}$ denotes the expectation over $\{s_n, a_n\}_{n=1}^{N}$ following the initial state probability density $p_1(s_1)$, the policy $\pi(a_n|s_n)$, and the transition probability density $p_T(s_{n+1}|s_n, a_n)$.

A fundamental problem of the above formulation is that the target function $Q^\pi(s,a)$ cannot be observed directly. To cope with this problem, we attempt to minimize the square of the Bellman residual instead [99]:

$$\boldsymbol{\theta}^* := \operatorname*{argmin}_{\boldsymbol{\theta}} G, \tag{7.5}$$

$$G := \mathbb{E}_{p_1,\pi,p_T}\left[\frac{1}{N}\sum_{n=1}^{N} g(s_n, a_n; \boldsymbol{\theta})\right], \tag{7.6}$$

$$g(s, a; \boldsymbol{\theta}) := \left(\widehat{Q}^\pi(s, a; \boldsymbol{\theta}) - R(s, a) - \gamma \mathop{\mathbb{E}}_{p_T(s'|s,a)} \mathop{\mathbb{E}}_{\pi(a'|s)}\left[\widehat{Q}^\pi(s', a'; \boldsymbol{\theta})\right]\right)^2,$$

where $g(s, a; \boldsymbol{\theta})$ is the approximation error for one step (s, a) derived from the Bellman equation[6] (equation 7.2).

7.6.4 Sample Reuse by Covariate Shift Adaptation

In policy iteration, the optimal policy is obtained by iteratively performing policy evaluation and improvement steps [174, 13]. When policies are updated, many popular policy iteration methods require the user to gather new samples following the updated policy, and the new samples are used for value function approximation. However, this approach is inefficient particularly when

---

6. Note that $g(s,a;\boldsymbol{\theta})$ with a reward observation r instead of the expected reward $R(s,a)$ corresponds to the square of the temporal difference (TD) error. That is,

$$g_{\mathrm{TD}}(s, a, r; \boldsymbol{\theta}) := \left(\widehat{Q}^\pi(s, a, \boldsymbol{\theta}) - r - \gamma \mathop{\mathbb{E}}_{p_T(s'|s,a)} \mathop{\mathbb{E}}_{\pi(a'|s)}\left[\widehat{Q}^\pi(s', a'; \boldsymbol{\theta})\right]\right)^2.$$

Although we use the Bellman residual for measuring the approximation error, it can be easily replaced with the TD error.

the sampling cost is high, and it will be more cost-efficient if one can reuse the data collected in the past. A situation where the sampling policy (a policy used for gathering data samples) and the current policy are different is called *off-policy* reinforcement learning [174].

In the off-policy setup, simply employing a standard policy iteration method such as least-squares policy iteration [99] does not lead to the optimal policy, as the sampling policy can introduce bias into value function approximation. This distribution mismatch problem can be eased by the use of importance-weighting techniques, which cancel the bias asymptotically. However, the approximation error is not necessarily small when the bias is reduced by importance weighting; the variance of estimators also needs to be taken into account since the approximation error is the sum of squared bias and variance. Due to large variance, naive importance-weighting techniques used in reinforcement learning tend to be unstable [174, 125].

To overcome the instability problem, an *adaptive importance-weighting* technique is useful. As shown in section 2.1.2, the adaptive importance-weighted estimator smoothly bridges the ordinary estimator and the importance-weighted estimator, allowing one to control the trade-off between bias and variance. Thus, given that the trade-off parameter is determined carefully, the optimal performance may be achieved in terms of both bias and variance. However, the optimal value of the trade-off parameter is heavily dependent on data samples and policies, and therefore using a predetermined parameter value may not always be effective in practice.

For optimally choosing the value of the trade-off parameter, importance-weighted cross-validation [160] (see section 3.3) enables one to estimate the approximation error of value functions in an almost unbiased manner even under off-policy situations. Thus, one can adaptively choose the trade-off parameter based on data samples at hand.

7.6.5 On-Policy vs. Off-Policy

Suppose that a data set consisting of M episodes of N steps is available. The agent initially starts from a randomly selected state s_1 following the initial state probability density $p_1(s)$ and chooses an action based on a *sampling policy* $\widetilde{\pi}(a_n|s_n)$. Then the agent makes a transition following $p_T(s_{n+1}|s_n, a_n)$, and receives a reward r_n $(= R(s_n, a_n, s_{n+1}))$. This is repeated for N steps—thus, the training data $\mathcal{D}^{\widetilde{\pi}}$ are expressed as

$$\mathcal{D}^{\widetilde{\pi}} := \{d_m^{\widetilde{\pi}}\}_{m=1}^M,$$

where each episodic sample $d_m^{\tilde{\pi}}$ consists of a set of quadruple elements as

$$d_m^{\tilde{\pi}} := \{(s_{m,n}^{\tilde{\pi}}, a_{m,n}^{\tilde{\pi}}, r_{m,n}^{\tilde{\pi}}, s_{m,n+1}^{\tilde{\pi}})\}_{n=1}^N.$$

Two types of policies which have different purposes are used here: the sampling policy $\tilde{\pi}(a|s)$ for collecting data samples and the current policy $\pi(a|s)$ for computing the value function $\widehat{Q}^\pi$. When $\tilde{\pi}(a|s)$ is equal to $\pi(a|s)$ (the situation called *on-policy*), just replacing the expectation contained in the error G defined in equation 7.6 by a sample average gives a consistent estimator (i.e., the estimated parameter converges to the optimal value as the number of episodes M goes to infinity):

$$\widehat{\boldsymbol{\theta}}_{\text{NIW}} := \underset{\boldsymbol{\theta}}{\arg\min}\, \widehat{G}_{\text{NIW}},$$

$$\widehat{G}_{\text{NIW}} := \frac{1}{MN}\sum_{m=1}^M \sum_{n=1}^N \widehat{g}_{m,n},$$

$$\widehat{g}_{m,n} := \widehat{g}(s_{m,n}^{\tilde{\pi}}, a_{m,n}^{\tilde{\pi}}; \boldsymbol{\theta}, \mathcal{D}^\pi),$$

$$\widehat{g}(s, a; \boldsymbol{\theta}, \mathcal{D}) := \left(\widehat{Q}^\pi(s, a; \boldsymbol{\theta}) - \frac{1}{|\mathcal{D}_{(s,a)}|}\sum_{r \in \mathcal{D}_{(s,a)}} r \right.$$

$$\left. - \frac{\gamma}{|\mathcal{D}_{(s,a)}|}\sum_{s' \in \mathcal{D}_{(s,a)}} \mathbb{E}_{\pi(a'|s')}[\widehat{Q}^\pi(s', a'; \boldsymbol{\theta})]\right)^2,$$

where $\mathcal{D}_{(s,a)}$ is a set of quadruple elements containing state s and action a in the training data $\mathcal{D}$, and $\sum_{r \in \mathcal{D}_{(s,a)}}$ and $\sum_{s' \in \mathcal{D}_{(s,a)}}$ denote the summation over r and s' in the set $\mathcal{D}_{(s,a)}$, respectively. Note that NIW stands for No Importance Weight.

However, in reality, $\tilde{\pi}(a|s)$ is usually different from $\pi(a|s)$, since the current policy is updated in policy iteration. The situation where $\tilde{\pi}(a|s)$ is different from $\pi(a|s)$ is called off-policy. In the off-policy setup, $\widehat{\boldsymbol{\theta}}_{\text{NIW}}$ is no longer consistent. This inconsistency can be avoided by gathering new samples. That is, when the current policy is updated, new samples are gathered following the updated policy, and the new samples are used for policy evaluation. However, when the data sampling cost is high, this is not cost-efficient—it would be more practical if one could reuse the previously gathered samples.

7.6.6 Importance Weighting in Value Function Approximation

For coping with the off-policy situation, we would like to use importance-weighting techniques. However, this is not that straightforward since our

7.6. Sample Reuse in Reinforcement Learning

training samples of state s and action a are not i.i.d. due to the sequential nature of MDPs. Below, standard importance-weighting techniques in the context of MDPs are reviewed.

7.6.6.1 Episodic Importance Weighting The method of *episodic importance weighting* (EIW) [174] utilizes the independence between episodes:

$$p(d, d') = p(d)p(d')$$
$$= p(s_1, a_1, s_2, a_2, \ldots, s_N, a_N, s_{N+1})$$
$$\times p(s'_1, a'_1, s'_2, a'_2, \ldots, s'_N, a'_N, s'_{N+1}).$$

Based on the independence between episodes, the error G defined by equation 7.6 can be rewritten as

$$G = \mathop{\mathbb{E}}_{p_\mathrm{I}, \widetilde{\pi}, p_\mathrm{T}} \left[\frac{1}{N} \sum_{n=1}^{N} g(s_n, a_n; \boldsymbol{\theta}) w_N \right],$$

where

$$w_N := \frac{p_\pi(d)}{p_{\widetilde{\pi}}(d)}.$$

$p_\pi(d)$ and $p_{\widetilde{\pi}}(d)$ are the probability densities of observing episodic data d under policy π and policy $\widetilde{\pi}$, respectively:

$$p_\pi(d) := p_\mathrm{I}(s_1) \prod_{n=1}^{N} \pi(a_n|s_n) p_\mathrm{T}(s_{n+1}|s_n, a_n),$$

$$p_{\widetilde{\pi}}(d) := p_\mathrm{I}(s_1) \prod_{n=1}^{N} \widetilde{\pi}(a_n|s_n) p_\mathrm{T}(s_{n+1}|s_n, a_n).$$

Note that the importance weights can be computed *without* explicitly knowing p_I and p_T since they are canceled out:

$$w_N = \frac{\prod_{n=1}^{N} \pi(a_n|s_n)}{\prod_{n=1}^{N} \widetilde{\pi}(a_n|s_n)}.$$

Thus, in the off-policy reinforcement learning scenario, importance estimation (chapter 4) is not necessary. Using the training data $\mathcal{D}^{\widetilde{\pi}}$, one can construct a consistent estimator of G as

$$\widehat{G}_{\text{EIW}} := \frac{1}{MN} \sum_{m=1}^{M} \sum_{n=1}^{N} \widehat{g}_{m,n} w_{m,N}, \qquad (7.7)$$

where

$$w_{m,N} := \frac{\prod_{n'=1}^{N} \pi(a_{m,n'}^{\widetilde{\pi}} | s_{m,n'}^{\widetilde{\pi}})}{\prod_{n'=1}^{N} \widetilde{\pi}(a_{m,n'}^{\widetilde{\pi}} | s_{m,n'}^{\widetilde{\pi}})}.$$

Based on this, the parameter θ is estimated by

$$\widehat{\theta}_{\text{EIW}} := \underset{\theta}{\operatorname{argmin}} \, \widehat{G}_{\text{EIW}}.$$

7.6.6.2 Per-Decision Importance Weighting A more sophisticated importance-weighting technique, called the *per-decision importance-weighting* (PIW) method, was proposed in [125]. A crucial observation in PIW is that the error at the n-th step does not depend on the samples after the n-th step, that is, the error G can be rewritten as

$$G = \underset{p_{\text{I}}, \widetilde{\pi}, p_{\text{T}}}{\mathbb{E}} \left[\frac{1}{N} \sum_{n=1}^{N} g(s_n, a_n; \theta) w_n \right].$$

Using the training data $\mathcal{D}^{\widetilde{\pi}}$, one can construct a consistent estimator as follows (see equation 7.7):

$$\widehat{G}_{\text{PIW}} := \frac{1}{MN} \sum_{m=1}^{M} \sum_{n=1}^{N} \widehat{g}_{m,n} w_{m,n}. \qquad (7.8)$$

$w_{m,n}$ in equation 7.8 contains only the relevant terms up to the n-th step, while $w_{m,N}$ in equation 7.7 includes all the terms upto the end of the episode.

Based on this, the parameter θ is estimated by

$$\widehat{\theta}_{\text{PIW}} := \underset{\theta}{\operatorname{argmin}} \, \widehat{G}_{\text{PIW}}.$$

7.6.6.3 Adaptive Per-Decision Importance Weighting The importance-weighted estimator $\widehat{\theta}_{\text{PIW}}$ (also $\widehat{\theta}_{\text{EIW}}$) is guaranteed to be consistent. However, both are not efficient in the statistical sense [145], that is, they do not have the smallest admissible variance. For this reason, $\widehat{\theta}_{\text{PIW}}$ can have large variance

7.6. Sample Reuse in Reinforcement Learning

in finite sample cases, and therefore learning with PIW can be unstable in practice. Below, an adaptive importance-weighting method (see section 2.1.2) is employed for enhancing stability.

In order to improve the estimation accuracy, it is important to control the trade-off between consistency and efficiency (or, similarly, bias and variance) based on the training data. Here, the *flattening parameter* ν $(\in [0, 1])$ is introduced to control the trade-off by slightly "flattening" the importance weights [145, 160]:

$$\widehat{G}_{\text{AIW}} := \frac{1}{MN} \sum_{m=1}^{M} \sum_{n=1}^{N} \widehat{g}_{m,n} \times (w_{m,n})^{\nu}, \quad (7.9)$$

where AIW stands for "Adaptive PIW." Based on this, the parameter θ is estimated as follows:

$$\widehat{\theta}_{\text{AIW}} := \operatorname*{argmin}_{\theta} \widehat{G}_{\text{AIW}}.$$

When $\nu = 0$, $\widehat{\theta}_{\text{AIW}}$ is reduced to the ordinary estimator $\widehat{\theta}_{\text{NIW}}$. Therefore, it has large bias but has relatively small variance. On the other hand, when $\nu = 1$, $\widehat{\theta}_{\text{AIW}}$ is reduced to the importance-weighted estimator $\widehat{\theta}_{\text{PIW}}$. Therefore, it has small bias but relatively large variance. In practice, an intermediate ν would yield the best performance.

The solution $\widehat{\theta}_{\text{AIW}}$ can be computed analytically as follows [66]:

$$\widehat{\theta}_{\text{AIW}} = \left(\sum_{m=1}^{M} \sum_{n=1}^{N} \widehat{\psi}(s_{m,n}^{\widetilde{\pi}}, a_{m,n}^{\widetilde{\pi}}; \mathcal{D}^{\widetilde{\pi}}) \widehat{\psi}(s_{m,n}^{\widetilde{\pi}}, a_{m,n}^{\widetilde{\pi}}; \mathcal{D}^{\widetilde{\pi}})^{\top} (w_{m,n})^{\nu} \right)^{-1}$$

$$\times \left(\sum_{m=1}^{M} \sum_{n=1}^{N} \left(\frac{1}{|\mathcal{D}_{(s_{m,n}^{\widetilde{\pi}}, a_{m,n}^{\widetilde{\pi}})}|} \sum_{r \in \mathcal{D}_{(s_{m,n}^{\widetilde{\pi}}, a_{m,n}^{\widetilde{\pi}})}} r \right) \right.$$

$$\left. \times \widehat{\psi}(s_{m,n}^{\widetilde{\pi}}, a_{m,n}^{\widetilde{\pi}}; \mathcal{D}^{\widetilde{\pi}}) (w_{m,n})^{\nu} \right), \quad (7.10)$$

where $\widehat{\psi}(s, a; \mathcal{D})$ is a B-dimensional column vector defined by

$$\widehat{\psi}(s, a; \mathcal{D}) := \phi(s, a) - \frac{\gamma}{|\mathcal{D}_{(s,a)}|} \sum_{s' \in \mathcal{D}_{(s,a)}} \mathbb{E}_{\pi(a'|s')} [\phi(s', a')].$$

This implies that the cost for computing $\widehat{\theta}_{\text{AIW}}$ is essentially the same as for $\widehat{\theta}_{\text{NIW}}$ and $\widehat{\theta}_{\text{PIW}}$.

7.6.7 Automatic Selection of the Flattening Parameter

As shown above, the performance of AIW depends on the choice of the flattening parameter ν. Ideally, ν is set so that the approximation error G is minimized. However, the true G is inaccessible in practice. To cope with this problem, the approximation error G may be replaced by its estimator obtained using IWCV [160] (see section 3.3). Below we explain how IWCV can be applied to the selection of the flattening parameter ν in the context of value function approximation.

Let us divide a training data set $\mathcal{D}^{\widetilde{\pi}}$ containing M episodes into K subsets $\{\mathcal{D}^{\widetilde{\pi}}_k\}_{k=1}^K$ of approximately the same size (we used $K = 5$ in experiments). For simplicity, assume that M is divisible by K. Let $\widehat{\boldsymbol{\theta}}^k_{\mathrm{AIW}}$ be the parameter learned from $\{\mathcal{D}^{\widetilde{\pi}}_{k'}\}_{k' \neq k}$ with AIW (see equation 7.9). Then, the approximation error is estimated by

$$\widehat{G}_{\mathrm{IWCV}} = \frac{1}{K} \sum_{k=1}^K \widehat{G}^k_{\mathrm{IWCV}},$$

where

$$\widehat{G}^k_{\mathrm{IWCV}} = \frac{K}{MN} \sum_{d^{\widetilde{\pi}}_m \in \mathcal{D}^{\widetilde{\pi}}_k} \sum_{n=1}^N \widehat{g}(s^{\widetilde{\pi}}_{m,n}, a^{\widetilde{\pi}}_{m,n}, r^{\widetilde{\pi}}_{m,n}; \widehat{\boldsymbol{\theta}}^k_{\mathrm{AIW}}, \mathcal{D}^{\widetilde{\pi}}_k) w_{m,n}.$$

The approximation error is estimated by the above K-fold IWCV method for all candidate models (in the current setting, a candidate model corresponds to a different value of the flattening parameter ν). Then the model candidate that minimizes the estimated error is selected:

$$\widehat{\nu}_{\mathrm{IWCV}} = \underset{\nu}{\mathrm{argmin}}\, \widehat{G}_{\mathrm{IWCV}}.$$

In general, the use of IWCV is computationally rather expensive since $\widehat{\boldsymbol{\theta}}^k_{\mathrm{AIW}}$ and $\widehat{G}^k_{\mathrm{IWCV}}$ need to be computed many times. For example, when performing fivefold IWCV for 11 candidates of the flattening parameter $\nu \in \{0.0, 0.1, \ldots, 0.9, 1.0\}$, $\widehat{\boldsymbol{\theta}}^k_{\mathrm{AIW}}$ and $\widehat{G}^k_{\mathrm{IWCV}}$ need to be computed 55 times. However, this would be acceptable in practice for two reasons. First, sensible model selection via IWCV allows one to obtain a much better solution with a small number of samples. Thus, in total, the computation time may not grow that much. The second reason is that cross-validation is suitable for parallel computing since error estimation for different flattening parameters and different folds are independent of one another. For instance, when performing fivefold

7.6. Sample Reuse in Reinforcement Learning

IWCV for 11 candidates of the flattening parameter, one can compute $\widehat{G}_{\text{IWCV}}$ for all candidates at once in parallel, using 55 CPUs; this would be highly realistic in the current computing environment. If a simulated problem is solved, the storage of all sequences can be more costly than resampling. However, for real-world applications, it is essential to reuse data, and IWCV will be one of the more promising approaches.

7.6.8 Sample Reuse Policy Iteration

So far, the AIW+IWCV method has been considered only in the context of policy evaluation. Here, this method is extended to the full policy iteration setup.

Let us denote the policy at the l-th iteration by π_l and the maximum number of iterations by L. In general policy iteration methods, new data samples $\mathcal{D}^{\pi_l}$ are collected following the new policy π_l during the policy evaluation step. Thus, previously collected data samples $\{\mathcal{D}^{\pi_1}, \mathcal{D}^{\pi_2}, \ldots, \mathcal{D}^{\pi_{l-1}}\}$ are not used:

$$\pi_1 \xrightarrow{E:\{\mathcal{D}^{\pi_1}\}} \widehat{Q}^{\pi_1} \xrightarrow{I} \pi_2 \xrightarrow{E:\{\mathcal{D}^{\pi_2}\}} \widehat{Q}^{\pi_2} \xrightarrow{I} \pi_3 \xrightarrow{E:\{\mathcal{D}^{\pi_3}\}} \cdots \xrightarrow{I} \pi_L,$$

where $E:\{\mathcal{D}\}$ indicates policy evaluation using the data sample $\mathcal{D}$. It would be more cost-efficient if one could reuse all previously collected data samples to perform policy evaluation with a growing data set as

$$\pi_1 \xrightarrow{E:\{\mathcal{D}^{\pi_1}\}} \widehat{Q}^{\pi_1} \xrightarrow{I} \pi_2 \xrightarrow{E:\{\mathcal{D}^{\pi_1},\mathcal{D}^{\pi_2}\}} \widehat{Q}^{\pi_2} \xrightarrow{I} \pi_3 \xrightarrow{E:\{\mathcal{D}^{\pi_1},\mathcal{D}^{\pi_2},\mathcal{D}^{\pi_3}\}} \cdots \xrightarrow{I} \pi_L.$$

Reusing previously collected data samples turns this into an *off-policy* scenario because the previous policies and the current policy are different unless the current policy has converged to the optimal one. Here, the AIW+IWCV method is applied to policy iteration. For this purpose, the definition of $\widehat{G}_{\text{AIW}}$ is extended so that multiple sampling policies $\{\pi_1, \pi_2, \ldots, \pi_l\}$ are taken into account:

$$\widehat{\boldsymbol{\theta}}^l_{\text{AIW}} := \operatorname*{argmin}_{\boldsymbol{\theta}} \widehat{G}^l_{\text{AIW}},$$

$$\widehat{G}^l_{\text{AIW}} := \frac{1}{lMN} \sum_{l'=1}^{l} \sum_{m=1}^{M} \sum_{n=1}^{N} \widehat{g}(s^{\pi_{l'}}_{m,n}, a^{\pi_{l'}}_{m,n}; \boldsymbol{\theta}, \{\mathcal{D}^{\pi_{l'}}\}^l_{l'=1})$$

$$\times \left(\frac{\prod_{n'=1}^{n} \pi_l(a^{\pi_{l'}}_{m,n'} | s^{\pi_{l'}}_{m,n'})}{\prod_{n'=1}^{n} \pi_{l'}(a^{\pi_{l'}}_{m,n'} | s^{\pi_{l'}}_{m,n'})} \right)^{\nu_l}, \qquad (7.11)$$

where $\widehat{G}^l_{\mathrm{AIW}}$ is the approximation error estimated at the l-th policy evaluation using AIW. The flattening parameter ν_l is chosen based on IWCV before performing policy evaluation. This method is called *sample reuse policy iteration* (SRPI) [66].

7.6.9 Robot Control Experiments

Here, the performance of the SRPI method is evaluated in a robot control task of an upward swinging inverted pendulum.

We consider the task of an upward swinging *inverted pendulum* illustrated in figure 7.6a, consisting of a rod hinged at the top of a cart. The goal of the task is to swing the rod up by moving the cart. We have three actions: applying positive force $+50$ $[kg \cdot m/s^2]$ to the cart to move right, negative force -50 to move left, and zero force just to coast. That is, the action space $\mathcal{A}$ is discrete and described by

$$\mathcal{A} = \{50, -50, 0\}\ [kg \cdot m/s^2].$$

Note that the force itself is not strong enough, so the cart needs to be moved back and forth several times to swing the rod up. The state space $\mathcal{S}$ is continuous and consists of the angle φ $[rad]$ ($\in [0, 2\pi]$) and the angular velocity $\dot{\varphi}$ $[rad/s]$ ($\in [-\pi, \pi]$)—thus, a state s is described by a two-dimensional vector

$$s = (\varphi, \dot{\varphi})^\top.$$

Figure 7.6b shows the parameter setting used in the simulation. The angle φ and angular velocity $\dot{\varphi}$ are updated as follows:

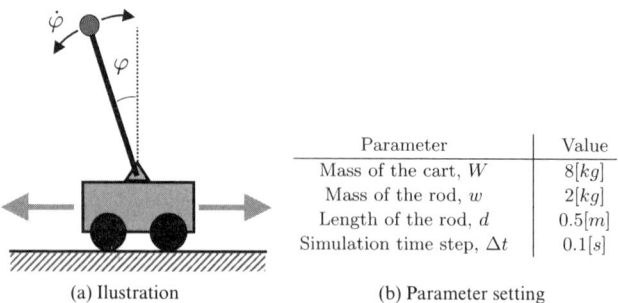

Figure 7.6
Illustration of the inverted pendulum task and parameters used in the simulation.

7.6. Sample Reuse in Reinforcement Learning

$$\varphi_{t+1} = \varphi_t + \dot{\varphi}_{t+1}\Delta t,$$

$$\dot{\varphi}_{t+1} = \dot{\varphi}_t + \frac{9.8\sin(\varphi_t) - \alpha wd(\dot{\varphi}_t)^2 \sin(2\varphi_t)/2 + \alpha \cos(\varphi_t)a_t}{4l/3 - \alpha wd \cos^2(\varphi_t)} \Delta t,$$

where $\alpha = 1/(W + w)$ and a_t is the action in $\mathcal{A}$ chosen at time t. The reward function $R(s, a, s')$ is defined as

$$R(s, a, s') = \cos(\varphi_{s'}),$$

where $\varphi_{s'}$ denotes the angle φ of state s'.

Forty-eight Gaussian kernels with standard deviation $\sigma = \pi$ are used as basis functions, and kernel centers are distributed over the following grid points:

$$\{0, 2/3\pi, 4/3\pi, 2\pi\} \times \{-3\pi, -\pi, \pi, 3\pi\}.$$

That is, the basis functions

$$\boldsymbol{\phi}(s, a) = (\phi_1(s, a), \phi_2(s, a), \ldots, \phi_{48}(s, a))^\top$$

are set to

$$\phi_{16(i-1)+j}(s, a) = I(a = a^{(i)}) \exp\left(-\frac{\|s - c_j\|^2}{2\sigma^2}\right),$$

for $i = 1, 2, 3$ and $j = 1, 2, \ldots, 16$, where

$$c_1 = (0, -3\pi)^\top, c_2 = (0, -\pi)^\top, \ldots, c_{16} = (2\pi, 3\pi)^\top.$$

The initial policy $\pi_1(a|s)$ is chosen randomly, and the initial state probability density $p_1(s)$ is set to be uniform. The agent collects data samples $\mathcal{D}^{\pi_l}$ ($M = 10$ and $N = 100$) at each policy iteration following the current policy π_l. The discounted factor is set to $\gamma = 0.95$, and the policy is improved by the Gibbs policy (equation 7.3) with $\tau = l$.

Figure 7.7a describes the performance of learned policies measured by the discounted sum of rewards as functions of the total number of episodes. The graph shows that SRPI nicely improves the performance throughout the entire policy iteration process. On the other hand, the performance when the flattening parameter is fixed to $\nu = 0$ or $\nu = 1$ is not properly improved after the middle iterations. The average flattening parameter value as a function of the

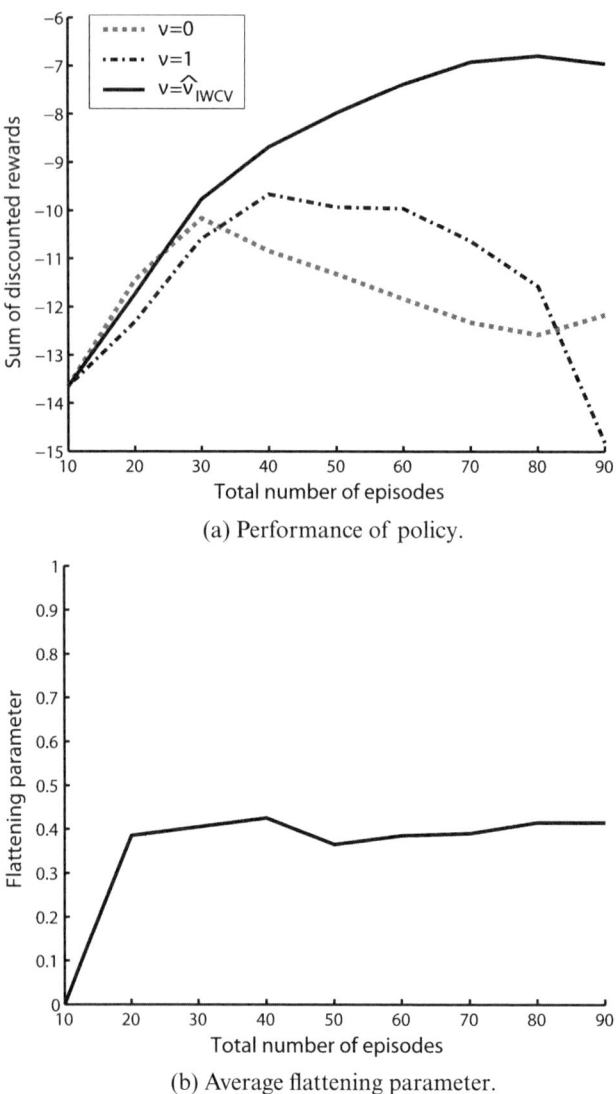

Figure 7.7
The results of sample reuse policy iteration in upward swing of an inverted pendulum. The agent collects training sample $\mathcal{D}^{\pi_l}$ ($M = 10$ and $N = 100$) at every iteration, and policy evaluation is performed using all collected samples $\{\mathcal{D}^{\pi_1}, \mathcal{D}^{\pi_2}, \ldots, \mathcal{D}^{\pi_l}\}$. (a) The performance of policies learned with $\nu = 0$, $\nu = 1$, and SRPI. The performance is measured by the average sum of discounted rewards computed from test samples over 20 trials. The total number of episodes is the number of training episodes ($M \times l$) collected by the agent in policy iteration. (b) Average flattening parameter used by SRPI over 20 trials.

total number of episodes is depicted in figure 7.7b, showing that the parameter value tends to increase quickly in the beginning and then is kept at medium values. These results indicate that the flattening parameter is well adjusted to reuse the previously collected samples effectively for policy evaluation, and thus SRPI can outperform the other methods.

LEARNING CAUSING COVARIATE SHIFT

8 Active Learning

Active learning [107,33,55]—also referred to as *experimental design* in statistics [93,48,127]—is the problem of determining the locations of training input points so that the generalization error is minimized (see figure 8.1). Active learning is particularly useful when the cost of sampling output value y is very expensive. In such cases, we want to find the best input points to observe output values within a fixed number of budgets (which corresponds to the number n_{tr} of training samples).

Since training input points are generated following a user-defined distribution, covariate shift naturally occurs in the active learning scenario. Thus, covariate shift adaptation techniques also play essential roles in the active learning scenario. In this chapter, we consider two types of active learning scenarios: *population-based* active learning, where one is allowed to sample output values at any input location (sections 8.2 and 8.3) and *pool-based* active learning, where input locations that are to have output values are chosen from a pool of (unlabeled) input samples (sections 8.4 and 8.5).

8.1 Preliminaries

In this section, we first summarize the common setup of this chapter. Then we describe a general strategy of active learning.

8.1.1 Setup

We focus on a linear regression setup throughout this chapter:

- The squared loss (see section 1.3.2) is used, and training output noise is assumed to be i.i.d. with mean zero and variance σ^2. Then the generalization

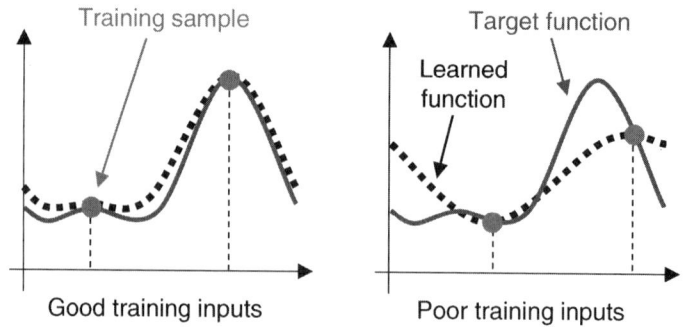

Figure 8.1
Active learning. In both cases, the target function is learned from two (noiseless) training samples. The only difference is the training input location.

error is expressed as follows (see section 3.2.2):

$$\text{Gen} := \mathop{\mathbb{E}}_{x^{te}} \mathop{\mathbb{E}}_{y^{te}} \left[\text{loss}(x^{te}, y^{te}, \widehat{f}(x^{te}; \theta)) \right]$$

$$= \mathop{\mathbb{E}}_{x^{te}} \left[\left(\widehat{f}(x^{te}; \theta) - f(x^{te}) \right)^2 \right] + \sigma^2,$$

where $\mathbb{E}_{x^{te}}$ denotes the expectation over x^{te} drawn from $p_{te}(x)$ and $\mathbb{E}_{y^{te}}$ denotes the expectation over y^{te} drawn from $p(y|x = x^{te})$.

- The test input density $p_{te}(x)$ is assumed to be known. This assumption is essential in the population-based active learning scenario since the training input points $\{x_i^{tr}\}_{i=1}^{n_{tr}}$ are designed so that prediction for the given $p_{te}(x)$ is improved (see sections 8.2 and 8.3 for details). In the pool-based active learning scenario, $p_{te}(x)$ is unknown, but a pool of (unlabeled) input samples drawn i.i.d. from $p_{te}(x)$ is assumed to be given (see sections 8.4 and 8.5 for details).
- A linear-in-parameter model (see section 1.3.5.1) is used:

$$\widehat{f}(x; \theta) = \sum_{\ell=1}^{b} \theta_\ell \varphi_\ell(x), \tag{8.1}$$

where θ is the parameter to be learned and $\{\varphi_\ell(x)\}_{\ell=1}^{b}$ are fixed linearly independent functions.

- A linear method is used for learning the parameter θ, that is, the learned parameter $\widehat{\theta}$ is given by

$$\widehat{\theta} = L y^{tr},$$

8.1. Preliminaries

where

$$\boldsymbol{y}^{\mathrm{tr}} := (y_1^{\mathrm{tr}}, y_2^{\mathrm{tr}}, \ldots, y_{n_{\mathrm{tr}}}^{\mathrm{tr}})^\top.$$

L is a $b \times n_{\mathrm{tr}}$ learning matrix that is independent of the training output noise; this independence assumption is essentially used as

$$\mathbb{E}_{\{y_i^{\mathrm{tr}}\}_{i=1}^{n_{\mathrm{tr}}}}\left[\widehat{\boldsymbol{\theta}}\right] = \mathbb{E}_{\{y_i^{\mathrm{tr}}\}_{i=1}^{n_{\mathrm{tr}}}}\left[L\boldsymbol{y}^{\mathrm{tr}}\right] = L\,\mathbb{E}_{\{y_i^{\mathrm{tr}}\}_{i=1}^{n_{\mathrm{tr}}}}\left[\boldsymbol{y}^{\mathrm{tr}}\right],$$

where $\mathbb{E}_{\{y_i^{\mathrm{tr}}\}_{i=1}^{n_{\mathrm{tr}}}}$ denotes the expectations over $\{y_i^{\mathrm{tr}}\}_{i=1}^{n_{\mathrm{tr}}}$, each of which is drawn from $p(y|\boldsymbol{x}=\boldsymbol{x}_i^{\mathrm{tr}})$.

8.1.2 Decomposition of Generalization Error

Let $\boldsymbol{\theta}^*$ be the optimal parameter under the generalization error:

$$\boldsymbol{\theta}^* := \operatorname*{argmin}_{\theta}[\mathrm{Gen}].$$

Let $\delta r(\boldsymbol{x})$ be the residual function

$$\delta r(\boldsymbol{x}) := \widehat{f}(\boldsymbol{x}; \boldsymbol{\theta}^*) - f(\boldsymbol{x}).$$

We normalize $r(\boldsymbol{x})$ as

$$\mathbb{E}_{\boldsymbol{x}^{\mathrm{te}}}\left[r^2(\boldsymbol{x}^{\mathrm{te}})\right] = 1,$$

so that δ governs the "magnitude" of the residual and $r(\boldsymbol{x})$ expresses the "direction" of the residual. Note that $r(\boldsymbol{x})$ is orthogonal to $\widehat{f}(\boldsymbol{x}; \boldsymbol{\theta})$ for any $\boldsymbol{\theta}$ under $p_{\mathrm{te}}(\boldsymbol{x})$ (see figure 3.2 in section 3.2.2):

$$\mathbb{E}_{\boldsymbol{x}^{\mathrm{te}}}\left[r(\boldsymbol{x}^{\mathrm{te}})\widehat{f}(\boldsymbol{x}^{\mathrm{te}}; \boldsymbol{\theta})\right] = 0 \text{ for any } \boldsymbol{\theta}.$$

Then the generalization error expected over the training output values $\{y_i^{\mathrm{tr}}\}_{i=1}^{n_{\mathrm{tr}}}$ can be decomposed as

$$\mathbb{E}_{\{y_i^{\mathrm{tr}}\}_{i=1}^{n_{\mathrm{tr}}}}[\mathrm{Gen}] = \mathbb{E}_{\{y_i^{\mathrm{tr}}\}_{i=1}^{n_{\mathrm{tr}}}} \mathbb{E}_{\boldsymbol{x}^{\mathrm{te}}}\left[\left(\widehat{f}(\boldsymbol{x}^{\mathrm{te}}; \widehat{\boldsymbol{\theta}}) - f(\boldsymbol{x}^{\mathrm{te}})\right)^2\right] + \sigma^2$$

$$= \mathbb{E}_{\{y_i^{\mathrm{tr}}\}_{i=1}^{n_{\mathrm{tr}}}} \mathbb{E}_{\boldsymbol{x}^{\mathrm{te}}}\left[\left(\widehat{f}(\boldsymbol{x}^{\mathrm{te}}; \widehat{\boldsymbol{\theta}}) - \widehat{f}(\boldsymbol{x}^{\mathrm{te}}; \boldsymbol{\theta}^*) + \delta r(\boldsymbol{x}^{\mathrm{te}})\right)^2\right] + \sigma^2$$

$$= \mathop{\mathbb{E}}_{\{y_i^{\text{tr}}\}_{i=1}^{n_{\text{tr}}}} \mathop{\mathbb{E}}_{x^{\text{te}}} \left[\left(\widehat{f}(x^{\text{te}}; \widehat{\theta}) - \widehat{f}(x^{\text{te}}; \theta^*) \right)^2 \right] + \delta^2 \mathop{\mathbb{E}}_{x^{\text{te}}} \left[r^2(x^{\text{te}}) \right]$$

$$+ 2 \mathop{\mathbb{E}}_{\{y_i^{\text{tr}}\}_{i=1}^{n_{\text{tr}}}} \mathop{\mathbb{E}}_{x^{\text{te}}} \left[\left(\widehat{f}(x^{\text{te}}; \widehat{\theta}) - \widehat{f}(x^{\text{te}}; \theta^*) \right) \left(\delta r(x^{\text{te}}) \right) \right] + \sigma^2$$

$$= \text{Gen}'' + \delta^2 + \sigma^2,$$

where

$$\text{Gen}'' := \mathop{\mathbb{E}}_{\{y_i^{\text{tr}}\}_{i=1}^{n_{\text{tr}}}} \mathop{\mathbb{E}}_{x^{\text{te}}} \left[\left(\widehat{f}(x^{\text{te}}; \widehat{\theta}) - \widehat{f}(x^{\text{te}}; \theta^*) \right) \right]. \tag{8.2}$$

Applying the standard *bias-variance decomposition* technique to Gen$''$, we have

$$\text{Gen}'' = \mathop{\mathbb{E}}_{\{y_i^{\text{tr}}\}_{i=1}^{n_{\text{tr}}}} \mathop{\mathbb{E}}_{x^{\text{te}}} \left[\left(\widehat{f}(x^{\text{te}}; \widehat{\theta}) - \widehat{f}(x^{\text{te}}; \theta^*) \right) \right]$$

$$= \mathop{\mathbb{E}}_{\{y_i^{\text{tr}}\}_{i=1}^{n_{\text{tr}}}} \mathop{\mathbb{E}}_{x^{\text{te}}} \Bigg[\bigg(\widehat{f}(x^{\text{te}}; \widehat{\theta}) - \mathop{\mathbb{E}}_{\{y_i^{\text{tr}}\}_{i=1}^{n_{\text{tr}}}} \left[\widehat{f}(x^{\text{te}}; \widehat{\theta}) \right]$$

$$+ \mathop{\mathbb{E}}_{\{y_i^{\text{tr}}\}_{i=1}^{n_{\text{tr}}}} \left[\widehat{f}(x^{\text{te}}; \widehat{\theta}) \right] - \widehat{f}(x^{\text{te}}; \theta^*) \bigg)^2 \Bigg]$$

$$= \mathop{\mathbb{E}}_{\{y_i^{\text{tr}}\}_{i=1}^{n_{\text{tr}}}} \mathop{\mathbb{E}}_{x^{\text{te}}} \Bigg[\bigg(\widehat{f}(x^{\text{te}}; \widehat{\theta}) - \mathop{\mathbb{E}}_{\{y_i^{\text{tr}}\}_{i=1}^{n_{\text{tr}}}} \left[\widehat{f}(x^{\text{te}}; \widehat{\theta}) \right] \bigg)^2 \Bigg]$$

$$+ 2 \mathop{\mathbb{E}}_{x^{\text{te}}} \Bigg[\bigg(\mathop{\mathbb{E}}_{\{y_i^{\text{tr}}\}_{i=1}^{n_{\text{tr}}}} \left[\widehat{f}(x^{\text{te}}; \widehat{\theta}) \right] - \mathop{\mathbb{E}}_{\{y_i^{\text{tr}}\}_{i=1}^{n_{\text{tr}}}} \left[\widehat{f}(x^{\text{te}}; \widehat{\theta}) \right] \bigg)$$

$$\times \bigg(\mathop{\mathbb{E}}_{\{y_i^{\text{tr}}\}_{i=1}^{n_{\text{tr}}}} \left[\widehat{f}(x^{\text{te}}; \widehat{\theta}) \right] - \widehat{f}(x^{\text{te}}; \theta^*) \bigg) \Bigg]$$

$$+ \mathop{\mathbb{E}}_{x^{\text{te}}} \Bigg[\bigg(\mathop{\mathbb{E}}_{\{y_i^{\text{tr}}\}_{i=1}^{n_{\text{tr}}}} \left[\widehat{f}(x^{\text{te}}; \widehat{\theta}) \right] - \widehat{f}(x^{\text{te}}; \theta^*) \bigg)^2 \Bigg]$$

$$= \text{Var} + \text{Bias}^2,$$

where Bias^2 and Var denote the squared bias and the variance defined as follows:

8.1. Preliminaries

$$\text{Bias}^2 := \mathbb{E}_{x^{\text{te}}} \left[\left(\mathbb{E}_{\{y_i^{\text{tr}}\}_{i=1}^{n_{\text{tr}}}} [\widehat{f}(x^{\text{te}}; \widehat{\theta})] - \widehat{f}(x^{\text{te}}; \theta^*) \right)^2 \right], \tag{8.3}$$

$$\text{Var} := \mathbb{E}_{\{y_i^{\text{tr}}\}_{i=1}^{n_{\text{tr}}}} \mathbb{E}_{x^{\text{te}}} \left[\left(\widehat{f}(x^{\text{te}}; \widehat{\theta}) - \mathbb{E}_{\{y_i^{\text{tr}}\}_{i=1}^{n_{\text{tr}}}} [\widehat{f}(x^{\text{te}}; \widehat{\theta})] \right)^2 \right]. \tag{8.4}$$

Under the linear learning setup (equation 8.1), Gen″, Bias² and Var are expressed in matrix/vector form as follows (see figure 8.2):

$$\text{Gen}'' = \mathbb{E}_{\{y_i^{\text{tr}}\}_{i=1}^{n_{\text{tr}}}} \left[\langle U(\widehat{\theta} - \theta^*), \widehat{\theta} - \theta^* \rangle \right],$$

$$\text{Bias}^2 = \mathbb{E}_{\{y_i^{\text{tr}}\}_{i=1}^{n_{\text{tr}}}} \left[\left\langle U\left(\mathbb{E}_{\{y_i^{\text{tr}}\}_{i=1}^{n_{\text{tr}}}} [\widehat{\theta}] - \theta^* \right), \mathbb{E}_{\{y_i^{\text{tr}}\}_{i=1}^{n_{\text{tr}}}} [\widehat{\theta}] - \theta^* \right\rangle \right],$$

$$\text{Var} = \mathbb{E}_{\{y_i^{\text{tr}}\}_{i=1}^{n_{\text{tr}}}} \left[\left\langle U\left(\widehat{\theta} - \mathbb{E}_{\{y_i^{\text{tr}}\}_{i=1}^{n_{\text{tr}}}} [\widehat{\theta}] \right), \widehat{\theta} - \mathbb{E}_{\{y_i^{\text{tr}}\}_{i=1}^{n_{\text{tr}}}} [\widehat{\theta}] \right\rangle \right]$$

$$= \sigma^2 \text{tr}(ULL^\top),$$

where U is the $b \times b$ matrix with the (ℓ, ℓ')-th element:

$$U_{\ell,\ell'} := \mathbb{E}_{x^{\text{te}}} [\varphi_\ell(x^{\text{te}}) \varphi_{\ell'}(x^{\text{te}})]. \tag{8.5}$$

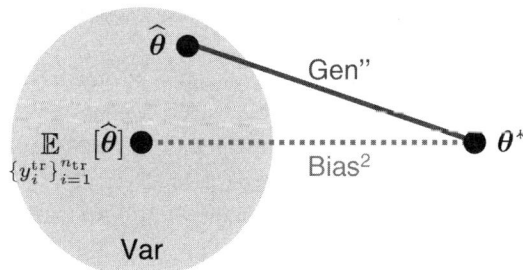

Figure 8.2
Bias-variance decomposition.

In some literature, $\text{Bias}^2 + \delta^2$ may be called the bias term:

$$\text{Bias}^2 + \delta^2 = \text{Bias}^2 + \delta^2 \underset{x^{\text{te}}}{\mathbb{E}} \left[r^2(x^{\text{te}}) \right]$$

$$= \underset{x^{\text{te}}}{\mathbb{E}} \left[\left(\underset{\{y_i^{\text{tr}}\}_{i=1}^{n_{\text{tr}}}}{\mathbb{E}} \left[\widehat{f}(x^{\text{te}}; \widehat{\boldsymbol{\theta}}) \right] - f(x^{\text{te}}) \right)^2 \right].$$

In our notation, we further decompose the above bias ($\text{Bias}^2 + \delta^2$) into the reducible part (Bias^2) and the *irreducible* part (δ^2), and refer to them as *bias* and *model error*, respectively.

8.1.3 Basic Strategy of Active Learning

The goal of active learning is to determine training input location $\{x_i^{\text{tr}}\}_{i=1}^{n_{\text{tr}}}$ so that the generalization error is minimized. Below, we focus on Gen'', the reducible part of Gen defined by equation 8.2, which is expressed as

$$\text{Gen}'' = \text{Gen} - \delta^2 - \sigma^2.$$

Note that the way the generalization error is decomposed here is different from that in model selection (cf. Gen' defined by equation 3.2).

Gen'' is unknown, so it needs to be estimated from samples. However, in active learning, we do not have training output values $\{y_i^{\text{tr}}\}_{i=1}^{n_{\text{tr}}}$ since the training input points $\{x_i^{\text{tr}}\}_{i=1}^{n_{\text{tr}}}$ have not yet been determined. Thus, the generalization error should be estimated without observing the training output values $\{y_i^{\text{tr}}\}_{i=1}^{n_{\text{tr}}}$. Therefore, generalization error estimation in active learning is generally more difficult than that in model selection, where both $\{x_i^{\text{tr}}\}_{i=1}^{n_{\text{tr}}}$ and $\{y_i^{\text{tr}}\}_{i=1}^{n_{\text{tr}}}$ are available.

Since we cannot use $\{y_i^{\text{tr}}\}_{i=1}^{n_{\text{tr}}}$ for estimating the generalization error, it is generally not possible to estimate the bias (equation 8.3), which depends on the true target function $f(x)$. A general strategy for coping with this problem is to find a setup where the bias is guaranteed to be zero (or small enough to be neglected), and design the location of training input points $\{x_i^{\text{tr}}\}_{i=1}^{n_{\text{tr}}}$ so that the variance (equation 8.4) is minimized.

Following this basic strategy, we describe several active learning methods below.

8.2 Population-Based Active Learning Methods

Population-based active learning indicates the situation where we know the distribution of test input points, and we are allowed to locate training input

8.2. Population-Based Active Learning Methods

points at any desired positions. The goal of population-based active learning is to find the optimal training input density $p_{tr}(x)$ (from which we generate training input points $\{x_i^{tr}\}_{i=1}^{n_{tr}}$) so that the generalization error is minimized.

8.2.1 Classical Method of Active Learning for Correct Models

A traditional variance-only active learning method assumes the following conditions (see, e.g., [48, 33, 55]):

- The model at hand is *correctly specified* (see section 1.3.6), that is, the model error δ is zero. In this case, we have

$$\widehat{f}(x; \theta^*) = f(x).$$

- The design matrix X^{tr}, which is the $n_{tr} \times b$ matrix with the (i, ℓ)-th element

$$X_{i,\ell} := \varphi_\ell(x_i^{tr}), \tag{8.6}$$

has rank b. Then the inverse of $X^{tr\top} X^{tr}$ exists.

- Ordinary least squares (OLS, which is an ERM method with the squared loss; see chapter 2) is used for parameter learning:

$$\widehat{\theta}_{OLS} := \underset{\theta}{\operatorname{argmin}} \left[\frac{1}{n_{tr}} \sum_{i=1}^{n_{tr}} \left(\widehat{f}(x_i^{tr}; \theta) - y_i^{tr} \right)^2 \right]. \tag{8.7}$$

The solution $\widehat{\theta}_{OLS}$ is given by

$$\widehat{\theta}_{OLS} = L_{OLS} y^{tr},$$

where

$$L_{OLS} := (X^{tr\top} X^{tr})^{-1} X^{tr\top},$$

$$y^{tr} := (y_1^{tr}, y_2^{tr}, \ldots, y_{n_{tr}}^{tr})^\top.$$

Under the above setup, Bias^2, defined in equation 8.3, is guaranteed to be zero, since

$$\underset{\{y_i^{tr}\}_{i=1}^{n_{tr}}}{\mathbb{E}} \left[\widehat{\theta}_{OLS} \right] = \underset{\{y_i^{tr}\}_{i=1}^{n_{tr}}}{\mathbb{E}} \left[L_{OLS} y^{tr} \right]$$

$$= L_{OLS} \underset{\{y_i^{tr}\}_{i=1}^{n_{tr}}}{\mathbb{E}} \left[y^{tr} \right]$$

$$= (X^{\text{tr}\top} X^{\text{tr}})^{-1} X^{\text{tr}\top} X^{\text{tr}} \theta^*$$
$$= \theta^*.$$

Then the training input points $\{x_i^{\text{tr}}\}_{i=1}^{n_{\text{tr}}}$ are optimized so that Var (equation 8.4) is minimized:

$$\min_{\{x_i^{\text{tr}}\}_{i=1}^{n_{\text{tr}}}} [\text{tr}(U(X^{\text{tr}\top} X^{\text{tr}})^{-1})]. \tag{8.8}$$

8.2.2 Limitations of Classical Approach and Countermeasures

In the traditional active learning method explained above (see also [48,33,55]), the minimizer of the variance really minimizes the generalization error since the bias is exactly zero under the correct model assumption. Thus, the minimizer is truly the optimal solution. However, this approach has two drawbacks.

The first drawback is that minimizing the variance with respect to $\{x_i^{\text{tr}}\}_{i=1}^{n_{\text{tr}}}$ may not be computationally tractable due to simultaneous optimization of n_{tr} input points. This problem can be eased by optimizing the training input density $p_{\text{tr}}(x)$ and drawing the training input points $\{x_i^{\text{tr}}\}_{i=1}^{n_{\text{tr}}}$ from the determined density.

The second, and more critical, problem is that correctness of the model may not be guaranteed in practice; then minimizing the variance does not necessarily result in minimizing the generalization error. In other words, the traditional active learning method based on OLS can have larger bias. This problem can be mitigated by the use of *importance-weighted least squares* (IWLS; see section 2.2.1):

$$\widehat{\theta}_{\text{IWLS}} := \underset{\theta}{\text{argmin}} \left[\frac{1}{n_{\text{tr}}} \sum_{i=1}^{n_{\text{tr}}} \frac{p_{\text{te}}(x_i^{\text{tr}})}{p_{\text{tr}}(x_i^{\text{tr}})} \left(\widehat{f}(x_i^{\text{tr}}; \theta) - y_i^{\text{tr}} \right)^2 \right]. \tag{8.9}$$

The solution $\widehat{\theta}_{\text{IWLS}}$ is given by

$$\widehat{\theta}_{\text{IWLS}} = L_{\text{IWLS}} y^{\text{tr}},$$

where

$$L_{\text{IWLS}} := \left(X^{\text{tr}\top} W X^{\text{tr}} \right)^{-1} X^{\text{tr}\top} W,$$

and W is the diagonal matrix with the i-th diagonal element

$$W_{i,i} := \frac{p_{\text{te}}(x_i^{\text{tr}})}{p_{\text{tr}}(x_i^{\text{tr}})}.$$

8.2. Population-Based Active Learning Methods

IWLS is shown to be asymptotically unbiased even when the model is misspecified; indeed, we have

$$
\begin{aligned}
\mathbb{E}_{\{y_i^{\text{tr}}\}_{i=1}^{n_{\text{tr}}}} \left[\widehat{\boldsymbol{\theta}}_{\text{IWLS}}\right] &= \mathbb{E}_{\{y_i^{\text{tr}}\}_{i=1}^{n_{\text{tr}}}} \left[\boldsymbol{L}_{\text{IWLS}} \boldsymbol{y}^{\text{tr}}\right] \\
&= \boldsymbol{L}_{\text{IWLS}} \mathbb{E}_{\{y_i^{\text{tr}}\}_{i=1}^{n_{\text{tr}}}} \left[\boldsymbol{y}^{\text{tr}}\right] \\
&= \left(\boldsymbol{X}^{\text{tr}\top} \boldsymbol{W} \boldsymbol{X}^{\text{tr}}\right)^{-1} \boldsymbol{X}^{\text{tr}\top} \boldsymbol{W} (\boldsymbol{X}^{\text{tr}} \boldsymbol{\theta}^* + \delta \boldsymbol{r}^{\text{tr}}) \\
&= \boldsymbol{\theta}^* + \left(\boldsymbol{X}^{\text{tr}\top} \boldsymbol{W} \boldsymbol{X}^{\text{tr}}\right)^{-1} \boldsymbol{X}^{\text{tr}\top} \boldsymbol{W} \boldsymbol{r}^{\text{tr}},
\end{aligned}
$$

where $\boldsymbol{r}^{\text{tr}}$ is the n_{tr}-dimensional vector defined by

$$\boldsymbol{r}^{\text{tr}} = (r(\boldsymbol{x}_1^{\text{tr}}), r(\boldsymbol{x}_2^{\text{tr}}), \ldots, r(\boldsymbol{x}_{n_{\text{tr}}}^{\text{tr}}))^\top.$$

As shown in section 3.2.3.2, the second term is of order $\mathcal{O}_p(n_{\text{tr}}^{-\frac{1}{2}})$:

$$\left(\boldsymbol{X}^{\text{tr}\top} \boldsymbol{W} \boldsymbol{X}^{\text{tr}}\right)^{-1} \boldsymbol{X}^{\text{tr}\top} \boldsymbol{W} \boldsymbol{r}^{\text{tr}} = \mathcal{O}_p(n_{\text{tr}}^{-\frac{1}{2}}),$$

where $\mathcal{O}_p$ denotes the asymptotic order in probability. Thus, we have

$$\mathbb{E}_{\{y_i^{\text{tr}}\}_{i=1}^{n_{\text{tr}}}} \left[\widehat{\boldsymbol{\theta}}_{\text{IWLS}}\right] = \boldsymbol{\theta}^* + \mathcal{O}_p(n_{\text{tr}}^{-\frac{1}{2}}).$$

Below, we introduce useful active learning methods which can overcome the limitations of the traditional OLS-based approach.

8.2.3 Input-Independent Variance-Only Method

For the IWLS estimator $\widehat{\boldsymbol{\theta}}_{\text{IWLS}}$, it has been proved [89] that the generalization error expected over training input points $\{\boldsymbol{x}_i^{\text{tr}}\}_{i=1}^{n_{\text{tr}}}$ and training output values $\{y_i\}_{i=1}^{n_{\text{tr}}}$ (i.e., input-independent analysis; see section 3.2.1) is asymptotically expressed as

$$\mathbb{E}_{\{\boldsymbol{x}_i^{\text{tr}}\}_{i=1}^{n_{\text{tr}}}} \mathbb{E}_{\{y_i^{\text{tr}}\}_{i=1}^{n_{\text{tr}}}} [\text{Gen}''] = \frac{1}{n_{\text{tr}}} \text{tr}(\boldsymbol{U}^{-1} \boldsymbol{H}) + \mathcal{O}(n_{\text{tr}}^{-\frac{3}{2}}), \qquad (8.10)$$

where $\boldsymbol{H}$ is the $b \times b$ matrix defined by

$$\boldsymbol{H} := \delta^2 \boldsymbol{S} + \sigma^2 \boldsymbol{T}. \qquad (8.11)$$

S and T are the $b \times b$ matrices with the (ℓ, ℓ')-th elements

$$S_{\ell,\ell'} := \mathbb{E}_{x^{te}} \left[\varphi_\ell(x^{te}) \varphi_{\ell'}(x^{te}) r(x^{te})^2 \frac{p_{te}(x^{te})}{p_{tr}(x^{te})} \right],$$

$$T_{\ell,\ell'} := \mathbb{E}_{x^{te}} \left[\varphi_\ell(x^{te}) \varphi_{\ell'}(x^{te}) \frac{p_{te}(x^{te})}{p_{tr}(x^{te})} \right], \qquad (8.12)$$

where $\mathbb{E}_{x^{te}}$ denotes the expectation over x^{te} drawn from $p_{te}(x)$. Note that $\frac{1}{n_{tr}}\mathrm{tr}(U^{-1}S)$ corresponds to the bias term and $\frac{\sigma^2}{n_{tr}}\mathrm{tr}(U^{-1}T)$ corresponds to the variance term. S is not accessible because unknown $r(x)$ is included, while T is accessible due to the assumption that the test input density $p_{te}(x)$ is known (see section 8.1.1).

Equation 8.10 suggests that $\mathrm{tr}(U^{-1}H)$ may be used as an active learning criterion. However, H includes the inaccessible quantities $r(x)$ and σ^2, so $\mathrm{tr}(U^{-1}H)$ cannot be calculated directly. To cope with this problem, Wiens [199] proposed[1] to ignore S (the bias term) and determine the training input density $p_{tr}(x)$ so that the variance term is minimized.

$$p_{tr}^* = \underset{p_{tr}}{\mathrm{argmin}} [\mathrm{tr}(U^{-1}T)]. \qquad (8.13)$$

As shown in [153], the above active learning method can be justified for *approximately correct models*, that is, for $\delta = o(1)$:

$$\mathbb{E}_{\{x_i^{tr}\}_{i=1}^{n_{tr}}} \mathbb{E}_{\{y_i^{tr}\}_{i=1}^{n_{tr}}} [\mathrm{Gen}''] = \frac{\sigma^2}{n_{tr}} \mathrm{tr}(U^{-1}T) + o(n_{tr}^{-1}).$$

A notable feature of the above active learning method is that the optimal training input density p_{tr}^* can be obtained analytically as

$$p_{tr}^*(x) \propto p_{te}(x) \left(\sum_{\ell,\ell'=1}^b [U^{-1}]_{\ell,\ell'} \varphi_\ell(x) \varphi_{\ell'}(x) \right)^{\frac{1}{2}}, \qquad (8.14)$$

which may be confirmed from the following equation [87]:

$$\mathrm{tr}(U^{-1}T) \propto \left(1 + \int \frac{(p_{tr}^*(x) - p_{tr}(x))^2}{p_{tr}(x)} dx \right).$$

---

1. In the original paper, the range of application was limited to the cases where the input domain is bounded and $p_{te}(x)$ is uniform over the domain. However, it may be easily extended to an arbitrary strictly positive $p_{te}(x)$. For this reason, we deal with the extended version here.

8.2. Population-Based Active Learning Methods

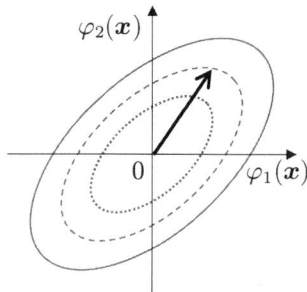

Figure 8.3
Illustration of the weights in the optimal training input density $p_{tr}^*(x)$.

Equation 8.14 implies that in the optimal training input density $p_{tr}^*(x)$, $p_{te}(x)$ is weighted according to the U^{-1}-norm of $(\varphi_1(x), \varphi_2(x), \ldots, \varphi_b(x))^\top$. Thus, the input points far from the origin tend to have higher weights in $p_{tr}^*(x)$. Note that the matrix U defined by equation 8.5 corresponds to the second-order moments of the basis functions $\{\varphi_\ell(x)\}_\ell^b$ around the origin, that is, it has ellipsoidal shapes (see figure 8.3).

8.2.4 Input-Dependent Variance-Only Method

As explained in section 3.2.1, estimating the generalization error without taking the expectation over the training input points $\{x_i^{tr}\}_{i=1}^{n_{tr}}$ is advantageous since the estimate is more data-dependent.

Following this idea, an input-dependent variance-only active learning method called *ALICE* (Active Learning using Importance-weighted least-squares learning based on Conditional Expectation of the generalization error) has been proposed [153]. ALICE minimizes the input-dependent variance (equation 8.4):

$$\min_{p_{tr}}[\text{tr}(U L_{\text{IWLS}} L_{\text{IWLS}}^\top)]. \tag{8.15}$$

This criterion can also be justified for approximately correct models, that is, for $\delta = o(1)$,

$$\mathbb{E}_{\{y_i^{tr}\}_{i=1}^{n_{tr}}}[\text{Gen}''] = \sigma^2 \text{tr}(U L_{\text{IWLS}} L_{\text{IWLS}}^\top) + o_p(n_{tr}^{-1}).$$

Input-dependent variance and input-independent variance are similar; indeed, they are actually asymptotically equivalent.

$$\mathrm{tr}(\boldsymbol{U}\boldsymbol{L}_{\mathrm{IWLS}}\boldsymbol{L}_{\mathrm{IWLS}}^\top) = \frac{1}{n_{\mathrm{tr}}}\mathrm{tr}(\boldsymbol{U}^{-1}\boldsymbol{T}) + \mathcal{O}_p(n_{\mathrm{tr}}^{-\frac{3}{2}}).$$

However, input-dependent variance is a more accurate estimator of the generalization error than input-independent variance. More precisely, the following inequality holds for approximately correct models with $\delta = o_p(n_{\mathrm{tr}}^{-\frac{1}{4}})$ [153]:

$$\mathop{\mathbb{E}}_{\{y_i^{\mathrm{tr}}\}_{i=1}^{n_{\mathrm{tr}}}} \left[\left(\frac{\sigma^2}{n_{\mathrm{tr}}}\mathrm{tr}(\boldsymbol{U}^{-1}\boldsymbol{T}) - \mathrm{Gen}''\right)^2\right]$$
$$\geq \mathop{\mathbb{E}}_{\{y_i^{\mathrm{tr}}\}_{i=1}^{n_{\mathrm{tr}}}} \left[\left(\sigma^2 \mathrm{tr}(\boldsymbol{U}\boldsymbol{L}_{\mathrm{IWLS}}\boldsymbol{L}_{\mathrm{IWLS}}^\top) - \mathrm{Gen}''\right)^2\right],$$

if terms of $o_p(n_{\mathrm{tr}}^{-3})$ are ignored. This difference is shown to cause a significant difference in practical performance (see section 8.3 for experimental performance).

As shown above, the input-dependent approach is more accurate than the input-independent approach. However, its downside is that no analytic solution is known for the ALICE criterion (equation 8.15). Thus, an exhaustive search strategy is needed to obtain a better training input density. A practical compromise for this problem would be to use the analytic optimal solution $p_{\mathrm{tr}}^*(\boldsymbol{x})$ of the input-independent variance-only active learning criterion (equation 8.13), and to search for a better solution around the vicinity of $p_{\mathrm{tr}}^*(\boldsymbol{x})$. Then we only need to perform a simple one-dimensional search: find the best training input density with respect to a scalar parameter ν:

$$p_\nu(\boldsymbol{x}) \propto p_{\mathrm{te}}(\boldsymbol{x}) \left(\sum_{\ell,\ell'=1}^{b} [\boldsymbol{U}^{-1}]_{\ell,\ell'} \varphi_\ell(\boldsymbol{x})\varphi_{\ell'}(\boldsymbol{x})\right)^{\frac{\nu}{2}}.$$

The parameter ν controls the "flatness" of the training input density; $\nu = 0$ corresponds to the test input density $p_{\mathrm{te}}(\boldsymbol{x})$ (i.e., *passive learning*—the training and test distributions are equivalent), $\nu = 1$ corresponds to the original $p_{\mathrm{tr}}^*(\boldsymbol{x})$, and $\nu > 1$ expresses a "sharper" density than $p_{\mathrm{tr}}^*(\boldsymbol{x})$. Searching intensively for a good value of ν intensively around $\nu = 1$ would be useful in practice.

A pseudo code of the ALICE algorithm is summarized in figure 8.4.

8.2. Population-Based Active Learning Methods

Input: A test input density $p_{\text{te}}(\boldsymbol{x})$ and basis functions $\{\varphi_\ell(\boldsymbol{x})\}_{\ell=1}^b$
Output: Learned parameter $\widehat{\boldsymbol{\theta}}$

Compute the $b \times b$ matrix $\boldsymbol{U}$ with $U_{\ell,\ell'} = \int \varphi_\ell(\boldsymbol{x})\varphi_{\ell'}(\boldsymbol{x})p_{\text{te}}(\boldsymbol{x})d\boldsymbol{x}$;
For several different values of ν (possibly around $\nu = 1$)
  Let $p_\nu(\boldsymbol{x}) = p_{\text{te}}(\boldsymbol{x}) \left(\sum_{\ell,\ell'=1}^b [\boldsymbol{U}^{-1}]_{\ell,\ell'} \varphi_\ell(\boldsymbol{x})\varphi_{\ell'}(\boldsymbol{x}) \right)^{\frac{\nu}{2}}$;
  Draw $\mathcal{X}_\nu^{\text{tr}} = \{\boldsymbol{x}_{\nu,i}^{\text{tr}}\}_{i=1}^{n_{\text{tr}}}$ following the density proportional to $p_\nu(\boldsymbol{x})$;
  Compute the $n_{\text{tr}} \times b$ matrix $\boldsymbol{X}_\nu^{\text{tr}}$ with $[X_\nu]_{i,\ell} = \varphi_\ell(\boldsymbol{x}_{\nu,i}^{\text{tr}})$;
  Compute the $n_{\text{tr}} \times n_{\text{tr}}$ diagonal matrix $\boldsymbol{W}_\nu$ with $[W_\nu]_{i,i} = \frac{p_\nu(\boldsymbol{x}_{\nu,i}^{\text{tr}})}{p_{\text{tr}}(\boldsymbol{x}_{\nu,i}^{\text{tr}})}$;
  Compute $\boldsymbol{L}_\nu = (\boldsymbol{X}_\nu^{\text{tr}\top} \boldsymbol{W}_\nu \boldsymbol{X}_\nu^{\text{tr}})^{-1} \boldsymbol{X}_\nu^{\text{tr}\top} \boldsymbol{W}_\nu$;
  Compute $\text{ALICE}(\nu) = \text{tr}(\boldsymbol{U}\boldsymbol{L}_\nu \boldsymbol{L}_\nu^\top)$;
End
Compute $\widehat{\nu} = \arg\min_\nu [\text{ALICE}(\nu)]$;
Gather training output values $\boldsymbol{y}^{\text{tr}} = (y_1^{\text{tr}}, y_2^{\text{tr}}, \ldots, y_{n_{\text{tr}}}^{\text{tr}})^\top$ at $\mathcal{X}_{\widehat{\nu}}^{\text{tr}}$;
Compute $\widehat{\boldsymbol{\theta}} = \boldsymbol{L}_{\widehat{\nu}} \boldsymbol{y}^{\text{tr}}$;

Figure 8.4
Pseudo code of the ALICE algorithm.

8.2.5 Input-Independent Bias-and-Variance Approach

The use of input-independent/dependent variance-only approaches is justified only for approximately correct models (i.e., the model error δ vanishes asymptotically). Although this condition turns out to be less problematic in practice (see section 8.3 for numerical results), it cannot be satisfied theoretically since the model error δ is a constant that does not depend on the number of samples.

To cope with this problem, a two-stage active learning method has been developed [89] which is theoretically justifiable for totally misspecified models within the input-independent framework (see section 8.2.3). The key idea is to use the samples gathered in the first stage for estimating the generalization error (i.e., both bias and variance), and the training input distribution is optimized based on the estimated generalization error in the second stage. Here, we explain the details of this algorithm.

In the first stage, $\widetilde{n}_{\text{tr}}$ ($\leq n_{\text{tr}}$) training input points $\{\widetilde{\boldsymbol{x}}_i^{\text{tr}}\}_{i=1}^{\widetilde{n}_{\text{tr}}}$ are created independently following the test input density $p_{\text{te}}(\boldsymbol{x})$, and corresponding training output values $\{\widetilde{y}_i^{\text{tr}}\}_{i=1}^{\widetilde{n}_{\text{tr}}}$ are observed.

Then we determine the training input density based on the above samples. More specifically, we prepare candidates for training input densities. Then, we estimate the generalization error for each candidate $p_{\text{tr}}(\boldsymbol{x})$, and the one that minimizes the estimated generalization error is chosen for the second stage. The generalization error for a candidate density $p_{tr}(x)$ is estimated as follows. Let $\widetilde{W}$ and $\widetilde{Q}$ be the $\widetilde{n}_{tr}$-dimensional diagonal matrices with i-th diagonal elements

$$\widetilde{W}_{i,i} = \frac{p_{te}(\widetilde{x}_i^{tr})}{p_{tr}(\widetilde{x}_i^{tr})},$$

$$\widetilde{Q}_{i,i} = [\widetilde{y}^{tr} - \widetilde{X}^{tr}(\widetilde{X}^{tr\top}\widetilde{X}^{tr})^{-1}\widetilde{X}^{tr\top}\widetilde{y}^{tr}]_i,$$

respectively, where $\widetilde{X}^{tr}$ is the design matrix for $\{\widetilde{x}_i^{tr}\}_{i=1}^{\widetilde{n}_{tr}}$ (i.e., the $\widetilde{n}_{tr} \times b$ matrix with the (i, ℓ)-th element)

$$\widetilde{X}_{i,\ell}^{tr} = \varphi_\ell(\widetilde{x}_i^{tr}),$$

and

$$\widetilde{y}^{tr} = (\widetilde{y}_1^{tr}, \widetilde{y}_2^{tr}, \ldots, \widetilde{y}_{\widetilde{n}_{tr}}^{tr})^\top.$$

Then an approximation $\widetilde{H}$ of the unknown matrix H defined by equation 8.10 is given as

$$\widetilde{H} = \frac{1}{\widetilde{n}_{tr}} \widetilde{X}^{tr\top} \widetilde{W} \widetilde{Q}^2 \widetilde{X}^{tr}. \tag{8.16}$$

Although U^{-1} is accessible in the current setting, it was also replaced by a consistent estimator $\widetilde{U}^{-1}$ [89], where

$$\widetilde{U} = \frac{1}{\widetilde{n}_{tr}} \widetilde{X}^{tr\top} \widetilde{X}^{tr}.$$

Based on the above approximations, the training input density $p_{tr}(x)$ is determined as follows:

$$\min_{p_{tr}}[\text{tr}(\widetilde{U}^{-1}\widetilde{H})]. \tag{8.17}$$

After determining the training input density $p_{tr}(x)$, the remaining $(n_{tr} - \widetilde{n}_{tr})$ training input points $\{x_i^{tr}\}_{i=\widetilde{n}_{tr}+1}^{n_{tr}-\widetilde{n}_{tr}}$ are created independently following the chosen $p_{tr}(x)$, and corresponding training output values $\{y_i^{tr}\}_{i=\widetilde{n}_{tr}+1}^{n_{tr}-\widetilde{n}_{tr}}$ are gathered. This is the second stage of sampling.

Finally, the learned parameter $\widehat{\theta}$ is obtained, using $\{(\widetilde{x}_i^{tr}, \widetilde{y}_i^{tr})\}_{i=1}^{\widetilde{n}_{tr}}$ and $\{(x_i^{tr}, y_i^{tr})\}_{i=\widetilde{n}_{tr}+1}^{n_{tr}-\widetilde{n}_{tr}}$, as

8.2. Population-Based Active Learning Methods

$$\widehat{\boldsymbol{\theta}} = \underset{\boldsymbol{\theta}}{\operatorname{argmin}} \left[\sum_{i=1}^{\widetilde{n}_{\mathrm{tr}}} \left(\widehat{f}(\widetilde{\boldsymbol{x}}_i^{\mathrm{tr}}; \boldsymbol{\theta}) - \widetilde{y}_i^{\mathrm{tr}} \right)^2 + \sum_{i=\widetilde{n}_{\mathrm{tr}}+1}^{n_{\mathrm{tr}}-\widetilde{n}_{\mathrm{tr}}} \frac{p_{\mathrm{te}}(\boldsymbol{x}_i^{\mathrm{tr}})}{p_{\mathrm{tr}}(\boldsymbol{x}_i^{\mathrm{tr}})} \left(\widehat{f}(\boldsymbol{x}_i^{\mathrm{tr}}; \boldsymbol{\theta}) - y_i^{\mathrm{tr}} \right)^2 \right]. \qquad (8.18)$$

The above active learning method has a strong theoretical property, that is, for $\widetilde{n}_{\mathrm{tr}} = o(n_{\mathrm{tr}})$, $\lim_{n_{\mathrm{tr}} \to \infty} \widetilde{n}_{\mathrm{tr}} = \infty$, and $\delta = \mathcal{O}(1)$,

$$\underset{\{\boldsymbol{x}_i^{\mathrm{tr}}\}_{i=1}^{n_{\mathrm{tr}}}}{\mathbb{E}} \underset{\{y_i^{\mathrm{tr}}\}_{i=1}^{n_{\mathrm{tr}}}}{\mathbb{E}} [\mathrm{Gen}''] = \frac{1}{n_{\mathrm{tr}}} \mathrm{tr}(\widetilde{\boldsymbol{U}}^{-1} \widetilde{\boldsymbol{H}}) + o(n_{\mathrm{tr}}^{-1}).$$

This means that the use of this two-stage active learning method can be justified for totally misspecified models (i.e., $\delta = \mathcal{O}(1)$). Furthermore, this method can be applied to more general scenarios beyond regression [89], such as classification with logistic regression (see section 2.3.2).

On the other hand, although the two-stage active learning method has good theoretical properties, this method seems not to perform very well in practice (see section 8.3 for numerical examples), which may be due to the following reasons.

- Since $\widetilde{n}_{\mathrm{tr}}$ training input points should be gathered following $p_{\mathrm{te}}(\boldsymbol{x})$ in the first stage, users are allowed to optimize the location of only $(n_{\mathrm{tr}} - \widetilde{n}_{\mathrm{tr}})$ remaining training input points. This is particularly critical when the total number n_{tr} is not very large, which is be a usual case in active learning.

- The performance depends on the choice of the number $\widetilde{n}_{\mathrm{tr}}$, and it is not straightforward to appropriately determine this number. Using $\widetilde{n}_{\mathrm{tr}} = \mathcal{O}(n_{\mathrm{tr}}^{\frac{1}{2}})$ is recommended in [89], but the exact choice of $\widetilde{n}_{\mathrm{tr}}$ seems still seems open.

- The estimated generalization error corresponds to the case where n_{tr} points are chosen from $p_{\mathrm{tr}}(\boldsymbol{x})$ and IWLS is used; but in reality, $\widetilde{n}_{\mathrm{tr}}$ points are taken from $p_{\mathrm{te}}(\boldsymbol{x})$ and $(n_{\mathrm{tr}} - \widetilde{n}_{\mathrm{tr}})$ points are taken from $p_{\mathrm{tr}}(\boldsymbol{x})$, and a combination of OLS and IWLS is used for parameter learning. Thus, this difference can degrade the performance. It is possible to resolve this problem by not using $\{(\widetilde{\boldsymbol{x}}_i^{\mathrm{tr}}, \widetilde{y}_i^{\mathrm{tr}})\}_{i=1}^{\widetilde{n}_{\mathrm{tr}}}$ gathered in the first stage for estimating the parameter. However, this may yield further degradation of the performance because only $(n_{\mathrm{tr}} - \widetilde{n}_{\mathrm{tr}})$ training examples are used for learning.

- Estimation of bias and noise variance is implicitly included (see equations 8.11 and 8.16). Practically, estimating the bias and noise variance from a small number of training samples is highly erroneous, and thus the performance of active learning can be degraded. On the other hand, the variance-only methods can avoid this difficulty by ignoring the bias; then the noise variance included in variance becomes just a proportional constant and can also justifiably be ignored.

Currently, bias-and-variance approaches in the input-dependent framework seem to be an open research issue.

8.3 Numerical Examples of Population-Based Active Learning Methods

In this section, we illustrate how the population-based active learning methods described in section 8.2 behave under a controlled setting.

8.3.1 Setup

Let the input dimension be $d = 1$ and the learning target function be

$$f(x) = 1 - x + x^2 + \delta r(x),$$

where

$$r(x) = \frac{z^3 - 3z}{\sqrt{6}} \quad \text{with} \quad z = \frac{x - 0.2}{0.4}. \tag{8.19}$$

Note that the above $r(x)$ is the *Hermite polynomial*, which ensures the orthonormality of $r(x)$ to the second-order polynomial model under a Gaussian test input distribution (see below for details). Let the number of training examples to gather be $n_{\text{tr}} = 100$, and we add i.i.d. Gaussian noise with mean zero and standard deviation 0.3 to output values:

$$y_i^{\text{tr}} = f(x_i^{\text{tr}}) + \epsilon_i^{\text{tr}},$$

$$\epsilon_i^{\text{tr}} \stackrel{i.i.d.}{\sim} N(\epsilon; 0, (0.3)^2),$$

where $N(\epsilon; \mu, \sigma^2)$ denotes the Gaussian density with mean μ and variance σ^2 with respect to a random variable ϵ. Let the test input density $p_{\text{te}}(x)$ be the Gaussian density with mean 0.2 and standard deviation 0.4:

$$p_{\text{te}}(x) = N(x; 0.2, (0.4)^2). \tag{8.20}$$

$p_{\text{te}}(x)$ is assumed to be known in this illustrative simulation. See the bottom graph of figure 8.5 for the profile of $p_{\text{te}}(x)$.

Let us use the following second-order polynomial model:

$$\widehat{f}(x; \boldsymbol{\theta}) = \theta_1 + \theta_2 x + \theta_3 x^2.$$

Note that for this model and the test input density $p_{\text{te}}(x)$ defined by equation 8.20, the residual function $r(x)$ in equation 8.19 is orthogonal to the model and normalized to 1 (see section 3.2.2).

8.3. Numerical Examples of Population-Based Active Learning Methods

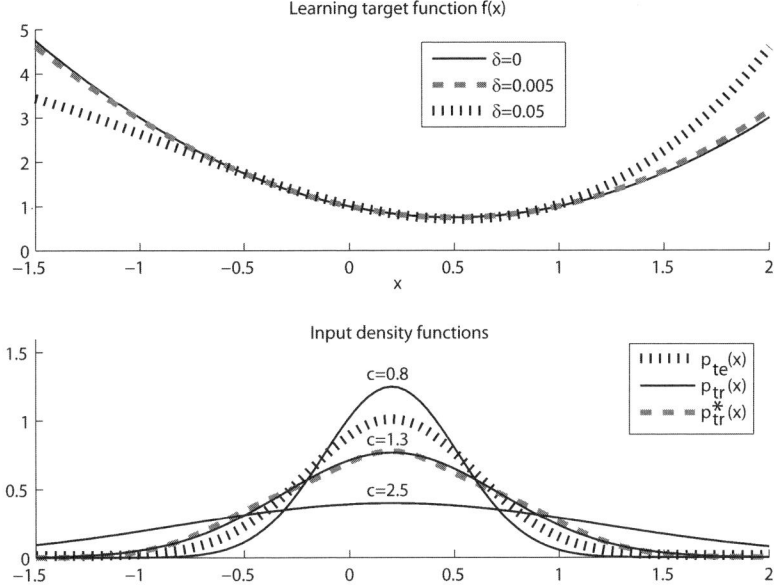

Figure 8.5
Learning target function (top) and input density functions (bottom).

Let us consider the following three setups for the experiments.

$$\delta = 0, 0.005, 0.05, \tag{8.21}$$

which roughly correspond to *correctly specified*, *approximately correct*, and *misspecified* cases, respectively. See the top graph of figure 8.5 for the profiles of $f(x)$ with different δ.

Training input densities are chosen from the Gaussian densities with mean 0.2 and standard deviation $0.4c$:

$$p_{tr}(x) = N(x; 0.2, (0.4c)^2),$$

where

$$c = 0.8, 0.9, 1.0, \ldots, 2.5.$$

See the bottom graph of figure 8.5 for the profiles of $p_{tr}(x)$ with different c.

In this experiment, we compare the performance of the following methods:

- **ALICE** c is determined by ALICE equation 8.15. IWLS (equation 8.9) is used for parameter learning.

- **Input-independent variance-only method (W)** c is determined by equation 8.13. IWLS (equation 8.9) is used for parameter learning. We denote this by W since it uses importance-weighted least squares.
- **Input-independent variance-only method* (W*)** The closed-form solution $p_{tr}^*(x)$ given by equation 8.14 is used as the training input density. The profile of $p_{tr}^*(x)$ under the current setting is illustrated in the bottom graph of figure 8.5, showing that $p_{tr}^*(x)$ is similar to the Gaussian density with $c = 1.3$. IWLS (equation 8.9) is used for parameter learning.
- **Input-independent bias-and-variance method (OW)** First, $\tilde{n}_{tr}$ training input points are created following the test input density $p_{te}(x)$, and corresponding training output values are observed. Based on the $\tilde{n}_{tr}$ training examples, c is determined by equation 8.17. Then $n_{tr} - \tilde{n}_{tr}$ remaining training input points are created following the determined input density. The combination of OLS and IWLS (see (equation 8.18) is used for estimating the parameters (the abbreviation OW comes from this). We set $\tilde{n}_{tr} = 25$, which we experimentally confirmed to be a reasonable choice in this illustrative simulation.
- **Traditional method (O)** c is determined by equation 8.8. OLS (equation 8.7) is used for parameter learning (the abbreviation O comes from this).
- **Passive method (P)** Following the test input density $p_{te}(x)$, training input points $\{x_i^{tr}\}_{i=1}^{n_{tr}}$ are created. OLS equation 8.7 is used for parameter learning.

For W*, we generate random samples following $p_{tr}^*(x)$ by *rejection sampling* (see, e.g., [95]). We repeat the simulation 1000 times for each δ in equation 8.21 by changing the random seed.

8.3.2 Accuracy of Generalization Error Estimation

First, we evaluate the accuracy of each active learning criterion as an estimator of the generalization error Gen″ (see equation 8.2). Note that ALICE and W are estimators of the generalization error by IWLS (which we denote by Gen″$_W$). OW is also derived as an estimator of Gen″$_W$, but the final solution is computed by the combination of OLS and IWLS given by equation 8.18. Therefore, OW should be regarded as an estimator of of the generalization error by this learning method (which we denote by Gen″$_{OW}$). O is an estimator of the generalization error by OLS, which we denote by Gen″$_O$.

In figure 8.6, the means and standard deviations of true generalization errors Gen″ and their estimates over 1000 runs are depicted as functions of c by the solid curves. The generalization error estimated by each method is denoted by $\widehat{\text{Gen}}$ in the figure. Here the upper and lower error bars are calculated separately since the distribution is not symmetric. The dashed curves show the means of

8.3. Numerical Examples of Population-Based Active Learning Methods

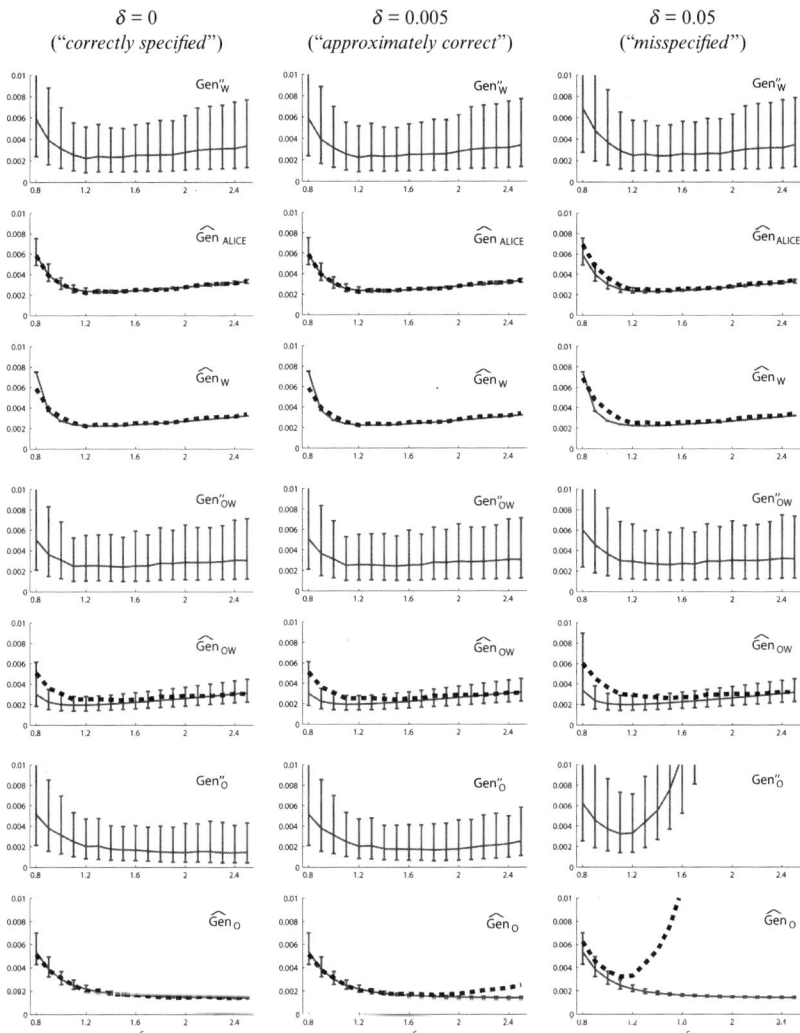

Figure 8.6
The means and (asymmetric) standard deviations of true generalization error Gen″ and its estimates over 1000 runs as functions of c. The generalization error estimated by each method is denoted by $\widehat{\text{Gen}}$. $\widehat{\text{Gen}}_{\text{ALICE}}$, $\widehat{\text{Gen}}_W$, and $\widehat{\text{Gen}}_O$ are multiplied by $\sigma^2 = (0.3)^2$ so that comparison with Gen''_W and Gen''_O is clear. The dashed curves show the means of the generalization error which corresponding active learning criteria are trying to estimate.

the generalization error which corresponding active learning criteria are trying to estimate. Note that the criterion values of ALICE, W, and O are multiplied by $\sigma^2 = (0.3)^2$ so that comparison with Gen''_W and Gen''_O is clear.

These graphs show that when $\delta = 0$ (*correctly specified*), ALICE and W give accurate estimates of Gen''_W. Note that the criterion value of W does not depend on the training input points $\{x_i^{\text{tr}}\}_{i=1}^{n_{\text{tr}}}$. Thus, it does not fluctuate over 1000 runs. OW is slightly biased in the negative direction for small c. We conjecture that this is caused by the small sample effect. However, the profile of OW still roughly approximates that of Gen''_{OW}. O gives accurate predictions of Gen''_O. When $\delta = 0.005$ (*approximately correct*), ALICE, W, and OW work similarly to the case with $\delta = 0$, that is, ALICE and W are accurate and OW is negatively biased. On the other hand, O behaves differently: it tends to be biased in the negative direction for large c. Finally, when $\delta = 0.05$ (*misspecified*), ALICE and W still give accurate estimates, although they have a slightly negative bias for small c. OW still roughly approximates Gen''_{OW}, and O gives a totally different profile from Gen''_O.

These results show that as estimators of the generalization error, ALICE and W are accurate and robust against the misspecification of models. OW is also reasonably accurate, although it tends to be rather inaccurate for small c. O is accurate in the correctly specified case, but it becomes totally inaccurate once the model correct assumption is violated.

Note that by definition, ALICE, W, and O do not depend on the learning target function. Therefore, in the simulation, they give the same values for all δ (ALICE and O depend on the realization of $\{x_i^{\text{tr}}\}_{i=1}^{n_{\text{tr}}}$, so they may have small fluctuations). On the other hand, the true generalization error of course depends on the learning target function even if the model error δ is subtracted, since the training output values depend on it. Note that the bias depends on δ, but the variance does not. The simulation results show that the profile of Gen''_O changes heavily as the degree of model misspecification increases. This would be caused by the increase of the bias since OLS is not unbiased even asymptotically. On the other hand, O stays the same even when δ increases. As a result, O becomes a very poor generalization error estimator for a large δ. In contrast, the profile of Gen''_W appears to be very stable against the change in δ, which is in good agreement with the theoretical fact that IWLS is asymptotically unbiased. Thanks to this property, ALICE and W are more accurate than O for misspecified models.

8.3.3 Obtained Generalization Error

In table 8.1, the mean and standard deviation of the generalization error obtained by each method are described. In each row of the table, the best

8.3. Numerical Examples of Population-Based Active Learning Methods

Table 8.1
The mean and standard deviation of the generalization error obtained by population-based active learning methods

	ALICE	W	W*	OW	O	P
$\delta = 0$	2.08 ± 1.95	2.40 ± 2.15	2.32 ± 2.02	3.09 ± 3.03	°1.31 ± 1.70	3.11 ± 2.78
$\delta = 0.005$	°2.10 ± 1.96	2.43 ± 2.15	2.35 ± 2.02	3.13 ± 3.00	2.53 ± 2.23	3.14 ± 2.78
$\delta = 0.05$	°2.11 ± 2.12	2.39 ± 2.26	2.34 ± 2.14	3.45 ± 3.58	121 ± 67.4	3.51 ± 3.43

For better comparison, the model error δ^2 is subtracted from the generalization error, and all values are multiplied by 10^3. In each row of the table, the best method and comparable ones by the t-test at the significance level 5 percent are indicated with o. The value of O for $\delta = 0.05$ is extremely large, but this is not a typo.

method and comparable ones by the t-test (e.g., [78]) at the significance level 5 percent are indicated with o. For better comparison, the model error δ^2 is subtracted from the generalization error and all values in the table are multiplied by 10^3. The value of O for $\delta = 0.05$ is extremely large, but this is not a typo.

When $\delta = 0$, O works significantly better than the other methods. Actually, in this case, training input densities that approximately minimize Gen''_W, Gen''_{OW}, and Gen''_O were successfully found by ALICE, W, OW, and O. This implies that the difference in the error is caused not by the quality of active learning criteria, but by the difference between IWLS and OLS: IWLS generally has larger variance than OLS [145]. Thus, OLS is more accurate than IWLS since both of them are unbiased when $\delta = 0$. Although ALICE, W, W*, and OW are outperformed by O, they still work better than P. Note that ALICE is significantly better than W, W*, OW, and P by the t-test.

When $\delta = 0.005$, ALICE gives significantly smaller errors than other methods. All the methods except O work similarly to the case with $\delta = 0$, while O tends to perform poorly. This result is surprising since the learning target functions with $\delta = 0$ and $\delta = 0.005$ are visually almost the same, as illustrated in the top graph of figure 8.5. Therefore, it intuitively seems that the result when $\delta = 0.005$ is not much different from the result when $\delta = 0$. However, this slight difference appears to make O unreliable.

When $\delta = 0.05$, ALICE again works significantly better than the other methods. W and W* still work reasonably well. The performance of OW is slightly degraded, although it is still better than P. O gives extremely large errors.

The above results are summarized as follows. For all three cases ($\delta = 0, 0.005, 0.05$), ALICE, W, W*, and OW work reasonably well and consistently outperform P. Among them, ALICE tends to be better than W, W*, and OW for all three cases. O works excellently when the model is correctly specified, but tends to perform very poorly once the model correct assumption is violated.

8.4 Pool-Based Active Learning Methods

Population-based active learning methods are applicable only when the test input density $p_{te}(x)$ is known (see section 8.1.1). On the other hand, *pool-based* active learning considers the situation where the test input distribution is unknown, but samples from that distribution are given. Let us denote the pooled test input samples by $\{x_j^{te}\}_{j=1}^{n_{te}}$.

The goal of pool-based active learning is, from the pool of test input points $\{x_j^{te}\}_{j=1}^{n_{te}}$, to choose the best input-point subset $\{x_i^{tr}\}_{i=1}^{n_{tr}}$ (with $n_{tr} \ll n_{te}$) for gathering output values $\{y_i^{tr}\}_{i=1}^{n_{tr}}$ that minimizes the generalization error. If we have infinitely many test input samples, the pool-based problem is reduced to the population-based problem. Due to the finite sample size, the pool-based active learning problem is generally harder to solve than the population-based problem. Note that the sample selection process of pool-based active learning (i.e., choosing a subset of test input points as training input points) resembles that of the sample selection bias model described in chapter 6.

8.4.1 Classical Active Learning Method for Correct Models and Its Limitations

The traditional active learning method explained in section 8.2.1 can be extended to the pool-based scenario in a straightforward way. Let us consider the same setup as section 8.2.1 here, except that $p_{te}(x)$ is unknown but its i.i.d. samples $\{x_j^{te}\}_{j=1}^{n_{te}}$ are given.

The active learning criterion (equation 8.8) contains only the design matrix X^{tr} and the matrix U. X^{tr} is still accessible even in the pool-based scenario (see equation 8.6), but U is not accessible since it includes the expectation over the *unknown* test input distribution (see equation 8.5). To cope with this problem, we simply replace U with an empirical estimate $\widehat{U}$, that is, $\widehat{U}$ is the $b \times b$ matrix with the (ℓ, ℓ')-th element

$$\widehat{U}_{\ell,\ell'} = \frac{1}{n_{te}} \sum_{j=1}^{n_{te}} \varphi_\ell(x_j^{te}) \varphi_{\ell'}(x_j^{te}). \tag{8.22}$$

Then we immediately have a pool-based active learning criterion:

$$\min_{\{x_i^{tr}\}_{i=1}^{n_{tr}} \subset \{x_j^{te}\}_{j=1}^{n_{te}}} [\text{tr}(\widehat{U}(X^{tr\top} X^{tr})^{-1})]. \tag{8.23}$$

8.4. Pool-Based Active Learning Methods

Unfortunately, this method has the same drawbacks as the population-based method:

- It requires an unrealistic assumption that the model at hand is correctly specified.
- n_{tr} input points need to be simultaneously optimized that may not be computationally tractable.

In order to overcome these drawbacks, we again employ *importance-weighted least squares* (IWLS; see section 2.2.1). However, in pool-based active learning, we cannot create training input points $\{x_i^{\mathrm{tr}}\}_{i=1}^{n_{\mathrm{tr}}}$ at arbitrary locations—we are allowed to choose only the training input points from $\{x_j^{\mathrm{te}}\}_{j=1}^{n_{\mathrm{te}}}$. In order to meet this requirement, we restrict the search space of the training input density $p_{\mathrm{tr}}(x)$ properly. More specifically, we consider a *resampling weight function* $\zeta(x_j^{\mathrm{te}})$, which is a discrete probability function over the pooled points $\{x_j^{\mathrm{te}}\}_{j=1}^{n_{\mathrm{te}}}$. This means that the training input probability $p_{\mathrm{tr}}(x_j^{\mathrm{te}})$ is defined *over* the test input probability $p_{\mathrm{te}}(x_j^{\mathrm{te}})$ as

$$p_{\mathrm{tr}}(x_j^{\mathrm{te}}) \propto p_{\mathrm{te}}(x_j^{\mathrm{te}})\zeta(x_j^{\mathrm{te}}), \tag{8.24}$$

where $\zeta(x_j^{\mathrm{te}}) > 0$ for $j = 1, 2, \ldots, n_{\mathrm{te}}$, and

$$\sum_{j=1}^{n_{\mathrm{te}}} \zeta(x_j^{\mathrm{te}}) = 1.$$

8.4.2 Input-Independent Variance-Only Method

The population-based input-independent variance-only active learning criterion (see section 8.2.3) can be extended to pool-based scenarios as follows.

The active learning criterion (equation 8.13) contains only the matrices U and T. The matrix U may be replaced by its empirical estimator $\widehat{U}$ (see equation 8.22), but approximating T is not straightforward since its empirical approximation $\widehat{T}$ still contains the importance values at training points (see equation 8.12):

$$\widehat{T}_{\ell,\ell'} := \frac{1}{n_{\mathrm{te}}} \sum_{j=1}^{n_{\mathrm{te}}} \varphi_\ell(x_j^{\mathrm{te}})\varphi_{\ell'}(x_j^{\mathrm{te}})w(x_j^{\mathrm{te}}),$$

where

$$w(x_j^{\mathrm{te}}) = \frac{p_{\mathrm{te}}(x_j^{\mathrm{te}})}{p_{\mathrm{tr}}(x_j^{\mathrm{te}})}.$$

Thus, $\widehat{T}$ still cannot be directly computed since $p_{\text{te}}(x_j^{\text{te}})$ is inaccessible in the pool-based scenarios. A possible solution to this problem is to use an importance estimation method described in chapter 4, but this produces some estimation error.

Here, we can utilize the fact that the training input probability $p_{\text{tr}}(x_j^{\text{te}})$ is defined over the test input probability $p_{\text{te}}(x_j^{\text{te}})$ using the resampling weight function $\zeta(x_j^{\text{te}})$ (see equation 8.24). Indeed, equation 8.24 immediately shows that the importance weight can be expressed as follows [87]:

$$w(x_j^{\text{te}}) \propto \frac{1}{\zeta(x_j^{\text{te}})}. \tag{8.25}$$

Note that the proportional constant is not needed in active learning since we are not interested in estimating the generalization error itself, but only in finding the minimizer of the generalization error. Thus, the right-hand side of equation 8.25 is sufficient for active learning purposes, which does not produce any estimation error.

$$\zeta^* = \underset{\zeta}{\operatorname{argmin}}[\operatorname{tr}(\widehat{U}^{-1}\widehat{T}')], \tag{8.26}$$

where $\widehat{T}'$ is the $b \times b$ matrix with the (ℓ, ℓ')-th element

$$\widehat{T}'_{\ell, \ell'} := \frac{1}{n_{\text{te}}} \sum_{j=1}^{n_{\text{te}}} \frac{\varphi_\ell(x_j^{\text{te}}) \varphi_{\ell'}(x_j^{\text{te}})}{\zeta(x_j^{\text{te}})}.$$

Note also that equation 8.25 is sufficient for computing the IWLS solution (see section 2.2.1):

$$\widehat{\theta}_{\text{IWLS}} = \underset{\theta}{\operatorname{argmin}} \left[\frac{1}{n_{\text{tr}}} \sum_{i=1}^{n_{\text{tr}}} \frac{\left(\widehat{f}(x_i^{\text{tr}}; \theta) - y_i^{\text{tr}}\right)^2}{\zeta(x_i^{\text{tr}})} \right]. \tag{8.27}$$

A notable feature of equation 8.26 is that the optimal resampling weight function $\zeta^*(x)$ can be obtained in a *closed form* [163]:

$$\zeta^*(x_j^{\text{te}}) \propto \left(\sum_{\ell, \ell'=1}^{b} [\widehat{U}^{-1}]_{\ell, \ell'} \varphi_\ell(x_j^{\text{te}}) \varphi_{\ell'}(x_j^{\text{te}}) \right)^{\frac{1}{2}}.$$

8.4.3 Input-Dependent Variance-Only Method

The population-based input-dependent variance-only active learning method (see section 8.2.4) can be extended to the pool-based scenarios in a similar way.

8.4. Pool-Based Active Learning Methods

We can obtain a pool-based version of the active learning criterion ALICE, given by equation 8.15, as follows. The metric matrix U is replaced with its empirical approximator $\widehat{U}$, and the importance value $p_{te}(x_i^{tr})/p_{tr}(x_i^{tr})$ (included in L_{IWLS}) is computed by equation 8.25. Then we have

$$\min_{\zeta}[\operatorname{tr}(\widehat{U} L_{IWLS} L_{IWLS}^{\top})]. \tag{8.28}$$

The criterion (equation 8.28) is called *PALICE* (Pool-based ALICE). Thanks to the input-dependence, PALICE would be more accurate than the input-independent counterpart (equation 8.26) as a generalization error estimator (see section 8.2.4).

However, no analytic solution is known for the PALICE criterion, and therefore an exhaustive search strategy is needed to obtain a better solution. Here, we can use the same idea as the population-based case, that is, the analytic optimal solution ζ^* of the input-independent variance-only active learning criterion (equation 8.26) is used as a baseline, and one searches for a better solution around the vicinity of ζ^*. In practice, we may adopt a simple one-dimensional search strategy: find the best resampling weight function with respect to a scalar parameter ν:

$$\zeta_\nu(x) \propto \left(\sum_{\ell,\ell'=1}^{t} [\widehat{U}^{-1}]_{\ell,\ell'} \varphi_\ell(x) \varphi_{\ell'}(x) \right)^{\frac{\nu}{2}}. \tag{8.29}$$

The parameter ν controls the "shape" of the training input distribution: when $\nu = 0$, the resampling weight is uniform over all test input samples. Thus, the above choice includes passive learning (the training and test distributions are equivalent) as a special case. In practice, solution search may be intensively carried out around $\nu = 1$.

A pseudo code of the PALICE algorithm is summarized in figure 8.7.

8.4.4 Input-Independent Bias-and-Variance Approach

Finally, we show how the population-based input-independent bias-and-variance active learning method (see section 8.2.5) can be extended to the pool-based scenarios.

As explained in section 8.2.3, if $\mathcal{O}(n_{tr}^{-\frac{3}{2}})$-terms are ignored, the generalization error in input-independent analysis is expressed as follows:

$$\mathbb{E}_{\{x_i^{tr}\}_{i=1}^{n_{tr}}} \mathbb{E}_{\{y_i^{tr}\}_{i=1}^{n_{tr}}} [\operatorname{Gen}''] = \frac{1}{n_{tr}} \operatorname{tr}(U^{-1} H),$$

Input: A pool of test input points $\{x_j^{\text{te}}\}_{j=1}^{n_{\text{te}}}$ and basis functions $\{\varphi_\ell(x)\}_{\ell=1}^{b}$
Output: Learned parameter $\widehat{\theta}$

Compute the $b \times b$ matrix $\widehat{U}$ with $\widehat{U}_{\ell,\ell'} = \frac{1}{n_{\text{te}}} \sum_{j=1}^{n_{\text{te}}} \varphi_\ell(x_j^{\text{te}}) \varphi_{\ell'}(x_j^{\text{te}})$;
For several different values of ν (possibly around $\nu = 1$)
　　Compute $\{\zeta_\nu(x_j^{\text{te}})\}_{j=1}^{n_{\text{te}}}$ with $\zeta_\nu(x) = \left(\sum_{\ell,\ell'=1}^{b} [\widehat{U}^{-1}]_{\ell,\ell'} \varphi_\ell(x)\varphi_{\ell'}(x)\right)^\nu$;
　　Choose $\mathcal{X}_\nu^{\text{tr}} = \{x_i^{\text{tr}}\}_{i=1}^{n_{\text{tr}}}$ from $\{x_j^{\text{te}}\}_{j=1}^{n_{\text{te}}}$
　　　　with probability proportional to $\{\zeta_\nu(x_j^{\text{te}})\}_{j=1}^{n_{\text{te}}}$;
　　Compute the $n_{\text{tr}} \times b$ matrix X_ν^{tr} with $[X_\nu]_{i,\ell} = \varphi_\ell(x_i^{\text{tr}})$;
　　Compute the $n_{\text{tr}} \times n_{\text{tr}}$ diagonal matrix W_ν with $[W_\nu]_{i,i} = \left(\zeta_\nu(x_i^{\text{tr}})\right)^{-1}$;
　　Compute $L_\nu = (X_\nu^{\text{tr}\top} W_\nu X_\nu^{\text{tr}})^{-1} X_\nu^{\text{tr}\top} W_\nu$;
　　Compute $\text{PALICE}(\nu) = \text{tr}(\widehat{U} L_\nu L_\nu^\top)$;
End
Compute $\widehat{\nu} = \text{argmin}_\nu [\text{PALICE}(\nu)]$;
Gather training output values $y^{\text{tr}} = (y_1^{\text{tr}}, y_2^{\text{tr}}, \ldots, y_{n_{\text{tr}}}^{\text{tr}})^\top$ at $\mathcal{X}_{\widehat{\nu}}^{\text{tr}}$;
Compute $\widehat{\theta} = L_{\widehat{\nu}} y^{\text{tr}}$;

Figure 8.7
Pseudo code of the PALICE algorithm.

where H is defined by equation 8.11. It has been shown [89] that the optimal training input density which minimizes the above asymptotic generalization error is proportional to

$$p_{\text{te}}(x) \left(\sum_{\ell,\ell'=1}^{b} [U^{-1}]_{\ell,\ell'} \varphi_\ell(x) \varphi_{\ell'}(x) (\delta^2 r^2(x) + \sigma^2) \right)^{\frac{1}{2}},$$

where $\delta r(x)$ is the residual function which cannot be approximated by the model at hand (see section 8.1.2 and also figure 3.2 in section 3.2.2). Then the optimal resampling weight function can be obtained as

$$\left(\sum_{\ell,\ell'=1}^{b} [\widehat{U}^{-1}]_{\ell,\ell'} \varphi_\ell(x) \varphi_{\ell'}(x) (\delta^2 r^2(x) + \sigma^2) \right)^{\frac{1}{2}}.$$

However, since $(\delta^2 r^2(x) + \sigma^2)$ is inaccessible, the above closed-form solution cannot be used directly used for active learning. To cope with this problem, a regression method can be used in a two-stage sampling framework [87]. In the first stage, $\widetilde{n}_{\text{tr}}$ ($\leq n_{\text{tr}}$) training input points $\{\widetilde{x}_i^{\text{tr}}\}_{i=1}^{\widetilde{n}_{\text{tr}}}$ are uniformly chosen from the pool $\{x_j^{\text{te}}\}_{j=1}^{n_{\text{te}}}$, and corresponding training output values $\{\widetilde{y}_i^{\text{tr}}\}_{i=1}^{\widetilde{n}_{\text{tr}}}$ are observed. It can be shown that a consistent estimator of the value of the optimal resampling weight function at $\widetilde{x}_i^{\text{tr}}$ ($i = 1, 2, \ldots, \widetilde{n}_{\text{tr}}$) is given by

8.5. Numerical Examples of Pool-Based Active Learning Methods

$$g_i = [\widetilde{Q}^2 \widetilde{X} \widetilde{U}^{-1} \widetilde{X}^\top]_{i,i}.$$

Based on the input–output samples $\{(\widetilde{x}_i^{tr}, g_i)\}_{i=1}^{\widetilde{n}_{tr}}$, the optimal resampling weight function can be learned by a regression method. Let us denote the learned resampling weight function by $\widehat{\zeta}(x)$. Since the value of $\widehat{\zeta}(x)$ is available at any input location x,

$$\{\widehat{\zeta}(x_j^{te})\}_{j=1}^{n_{te}} \tag{8.30}$$

can be computed and used for resampling from the pooled input points. Then, in the second stage, the remaining $(n_{tr} - \widetilde{n}_{tr})$ training input points $\{x_i^{tr}\}_{i=\widetilde{n}_{tr}+1}^{n_{tr}-\widetilde{n}_{tr}}$ are chosen following the learned resampling weight function, and corresponding training output values $\{y_i^{tr}\}_{i=\widetilde{n}_{tr}+1}^{n_{tr}-\widetilde{n}_{tr}}$ are gathered. Finally, the parameter θ is learned, using $\{(\widetilde{x}_i^{tr}, \widetilde{y}_i^{tr})\}_{i=1}^{\widetilde{n}_{tr}}$ and $\{(x_i^{tr}, y_i^{tr})\}_{i=\widetilde{n}_{tr}+1}^{n_{tr}-\widetilde{n}_{tr}}$, as

$$\widehat{\theta} = \underset{\theta}{\mathrm{argmin}} \left[\sum_{i=1}^{\widetilde{n}_{tr}} \left(\widehat{f}(\widetilde{x}_i^{tr}; \theta) - \widetilde{y}_i^{tr}\right)^2 + \sum_{i=\widetilde{n}_{tr}+1}^{n_{tr}-\widetilde{n}_{tr}} \frac{\left(\widehat{f}(x_i^{tr}; \theta) - y_i^{tr}\right)^2}{\widehat{\zeta}(x_i^{tr})} \right]. \tag{8.31}$$

However, this method suffers from the limitations caused by the two-stage approach pointed out in section 8.2.5. Furthermore, obtaining a good approximation $\widehat{\zeta}(x)$ by regression is generally difficult, so this method may not be so reliable in practice.

8.5 Numerical Examples of Pool-Based Active Learning Methods

In this section, we illustrate the behavior of the pool-based active learning methods described in section 8.4.

Let the input dimension be $d = 1$, and let the learning target function be

$$f(x) = 1 - x + x^2 + \delta r(x),$$

where

$$r(x) = \frac{z^3 - 3z}{\sqrt{6}} \quad \text{with} \quad z = \frac{x - 0.2}{0.4}. \tag{8.32}$$

The reason for the choice of $r(x)$ will be explained later. Let us consider the following three cases.

$\delta = 0, 0.03, 0.06.$

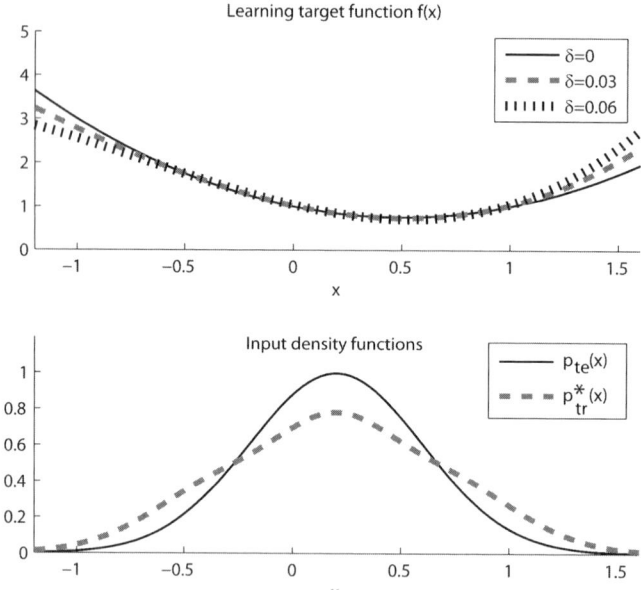

Figure 8.8
Learning target function (top) and test input density functions (bottom).

See the top graph of figure 8.8 for the profiles of $f(x)$ with different δ.

Let the number of training samples to gather be $n_{tr} = 100$. Add i.i.d. Gaussian noise with mean zero and standard deviation $\sigma = 0.3$ to output values. Let the test input density $p_{te}(x)$ be the Gaussian density with mean 0.2 and standard deviation 0.4; however, $p_{te}(x)$ is treated as unknown here. See the bottom graph of figure 8.8 for the profile of $p_{te}(x)$. Let us draw $n_{te} = 1000$ test input points independently from the test input distribution.

A polynomial model of order 2 is used for learning:

$$\widehat{f}(x) = \theta_1 + \theta_2 x + \theta_3 x^2. \tag{8.33}$$

Note that for these basis functions, the residual function $r(x)$ in equation 8.32 is orthogonal to the model and normalized to 1 (see section 3.2.2).

In this experiment, we compare the performance of the following sampling strategies:

- **PALICE** Training input points are chosen following equation 8.29 for

$$\nu \in \{0, 0.2, 0.4 \ldots, 2\} \cup \{0.8, 0.82, 0.84, \ldots, 1.2\}. \tag{8.34}$$

8.5. Numerical Examples of Pool-Based Active Learning Methods

Then the best value of ν is chosen from the above candidates based on equation 8.28. IWLS (equation 8.27) is used for parameter learning.

- **Pool-based input-independent variance-only method (PW)** Training input points are chosen following equation 8.26 (or equivalently equation 8.29 with $\nu = 1$). IWLS (equation 8.27) is used for parameter learning.

- **Pool-based traditional method (PO)** Training input points are chosen following equation 8.29 for equation 8.34, and the best value of ν is chosen based on equation 8.23. OLS (equation 8.7) is used for parameter learning.

- **Pool-based input-independent bias-and-variance method (POW)** Initially, $\widetilde{n}_{\text{tr}}$ training input–output samples are gathered based on the test input distribution, and they are used for learning the resampling bias function. The resampling bias function is learned by kernel ridge regression with Gaussian kernels, where the Gaussian width and ridge parameter are optimized based on fivefold cross-validation with exhaustive grid search. Then the remaining $n_{\text{tr}} - \widetilde{n}_{\text{tr}}$ training input points are chosen based on equation 8.30. The combination of OLS and IWLS (see equation 8.31) is used for parameter learning. We set $\widetilde{n}_{\text{tr}} = 25$.

- **Passive method (P)** Training input points are drawn uniformly from the pool of test input samples (or equivalently equation 8.29 with $\nu = 0$). OLS is used for parameter learning.

For references, the profile of $p_{\text{tr}}^*(x)$ ($= p_{\text{te}}(x)\zeta^*(x)$) is also depicted in the bottom graph of figure 8.8, which is the optimal training input density by PW (see section 8.4.2).

In table 8.2, the generalization error obtained by each method is described. The numbers in the table are means and standard deviations over 100 trials. For better comparison, the model error δ^2 is subtracted from the obtained error and all values are multiplied by 10^3. In each row of the table, the best method and comparable ones by the Wilcoxon signed-rank test (e.g., [78]) at the significance level 5% percent are indicated with o.

When $\delta = 0$, PO works the best and is followed by PALICE. These two methods have no statistically significant difference and are significantly better than the other methods. When δ is increased from 0 to 0.03, the performances of PALICE and PW are almost unchanged, while the performance of PO is considerably degraded. Consequently, PALICE gives the best performance among all. When δ is further increased to 0.06, the performance of PALICE and PW is still almost unchanged. On the other hand, PO performs very poorly and is outperformed even by the baseline Passive method. POW does not seem to work well for all three cases.

Table 8.2
The mean and standard deviation of the generalization error obtained by pool-based active learning methods

	PALICE	PW	PO	POW	P
$\delta = 0$	°2.03 ± 1.81	2.59 ± 1.83	°1.82 ± 1.69	6.43 ± 6.61	3.10 ± 3.09
$\delta = 0.03$	°2.17 ± 2.04	2.81 ± 2.01	2.62 ± 2.05	6.66 ± 6.54	3.40 ± 3.55
$\delta = 0.06$	°2.42 ± 2.65	3.19 ± 2.59	4.85 ± 3.37	7.65 ± 7.21	4.12 ± 4.71
Average	°2.21 ± 2.19	2.86 ± 2.18	3.10 ± 2.78	6.91 ± 6.79	3.54 ± 3.85

For better comparison, the model error δ^2 is subtracted from the error, and all values are multiplied by 10^3. In each row of the table, the best method and comparable ones by the Wilcoxon signed-rank test at the significance level 5 percent are indicated with o.

Overall, PALICE and PW are shown to be highly robust against model misspecification, while PO is very sensitive to the violation of the correct model assumption. PALICE significantly outperforms PW, because ALICE is a more accurate estimator of the single-trial generalization error than W (see section 8.2.4).

8.6 Summary and Discussion

Active learning is an important issue particularly when the cost of sampling output value is very expensive. However, estimating the generalization error before observing samples is hard. A standard strategy for generalization error estimation in active learning scenarios is to assume that the bias is small enough to be neglected, and focus on the variance (section 8.1.3).

We first addressed the population-based active learning problems, where the test input distribution is known. We began our discussion by pointing out that the traditional active learning method based on ordinary least squares is not practical since it requires the model to be correctly specified (section 8.2.1). To overcome this problem, active learning methods based on importance-weighted least squares have been developed (sections 8.2.3, 8.2.4, and 8.2.5); among them the input-dependent variance-only method called ALICE was shown to perform excellently in experiments (section 8.3).

We then turned our focus to the pool-based active learning scenarios where the test input distribution is unknown but a pool of test input samples is given. We showed that all the population-based methods explained above can be extended to the pool-based scenarios (sections 8.4.2, 8.4.3, and 8.4.4). The simulations showed that the method called PALICE works very well (section 8.5).

8.6. Summary and Discussion

Table 8.3
Active learning methods

	Population-based		Pool-based	
	Input independent	Input dependent	Input independent	Input dependent
Correct	—	section 8.2.1	—	section 8.4.1
Approximately correct	section 8.2.3	section 8.2.4	section 8.4.2	section 8.4.3
Completely misspecified	section 8.2.5	—	section 8.4.4	—

In ALICE or PALICE, we need to prepare reasonable candidates for training input distributions. We introduced practical heuristics of searching around the analytic solution obtained by other methods (sections 8.2.4 and 8.4.3), which were shown to be reasonable through experiments. However, there may still be room for further improvement, and it is important to explore alternative strategies for preparing better candidates.

The active learning methods covered in this chapter are summarized in table 8.3.

We have focused on regression scenarios in this chapter. A natural desire is to extend the same idea to classification scenarios. The conceptual issues we have addressed in this chapter—the usefulness of the input-dependent analysis of the generalization error and the practical importance of dealing with approximately correct models—will still be valid in classification scenarios. Developing active learning methods in classification scenarios based on these conceptual ideas will be promising.

The ALICE and PALICE criteria are random variables which depend not only on training input distributions, but also on realizations of training input points. This is why the minimizer of ALICE or PALICE cannot be obtained analytically. On the other hand, this fact implies that ALICE and PALICE allow one to evaluate the goodness not only of training input distributions but also of realizations of training input points. It will be interesting to investigate this issue systematically.

The ALICE and PALICE methods have been shown to be robust against the existence of bias. However, if the input dimensionality is very high, the variance tends to dominate the bias due to small sample size, and therefore advantages of these methods tend to be lost. More critically, regression from data samples is highly unreliable in such high-dimensional problems due to extremely large variance. To address this issue, it will be important to first reduce the dimensionality of the data [154, 178, 156, 175], which is another challenge in active learning research. Active learning for classification in high-dimensional problems is discussed in, for instance, [115, 139].

We have focused on linear models. However, the importance-weighting technique used to compensate for the bias caused by model misspecification is valid for any empirical error-based methods (see chapter 2). Thus, another important direction to be pursued is extending the current active learning ideas to more complex models, such as support vector machines [193] and neural networks [20].

9 Active Learning with Model Selection

In chapters 3 and 8, we addressed the problems of model selection[1] and active learning. When discussing model selection strategies, we assumed that the training input points have been fixed. On the other hand, when discussing active learning strategies, we assumed that the model had been fixed.

Although the problems of active learning and model selection share the common goal of minimizing the generalization error, they have been studied as two independent problems so far. If active learning and model selection are performed at the same time, the generalization performance will be further improved. We call the problem of simultaneously optimizing the training input distribution and model *active learning with model selection*. This is the problem we address in this chapter.

Below, we focus on the model selection criterion IWSIC (equation 3.11) and the population-based active learning criterion ALICE (equation 8.15). However, the fundamental idea explained in this chapter is applicable to any model selection and active learning criteria.

9.1 Direct Approach and the Active Learning/Model Selection Dilemma

A naive and direct solution to the problem of active learning with model selection is to simultaneously optimize the training input distribution and model. However, this direct approach may not be possible simply by combining existing active learning methods and model selection methods in a batch manner, due to the *active learning/model selection dilemma* [166]: When selecting the training input density $p_{tr}(x)$ with existing active learning methods, the model must have been fixed [48, 107, 33, 55, 199, 89, 153]. On the other hand,

---

[1]. "Model selection" refers to the selection of various tunable factors M including basis functions, the regularization parameter, and the flattening parameter.

when choosing the model with existing model selection methods, the training input points $\{x_i^{tr}\}_{i=1}^{n_{tr}}$ (or the training input density $p_{tr}(x)$) must have been fixed and the corresponding training output values $\{y_i^{tr}\}_{i=1}^{n_{tr}}$ must have been gathered [2, 135, 142, 35, 145, 162]. For example, the active learning criterion (equation 8.15) cannot be computed without fixing the model M, and the model selection criterion (equation 3.11) cannot be computed without fixing the training input density $p_{tr}(x)$.

If training input points that are optimal for all model candidates exist, it is possible to perform active learning and model selection at the same time without regard to the active learning/model selection dilemma: Choose the training input points $\{x_i^{tr}\}_{i=1}^{n_{tr}}$ for some model M by an active learning method (e.g., equation 8.15), gather corresponding output values $\{y_i^{tr}\}_{i=1}^{n_{tr}}$, and choose a model by a selection method (e.g., equation 3.11). It has been shown that such common optimal training input points exist for a class of correctly specified trigonometric polynomial regression models [166]. However, the common optimal training input points may not exist in general, and thus the range of application of this approach is limited.

9.2 Sequential Approach

A standard approach to coping with the above active learning/model selection dilemma for arbitrary models is the *sequential approach* [106]. That is, a model is iteratively chosen by a model selection method, and the next input point (or a small batch) is optimized for the chosen model by an active learning method (see figure 9.1a).

In the sequential approach, the chosen model varies through the sequential learning process (see the dashed line in figure 9.1b). We refer to this phenomenon as the *model drift*. The model drift phenomenon could be a weakness of the sequential approach since the location of optimal training input points depends on the target model in active learning; thus a good training input point for one model could be poor for another model. Depending on the transition of the chosen models, the sequential approach can work very well. For example, when the transition of the model is the solid line in figure 9.1b, most of the training input points are chosen for the finally selected model $M_{n_{tr}}$ and the sequential approach will have an excellent performance. However, when the transition of the model is the dotted line in figure 9.1b, the performance becomes poor since most of the training input points are chosen for other models. Note that we cannot control the transition of the model as desired since we do not know a priori which model will be chosen in the end. For this reason, the sequential approach will be unreliable in practice.

9.2. Sequential Approach

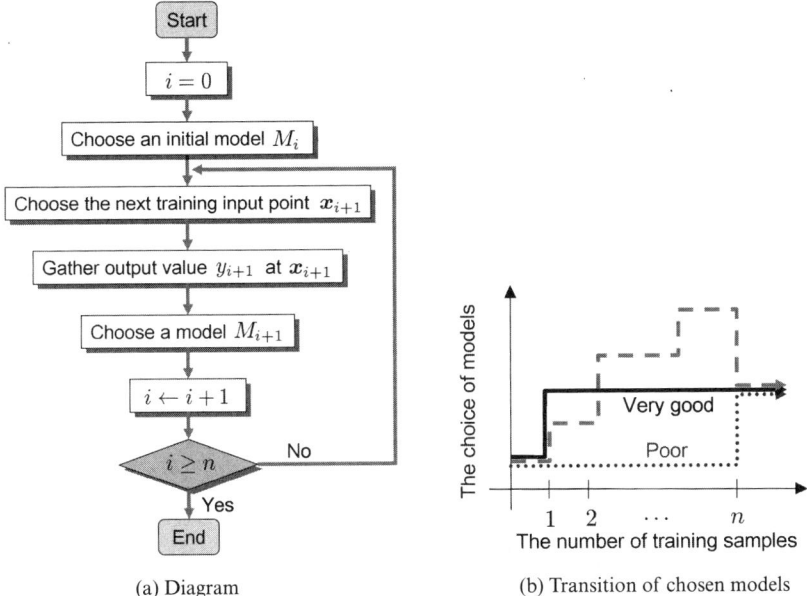

Figure 9.1
Sequential approach.

Another issue that needs to be taken into account in the sequential approach is that the training input points are not i.i.d. in general—the choice of the $(i+1)$-th training input point x_{i+1}^{tr} depends on the previously gathered samples $\{(x_{i'}^{\text{tr}}, y_{i'}^{\text{tr}})\}_{i'=1}^{i}$. Since standard active learning and model selection methods require the i.i.d. assumption for establishing their statistical properties such as consistency or unbiasedness, they may not be directly employed in the sequential approach [9]. The active learning criterion ALICE (equation 8.15) and the model selection criterion IWSIC (equation 3.11) also suffer from the violation of the i.i.d. condition, and they may lose their consistency and unbiasedness. However, this problem can be settled by slightly modifying the criteria, which is an advantage of ALICE and IWSIC: Suppose we draw u input points from $p_{\text{tr}}^{(i)}(x)$ in each iteration (let $n_{\text{tr}} = uv$, where v is the number of iterations). If u tends to infinity, simply redefining the diagonal matrix W as follows makes ALICE and IWSIC still consistent and asymptotically unbiased:

$$W_{k,k} = \frac{p_{\text{te}}(x_k^{\text{tr}})}{p_{\text{tr}}^{(i)}(x_k^{\text{tr}})}, \tag{9.1}$$

where $k = (i-1)u + j$, $i = 1, 2, \ldots, v$, and $j = 1, 2, \ldots, u$.

9.3 Batch Approach

An alternative approach to active learning with model selection is to choose all the training input points for an initially chosen model M_0. We refer to this approach as the *batch approach* (see figure 9.2a). Due to its nature, this approach does not suffer from the model drift (cf. figure 9.1b); the batch approach can be optimal in terms of active learning if an initially chosen model M_0 agrees with the finally chosen model $M_{n_{\mathrm{tr}}}$ (see the solid line in figure 9.2b).

In order to choose the initial model M_0, we may need a generalization error estimator that can be computed before observing training samples—for example, the generalization error estimator (equation 8.15). However, this does not work well since equation 8.15 only evaluates the variance of the estimator (see equation 8.4); thus, using equation 8.15 for choosing the initial model M_0 always results in selecting the simplest model from among the candidates. Note that this problem is not specific to the generalization error estimator (equation 8.15), but is common to most generalization error estimators since it is generally not possible to estimate the bias of the estimator (see equation 8.3) before observing training samples. Therefore, in practice, one may have to choose the initial model M_0 randomly. If one has some prior preference of models, $p(M)$, the initial model may be drawn according to it; otherwise, one has to choose the initial model M_0 randomly from the uniform distribution.

Due to the randomness of the initial model choice, the performance of the batch approach may be unreliable in practice (see the dashed line in figure 9.2b).

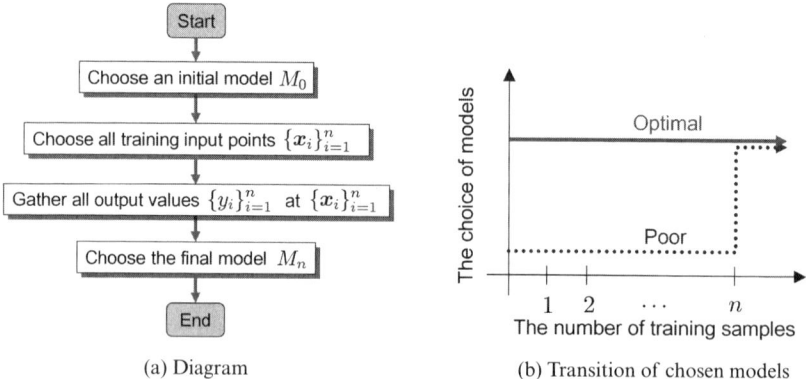

(a) Diagram (b) Transition of chosen models

Figure 9.2
Batch approach.

9.4 Ensemble Active Learning

As pointed out above, the sequential and batch approaches have potential limitations. In this section, we describe a method of active learning with model selection that can cope with the above limitations [167].

The weakness of the batch approach lies in the fact that the training input points chosen by an active learning method are overfitted to the initially chosen model—the training input points optimized for the initial model could be poor if a different model is chosen later.

We may reduce the risk of overfitting by not optimizing the training input distribution specifically for a single model, but by optimizing it for all model candidates (see figure 9.3). This allows all the models to contribute to the optimization of the training input distribution, and thus we can hedge the risk of overfitting to a single (possibly inferior) model. Since this idea can be viewed as applying a popular idea of *ensemble learning* to the problem of active learning, this approach is called *ensemble active learning* (EAL).

The idea of ensemble active learning can be realized by determining the training input density $p_{tr}(x)$ so that the expected generalization error over all model candidates is minimized:

$$\min_{p_{tr}} \left[\sum_M \text{ALICE}_M(p_{tr}) p(M) \right],$$

where ALICE_M denotes the value of the active learning criterion ALICE for a model M (see equation 8.15), and $p(M)$ is the prior preference of the model M.

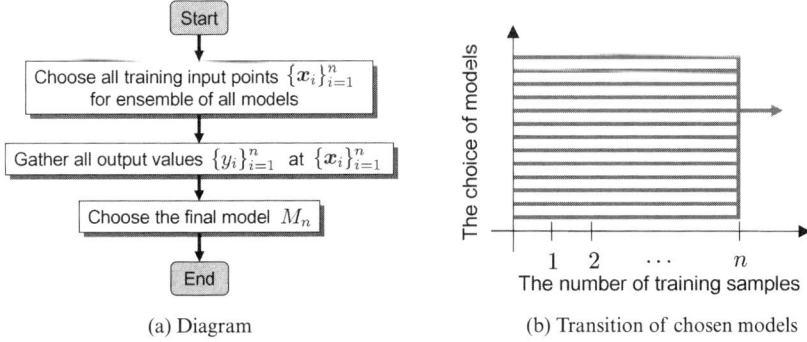

(a) Diagram   (b) Transition of chosen models

Figure 9.3
The ensemble approach.

If no prior information on the goodness/preference of the models is available, the uniform prior may be used. In the next section, we experimentally show that this ensemble approach significantly outperforms the sequential and batch approaches.

9.5 Numerical Examples

Here, we illustrate how the sequential (section 9.2), batch (section 9.3), and ensemble (section 9.4) methods behave using a one-dimensional data set.

9.5.1 Setting

Let the input dimension be $d = 1$, and the target function $f(x)$ be the following third-order polynomial (see the top graph of figure 9.4):

$$f(x) = 1 - x + x^2 + 0.05r(x),$$

where

$$r(x) = \frac{z^3 - 3z}{\sqrt{6}} \quad \text{with} \quad z = \frac{x - 0.2}{0.4}.$$

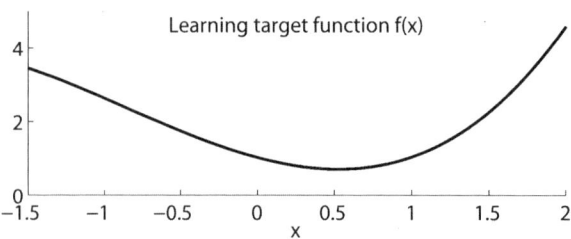

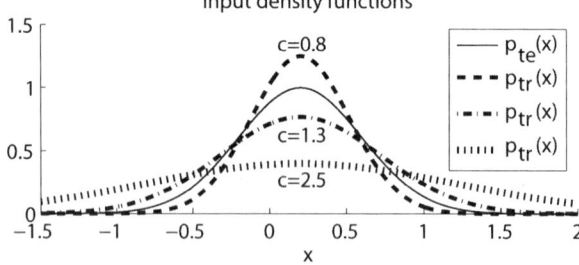

Figure 9.4
Target function, training input densities $p_{tr}(x)$, and test input density $p_{te}(x)$.

9.5. Numerical Examples

Let the test input density $p_{te}(x)$ be the Gaussian density with mean 0.2 and standard deviation 0.4, which is assumed to be known in this illustrative simulation. We choose the training input density $p_{tr}(x)$ from a set of Gaussian densities with mean 0.2 and standard deviation $0.4c$, where

$$c = 0.8, 0.9, 1.0, \ldots, 2.5.$$

These density functions are illustrated in the bottom graph of figure 9.4. We add i.i.d. Gaussian noise with mean zero and standard deviation 0.3 to the training output values.

Let us use the second-order polynomial model:

$$\widehat{f}(x; \boldsymbol{\theta}) = \theta_1 + \theta_2 x + \theta_3 x^2.$$

Note that the target function $f(x)$, which is the third-order polynomial, is not realizable by the second-order model.

The parameters are learned by *adaptive importance-weighted least squares* (AIWLS; see section 2.2.1):

$$\min_{\boldsymbol{\theta}} \left[\frac{1}{n_{tr}} \sum_{i=1}^{n_{tr}} \left(\frac{p_{te}(x_i^{tr})}{p_{tr}(x_i^{tr})} \right)^\gamma \left(\widehat{f}(x_i^{tr}; \boldsymbol{\theta}) - y_i^{tr} \right)^2 \right],$$

where γ is the *flattening parameter* ($0 \leq \gamma \leq 1$) for controlling the bias-variance trade-off. Here, we focus on choosing the flattening parameter γ by model selection; γ is selected from

$$\gamma = 0, 0.5, 1.$$

9.5.2 Analysis of Batch Approach

First, we investigate the dependency between the goodness of the training input density (i.e., c) and the model (i.e., γ). For each γ and each c, we draw training input points $\{x_i^{tr}\}_{i=1}^{100}$ and gather output values $\{y_i^{tr}\}_{i=1}^{100}$. Then we learn the parameter $\boldsymbol{\theta}$ of the model by AIWLS and compute the generalization error Gen. The mean Gen over 500 trials as a function of c for each γ is depicted in figure 9.5a. This graph underlines that the best training input density c could strongly depend on the model γ, implying that a training input density that is good for one model could be poor for others. For example, when the training input density is optimized for the model $\gamma = 0$, $c = 1.1$ would be an excellent choice. However, $c = 1.1$ is not so suitable for models $\gamma = 0.5, 1$. This figure illustrates a possible weakness of the batch method: When an initially chosen model is significantly different from the finally chosen model, the training

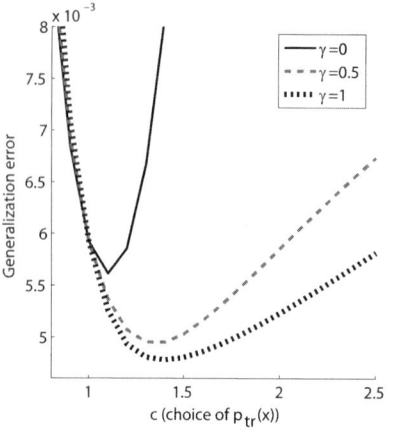 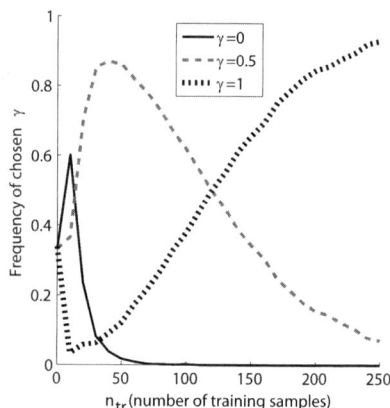

(a) The mean generalization error over 500 trials as a function of training input density c for each γ (when $n_{tr} = 100$)

(b) Frequency of chosen γ over 500 trials as a function of the number of training samples

Figure 9.5
Simulation results of active learning with model selection.

input points optimized for the initial model could be less useful for the final model, and the performance is degraded.

9.5.3 Analysis of Sequential Approach

Next, we investigate the behavior of the sequential approach. In our implementation, ten training input points are chosen at each iteration. Figure 9.5b depicts the transition of the frequency of chosen γ in the sequential learning process over 500 trials. It shows that the choice of models varies over the learning process; a smaller γ (which has smaller variance, and thus low complexity) is favored in the beginning, but a larger γ (which has larger variance, and thus higher complexity) tends to be chosen as the number of training samples increases. Figure 9.5 illustrates a possible weakness of the sequential method: The target model drifts during the sequential learning process (from small γ to large γ), and the training input points designed in an early stage (for $\gamma = 0$) could be poor for the finally chosen model ($\gamma = 1$).

9.5.4 Comparison of Obtained Generalization Error

Finally, we investigate the generalization performance of each method when the number of training samples to be gathered is

$n_{tr} = 50, 100, 150, 200, 250$.

9.6. Summary and Discussion

Table 9.1
Means and standard deviations of generalization error when the flattening parameter γ is chosen from $\{0, 0.5, 1\}$ by model selection

n_{tr}	Passive	Sequential	Batch	Ensemble
50	10.63 ± 8.33	7.98 ± 4.57	8.04 ± 4.39	°7.59 ± 4.27
100	5.90 ± 3.42	5.66 ± 2.75	5.73 ± 3.01	°5.15 ± 2.49
150	4.80 ± 2.38	4.40 ± 1.74	4.61 ± 1.85	°4.13 ± 1.56
200	4.21 ± 1.66	3.97 ± 1.54	4.26 ± 1.63	°3.73 ± 1.25
250	3.79 ± 1.31	3.46 ± 1.00	3.88 ± 1.41	°3.35 ± 0.95

All values in the table are multiplied by 10^3. The best method in terms of the mean generalization error and comparable methods according to the Wilcoxon signed-rank test at the significance level 5% are marked by 'o'.

Table 9.1 describes the means and standard deviations of the generalization error obtained by the sequential, batch, and ensemble methods; as a baseline, we included the result of passive learning, that is, the training input points $\{x_i^{tr}\}_{i=1}^{n_{tr}}$ are drawn from the test input density $p_{te}(x)$ (or equivalently $c = 1$). The table shows that all three methods of active learning with model selection tend to outperform passive learning. However, the improvement of the sequential method is not so significant, as a result the model drift phenomenon (see figure 9.5). The batch method also does not provide significant improvement, due to overfitting to the randomly chosen initial model (see figure 9.5a). On the other hand, the EAL method does not suffer from these problems and works significantly better than the other methods. The best method in terms of the mean generalization error and comparable methods by the *Wilcoxon signed-rank test* at the significance level 5 percent [78] are marked by o in the table.

9.6 Summary and Discussion

Historically, the problems of active learning and model selection have been studied as two independent problems, although they share a common goal of minimizing the generalization error. We suggested that by simultaneously performing active learning and model selection—which is called *active learning with model selection*—a better generalization capability can be achieved.

We pointed out that the sequential approach, which would be a common approach to active learning with model selection, can perform poorly due to the model drift phenomenon (section 9.2). A batch approach does not suffer from the model drift problem, but it is hard to choose the initial model appropriately. For this reason, the batch approach is not reliable in practice (section 9.3). To overcome the limitations of the sequential and batch approaches, we introduced an approach called ensemble active learning (EAL), which performs active learning not only for a single model, but also for an ensemble of models (section 9.4). The EAL method was shown to compare favorably with other approaches through simulations (section 9.5).

Although we focused on regression problems in this chapter, EAL is applicable to any supervised learning scenario, given that a suitable batch active learning method is available. This implies that, in principle, it is possible to extend the EAL method to classification problems. However, to the best of our knowledge, there is no reliable batch active learning method in classification tasks. Therefore, developing a method of active learning with model selection for classification is still a challenging open problem which needs to be further investigated.

10 Applications of Active Learning

In this chapter, we describe real-world applications of active learning techniques: sampling policy design in reinforcement learning (section 10.1) and wafer alignment in semiconductor exposure apparatus (section 10.2).

10.1 Design of Efficient Exploration Strategies in Reinforcement Learning

As shown in section 7.6, *reinforcement learning* [174] is a useful framework to let a robot agent learn optimal behavior in an unknown environment.

The accuracy of estimated value functions depends on the training samples collected following sampling policy $\widetilde{\pi}(a|s)$. In this section, we apply the population-based active learning method described in section 8.2.4 to designing good sampling policies [4]. The contents of this section are based on the framework of *sample reuse policy iteration* described in section 7.6.

10.1.1 Efficient Exploration with Active Learning

Let us consider a situation where collecting state-action trajectory samples is easy and cheap, but gathering immediate reward samples is hard and expensive.

For example, let us consider a robot-arm control task of hitting a ball with a bat and driving the ball as far away as possible (see section 10.1.). Let us adopt the carry of the ball as the immediate reward. In this setting, obtaining state-action trajectory samples of the robot arm is easy and relatively cheap since we just need to control the robot arm and record its state-action trajectories over time. On the other hand, explicitly computing the carry of the ball from the state-action samples is hard due to friction and elasticity of links, air resistance, unpredictable disturbances such a current of air, and so on. Thus, in practice, we may need to put the robot in open space, let it really hit the ball, and measure the carry of the ball manually. Thus, gathering immediate reward samples is much more expensive than gathering the state-action trajectory samples.

The goal of active learning in the current setup is to determine the sampling policy so that the expected generalization error is minimized. The generalization error is not accessible in practice since the expected reward function $R(s, a)$ and the transition probability $p_T(s'|s, a)$ are unknown. Thus, for performing active learning, the generalization error needs to be estimated from samples. A difficulty of estimating the generalization error in the context of active learning is that its estimation needs to be carried out only from state-action trajectory samples without using immediate reward samples, because gathering immediate reward samples is hard and expensive. Below, we explain how the generalization error for active learning is estimated without reward samples.

10.1.2 Reinforcement Learning Revisited

Here, we briefly revisit essential ingredients of reinforcement learning. See section 7.6 for more details.

For state s, action a, reward r, and discount factor γ, the state-action value function $Q^\pi(s, a) \in \mathbb{R}$ for policy π is defined as the expected discounted sum of rewards the agent will receive when taking action a in state s and following policy π thereafter. That is,

$$Q^\pi(s, a) := \mathbb{E}_{\pi, p_T}\left[\sum_{n=1}^{\infty} \gamma^{n-1} R(s_n, a_n, s_{n+1}) \,\bigg|\, s_1 = s, a_1 = a\right],$$

where $\mathbb{E}_{\pi, p_T}$ denotes the expectation over $\{s_n, a_n\}_{n=1}^{\infty}$ following policy $\pi(a_n|s_n)$ and transition probability $p_T(s_{n+1}|s_n, a_n)$.

We approximate the state-action value function $Q^\pi(s, a)$ using the following linear model:

$$\widehat{Q}^\pi(s, a; \boldsymbol{\theta}) := \sum_{b=1}^{B} \theta_b \phi_b(s, a) = \boldsymbol{\theta}^\top \boldsymbol{\phi}(s, a),$$

where

$$\boldsymbol{\phi}(s, a) = (\phi_1(s, a), \phi_2(s, a), \ldots, \phi_B(s, a))^\top$$

are the fixed basis functions, B is the number of basis functions, and

$$\boldsymbol{\theta} = (\theta_1, \theta_2, \ldots, \theta_B)^\top$$

are model parameters.

10.1. Design of Efficient Exploration Strategies in Reinforcement Learning

We want to learn θ so that the true value function $Q^\pi(s, a)$ is well approximated. As explained in section 7.6, this can be achieved by regressing the immediate reward function $R(s, a)$, using the following transformed basis function:

$$\widehat{\psi}(s, a; \mathcal{D}) := \phi(s, a) - \frac{\gamma}{|\mathcal{D}_{(s,a)}|} \sum_{s' \in \mathcal{D}_{(s,a)}} \mathbb{E}_{\pi(a'|s')} \left[\phi(s', a') \right],$$

where $\mathcal{D}$ is a set of training samples, $\mathcal{D}_{(s,a)}$ is a set of four-quadruple elements containing state s and action a in the training data $\mathcal{D}$, and $\mathbb{E}_{\pi(a'|s')}$ denotes the conditional expectation of a' over $\pi(a'|s')$, given s'.

The generalization error of a parameter θ is measured by the following squared Bellman residual G:

$$G := \mathbb{E}_{p_1, \pi, p_T} \left[\frac{1}{N} \sum_{n=1}^{N} (\theta^\top \widehat{\psi}(s_n, a_n; \mathcal{D}) - R(s_n, a_n))^2 \right],$$

where $\mathbb{E}_{p_1, \pi, p_T}$ denotes the expectation over $\{s_n, a_n\}_{n=1}^{N}$ following the initial state probability density $p_1(s_1)$, the policy $\pi(a_n|s_n)$, and the transition probability density $p_T(s_{n+1}|s_n, a_n)$.

Here, we consider the off-policy setup (see section 7.6.5), where the current policy $\pi(a|s)$ is used for evaluating the generalization error, and a sampling policy $\widetilde{\pi}(a|s)$ is used for collecting data samples. We use the *per-decision importance-weighting* (PIW) method for parameter learning (see section 7.6.6.2):

$$\widehat{\theta} := \underset{\theta}{\operatorname{argmin}} \left[\frac{1}{MN} \sum_{m=1}^{M} \sum_{n=1}^{N} \left(\theta^\top \widehat{\psi}(s_{m,n}^{\widetilde{\pi}}, a_{m,n}^{\widetilde{\pi}}; \mathcal{D}^{\widetilde{\pi}}) \right.\right.$$
$$\left.\left. - \frac{1}{|\mathcal{D}^{\widetilde{\pi}}_{(s_{m,n}^{\widetilde{\pi}}, a_{m,n}^{\widetilde{\pi}})}|} \sum_{r \in \mathcal{D}^{\widetilde{\pi}}_{(s_{m,n}^{\widetilde{\pi}}, a_{m,n}^{\widetilde{\pi}})}} r \right)^2 w_{m,n}^{\widetilde{\pi}} \right],$$

where

$$w_{m,n}^{\widetilde{\pi}} := \frac{\prod_{n'=1}^{n} \pi(a_{m,n'}^{\widetilde{\pi}}|s_{m,n'}^{\widetilde{\pi}})}{\prod_{n'=1}^{n} \widetilde{\pi}(a_{m,n'}^{\widetilde{\pi}}|s_{m,n'}^{\widetilde{\pi}})}$$

is the *importance weight*.

The goal of active learning here is to find the best sampling policy $\widetilde{\pi}(a|s)$ that minimizes the generalization error.

10.1.3 Decomposition of Generalization Error

The information we are allowed to use for estimating the generalization error is a set of roll-out samples without immediate rewards:

$$\overline{\mathcal{D}}^{\widetilde{\pi}} := \{\overline{d}_m^{\widetilde{\pi}}\}_{m=1}^M,$$

$$\overline{d}_m^{\widetilde{\pi}} := \{(s_{m,n}^{\widetilde{\pi}}, a_{m,n}^{\widetilde{\pi}}, s_{m,n+1}^{\widetilde{\pi}})\}_{n=1}^N.$$

Let us define the deviation of immediate rewards from the mean as

$$\epsilon_{m,n}^{\widetilde{\pi}} := r_{m,n}^{\widetilde{\pi}} - R(s_{m,n}^{\widetilde{\pi}}, a_{m,n}^{\widetilde{\pi}}).$$

Note that $\epsilon_{m,n}^{\widetilde{\pi}}$ can be regarded as additive noise in the context of least-squares function fitting. By definition, $\epsilon_{m,n}^{\widetilde{\pi}}$ has mean zero and its variance generally depends on $s_{m,n}^{\widetilde{\pi}}$ and $a_{m,n}^{\widetilde{\pi}}$ (i.e., *heteroscedastic* noise [21]). However, since estimating the variance of $\epsilon_{m,n}^{\widetilde{\pi}}$ without using reward samples is not generally possible, we ignore the dependence of the variance on $s_{m,n}^{\widetilde{\pi}}$ and $a_{m,n}^{\widetilde{\pi}}$. Let us denote the input-independent common variance by σ^2.

Now we would like to estimate the generalization error

$$\overline{G}(\widehat{\theta}) := \mathbb{E}_{p_{\mathrm{I}},\pi,p_{\mathrm{T}}}\left[\frac{1}{N}\sum_{n=1}^N (\widehat{\theta}^\top \widehat{\psi}(s_n, a_n; \overline{\mathcal{D}}^{\widetilde{\pi}}) - R(s_n, a_n))^2\right]$$

from $\overline{\mathcal{D}}^{\widetilde{\pi}}$, where $\widehat{\theta}$ is a PIW estimator given by

$$\widehat{\theta} = \widehat{L}r,$$

$$\widehat{L} = (\widehat{X}^\top W \widehat{X})^{-1}\widehat{X}^\top W,$$

$$\widehat{X}_{N(m-1)+n,b} = \widehat{\psi}_b(s_{m,n}^{\widetilde{\pi}}, a_{m,n}^{\widetilde{\pi}}; \overline{\mathcal{D}}^{\widetilde{\pi}}),$$

$$r_{N(m-1)+n} = r_{m,n}^{\widetilde{\pi}}.$$

W is the diagonal matrix with the $(N(m-1)+n)$-th diagonal element given by

$$W_{N(m-1)+n,N(m-1)+n} = w_{m,n}^{\widetilde{\pi}}.$$

10.1. Design of Efficient Exploration Strategies in Reinforcement Learning

Note that in the above calculation of $\widehat{\boldsymbol{\theta}}$, $\overline{\mathcal{D}}^{\widetilde{\pi}}$ (a data set without immediate rewards) is used instead of $\mathcal{D}^{\widetilde{\pi}}$ (a data set with immediate rewards) since $\mathcal{D}^{\widetilde{\pi}}$ is not available in the active learning setup.

The expectation of the above generalization error over "noise" can be decomposed as follows:

$$\mathbb{E}_{\epsilon^{\widetilde{\pi}}}\left[G(\widehat{\boldsymbol{\theta}})\right] = \text{Bias}^2 + \text{Variance} + \delta^2,$$

where $\mathbb{E}_{\epsilon^{\widetilde{\pi}}}$ denotes the expectation over "noise" $\{\epsilon_{m,n}^{\widetilde{\pi}}\}_{m=1,n=1}^{M,N}$. Bias^2, Variance, and δ^2 are the *bias* term, the *variance* term, and the *model error* term (respectively) defined by

$$\text{Bias}^2 := \mathbb{E}_{p_\text{I},\pi,p_\text{T}}\left[\frac{1}{N}\sum_{n=1}^{N}\left\{(\mathbb{E}_{\epsilon^{\widetilde{\pi}}}[\widehat{\boldsymbol{\theta}}] - \boldsymbol{\theta}^*)^\top \widehat{\boldsymbol{\psi}}(s_n, a_n; \overline{\mathcal{D}}^{\widetilde{\pi}})\right\}^2\right],$$

$$\text{Variance} := \mathbb{E}_{p_\text{I},\pi,p_\text{T}} \mathbb{E}_{\epsilon^{\widetilde{\pi}}}\left[\frac{1}{N}\sum_{n=1}^{N}\left\{(\widehat{\boldsymbol{\theta}} - \mathbb{E}_{\epsilon^{\widetilde{\pi}}}[\widehat{\boldsymbol{\theta}}])^\top \widehat{\boldsymbol{\psi}}(s_n, a_n; \overline{\mathcal{D}}^{\widetilde{\pi}})\right\}^2\right],$$

$$\delta^2 := \mathbb{E}_{p_\text{I},\pi,p_\text{T}}\left[\frac{1}{N}\sum_{n=1}^{N}(\boldsymbol{\theta}^{*\top} \widehat{\boldsymbol{\psi}}(s_n, a_n; \overline{\mathcal{D}}^{\widetilde{\pi}}) - R(s_n, a_n))^2\right].$$

$\boldsymbol{\theta}^*$ is the optimal parameter in the model, defined by equation 7.5 in section 7.6. Note that the variance term can be expressed in a compact form as

$$\text{Variance} = \sigma^2 \text{tr}(\boldsymbol{U}\widehat{\boldsymbol{L}}\widehat{\boldsymbol{L}}^\top),$$

where $\boldsymbol{U}$ is the $B \times B$ matrix with the (b, b')-th element

$$U_{b,b'} := \mathbb{E}_{p_\text{I},\pi,p_\text{T}}\left[\frac{1}{N}\sum_{n=1}^{N} \widehat{\psi}_b(s_n, a_n; \overline{\mathcal{D}}^{\widetilde{\pi}}) \widehat{\psi}_{b'}(s_n, a_n; \overline{\mathcal{D}}^{\widetilde{\pi}})\right]. \tag{10.1}$$

10.1.4 Estimating Generalization Error for Active Learning

The model error is constant, and thus can be safely ignored in generalization error estimation, since we are interested in finding a minimizer of the generalization error with respect to $\widetilde{\pi}$. For this reason, we focus on the bias term and the variance term. However, the bias term includes the unknown optimal parameter $\boldsymbol{\theta}^*$, and thus it may not be possible to estimate the bias term without using reward samples; similarly, it may not be possible to estimate the "noise" variance σ^2 included in the variance term without using reward samples.

As explained in section 8.2.4, the bias term is small enough to be neglected when the model is approximately correct, that is, $\boldsymbol{\theta}^{*\top}\widehat{\boldsymbol{\psi}}(s,a)$ approximately agrees with the true function $R(s,a)$. Then we have

$$\mathbb{E}_{\epsilon^{\widetilde{\pi}}}\left[\overline{G(\widehat{\boldsymbol{\theta}})}\right] - \delta^2 - \text{Bias}^2 \propto \text{tr}(\boldsymbol{U}\widehat{\boldsymbol{L}}\widehat{\boldsymbol{L}}^{\top}), \tag{10.2}$$

which does not require immediate reward samples for its computation. Since $\mathbb{E}_{p_I,\pi,p_T}$ included in $\boldsymbol{U}$ is not accessible (see equation 10.1), we replace $\boldsymbol{U}$ by its consistent estimator $\widehat{\boldsymbol{U}}$:

$$\widehat{\boldsymbol{U}} := \frac{1}{MN} \sum_{m=1}^{M}\sum_{n=1}^{N} \widehat{\boldsymbol{\psi}}(s_{m,n}^{\widetilde{\pi}}, a_{m,n}^{\widetilde{\pi}}; \overline{\mathcal{D}}^{\widetilde{\pi}})\widehat{\boldsymbol{\psi}}(s_{m,n}^{\widetilde{\pi}}, a_{m,n}^{\widetilde{\pi}}; \overline{\mathcal{D}}^{\widetilde{\pi}})^{\top} w_{m,n}^{\widetilde{\pi}}.$$

Consequently, we have the following generalization error estimator:

$$J := \text{tr}(\widehat{\boldsymbol{U}}\widehat{\boldsymbol{L}}\widehat{\boldsymbol{L}}^{\top}),$$

which can be computed only from $\overline{\mathcal{D}}^{\widetilde{\pi}}$, and thus can be employed in the active learning scenarios.

10.1.5 Designing Sampling Policies

Based on the generalization error estimator derived above, we give an algorithm for designing a good sampling policy which fully makes use of the roll-out samples without immediate rewards.

1. Prepare K candidates of sampling policy: $\{\widetilde{\pi}_k\}_{k=1}^{K}$.
2. Collect episodic samples without immediate rewards for each sampling policy candidate: $\{\overline{\mathcal{D}}^{\widetilde{\pi}_k}\}_{k=1}^{K}$.
3. Estimate $\boldsymbol{U}$ using all samples $\{\overline{\mathcal{D}}^{\widetilde{\pi}_k}\}_{k=1}^{K}$:

$$\widetilde{\boldsymbol{U}} = \frac{1}{KMN} \sum_{k=1}^{K}\sum_{m=1}^{M}\sum_{n=1}^{N} \widehat{\boldsymbol{\psi}}(s_{m,n}^{\widetilde{\pi}_k}, a_{m,n}^{\widetilde{\pi}_k}; \{\overline{\mathcal{D}}^{\widetilde{\pi}_k}\}_{k=1}^{K})$$
$$\times \widehat{\boldsymbol{\psi}}(s_{m,n}^{\widetilde{\pi}_k}, a_{m,n}^{\widetilde{\pi}_k}; \{\overline{\mathcal{D}}^{\widetilde{\pi}_k}\}_{k=1}^{K})^{\top} w_{m,n}^{\widetilde{\pi}_k}.$$

4. Estimate the generalization error for each k:

$$J_k := \text{tr}(\widetilde{\boldsymbol{U}}\widehat{\boldsymbol{L}}^{\widetilde{\pi}_k}\widehat{\boldsymbol{L}}^{\widetilde{\pi}_k\top}),$$
$$\widehat{\boldsymbol{L}}^{\widetilde{\pi}_k} := (\widehat{\boldsymbol{X}}^{\widetilde{\pi}_k\top}\boldsymbol{W}^{\widetilde{\pi}_k}\widehat{\boldsymbol{X}}^{\widetilde{\pi}_k})^{-1}\widehat{\boldsymbol{X}}^{\widetilde{\pi}_k\top}\boldsymbol{W}^{\widetilde{\pi}_k},$$

10.1. Design of Efficient Exploration Strategies in Reinforcement Learning 231

$$\widehat{X}^{\widetilde{\pi}_k}_{N(m-1)+n,b} := \widehat{\psi}_b(s^{\widetilde{\pi}_k}_{m,n}, a^{\widetilde{\pi}_k}_{m,n}; \{\overline{\mathcal{D}}^{\widetilde{\pi}_k}\}_{k=1}^K),$$

$W^{\widetilde{\pi}_k}$ is the diagonal matrix with the $(N(m-1)+n)$-th diagonal element given by

$$W^{\widetilde{\pi}_k}_{N(m-1)+n, N(m-1)+n} = w^{\widetilde{\pi}_k}_{m,n}.$$

5. (If possible) repeat 2 to 4 several times and calculate the average for each k: $\{J'_k\}_{k=1}^K$.
6. Determine the sampling policy: $\widetilde{\pi}_{\mathrm{AL}} := \mathrm{argmin}_k J'_k$.
7. Collect training samples with immediate rewards following $\widetilde{\pi}_{\mathrm{AL}}$: $\mathcal{D}^{\widetilde{\pi}_{\mathrm{AL}}}$.
8. Learn the value function by LSPI using $\mathcal{D}^{\widetilde{\pi}_{\mathrm{AL}}}$.

10.1.6 Active Learning in Policy Iteration

As shown above, the unknown generalization error can be accurately estimated without using immediate reward samples in one-step policy evaluation. Here, we extend the idea to the full policy iteration setup.

Sample reuse policy iteration (SRPI) [66], described in section 7.6, is a framework of *off-policy reinforcement learning* [174, 125] which allows one to reuse previously collected samples effectively. Let us denote the evaluation policy at the l-th iteration by π_l and the maximum number of iterations by L.

In the policy iteration framework, new data samples $\mathcal{D}^{\pi_l}$ are collected following the new policy π_l for the next policy evaluation step. In ordinary policy iteration methods, only the new samples $\mathcal{D}^{\pi_l}$ are used for policy evaluation. Thus, the previously collected data samples $\{\mathcal{D}^{\pi_1}, \mathcal{D}^{\pi_2}, \ldots, \mathcal{D}^{\pi_{l-1}}\}$ are not utilized:

$$\pi_1 \overset{\mathrm{E}:\{\mathcal{D}^{\pi_1}\}}{\to} \widehat{Q}^{\pi_1} \overset{\mathrm{I}}{\to} \pi_2 \overset{\mathrm{E}:\{\mathcal{D}^{\pi_2}\}}{\to} \widehat{Q}^{\pi_2} \overset{\mathrm{I}}{\to} \pi_3 \overset{\mathrm{E}:\{\mathcal{D}^{\pi_3}\}}{\to} \cdots \overset{\mathrm{I}}{\to} \pi_{L+1},$$

where $\mathrm{E}:\{\mathcal{D}\}$ indicates policy evaluation using the data sample $\mathcal{D}$, and I denotes policy improvement. On the other hand, in SRPI, all previously collected data samples are reused for policy evaluation as

$$\pi_1 \overset{\mathrm{E}:\{\mathcal{D}^{\pi_1}\}}{\to} \widehat{Q}^{\pi_1} \overset{\mathrm{I}}{\to} \pi_2 \overset{\mathrm{E}:\{\mathcal{D}^{\pi_1},\mathcal{D}^{\pi_2}\}}{\to} \widehat{Q}^{\pi_2} \overset{\mathrm{I}}{\to} \pi_3 \overset{\mathrm{E}:\{\mathcal{D}^{\pi_1},\mathcal{D}^{\pi_2},\mathcal{D}^{\pi_3}\}}{\to} \cdots \overset{\mathrm{I}}{\to} \pi_{L+1},$$

where appropriate importance weights are applied to each set of previously collected samples in the policy evaluation step.

Here, we apply the active learning technique to the SRPI framework. More specifically, we optimize the sampling policy at each iteration. Then the iteration process becomes

$$\pi_1 \xrightarrow{\mathrm{E:}\{\mathcal{D}^{\widetilde{\pi}_1}\}} \widehat{Q}^{\pi_1} \xrightarrow{\mathrm{I}} \pi_2 \xrightarrow{\mathrm{E:}\{\mathcal{D}^{\widetilde{\pi}_1},\mathcal{D}^{\widetilde{\pi}_2}\}} \widehat{Q}^{\pi_2} \xrightarrow{\mathrm{I}} \pi_3 \xrightarrow{\mathrm{E:}\{\mathcal{D}^{\widetilde{\pi}_1},\mathcal{D}^{\widetilde{\pi}_2},\mathcal{D}^{\widetilde{\pi}_3}\}} \cdots \xrightarrow{\mathrm{I}} \pi_{L+1}.$$

Thus, we do not gather samples following the current policy π_l, but following the sampling policy $\widetilde{\pi}_l$ optimized on the basis of the active learning method. We call this framework *active policy iteration* (API).

10.1.7 Robot Control Experiments

Here, we evaluate the performance of the API method using a ball-batting robot (see figure 10.1), which consists of two links and two joints. The goal of the ball-batting task is to control the robot arm so that it drives the ball as far as possible.

The state space $\mathcal{S}$ is continuous and consists of angles φ_1[rad] ($\in [0, \pi/4]$) and φ_2[rad] ($\in [-\pi/4, \pi/4]$), and angular velocities $\dot{\varphi}_1$[rad/s] and $\dot{\varphi}_2$[rad/s]. Thus, a state s ($\in \mathcal{S}$) is described by a four-dimensional vector:

$$s = (\varphi_1, \dot{\varphi}_1, \varphi_2, \dot{\varphi}_2)^\top.$$

The action space $\mathcal{A}$ is discrete and contains two elements:

$$\mathcal{A} = \{a^{(i)}\}_{i=1}^2 = \{(50, -35)^\top, (-50, 10)^\top\},$$

where the i-th element ($i = 1, 2$) of each vector corresponds to the torque [N · m] added to joint i.

We use the *open dynamics engine* (ODE), which is available at http://ode.org/, for physical calculations including the update of the angles and

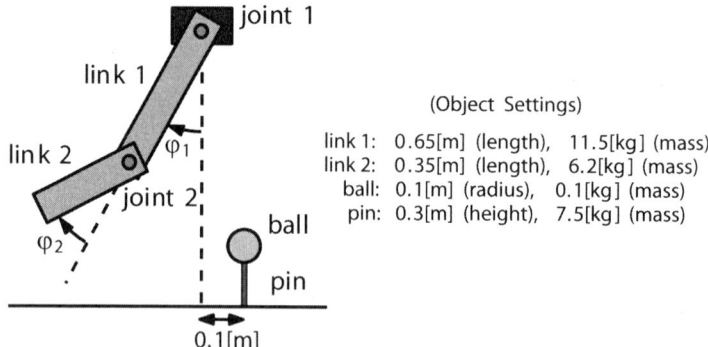

Figure 10.1
A ball-batting robot.

10.1. Design of Efficient Exploration Strategies in Reinforcement Learning

angular velocities, and collision detection between the robot arm, ball, and pin. The simulation time step is set to 7.5 [ms] and the next state is observed after 10 time steps. The action chosen in the current state is kept taken for 10 time steps. To make the experiments realistic, we add noise to actions: If action $(f_1, f_2)^\top$ is taken, the actual torques applied to the joints are $f_1 + \varepsilon_1$ and $f_2 + \varepsilon_2$, where ε_1 and ε_2 are drawn independently from the Gaussian distribution with mean 0 and variance 3.

The immediate reward is defined as the carry of the ball. This reward is given only when the robot arm hits the ball for the first time at state s' after taking action a at current state s. For value function approximation, we use the 110 basis functions defined as

$$\phi_{2(i-1)+j} = \begin{cases} I(a = a^{(j)}) \exp\left(-\dfrac{\|s - c_i\|^2}{2\tau^2}\right) \\ \qquad \text{for } i = 1, \ldots, 54 \text{ and } j = 1, 2, \\ I(a = a^{(j)}) \quad \text{for } i = 55 \text{ and } j = 1, 2, \end{cases}$$

where τ is set to $3\pi/2$ and the Gaussian centers c_i ($i = 1, \ldots, 54$) are located on the regular grid

$$\{0, \pi/4\} \times \{-\pi, 0, \pi\} \times \{-\pi/4, 0, \pi/4\} \times \{-\pi, 0, \pi\}.$$

$I(c)$ denotes the indicator function:

$$I(c) = \begin{cases} 1 & \text{if the condition } c \text{ is true,} \\ 0 & \text{otherwise.} \end{cases}$$

We set $L = 7$ and $N = 10$. As for the number of episodes M, we compare the "decreasing M" strategy (M is decreased as 10, 10, 7, 7, 7, 4, and 4 from iteration 1 to iteration 7) and the "fixed M" strategy (M is fixed to 7 throughout iterations). The initial state is always set to $s = (\pi/4, 0, 0, 0)^\top$. The initial evaluation policy π_1 is set to the ϵ-greedy policy, defined as

$$\pi_1(a|s) := 0.15\, p_\mathrm{u}(a) + 0.85\, I(a = \underset{a'}{\operatorname{argmax}}\, \widehat{Q}_0(s, a')),$$

$$\widehat{Q}_0(s, a) := \sum_{b=1}^{110} \phi_b(s, a),$$

where $p_\mathrm{u}(a)$ denotes the uniform distribution over actions. Policies are updated using the ϵ-greedy rule with $\epsilon = 0.15/l$ in the l-th iteration. We prepare the following four sampling policy candidates in the sampling policy selection step of the l-th iteration:

$$\{\overline{\pi}_l^{0.15/l}, \overline{\pi}_l^{0.15/l+0.15}, \overline{\pi}_l^{0.15/l+0.5}, \overline{\pi}_l^{0.15/l+0.85}\},$$

where $\overline{\pi}_l$ denotes the policy obtained by greedy update using $\widehat{Q}^{\pi_{l-1}}$, and $\overline{\pi}_l^\epsilon$ is the "ϵ-greedy" version of the base policy $\overline{\pi}_l$. That is, the intended action can be successfully chosen with probability $1 - \epsilon/2$, and the other action is chosen with probability $\epsilon/2$.

The discount factor γ is set to 1, and the performance of learned policy π_{L+1} is measured by the discounted sum of immediate rewards for test samples $\{r_{m,n}^{\pi_{L+1}}\}_{m=1,n=1}^{20,10}$ (20 episodes with 10 steps collected following π_{L+1}):

$$\text{Performance} = \sum_{m=1}^{M}\sum_{n=1}^{N} r_{m,n}^{\pi_{L+1}}.$$

The experiment is repeated 500 times with different random seeds, and the average performance of each learning method is evaluated. The results, are depicted in figure 10.2, showing that the API method outperforms the passive learning strategy; for the "decreasing M" strategy, the performance difference is statistically significant by the t-test at the significance level 1 percent for the error values at the seventh iteration.

The above experimental evaluation showed that the sampling policy design method, API, is useful for improving the performance of reinforcement learning. Moreover, the "decreasing M" strategy was shown to be a useful heuristic to further enhance the performance of API.

10.2 Wafer Alignment in Semiconductor Exposure Apparatus

In this section, we describe an application of pool-based active learning methods to a wafer alignment problem in semiconductor exposure apparatus [163]. A profile of the exposure apparatus is illustrated in figure 10.3.

Recent semiconductors have the layered circuit structure, which is built by exposing circuit patterns multiple times. In this process, it is extremely important to align the wafers at the same position with very high accuracy. To this end, the location of markers is measured to adjust the shift and rotation of wafers. However, measuring the location of markers is time-consuming, and therefore there is a strong need to reduce the number of markers to be measured in order to speed up the semiconductor production process.

10.2. Wafer Alignment in Semiconductor Exposure Apparatus

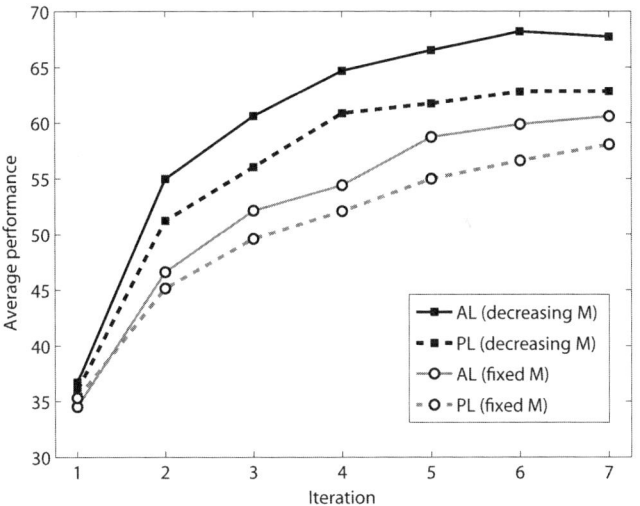

Figure 10.2
The mean performance over 500 runs in the ball-batting experiment. The dotted lines denote the performance of passive learning (PL), and the solid lines denote the performance of the active learning (AL) method. The error bars are omitted for clear visibility. For the "decreasing M" strategy, the performance of active learning after the seventh iteration is significantly better than that of PL according to the t-test at the significance level 1 percent for the error values at the seventh iteration.

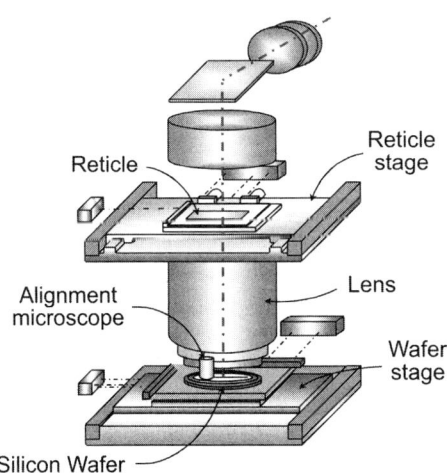

Figure 10.3
Semiconductor exposure apparatus.

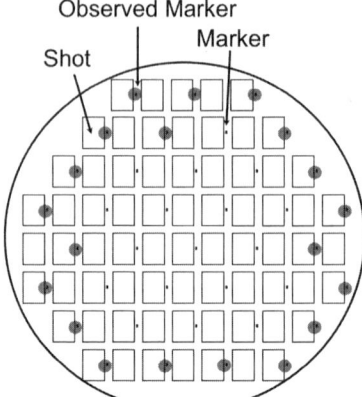

Figure 10.4
Silicon wafer with markers. Observed markers based on the conventional heuristic are also shown.

Figure 10.4 illustrates a wafer on which markers are printed uniformly. The goal is to choose the most "informative" markers to be measured for better alignment of the wafer. A conventional choice is to measure markers far from the center in a symmetric way, which will provide robust estimation of the rotation angle (see figure 10.4). However, this naive approach is not necessarily the best since misalignment is caused not only by affine transformation but also by several other nonlinear factors, such as a warp, a biased characteristic of measurement apparatus, and different temperature conditions. In practice, it is not easy to model such nonlinear factors accurately. For this reason, the linear affine model or the second-order model is often used in wafer alignment. However, this causes model misspecification, and therefore active learning methods for approximately correct models explained in chapter 8 would be useful in this application.

Let us consider the functions whose input $x = (u, v)^\top$ is the location on the wafer and whose output is the horizontal discrepancy Δu or the vertical discrepancy Δv. These functions are learned using the following second-order model:

$$\Delta u \text{ or } \Delta v = \theta_0 + \theta_1 u + \theta_2 v + \theta_3 uv + \theta_4 u^2 + \theta_5 v^2.$$

For 220 wafer samples, experiments are carried out as follows. For each wafer, $n_{tr} = 20$ points are chosen from $n_{te} = 38$ markers, and the horizontal and the vertical discrepancies are observed. Then the above model is trained and its prediction performance is tested using all 38 markers in the 220 wafers. This

10.2. Wafer Alignment in Semiconductor Exposure Apparatus

Table 10.1
The mean squared test error for the wafer alignment problem (means and standard deviations over 220 wafers)

Order	PALICE	PW	PO	Passive	Conv.
1	°2.27 ± 1.08	2.29 ± 1.08	2.37 ± 1.15	2.32 ± 1.11	2.36 ± 1.15
2	°1.93 ± 0.89	2.09 ± 0.98	1.96 ± 0.91	2.32 ± 1.15	2.13 ± 1.08

PALICE, PW, and PO denote the active learning methods described in sections 8.4.3, 8.4.2, and 8.4.1, respectively. "Passive" indicates the passive sampling strategy where training input points are randomly chosen from all markers. "Conv." indicates the conventional heuristic of choosing the outer markers.

process is repeated for all 220 wafers. Since the choice of the sampling location by active learning methods is stochastic, the above experiment is repeated 100 times with different random seeds.

The mean and standard deviation of the squared test error over 220 wafers are summarized in table 10.1. This shows that the PALICE method (see section 8.4.3) works significantly better than the other sampling strategies, and it provides about a 10 percent reduction in the squared error from the conventional heuristic of choosing the outer markers.

IV CONCLUSIONS

11 Conclusions and Future Prospects

In this book, we provided a comprehensive overview of theory, algorithms, and applications of machine learning under covariate shift.

11.1 Conclusions

Part II of the book covered topics on learning under covariate shift. In chapters 2 and 3, importance sampling techniques were shown to form the theoretical basis of covariate shift adaptation in function learning and model selection. In practice, importance weights needed in importance sampling are unknown. Thus, estimating the importance weights is a key component in covariate shift adaptation, which was covered in chapter 4. In chapter 5, a novel idea for estimating the importance weights in high-dimensional problems was explained. Chapter 6 was devoted to the review of a Nobel Prize-winning work on sample selection bias, and its relation to covariate shift adaptation was discussed. In chapter 7, applications of covariate shift adaptation techniques to various real-world problems were shown.

In part II, we considered the occurrence of covariate shift and how to cope with it. On the other hand, in part III, we considered the situation where covariate shift is intentionally caused by users in order to improve generalization ability. In chapter 8, the problem of active learning, where the training input distribution is designed by users, was addressed. Since active learning naturally induces covariate shift, its adaptation was shown to be essential for designing better active learning algorithms. In chapter 9, a challenging problem of active learning with model selection where active learning and model selection are performed at the same time, was addressed. The ensemble approach was shown to be a promising method for this chicken-or-egg problem. In chapter 10, applications of active learning techniques to real-world problems were shown.

11.2 Future Prospects

In the context of covariate shift adaptation, the importance weights played an essential role in systematically adjusting the difference of distributions in the training and test phases. In chapter 4, we showed various methods for estimating the importance weights.

Beyond covariate shift adaptation, it has been shown recently that the ratio of probability densities can be used for solving machine learning tasks [157, 170]. This novel machine learning framework includes multitask learning [16], privacy-preserving data mining [46], outlier detection [79, 146, 80], change detection in time series [91], two-sample test [169], conditional density estimation [172], and probabilistic classification [155]. Furthermore, mutual information—which plays a central role in information theory [34]—can be estimated via density ratio estimation [178, 179]. Since mutual information is a measure of statistical independence between random variables, density ratio estimation also can be used for variable selection [177], dimensionality reduction [175], independence test [168], clustering [94], independent component analysis [176], and causal inference [203]. Thus, density ratio estimation is a promising versatile tool for machine learning which needs to be further investigated.

Appendix: List of Symbols and Abbreviations

$\mathcal{X}$	Input domain
d	Input dimensionality
$\mathcal{Y}$	Output domain
$\boldsymbol{x}_i^{\text{tr}}$	i-th training input
y_i^{tr}	i-th training output
$\boldsymbol{y}^{\text{tr}}$	Training output vector
ϵ_i^{tr}	i-th training output noise
$\boldsymbol{\epsilon}^{\text{tr}}$	Training output noise vector
σ	Standard deviation of output noise
n_{tr}	Number of training samples
$p_{\text{tr}}(\boldsymbol{x})$	Training input density
$p(y\|\boldsymbol{x})$	Conditional density of output y, given input $\boldsymbol{x}$
$f(\boldsymbol{x})$	Conditional mean of output y, given input $\boldsymbol{x}$
$\boldsymbol{x}_j^{\text{te}}$	j-th test input
y_j^{te}	j-th test output
n_{te}	Number of test samples
$p_{\text{te}}(\boldsymbol{x})$	Test input density
$w(\boldsymbol{x})$	Importance weight
$\text{loss}(\boldsymbol{x}, y, \widehat{y})$	Loss when output y at input $\boldsymbol{x}$ is estimated by $\widehat{y}$
Gen	Generalization error
Gen$'$, Gen$''$	Generalization error without irrelevant constant
$\widehat{\text{Gen}}$	Generalization error estimator
Bias^2	(Squared) bias term in generalization error
Var	Variance term in generalization error
$\mathbb{E}_{\{\boldsymbol{x}_i^{\text{tr}}\}_{i=1}^{n_{\text{tr}}}}$	Expectation over $\{\boldsymbol{x}_i^{\text{tr}}\}_{i=1}^{n_{\text{tr}}}$ drawn i.i.d. from $p_{\text{tr}}(\boldsymbol{x})$
$\mathbb{E}_{\{y_i^{\text{tr}}\}_{i=1}^{n_{\text{tr}}}}$	Expectation over $\{y_i^{\text{tr}}\}_{i=1}^{n_{\text{tr}}}$, each drawn from $p(y\|\boldsymbol{x}=\boldsymbol{x}_i^{\text{tr}})$
$\mathbb{E}_{\boldsymbol{x}^{\text{te}}}$	Expectation over $\boldsymbol{x}^{\text{te}}$ drawn from $p_{\text{te}}(\boldsymbol{x})$
$\mathbb{E}_{y^{\text{te}}}$	Expectation over y^{te} drawn from $p(y\|\boldsymbol{x}=\boldsymbol{x}^{\text{te}})$
M	Model

$\widehat{f}(\boldsymbol{x};\boldsymbol{\theta})$	Function model
θ_ℓ	ℓ-th parameter
$\varphi_\ell(\boldsymbol{x})$	ℓ-th basis function
$\boldsymbol{\theta}$	Parameter vector
b	Number of parameters
$K(\boldsymbol{x},\boldsymbol{x}')$	Kernel function
$\widehat{\boldsymbol{\theta}}$	Learned parameter
$\boldsymbol{\theta}^*$	Optimal parameter
γ	Flattening parameter for importance weights
λ	Regularization parameter
$R(\boldsymbol{\theta})$	Regularization function
$\boldsymbol{X}^{\mathrm{tr}}$	Training design matrix
$\boldsymbol{W}$	Importance-weight matrix
$\boldsymbol{L}$	Learning matrix
$\boldsymbol{U}$	Metric matrix
$\boldsymbol{K}^{\mathrm{tr}}$	Training kernel matrix
$N(x;\mu,\sigma^2)$	Gaussian density with mean μ and variance σ^2
$N(\boldsymbol{x};\boldsymbol{\mu},\boldsymbol{\Sigma})$	Multidimensional Gaussian density with mean $\boldsymbol{\mu}$ and covariance matrix $\boldsymbol{\Sigma}$
$r(\boldsymbol{x})$	Residual function
δ	Model error
$p^*_{\mathrm{tr}}(\boldsymbol{x})$	"Optimal" training input density
$\zeta(\boldsymbol{x})$	Resampling weight function
$\zeta^*(\boldsymbol{x})$	"Optimal" resampling weight function
ν	Flattening parameter of training input density
$\mathcal{O}$	Asymptotic order ("big o")
$\mathcal{O}_p$	Asymptotic order in probability ("big o")
o	Asymptotic order ("small o")
o_p	Asymptotic order in probability ("small o")
$\top$	Transpose of matrix or vector
$\langle\cdot,\cdot\rangle$	Inner product
$\|\cdot\|$	Norm

AIC	Akaike information criterion
AIWERM	Adaptive IWERM
AIWLS	Adaptive IWLS
ALICE	Active learning using IWLS learning based on conditional expectation of generalization error
API	Active policy iteration
BASIC	Bootstrap approximated SIC

Appendix: List of Symbols and Abbreviations

CRF	Conditional random field
CSP	Common spatial pattern
CV	Cross-validation
D^3	Direct density-ratio estimation with dimensionality reduction
EAL	Ensemble active learning
ERM	Empirical risk minimization
FDA	Fisher discriminant analysis
GMM	Gaussian mixture model
IWERM	Importance-weighted ERM
IWLS	Importance-weighted LS
KDE	Kernel density estimation
KKT	Karush–Kuhn–Tucker
KL	Kullback–Leibler
KLIEP	KL importance estimation procedure
KMM	Kernel mean matching
LASIC	Linearly approximated SIC
LFDA	Local FDA
LOOCV	Leave-one-out CV
LR	Logistic regression
LS	Least squares
LSIF	Least-squares importance fitting
MDP	Markov decision problem
MFCC	Mel-frequency cepstrum coefficient
MLE	Maximum likelihood estimation
MSE	Mean squared error
NLP	Natural language processing
OLS	Ordinary LS
PALICE	Pool-based ALICE
QP	Quadratic program
RIWERM	Regularized IWERM
RL	Reinforcement learning
SIC	Subspace information criterion
SRPI	Sample reuse policy iteration
SVM	Support vector machine
TD	Temporal difference
uLSIF	Unconstrained LSIF

Bibliography

1. H. Akaike. Statistical predictor identification. *Annals of the Institute of Statistical Mathematics*, 22(1):203–217, 1970.
2. H. Akaike. A new look at the statistical model identification. *IEEE Transactions on Automatic Control*, AC-19(6):716–723, 1974.
3. H. Akaike. Likelihood and the Bayes procedure. In J. M. Bernardo, M. H. DeGroot, D. V. Lindley, and A. F. M. Smith, editors, *Bayesian Statistics*, pages 141–166. University of Valencia Press, Vlencia, Spain, 1980.
4. T. Akiyama, H. Hachiya, and M. Sugiyama. Efficient exploration through active learning for value function approximation in reinforcement learning. *Neural Networks*, 23(5):639–648, 2010.
5. A. Albert. *Regression and the Moore-Penrose Pseudoinverse*. Academic Press, New York and London, 1972.
6. N. Altman and C. Léger. On the optimality of prediction-based selection criteria and the convergence rates of estimators. *Journal of the Royal Statistical Society*, series B, 59(1):205–216, 1997.
7. S. Amari. Theory of adaptive pattern classifiers. *IEEE Transactions on Electronic Computers*, EC-16(3):299–307, 1967.
8. F. Babiloni, F. Cincotti, L. Lazzarini, J. del R. Millán, J. Mouriño, M. Varsta, J. Heikkonen, L. Bianchi, and M. G. Marciani. Linear classification of low-resolution EEG patterns produced by imagined hand movements. *IEEE Transactions on Rehabilitation Engineering*, 8(2):186–188, June 2000.
9. F. R. Bach. Active learning for misspecified generalized linear models. In B. Schölkopf, J. Platt, and T. Hoffman, editors, *Advances in Neural Information Processing Systems*, volume 19, pages 65–72. MIT Press, Cambridge, MA, 2007.
10. P. Baldi and S. Brunak. *Bioinformatics: The Machine Learning Approach*. MIT Press, Cambridge, MA, 1998.
11. L. Bao and S. S. Intille. Activity recognition from user-annotated acceleration data. In *Proceedings of the 2nd IEEE International Conference on Pervasive Computing*, pages 1–17. Springer, New York, 2004.
12. R. Bellman. *Adaptive Control Processes: A Guided Tour*. Princeton University Press, Princeton, NJ, 1961.
13. P. D. Bertsekas and J. Tsitsiklis. *Neuro-Dynamic Programming*. Athena Scientific, Nashua, NH, 1996.
14. M. J. Best. An algorithm for the solution of the parametric quadratic programming problem. CORR Report 82-24, Faculty of Mathematics, University of Waterloo, Ontaris, Canada, 1982.
15. N. B. Bharatula, M. Stäger, P. Lukowicz, and G. Tröster. Empirical study of design choices in multi-sensor context recognition. In *Proceedings of the 2nd International Form on Applied Wearable Computing*, pages 79–93. 2005.

16. S. Bickel, J. Bogojeska, T. Lengauer, and T. Scheffer. Multi-task learning for HIV therapy screening. In A. McCallum and S. Roweis, editors, *Proceedings of the 25th Annual International Conference on Machine Learning*, pages 56–63. Madison, WI, Omnipress, 2008.

17. S. Bickel, M. Brückner, and T. Scheffer. Discriminative learning for differing training and test distributions. In Z. Ghahramani, editor, *Proceedings of the 24th International Conference on Machine Learning*, pages 81–88. 2007.

18. S. Bickel and T. Scheffer. Dirichlet-enhanced spam filtering based on biased samples. In B. Schölkopf, J. Platt, and T. Hoffman, editors, *Advances in Neural Information Processing Systems*, volume 19, pages 161–168. MIT Press, Cambridge, MA, 2007.

19. H. J. Bierens. Maximum likelihood estimation of Heckman's sample selection model. Unpublished manuscript, Pennsylvania State University, 2002. Available at http://econ.la.psu.edu/˜hbierens/EasyRegTours/HECKMAN_Tourfiles/Heckman.PDF.

20. C. M. Bishop. *Neural Networks for Pattern Recognition*. Clarendon Press, Oxford, 1995.

21. C. M. Bishop. *Pattern Recognition and Machine Learning*. Springer, New York, 2006.

22. B. Blankertz, G. Dornhege, M. Krauledat, and K.-R. Müller. The Berlin brain-computer interface: EEG-based communication without subject training. *IEEE Transactions on Neural Systems and Rehabilitation Engineering*, 14(2):147–152, 2006.

23. B. Blankertz, G. Dornhege, M. Krauledat, K.-R. Müller, and G. Curio. The Berlin brain-computer interface: Report from the feedback sessions. Technical Report 1, Fraunhofer FIRST, 2005.

24. J. Blitzer, R. McDonald, and F. Pereira. Domain adaptation with structural correspondence learning. In *Proceedings of the Conference on Empirical Methods in Natural Language Processing*, pages 120–128. 2006.

25. K. M. Borgwardt, A. Gretton, M. J. Rasch, H.-P. Kriegel, B. Schölkopf, and A. J. Smola. Integrating structured biological data by kernel maximum mean discrepancy. *Bioinformatics*, 22(14):e49–e57, 2006.

26. B. E. Boser, I. M. Guyon, and V. N. Vapnik. A training algorithm for optimal margin classifiers. In D. Haussler, editor, *Proceedings of the Fifth Annual ACM Workshop on Computational Learning Theory*, pages 144–152. ACM Press, New York, 1992.

27. S. Boyd and L. Vandenberghe. *Convex Optimization*. Cambridge University Press, Cambridge, 2004.

28. L. Breiman. Arcing classifiers. *Annals of Statistics*, 26(3):801–849, 1998.

29. W. Campbell. Generalized linear discriminant sequence kernels for speaker recognition. In *Proceedings of the IEEE International Conference on Acoustics, Speech, and Signal Processing*, volume 1, pages 161–164. 2002.

30. O. Chapelle, B. Schölkopf, and A. Zien, editors. *Semi-Supervised Learning*. MIT Press, Cambridge, MA, 2006.

31. S. S. Chen, D. L. Donoho, and M. A. Saunders. Atomic decomposition by basis pursuit. *SIAM Journal on Scientific Computing*, 20(1):33–61, 1998.

32. K. F. Cheng and C. K. Chu. Semiparametric density estimation under a two-sample density ratio model. *Bernoulli*, 10(4):583–604, 2004.

33. D. A. Cohn, Z. Ghahramani, and M. I. Jordan. Active learning with statistical models. *Journal of Artificial Intelligence Research*, 4:129–145, 1996.

34. T. M. Cover and J. A. Thomas. *Elements of Information Theory*. Wiley-Interscience, New York, 1991.

35. P. Craven and G. Wahba. Smoothing noisy data with spline functions: Estimating the correct degree of smoothing by the method of generalized cross-validation. *Numerische Mathematik*, 31:377–403, 1979.

36. H. Daumé III. Frustratingly easy domain adaptation. In *Proceedings of the 45th Annual Meeting of the Association for Computational Linguistics*, pages 256–263. 2007.
37. A. Demiriz, K. P. Bennett, and J. Shawe-Taylor. Linear programming boosting via column generation. *Machine Learning*, 46(1/3):225–254, 2002.
38. A. P. Dempster, N. M. Laird, and D. B. Rubin. Maximum likelihood from incomplete data via the EM algorithm. *Journal of the Royal Statistical Society*, series B, 39(1):1–38, 1977.
39. G. Dornhege, B. Blankertz, G. Curio, and K.-R. Müller. Boosting bit rates in noninvasive EEG single-trial classifications by feature combination and multiclass paradigms. *IEEE Transactions on Biomedical Engineering*, 51(6):993–1002, June 2004.
40. G. Dornhege, J. del R. Millán, T. Hinterberger, D. McFarland, and K.-R. Müller, editors. *Toward Brain–Computer Interfacing*. MIT Press, Cambridge, MA, 2007.
41. N. R. Draper and H. Smith. *Applied Regression Analysis*, third edition. Wiley-Interscience, New York, 1998.
42. R. O. Duda, P. E. Hart, and D. G. Stork. *Pattern Classification*, second edition. Wiley-Interscience, New York, 2000.
43. B. Efron. Bootstrap methods: Another look at the jackknife. *Annals of Statistics*, 7(1):1–26, 1979.
44. B. Efron, T. Hastie, I. Johnstone, and R. Tibshirani. Least angle regression. *Annals of Statistics*, 32(2):407–499, 2004.
45. B. Efron and R. J. Tibshirani. *An Introduction to the Bootstrap*. Chapman & Hall/CRC, New York, 1994.
46. C. Elkan. Privacy-preserving data mining via importance weighting. In *Proceedings of the ECML/PKDD Workshop on Privacy and Security Issues in Data Mining and Machine Learning*, pages 15–21, Springer, 2010.
47. T. Evgeniou, M. Pontil, and T. Poggio. Regularization networks and support vector machines. *Advances in Computational Mathematics*, 13(1):1–50, 2000.
48. V. V. Fedorov. *Theory of Optimal Experiments*. Academic Press, New York, 1972.
49. FG-NET Consortium. The FG-NET Aging Database. http://www.fgnet.rsunit.com/.
50. R. A. Fisher. The use of multiple measurements in taxonomic problems. *Annals of Eugenics*, 7(2):179–188, 1936.
51. G. S. Fishman. *Monte Carlo: Concepts, Algorithms, and Applications*. Springer-Verlag, Berlin, 1996.
52. Y. Freund and R. E. Schapire. Experiments with a new boosting algorithm. In *Proceedings of the 13th International Conference on Machine Learning*, pages 148–156. Morgan Kaufmann, San Francisco, 1996.
53. J. Friedman, T. Hastie, and R. Tibshirani. Additive logistic regression: A statistical view of boosting. *Annals of Statistics*, 28(2):337–407, 2000.
54. Y. Fu, Y. Xu, and T. S. Huang. Estimating human age by manifold analysis of face pictures and regression on aging features. In *Proceedings of the IEEE International Conference on Multimedia and Expo*, pages 1383–1386. 2007.
55. K. Fukumizu. Statistical active learning in multilayer perceptrons. *IEEE Transactions on Neural Networks*, 11(1):17–26, 2000.
56. K. Fukumizu, F. R. Bach, and M. I. Jordan. Dimensionality reduction for supervised learning with reproducing kernel Hilbert spaces. *Journal of Machine Learning Research*, 5(1):73–99, January 2004.
57. K. Fukunaga. *Introduction to Statistical Pattern Recognition*, second edition. Academic Press, Boston, 1990.
58. S. Furui. Cepstral analysis technique for automatic speaker verification. *IEEE Transactions on Acoustics, Speech, and Signal Processing*, 29(2):254–272, 1981.

59. S. Furui. Comparison of speaker recognition methods using statistical features and dynamic features. *IEEE Transactions on Acoustics, Speech and Signal Processing*, 29(3):342–350, 1981.

60. C. Gao, F. Kong, and J. Tan. HealthAware: Tackling obesity with Health Aware smart phone systems. In *Proceedings of the IEEE International Conference on Robotics and Biomimetics*, pages 1549–1554. IEEE Press, Piscataway, NJ, 2009.

61. X. Geng, Z. Zhou, Y. Zhang, G. Li, and H. Dai. Learning from facial aging patterns for automatic age estimation. In *Proceedings of the 14th ACM International Conference on Multimedia*, pages 307–316. 2006.

62. A. Globerson and S. Roweis. Metric learning by collapsing classes. In Y. Weiss, B. Schölkopf, and J. Platt, editors, *Advances in Neural Information Processing Systems*, volume 18, pages 451–458, MIT Press, Cambridge, MA, 2006.

63. J. Goldberger, S. Roweis, G. Hinton, and R. Salakhutdinov. Neighbourhood components analysis. In L. K. Saul, Y. Weiss, and L. Bottou, editors, *Advances in Neural Information Processing Systems*, volume 17, pages 513–520. MIT Press, Cambridge, MA, 2005.

64. G. H. Golub and C. F. van Loan. *Matrix Computations*, third edition. Johns Hopkins University Press, Baltimore, 1996.

65. G. Guo, G. Mu, Y. Fu, C. Dyer, and T. Huang. A study on automatic age estimation using a large database. In *Proceedings of the IEEE International Conference on Computer Vision*, pages 1986–1991. 2009.

66. H. Hachiya, T. Akiyama, M. Sugiyama, and J. Peters. Adaptive importance sampling for value function approximation in off-policy reinforcement learning. *Neural Networks*, 22(10):1399–1410, 2009.

67. H. Hachiya, J. Peters, and M. Sugiyama. Efficient sample reuse in EM-based policy search. In W. Buntine, M. Grobelnik, D. Mladenic, and J. Shawe-Taylor, editors, *Machine Learning and Knowledge Discovery in Databases*. Volume 5781 of Lecture Notes in Artificial Intelligence, pages 469–484. Springer, Berlin, 2009.

68. H. Hachiya, M. Sugiyama, and N. Ueda. Importance-weighted least-squares probabilistic classifier for covariate shift adaptation with application to human activity recognition. *Neurocomputing*, 2011. In press.

69. W. Härdle, M. Müller, S. Sperlich, and A. Werwatz. *Nonparametric and Semiparametric Models*. Springer, Berlin, 2004.

70. T. Hastie, S. Rosset, R. Tibshirani, and J. Zhu. The entire regularization path for the support vector machine. *Journal of Machine Learning Research*, 5:1391–1415, 2004.

71. T. Hastie and R. Tibshirani. *Generalized Additive Models*, volume 43 of Monographs on Statistics and Applied Probability. Chapman & Hall/CRC, London, 1990.

72. T. Hastie and R. Tibshirani. Discriminant adaptive nearest neighbor classification. *IEEE Transactions on Pattern Analysis and Machine Intelligence*, 18(6):607–616, 1996.

73. T. Hastie and R. Tibshirani. Discriminant analysis by Gaussian mixtures. *Journal of the Royal Statistical Society*, Series B, 58(1):155–176, 1996.

74. T. Hastie, R. Tibshirani, and J. Friedman. *The Elements of Statistical Learning: Data Mining, Inference, and Prediction*. Springer, New York, 2001.

75. Y. Hattori, S. Inoue, T. Masaki, G. Hirakawa, and O. Sudo. Gathering large scale human activity information using mobile sensor devices. In *Proceedings of the Second International Workshop on Network Traffic Control, Analysis and Applications*, pages 708–713. 2010.

76. J. J. Heckman. The common structure of statistical models of truncation, sample selection and limited dependent variables and a simple estimator for such models. *Annals of Economic and Social Measurement*, 5(4):120–137, 1976.

77. J. J. Heckman. Sample selection bias as a specification error. *Econometrica*, 47(1):153–161, 1979.

78. R. E. Henkel. *Tests of Significance*. Sage Publications, Beverly Hills, CA, 1976.

79. S. Hido, Y. Tsuboi, H. Kashima, M. Sugiyama, and T. Kanamori. Inlier-based outlier detection via direct density ratio estimation. In F. Giannotti, D. Gunopulos, F. Turini, C. Zaniolo, N. Ramakrishnan, and X. Wu, editors, *Proceedings of the IEEE International Conference on Data Mining*, pages 223–232. 2008.

80. S. Hido, Y. Tsuboi, H. Kashima, M. Sugiyama, and T. Kanamori. Statistical outlier detection using direct density ratio estimation. *Knowledge and Information Systems*, 26(2):309–336, 2011.

81. G. E. Hinton. Training products of experts by minimizing contrastive divergence. *Neural Computation*, 14(8):1771–1800, 2002.

82. J. Huang, A. Smola, A. Gretton, K. M. Borgwardt, and B. Schölkopf. Correcting sample selection bias by unlabeled data. In B. Schölkopf, J. Platt, and T. Hoffman, editors, *Advances in Neural Information Processing Systems*, volume 19, pages 601–608. MIT Press, Cambridge, MA, 2007.

83. P. J. Huber. *Robust Statistics*. Wiley-Interscience, New York, 1981.

84. A. Hyvärinen, J. Karhunen, and E. Oja. *Independent Component Analysis*. Wiley, New York, 2001.

85. M. Ishiguro, Y. Sakamoto, and G. Kitagawa. Bootstrapping log likelihood and EIC, an extension of AIC. *Annals of the Institute of Statistical Mathematics*, 49(3):411–434, 1997.

86. J. Jiang and C. Zhai. Instance weighting for domain adaptation in NLP. In *Proceedings of the 45th Annual Meeting of the Association for Computational Linguistics*, pages 264–271. Association for Computational Linguistics, 2007.

87. T. Kanamori. Pool-based active learning with optimal sampling distribution and its information geometrical interpretation. *Neurocomputing*, 71(1–3):353–362, 2007.

88. T. Kanamori, S. Hido, and M. Sugiyama. A least-squares approach to direct importance estimation. *Journal of Machine Learning Research*, 10:1391–1445, July 2009.

89. T. Kanamori and H. Shimodaira. Active learning algorithm using the maximum weighted log-likelihood estimator. *Journal of Statistical Planning and Inference*, 116(1):149–162, 2003.

90. T. Kanamori, T. Suzuki, and M. Sugiyama. Condition number analysis of kernel-based density ratio estimation. Technical report TR09-0006, Department of Computer Science, Tokyo Institute of Technology, 2009. Available at: http://arxiv.org/abs/0912.2800.

91. Y. Kawahara and M. Sugiyama. Change-point detection in time-series data by direct density-ratio estimation. In H. Park, S. Parthasarathy, H. Liu, and Z. Obradovic, editors, *Proceedings of the SIAM International Conference on Data Mining*, pages 389–400. SIAM, 2009.

92. M. Kawanabe, M. Sugiyama, G. Blanchard, and K.-R. Müller. A new algorithm of non-Gaussian component analysis with radial kernel functions. *Annals of the Institute of Statistical Mathematics*, 59(1):57–75, 2007.

93. J. Kiefer. Optimum experimental designs. *Journal of the Royal Statistical Society*, Series B, 21:272 304, 1959.

94. M. Kimura and M. Sugiyama. Dependence-maximization clustering with least-squares mutual information. *Journal of Advanced Computational Intelligence and Intelligent Informatics*, 15(7): 800–805, 2011.

95. D. E. Knuth. *Seminumerical Algorithms*, volume 2 of *The Art of Computer Programming*, third edition. Addison-Wesley Professional, Boston, 1998.

96. S. Konishi and G. Kitagawa. Generalised information criteria in model selection. *Biometrika*, 83(4):875–890, 1996.

97. S. Kullback and R. A. Leibler. On information and sufficiency. *Annals of Mathematical Statistics*, 22(1):79–86, 1951.

98. J. Lafferty, A. McCallum, and F. Pereira. Conditional random fields: Probabilistic models for segmenting and labeling sequence data. In *Proceedings of the 18th International Conference on Machine Learning*, pages 282–289. Morgan Kaufmann, San Francisco, 2001.

99. M. G. Lagoudakis and R. Parr. Least-squares policy iteration. *Journal of Machine Learning Research*, 4:1107–1149, December 2003.

100. P. Leijdekkers and V. Gay. A self-test to detect a heart attack using a mobile phone and wearable sensors. In *Proceedings of the 21st IEEE International Symposium on Computer-Based Medical Systems*, pages 93–98. IEEE Computer Society, Washington, DC, 2008.

101. S. Lemm, B. Blankertz, G. Curio, and K.-R. Müller. Spatio-spectral filters for improving the classification of single trial EEG. *IEEE Transactions on Biomedical Engineering*, 52(9):1541–1548, September 2005.

102. Y. Li, H. Kambara, Y. Koike, and M. Sugiyama. Application of covariate shift adaptation techniques in brain computer interfaces. *IEEE Transactions on Biomedical Engineering*, 57(6):1318–1324, 2010.

103. C.-J. Lin, R. C. Weng, and S. S. Keerthi. Trust region Newton method for large-scale logistic regression. *Journal of Machine Learning Research*, 9:627–650, April 2008.

104. R. J. A. Little and D. B. Rubin. *Statistical Analysis with Missing Data*. Wiley, New York, 1987.

105. A. Luntz and V. Brailovsky. On estimation of characters obtained in statistical procedure of recognition. *Technicheskaya Kibernetica*, 3, 1969. (In Russian).

106. D. J. C. MacKay. Bayesian interpolation. *Neural Computation*, 4(3):415–447, 1992.

107. D. J. C. MacKay. Information-based objective functions for active data selection. *Neural Computation*, 4(4):590–604, 1992.

108. C. L. Mallows. Some comments on C_P. *Technometrics*, 15(4):661–675, 1973.

109. O. L. Mangasarian and D. R. Musicant. Robust linear and support vector regression. *IEEE Transactions on Pattern Analysis and Machine Intelligence*, 22(9):950–955, 2000.

110. J. Mariéthoz and S. Bengio. A kernel trick for sequences applied to text-independent speaker verification systems. *Pattern Recognition*, 40(8):2315–2324, 2007.

111. T. Matsui and K. Aikawa. Robust model for speaker verification against session-dependent utterance variation. *IEICE Transactions on Information and Systems*, E86-D(4):712–718, 2003.

112. T. Matsui and S. Furui. Concatenated phoneme models for text-variable speaker recognition. In *Proceedings of the IEEE International Conference on Audio Speech and Signal Processing*, pages 391–394. 1993.

113. T. Matsui and K. Tanabe. Comparative study of speaker identification methods: dPLRM, SVM, and GMM. *IEICE Transactions on Information and Systems*, E89-D(3):1066–1073, 2006.

114. P. McCullagh and J. A. Nelder. *Generalized Linear Models*, second edition. Chapman & Hall/CRC, London, 1989.

115. P. Melville and R. J. Mooney. Diverse ensembles for active learning. In *Proceedings of the 21st International Conference on Machine Learning*, pages 584–591. ACM Press, New York, 2004.

116. J. del R. Millán. On the need for on-line learning in brain-computer interfaces. In *Proceedings of the International Joint Conference on Neural Networks*, volume 4, pages 2877–2882. 2004.

117. T. P. Minka. A comparison of numerical optimizers for logistic regression. Technical report, Microsoft Research. 2007.

118. N. Murata, S. Yoshizawa, and S. Amari. Network information criterion—Determining the number of hidden units for an artificial neural network model. *IEEE Transactions on Neural Networks*, 5(6):865–872, 1994.

119. W. K. Newey, J. L. Powell, and J. R. Walker. Semiparametric estimation of selection models: Some empirical results. *American Economic Review Papers and Proceedings*, 80(2):324–328, 1990.

120. X. Nguyen, M. J. Wainwright, and M. I. Jordan. Estimating divergence functionals and the likelihood ratio by convex risk minimization. *IEEE Transactions on Information Theory*, 56(11):5847–5861, 2010.

121. K. Pelckmans, J. A. K. Suykens, and B. de Moor. Additive regularization trade-off: Fusion of training and validation levels in kernel methods. *Machine Learning*, 62(3):217–252, 2006.

122. G. Pfurtscheller and F. H. Lopes da Silva. Event-related EEG/MEG synchronization and desynchronization: Basic principles. *Clinical Neurophysiology*, 110(11):1842–1857, November 1999.

123. P. J. Phillips, P. J. Flynn, T. Scruggs, K. W. Bowyer, J. Chang, K. Hoffman, J. Marques, J. Min, and W. J. Worek. Overview of the face recognition grand challenge. In *Proceedings of the IEEE Computer Society Conference on Computer Vision and Pattern Recognition*, pages 947–954. 2005.

124. D. Precup, R. S. Sutton, and S. Dasgupta. Off-policy temporal-difference learning with function approximation. In *Proceedings of the 18th International Conference on Machine Learning*, pages 417–424. 2001.

125. D. Precup, R. S. Sutton, and S. Singh. Eligibility traces for off-policy policy evaluation. In *Proceedings of the 17th International Conference on Machine Learning*, pages 759–766. Morgan Kaufmann, San Franciscs, 2000.

126. P. A. Puhani. The heckman correction for sample selection and its critique: A short survey. *Journal of Economic Surveys*, 14(1):53–68, 2000.

127. F. Pukelsheim. *Optimal Design of Experiments*. Wiley, New York, 1993.

128. J. Qin. Inferences for case-control and semiparametric two-sample density ratio models. *Biometrika*, 85(3):619–630, 1998.

129. L. Rabiner and B-H. Juang. *Fundamentals of Speech Recognition*. Prentice Hall, Englewood Cliffs, NJ, 1993.

130. H. Ramoser, J. Müller-Gerking, and G. Pfurtscheller. Optimal spatial filtering of single trial EEG during imagined hand movement. *IEEE Transactions on Rehabilitation Engineering*, 8(4):441–446, 2000.

131. C. R. Rao. *Linear Statistical Inference and Its Applications*. Wiley, New York, 1965.

132. D. A. Reynolds, T. F. Quatieri, and R. B. Dunn. Speaker verification using adapted Gaussian mixture models. *Digital Signal Processing*, 10(1–3):19–41, 2000.

133. D. A. Reynolds and R. C. Rose. Robust text-independent speaker verification using Gaussian mixture speaker models. *IEEE Transactions on Speech and Audio Processing*, 3(1):72–83, 1995.

134. K. Ricanek and T. Tesafaye. MORPH: A longitudinal image database of normal adult age-progression. In *Proceedings of the IEEE 7th International Conference on Automatic Face and Gesture Recognition*, pages 341–345. 2006.

135. J. Rissanen. Modeling by shortest data description. *Automatica*, 14(5):465–471, 1978.

136. J. Rissanen. Stochastic complexity. *Journal of the Royal Statistical Society*, Series B, 49(3):223–239, 1987.

137. R. T. Rockafellar and S. Uryasev. Conditional value-at-risk for general loss distributions. *Journal of Banking & Finance*, 26(7):1443–1471, 2002.

138. P. J. Rousseeuw and A. M. Leroy. *Robust Regression and Outlier Detection*. Wiley, New York, 1987.

139. A. I. Schein and L. H. Ungar. Active learning for logistic regression: An evaluation. *Machine Learning*, 68(3):235–265, 2007.

140. M. Schmidt. *minFunc*, 2005. http://people.cs.ubc.ca/˜schmidtm/ Software/minFunc.html.

141. B. Schölkopf and A. J. Smola. *Learning with Kernels*. MIT Press, Cambridge, MA, 2001.

142. G. Schwarz. Estimating the dimension of a model. *Annals of Statistics*, 6(2):461–464, 1978.

143. P. Shenoy, M. Krauledat, B. Blankertz, R. P. N. Rao, and K.-R. Müller. Towards adaptive classification for BCI. *Journal of Neural Engineering*, 3(1):R13–R23, 2006.

144. R. Shibata. Statistical aspects of model selection. In J. C. Willems, editor, *From Data to Model*, pages 215–240. Springer-Verlag, New York, 1989.

145. H. Shimodaira. Improving predictive inference under covariate shift by weighting the log-likelihood function. *Journal of Statistical Planning and Inference*, 90(2):227–244, 2000.

146. A. Smola, L. Song, and C. H. Teo. Relative novelty detection. In D. van Dyk and M. Welling, editors, *Proceedings of the 12th International Conference on Artificial Intelligence and Statistics*, volume 5 of *JMLR Workshop and Conference Proceedings*, pages 536–543. 2009.

147. L. Song, A. Smola, A. Gretton, K. M. Borgwardt, and J. Bedo. Supervised feature selection via dependence estimation. In *Proceedings of the 24th International Conference on Machine Learning*, pages 823–830. ACM Press, New York, 2007.

148. C. M. Stein. Estimation of the mean of a multivariate normal distribution. *Annals of Statistics*, 9(6):1135–1151, 1981.

149. I. Steinwart. On the influence of the kernel on the consistency of support vector machines. *Journal of Machine Learning Research*, 2:67–93, 2001.

150. M. Stone. Cross-validatory choice and assessment of statistical predictions. *Journal of the Royal Statistical Society*, Series B, 36(2):111–147, 1974.

151. M. Stone. Asymptotics for and against cross-validation. *Biometrika*, 64(1):29–35, 1977.

152. E. P. Stuntebeck, J. S. Davis II, G. D. Abowd, and M. Blount. Healthsense: Classification of health-related sensor data through user-assisted machine learning. In *Proceedings of the 9th Workshop on Mobile Computing Systems and Applications*, pages 1–5. ACM, New York, 2008.

153. M. Sugiyama. Active learning in approximately linear regression based on conditional expectation of generalization error. *Journal of Machine Learning Research*, 7:141–166, January 2006.

154. M. Sugiyama. Dimensionality reduction of multimodal labeled data by local Fisher discriminant analysis. *Journal of Machine Learning Research*, 8:1027–1061, May 2007.

155. M. Sugiyama. Superfast-trainable multi-class probabilistic classifier by least-squares posterior fitting. *IEICE Transactions on Information and Systems*, E93-D(10):2690–2701, 2010.

156. M. Sugiyama, T. Idé, S. Nakajima, and J. Sese. Semi-supervised local Fisher discriminant analysis for dimensionality reduction. *Machine Learning*, 78(1–2):35–61, 2010.

157. M. Sugiyama, T. Kanamori, T. Suzuki, S. Hido, J. Sese, I. Takeuchi, and L. Wang. A density-ratio framework for statistical data processing. *IPSJ Transactions on Computer Vision and Applications*, 1:183–208, 2009.

158. M. Sugiyama, M. Kawanabe, and P. L. Chui. Dimensionality reduction for density ratio estimation in high-dimensional spaces. *Neural Networks*, 23(1):44–59, 2010.

159. M. Sugiyama, M. Kawanabe, and K.-R. Müller. Trading variance reduction with unbiasedness: The regularized subspace information criterion for robust model selection in kernel regression. *Neural Computation*, 16(5):1077–1104, 2004.

160. M. Sugiyama, M. Krauledat, and K.-R. Müller. Covariate shift adaptation by importance weighted cross validation. *Journal of Machine Learning Research*, 8:985–1005, May 2007.

161. M. Sugiyama and K.-R. Müller. The subspace information criterion for infinite dimensional hypothesis spaces. *Journal of Machine Learning Research*, 3:323–359, November 2002.

162. M. Sugiyama and K.-R. Müller. Input-dependent estimation of generalization error under covariate shift. *Statistics & Decisions*, 23(4):249–279, 2005.

163. M. Sugiyama and S. Nakajima. Pool-based active learning in approximate linear regression. *Machine Learning*, 75(3):249–274, 2009.

164. M. Sugiyama, S. Nakajima, H. Kashima, P. von Bünau, and M. Kawanabe. Direct importance estimation with model selection and its application to covariate shift adaptation. In J. C. Platt, D. Koller, Y. Singer, and S. Roweis, editors, *Advances in Neural Information Processing Systems* volume 20, pages 1433–1440. Cambridge, MA, MIT Press, 2008.

165. M. Sugiyama and H. Ogawa. Subspace information criterion for model selection. *Neural Computation*, 13(8):1863–1889, 2001.

166. M. Sugiyama and H. Ogawa. Active learning with model selection—Simultaneous optimization of sample points and models for trigonometric polynomial models. *IEICE Transactions on Information and Systems*, E86-D(12):2753–2763, 2003.

167. M. Sugiyama and N. Rubens. A batch ensemble approach to active learning with model selection. *Neural Networks*, 21(9):1278–1286, 2008.

168. M. Sugiyama and T. Suzuki. Least-squares independence test. *IEICE Transactions on Information and Systems*, E94-D(6):1333–1336, 2011.

169. M. Sugiyama, T. Suzuki, Y. Itoh, T. Kanamori, and M. Kimura. Least-squares two-sample test. *Neural Networks*, 24(7):735–751, 2011.

170. M. Sugiyama, T. Suzuki, and T. Kanamori. *Density Ratio Estimation in Machine Learning*. Cambridge, UK: Cambridge University Press, 2012.

171. M. Sugiyama, T. Suzuki, S. Nakajima, H. Kashima, P. von Bünau, and M. Kawanabe. Direct importance estimation for covariate shift adaptation. *Annals of the Institute of Statistical Mathematics*, 60(4):699–746, 2008.

172. M. Sugiyama, I. Takeuchi, T. Suzuki, T. Kanamori, H. Hachiya, and D. Okanohara. Least-squares conditional density estimation. *IEICE Transactions on Information and Systems*, E93-D(3):583–594, 2010.

173. M. Sugiyama, M. Yamada, P. von Bünau, T. Suzuki, T. Kanamori, and M. Kawanabe. Direct density-ratio estimation with dimensionality reduction via least-squares hetero-distributional subspace search. *Neural Networks*, 24(2):183–198, 2011.

174. R. S. Sutton and G. A. Barto. *Reinforcement Learning: An Introduction*. Cambridge, MA, MIT Press, 1998.

175. T. Suzuki and M. Sugiyama. Sufficient dimension reduction via squared-loss mutual information estimation. In Y. W. Teh and M. Tiggerington, editors, *Proceedings of the 13th International Conference on Artificial Intelligence and Statistics*, volume 9 of *JMLR Workshop and Conference Proceedings*, pages 804–811. 2010.

176. T. Suzuki and M. Sugiyama. Least-squares independent component analysis. *Neural Computation*, 23(1):284–301, 2011.

177. T. Suzuki, M. Sugiyama, T. Kanamori, and J. Sese. Mutual information estimation reveals global associations between stimuli and biological processes. *BMC Bioinformatics*, 10(1):S52, 2009.

178. T. Suzuki, M. Sugiyama, J. Sese, and T. Kanamori. Approximating mutual information by maximum likelihood density ratio estimation. In Y. Saeys, H. Liu, I. Inza, L. Wehenkel, and Y. Van de Peer, editors, *Proceedings of the ECML-PKDD2008 Workshop on New Challenges for Feature Selection in Data Mining and Knowledge Discovery*, volume 4 of *JMLR Workshop and Conference Proceedings*, pages 5–20. 2008.

179. T. Suzuki, M. Sugiyama, and T. Tanaka. Mutual information approximation via maximum likelihood estimation of density ratio. In *Proceedings of the IEEE International Symposium on Information Theory*, pages 463–467. 2009.

180. A. Takeda, J. Gotoh, and M. Sugiyama. Support vector regression as conditional value-at-risk minimization with application to financial time-series analysis. In S. Kaski, D. J. Miller, E. Oja, and A. Honkela, editors, *IEEE International Workshop on Machine Learning for Signal Processing*, pages 118–123. 2010.

181. A. Takeda and M. Sugiyama. On generalization performance and non-convex optimization of extended ν-support vector machine. *New Generation Computing*, 27(3):259–279, 2009.

182. K. Takeuchi. Distribution of information statistics and validity criteria of models. *Mathematical Sciences*, 153:12–18, 1976. (In Japanese).

183. R. Tibshirani. Regression shrinkage and subset selection with the Lasso. *Journal of the Royal Statistical Society*, Series B, 58(1):267–288, 1996.

184. F. H. C. Tivive and A. Bouzerdoum. A gender recognition system using shunting inhibitory convolutional neural networks. In *Proceedings of the IEEE International Joint Conference on Neural Networks*, volume 10, pages 5336–5341. 2006.

185. Y. Tsuboi, H. Kashima, S. Hido, S. Bickel, and M. Sugiyama. Direct density ratio estimation for large-scale covariate shift adaptation. In M. J. Zaki, K. Wang, C. Apte, and H. Park, editors, *Proceedings of the 8th SIAM International Conference on Data Mining*, pages 443–454. SIAM, 2008.

186. Y. Tsuboi, H. Kashima, S. Hido, S. Bickel, and M. Sugiyama. Direct density ratio estimation for large-scale covariate shift adaptation. *Journal of Information Processing*, 17:138–155, 2009.

187. Y. Tsuboi, H. Kashima, S. Mori, H. Oda, and Y. Matsumoto. Training conditional random fields using incomplete annotations. In *Proceedings of the 22nd International Conference on Computational Linguistics*, pages 897–904. 2008.

188. K. Ueki, M. Sugiyama, and Y. Ihara. Perceived age estimation under lighting condition change by covariate shift adaptation. In *Proceedings of the 20th International Conference on Pattern Recognition*, pages 3400–3403. 2010.

189. K. Ueki, M. Sugiyama, and Y. Ihara. Semi-supervised estimation of perceived age from face images. In *Proceedings of the International Conference on Computer Vision Theory and Applications*, pages 319–324. 2010.

190. L. G. Valiant. A theory of the learnable. *Communications of the Association for Computing Machinery*, 27:1134–1142, 1984.

191. S. van de Geer. *Empirical Processes in M-Estimation*. Cambridge University Press, 2000.

192. A. W. van der Vaart and J. A. Wellner. *Weak Convergence and Empirical Processes: With Applications to Statistics*. Springer, New York, 1996.

193. V. N. Vapnik. *Statistical Learning Theory*. Wiley-Interscience, New York, 1998.

194. C. Vidaurre, A. Schlögl, R. Cabeza, and G. Pfurtscheller. About adaptive classifiers for brain computer interfaces. *Biomedizinische Technik*, 49(1):85–86, 2004.

195. G. Wahba. *Spline Models for Observational Data*. Philadelphia, SIAM, 1990.

196. S. Watanabe. *Algebraic Geometry and Statistical Learning Theory*. Cambridge University Press, Cambridge, UK, 2009.

197. H. White. Maximum likelihood estimation of misspecified models. *Econometrica*, 50(1):1–25, 1982.

198. G. Wichern, M. Yamada, H. Thornburg, M. Sugiyama, and A. Spanias. Automatic audio tagging using covariate shift adaptation. In *Proceedings of the IEEE International Conference on Acoustics, Speech, and Signal Processing*, pages 253–256. 2010.

199. D. P. Wiens. Robust weights and designs for biased regression models: Least squares and generalized M-estimation. *Journal of Statistical Planning and Inference*, 83(2):395–412, 2000.

200. P. M. Williams. Bayesian regularization and pruning using a Laplace prior. *Neural Computation*, 7(1):117–143, 1995.

201. J. R. Wolpaw, N. Birbaumer, D. J. McFarland, G. Pfurtscheller, and T. M. Vaughan. Brain-computer interfaces for communication and control. *Clinical Neurophysiology*, 113(6):767–791, 2002.

202. M. Yamada and M. Sugiyama. Direct importance estimation with Gaussian mixture models. *IEICE Transactions on Information and Systems*, E92-D(10):2159–2162, 2009.

203. M. Yamada and M. Sugiyama. Dependence minimizing regression with model selection for non-linear causal inference under non-Gaussian noise. In *Proceedings of the 24th AAAI Conference on Artificial Intelligence*, pages 643–648. AAAI Press, 2010.

204. M. Yamada, M. Sugiyama, and T. Matsui. Semi-supervised speaker identification under covariate shift. *Signal Processing*, 90(8):2353–2361, 2010.

205. M. Yamada, M. Sugiyama, G. Wichern, and J. Simm. Direct importance estimation with a mixture of probabilistic principal component analyzers. *IEICE Transactions on Information and Systems*, E93-D(10):2846–2849, 2010.

206. M. Yamada, M. Sugiyama, G. Wichern, and J. Simm. Improving the accuracy of least-squares probabilistic classifiers. *IEICE Transactions on Information and Systems*, E94-D(6):1337–1340, 2011.

207. K. Yamagishi, N. Ito, H. Kosuga, N. Yasuda, K. Isogami, and N. Kozuno. A simplified measurement of farm worker's load using an accelerometer. *Journal of the Japanese Society of Agricultural Technology Management*, 9(2):127–132, 2002. (In Japanese.)

208. L. Zelnik-Manor and P. Perona. Self-tuning spectral clustering. In L. K. Saul, Y. Weiss, and L. Bottou, editors, *Advances in Neural Information Processing Systems*, volume 17, pages 1601–1608. MIT Press, Cambridge, MA, 2005.

Index

Active learning, 183
  ensemble, 219
  with model selection, 215
  pool-based, 204, 234
  population-based, 188, 225
Active learning/model selection dilemma, 215
Active policy iteration, 231
Affine transform, 236
Age prediction, 152
Akaike information criterion
  importance-weighted, 47

Ball batting, 232
Basis
  polynomial, 10, 198, 210, 221, 236
  trigonometric polynomial, 10, 216
Bayes decision rule, 143
Bellman equation, 166
Bellman residual, 168
Bi-orthogonality, 104
Bias-variance decomposition, 186, 228
Bias-variance trade-off, 23
Boosting
  importance-weighted, 40

Cepstral mean normalization, 142
Chebyshev approximation, 35
Classification, 8, 35, 41
Common spatial patterns, 138
Conditional random field, 150
Conditional value-at-risk, 34, 40
Confidence, 38, 160
Consistency, 21
Covariate shift, 3, 9
Cross-validation, 74, 77, 80, 84
  importance-weighted, 64, 144, 156, 169, 174
  leave-one-out, 65, 88, 113
Curse of dimensionality, 11, 74

Design matrix, 27
Dimensionality reduction, 103

Dirac delta function, 166
Direct density-ratio estimation with
    dimensionality reduction, 103
Distribution
  conditional, 8
  test input, 9, 73
  training input, 7, 73
Domain adaptation, 149
Dual basis, 104

EM algorithm, 146
Empirical risk minimization, 21
  importance-weighted, 23
Error function, 129
Event-related desynchronization, 138
Expected shortfall, 35
Experimental design, 183
Extrapolation, 5

Feasible region, 25
Feature selection, 25
Fisher discriminant analysis, 108, 137
  importance-weighted, 36, 43, 138
  local, 109
Flattening parameter, 23, 47, 140
F-measure, 151

Generalization error, 9, 53, 183
  estimation, 47
  input-dependent analysis, 51, 54, 193, 206
  input-independent analysis, 51, 64, 191, 195, 205, 207
  single-trial, 51
Generalized eigenvalue problem, 37
Gradient method, 28, 32
  conjugate, 39
  stochastic, 29, 33
Gram-Schmidt orthonormalization, 112

Hazard ratio, 131
Heteroscedastic noise, 228

Huber regression importance-weighted, 31
Human activity recognition, 157

Idempotence, 105
Importance estimation
 kernel density estimation, 73
 kernel mean matching, 75
 Kullback–Leibler importance estimation procedure, 78, 144, 156
 least-squares importance fitting, 83
 logistic regression, 76
 unconstrained least-squares importance fitting, 87
Importance sampling, 22
Importance weight, 9, 22
 adaptive, 23, 169
 Akaike information criterion, 47
 boosting, 40
 classification, 35
 cross-validation, 64, 144, 156, 169, 174
 empirical risk minimization, 23
 estimation, 73, 103
 Fisher discriminant analysis, 138
 least squares, 26, 41, 66, 190
 logistic regression, 38, 144
 regression, 25
 regularized, 23, 153
 subspace information criterion, 54
 support vector machine, 39
Inverse Mills ratio, 131
Inverted pendulum, 176

Jacobian, 104

Kernel
 Gaussian, 12, 29, 73, 75, 84, 144, 153
 model, 12, 29, 143, 153
 sequence, 143
Kernel density estimation, 73
Kernel mean matching, 75
k-means clustering, 146
Kullback–Leibler divergence, 47, 78
Kullback–Leibler importance estimation procedure, 78, 144, 150, 156

Learning matrix, 27
Least squares, 38, 41, 55
 general, 133
 importance-weighted, 26, 41, 66, 205
Least-squares importance fitting, 83
Linear discriminant analysis, *see* Fisher discriminant analysis
Linear learning, 49, 59, 184
Linear program, 30
Logistic regression, 76
 importance weight, 38, 144

Loss
 0/1, 8, 35, 64
 absolute, 30
 classification, 38
 deadzone-linear, 33
 exponential, 40
 hinge, 39
 Huber, 31
 logistic, 39
 regression, 25
 squared, 8, 26, 38, 41, 49, 53, 55, 83, 183

Machine learning, 3
Mapping
 hetero-distributional, 106
 homo-distributional, 106
Markov decision problem, 165
Maximum likelihood, 38
Mel-frequency cepstrum coefficient, 142
Model
 additive, 11
 approximately correct, 14, 53, 192, 193, 195, 229
 correctly specified, 13, 189
 Gaussian mixture, 80, 142
 kernel, 12, 29, 143, 153
 linear-in-input, 10, 25, 37, 39, 41, 43
 linear-in-parameter, 10, 27, 32, 49, 54, 78, 80, 83, 184, 198, 221
 log-linear, 77, 80, 150
 logistic, 38, 143, 150
 misspecified, 14, 53, 190
 multiplicative, 11
 nonparametric, 13, 73
 parametric, 13
 probabilistic principal-component-analyzer mixture, 80, 123
Model drift, 216
Model error, 54, 57, 186, 188, 229
Model overfitting, 219
Model selection, 23, 47, 174

Natural language processing, 149
Newton's method, 39

Oblique projection, 104
Off-policy reinforcement learning, 169
Outliers, 30, 31

Parametric optimization, 85
Policy iteration, 166
Probit model, 129

Quadratic program, 32, 75, 84

Regression, 8, 25, 40, 66
Regularization parameter, 24

Index

Regularization path tracking, 85
Regularizer
  absolute, 24
  squared, 24
Reinforcement learning, 4, 165, 225
Rejection sampling, 200
Resampling weight function, 205
Robustness parameter, 31

Sample
  test, 9, 73
  training, 7, 73
Sample selection bias, 125
Sample reuse policy iteration, 175, 225
Scatter matrix
  between-class, 36, 108
  local between-class, 110
  local within-class, 110
  within-class, 36, 108
Semisupervised learning, 4, 142
Sherman-Woodbury-Morrison formula, 88
Speaker identification, 142
Sphering, 105
Subspace
  hetero-distributional, 104
  homo-distributional, 104
Subspace information criterion
  importance-weighted, 54
Supervised learning, 3, 7
Support vector machine, 75, 142
  importance-weighted, 39
Support vector regression, 33

Test
  input distribution, 9, 73
  samples, 9, 73
Training
  input distribution, 7, 73
  samples, 7, 73

Unbiasedness, 66
  asymptotic, 50, 60, 66
Unconstrained least-squares importance
    fitting, 87, 113
Universal reproducing kernel Hilbert space, 75
Unsupervised learning, 3

Value function, 166
Value-at-risk, 34
Variable selection, 25

Wafer alignment, 234

Adaptive Computation and Machine Learning

Thomas Dietterich, Editor

Christopher Bishop, David Heckerman, Michael Jordan, and Michael Kearns, Associate Editors

Bioinformatics: The Machine Learning Approach, Pierre Baldi and Søren Brunak

Reinforcement Learning: An Introduction, Richard S. Sutton and Andrew G. Barto

Graphical Models for Machine Learning and Digital Communication, Brendan J. Frey

Learning in Graphical Models, Michael I. Jordan

Causation, Prediction, and Search, second edition, Peter Spirtes, Clark Glymour, and Richard Scheines

Principles of Data Mining, David Hand, Heikki Mannila, and Padhraic Smyth

Bioinformatics: The Machine Learning Approach, second edition, Pierre Baldi and Søren Brunak

Learning Kernel Classifiers: Theory and Algorithms, Ralf Herbrich

Learning with Kernels: Support Vector Machines, Regularization, Optimization, and Beyond, Bernhard Schölkopf and Alexander J. Smola

Introduction to Machine Learning, Ethem Alpaydin

Gaussian Processes for Machine Learning, Carl Edward Rasmussen and Christopher K.I. Williams

Semi-Supervised Learning, Olivier Chapelle, Bernhard Schölkopf, and Alexander Zien, Eds.

The Minimum Description Length Principle, Peter D. Grünwald

Introduction to Statistical Relational Learning, Lise Getoor and Ben Taskar, Eds.

Probabilistic Graphical Models: Principles and Techniques, Daphne Koller and Nir Friedman

Introduction to Machine Learning, second edition, Ethem Alpaydin

Machine Learning in Non-Stationary Environments: Introduction to Covariate Shift Adaptation, Masashi Sugiyama and Motoaki Kawanabe

Boosting: Foundations and Algorithms, Robert E. Schapire and Yoav Freund